Mastering the
COMMODORE 64

ELLIS HORWOOD BOOKS IN COMPUTING

Mastering the
COMMODORE 64

A. J. Jones and G. J. Carpenter

ELLIS HORWOOD LIMITED
Publishers · Chichester

JOHN WILEY & SONS INC.
New York · Brisbane · Chichester · Toronto · Singapore

17003

First published in 1984 by
ELLIS HORWOOD LIMITED
Market Cross House, Cooper Street, Chichester,
West Sussex PO19 1EB, England

Distributors:

Australia, New Zealand, South-east Asia:
Jacardand-Wiley Ltd., Jacaranda Press
JOHN WILEY & SONS INC.
GPO Box 859, Brisbane, Queensland 4001, Australia

Canada:
JOHN WILEY & SONS CANADA LIMITED
22 Worcester Road, Rexdale, Ontario, Canada

Europe, Africa:
JOHN WILEY & SONS LIMITED
Baffins Lane, Chichester, West Sussex, England

North and South America and the rest of the world:
JOHN WILEY & SONS INC.
605 Third Avenue, New York, NY 10158, USA

©1984 A.J. Jones and G.J. Carpenter/Ellis Horwood Ltd.

British Library Cataloguing in Publication Data
Jones, A.J. (Antonia Jane)
Mastering the Commodore 64. — (Ellis Horwood series in
home computing)
1. Commodore 64 (Computer)
I. Title II. Carpenter, G.J.
001.64'04 QA76.8.C64

Library of Congress Card No. 84-726

ISBN 0-85312-654-2 (Ellis Horwood Limited)
ISBN 0-471-80755-9 (John Wiley & Sons Inc.)

Typeset by Ellis Horwood Limited.
Printed in Great Britain by R.J. Acford, Chichester.

Contents

Disk directory

3	"SYS EXAMPLE"	PRG	5	"MULTICOL DEMO"	PRG	1	"PARAWEDGE.HEX"	PRG
1	"WAIT/KEYPRESS"	PRG	6	"EXTEN COL DEMO"	PRG	22	"2BYTJOY.SRC"	SEQ
1	"WAIT/NO KEY"	PRG	4	"HIRES DEMO"	PRG	3	"2BYTJOY.OB"	SEQ
2	"CHASE"	PRG	24	"SPRITE EDITOR"	PRG	2	"2BYTJOY.HEX"	PRG
3	"AUTOMERGE"	PRG	18	"HELLO HOUSE"	PRG	22	"PLOTSUB.SRC"	SEQ
2	"SCROLL MESSAGE"	PRG	6	"LOAD.SRC"	SEQ	4	"PLOTSUB.OB"	SEQ
3	"BIT PATTERNS"	PRG	1	"LOAD.OB"	SEQ	2	"PLOTSUB.HEX"	PRG
5	"HYPERPEEK"	PRG	1	"LOAD.HEX"	PRG	140	"GINRUMMY"	PRG
2	"ARRAY FILLING EX"	PRG	9	"SAVE.SRC"	SEQ	3	"LOAD.BAS"	PRG
3	"SHUFFLES"	PRG	1	"SAVE.OB"	SEQ	1	"TESTLOAD"	PRG
8	"TEST CARD DISPL"	PRG	1	"SAVE.HEX"	PRG	4	"SAVE.BAS"	PRG
18	"BLACKJACK64"	PRG	9	"COPY.SRC"	SEQ	1	"TESTSAVE"	PRG
4	"HEX/DEC CONVERT"	PRG	1	"COPY.OB"	SEQ	4	"COPY.BAS"	PRG
2	"BINARY SEARCH"	PRG	1	"COPY.HEX"	PRG	2	"TESTCOPY"	PRG
4	"INSERTION SORT"	PRG	20	"CLOCK.SRC"	SEQ	8	"CLOCK.BAS"	PRG
15	"INDEX PREP"	PRG	4	"CLOCK.OB"	SEQ	1	"TESTCLOCK"	PRG
4	"QUICKSORT"	PRG	2	"CLOCK.HEX"	PRG	4	"CHARGET.BAS"	PRG
2	"FIND AN INTEGER"	PRG	9	"CHARGET.SRC"	SEQ	5	"PARCOMS.BAS"	PRG
2	"FIND A FPVAR"	PRG	2	"CHARGET.OB"	SEQ	5	"PARAWEDGE.BAS"	PRG
2	"FIND A STRING"	PRG	1	"CHARGET.HEX"	PRG	7	"2BYTJOY.BAS"	PRG
23	"DATASTATE"	PRG	11	"PARCOMS.SRC"	SEQ	5	"TEST2BYTJOY"	PRG
35	"64-SYN"	PRG	2	"PARCOMS.OB"	SEQ	3	"PLOTSUB.BAS"	PRG
37	"SCREEN EDITOR"	PRG	1	"PARCOMS.HEX"	PRG	3	"TESTPLOTSUB"	PRG
9	" DRAGON.S"	PRG	14	"PARAWEDGE.SRC"	SEQ	51	BLOCKS FREE.	
9	" ABSTRACT.S"	PRG	3	"PARAWEDGE.OB"	SEQ			

Cassette tapes or floppy diskettes containing these programs are available from:

USA – John Wiley & Sons Inc., 605 Third Avenue, New York, NY10158, USA.

UK/Europe – John Wiley & Sons Limited, Baffins Lane, Chichester, West Sussex, England.

Preface

This book is not intended as a 'Let's Get Started' introduction to microcomputers using the Commodore 64. We assume that you have read some material of this type, in particular the manual which is supplied with the Commodore 64. This book attempts to bridge the gap between the beginner's knowledge of BASIC and a real understanding of what is going on inside your Commodore 64, eventually leading to machine language programming.

A book of this type is a demanding project and we should like to extend our thanks to a number of people. Firstly, particular thanks are due to David Briggs, Gail Wellington and Nick Green of Commodore UK. David supplied invaluable technical information, without which no book of this type could be written; Nick helped in many less easily defined ways; Gail helped by letting us have an early copy of Easyscript (on which most of this book was written) and allowing us to borrow various bits of equipment. Thanks are also due to Peter Raybaud of Adda who got hold of a Commodore 64 for us when machines were like gold dust and then kept our equipment running through an incredibly hot summer (Oh, to lie in the sun!). Peter also let us have advance copies of POWER (no way we could have developed the programs without it) and PAL, both excellent examples of Proline software. Oxford Computer Systems also deserve a vote of thanks for letting us have Interpod (which meant we could use a 4040 disk drive) and a copy of the Commodore 64 PETSPEED compiler (which opened new horizons). Our local microstore the 'Wokingham Computer Centre', who did a brilliant job of getting our 4040 fixed in a hurry, also deserve our thanks — thanks guys. Many other people helped our efforts but three deserve special mention. Mary Radcliffe did all the flow charting and a lot of the coding for GINRUMMY, a huge task. We both agree that Mary is a very special person. Liz Coley did a lot of rushing around and phoning when the pressure was on, thanks Liz. Finally, when things were getting very tough Joan Frazier provided essential life-support functions for Antonia — like making sure she ate!

In the time available to us we have made every attempt to ensure the accuracy of the information given. Inevitably there will be errors, hopefully very few, and we apologize in advance for those that slip through. All the main software developed in this book is available on tape or disk. These programs have been tested and are, to the best of our knowledge, bug-free. All long listings are reproduced directly from the software disk. There are some conventions used in the file names which will help you find your way around the disk. These are

FILENAME.SRC

This denotes a machine language Source file prepared by using the Commodore Assembler/Editor. It will be an SEQ file (the Editor uses GET and PUT to load and save such files) and even if you don't have the Commodore Assembler/Editor it can be read as any other sequential file, for example, as text file on a word processor. When the Assembler is RUN it produces an Object code file. We have used the convention

FILENAME.OB

to denote files of this type. When HILOAD or LOLOAD are used to put the object code into memory the program can then be saved as a program file using 64-MON. We have used the convention

FILENAME.HEX

to denote these files. They should be LOADed using LOAD"FILENAME.HEX",8,1. Finally the program has been SAVEd as a series of DATA statements to be POKEd into memory by a BASIC loader. These loaders are denoted by

FILENAME.BAS

Where appropriate there is a BASIC program to test the machine code and this has been SAVEd as
TESTFILENAME

Wokingham, Berkshire
January 1984

ACKNOWLEDGEMENTS

We are grateful to CBM (UK) for permission to reproduce a number of tables from the *Commodore 64 Programmer's Reference Guide* and to Mike Todd for permission to use material from his *ICPUG Newsletter* articles.

To our parents
and to Mary with thanks

SECTION I

A review of BASIC

INTRODUCTION

The aim of this section is to provide a detailed review of CBM BASIC V2. After a brief discussion of data 'types' each BASIC keyword is discussed in detail. You might prefer to treat this material as a convenient reference whilst reading through the other chapters. Still, even if you know BASIC pretty well, you may find a quick browse through the following paragraphs will throw up some points of interest, specific to the CBM 64, which you can put to good use.

As we have said, this book is not intended to be a first course in BASIC, so there are several things we shall take for granted. The first of these concerns the screen editor. When the machine is first turned on, you are inviting a 'dialog' in BASIC, specifically you need to LOAD or write a program. However, before a program can be LOADed it must first be written, by you or somebody else, and this is where the screen editor comes in. Those who have had the dubious pleasure of working with mainframe computers will know that the Commodore BASIC screen editor makes most mainframe terminal editing facilities look as if they were invented before the wheel! So when you are struggling with getting things right inside quote marks (hit 'SHIFT+RETURN' and try again: the line will not have been entered) just remember things could be far worse. Seriously though, the fundamentals of using the screen editor are quite well covered in the manual which comes with your CBM 64, and the rest soon comes with practice (there are neat solutions to all the usual editorial snags).

There is a great satisfaction to be gained from using a good tool well, and as one of us remarked (but I bet he didn't say it first). "the microcomputer is the most versatile tool mankind has ever had". So it is worth a little time to learn how to get the best from your CBM 64's BASIC.

VARIABLES AND STRINGS

Given that a microcomputer is a device for manipulating data, we can reasonably ask what kind of data can a microcomputer manipulate? Although all data is eventually expressed as zeros and ones, at BASIC programming level there are three types of data which can be distinguished.

Integer variables – whole numbers such as $0,1,2,3,\ldots,-1,-2,-3,\ldots$ etc. in the range -32768 to $+32767$.

Real number or floating point variables such as

$$3.14159265E-20.$$

In this example the number represented is 3.14159265 multiplied by 10 raised to the power -20 (shift the decimal point left 20 places), and -20 is called the exponent of 10. Thus every floating point variable may be represented as a decimal part multiplied by 10 raised to the power of some exponent. The range of usable exponents is -38 to $+38$, a CBM 64 counts $10\uparrow-39$ as zero and gives an overflow error for $10\uparrow39$.

An integer variable is defined by a statement like $X\%=10$, the $\%$ sign signifies an integer, and a floating variable by simply $X=10$. Strictly speaking $X=10$ means LET $X=10$ but LET takes up space and is unnecessary as long as we realize that $=$ is not symmetric in BASIC, that is $X=10$ is not the same as $10=X$. To illustrate this, the program

1000 X=10:PRINTX

will RUN and print the number 10, but the program

1000 10=X:PRINTX

will give a SYNTAX ERROR.

String of character variables such as

"ABCD1230<>*="

which is a string of length 12. A string is defined by a statement like $X\$="AB"$, the $ sign signifies a string, and consists of a sequence of characters of any length up to 255. The characters of a string may include color control or cursor control characters.

In order to store values of variables and programs the CBM 64 needs memory. There are two kinds of internal memory used in microcomputers: ROM, Read Only Memory, and RAM, Random Access Memory. Read Only Memory, as the name implies, is memory which can only be read from, that is the contents of ROM are determined by the manufacturer and cannot be changed by the user. Memory of this type contains the machine code which enables the CBM 64 to understand BASIC. This program is called the Interpreter and is effectively the 'operating system' of the CBM 64. The other large machine code program in ROM is the Kernal which provides all the necessary input/output (I/O) functions, such as the keyboard, screen, cassette, printer and disk drive. The term Random Access Memory is a bit misleading, for our purposes it means memory which can be both read from and written to. RAM is the memory used to store BASIC programs and the variables used by the programs. More generally RAM is used to store any variable data. The total memory of the CBM 64 consists of 65536 ($2\uparrow64$) 'cells', each of which can be identified by a unique number which is called its *address*. Valid addresses lie in the range 0 to 65535. Each 'cell' contains a number in the range 0 to 255, just why this should be so we shall see later. The information held in a 'cell' is called a *byte* and memory capacity is usually measured in units of 1024 bytes, called 1K; thus the CBM 64 has a 64K memory.

One might think that a floating point variable would take up more memory than an integer in the range −36768 to 32767, but because of the way BASIC V2 works this is not the case unless the variables are elements of an array. In fact both types of variable occupy 7 bytes of memory. However, when using numbers as array elements, there is a saving of 3 bytes per element using integers rather than floating point variables, for large arrays this gain is significant. A string variable, discounting space for the variable name, uses one byte per character.

Up to two characters can be used to identify variables the first of which must be alphabetic, you can use more but only the first two will be recognized; of course XY% is recognized as being a different variable from XY or XY$. Thus FLAG, a floating point variable, is only seen by the operating system as FL and so would be equivalent to FLAT or FLOG. For this reason it is best to stick to two characters, possibly using a third to help identify the purpose of the variable in the program, e.g. BLF, EDF could be flags. Variable names which contain BASIC words as a subword must be avoided. Other names to avoid are ST, TI and TI$ as these are already assigned by the operating system: ST (STATUS) is a variable which represents the status of the last I/O operation, TI (TIME) is the time in jiffys (1/60 second) since the machine was turned on (it is reset to zero after 24 hours) and TI$ (TIME$) is TI expressed in hours, minutes, seconds. The string variable TI$ can easily be reset from BASIC by the user (e.g. TI$ = "000000") whereas TI cannot.

Each kind of variable has special commands in BASIC to enable the programmer (you) to manipulate it.

BASIC KEYWORDS

If you have ever tried to learn a foreign language then you will know that two sources of difficulty are building up an adequate vocabulary, and the fact that frequently a particular word can have several meanings depending upon its context. Well, learning BASIC is a bit like learning a new language but it is comforting to know that CBM BASIC V2, as used on a CBM 64 with no special add-ons, has only 76 words! Even better, each word has only ever got one meaning. So as languages go BASIC is pretty easy to learn. It should be, because BASIC stands for Beginners All-purpose Symbolic Instruction Code, an easy but powerful way for you to give the computer instructions.

Apart from relational operators, π, the arithmetic symbols $+, -, *, /$ and $\uparrow$, the following is a complete list of BASIC words, or *keywords* as they are often called:

ABS	DATA	GOTO
AND	DEFN and FN	ON ... GOTO
ASC	DIM	IF ... THEN
ATN	END	INPUT and INPUT#
CHR$	EXP	INT
CLOSE	FOR ... TO ... STEP	LEFT$ and RIGHT$
CLR	FRE	LEN
CMD	GET and GET#	LET
CONT	GOSUB	LIST
COS	ON ... GOSUB	LOAD

LOG	REM	STR$
MID$	RESTORE	SYS
NEW	RETURN	TAB(
NEXT	RND	TAN
NOT	RUN	TI
OPEN	SAVE	TI$
OR	SGN	USR
PEEK	SIN	VAL
POKE	SPC(	VERIFY
POS	SQR	WAIT
PRINT and PRINT#	ST	
READ	STOP	

We shall survey these BASIC keywords under six main headings: *Program handling commands, BASIC program statements, Arithmetic functions, String functions, Logical operators,* and *Input/ Output statements.* Many of these are discussed in detail later on, so you can treat what follows as a handy reference section for the words of BASIC.

(Note. In what follows two slashes, //, are used to indicate that whatever is within is optional. If optional parameters are omitted the operating system will substitute default values. The particular default values assumed vary from one command to another but are chosen to make for ease of operation.

Another convention used is that items inside angle brackets '<>' denote variable data which you provide, the angle brackets are not part of the syntax.)

PROGRAM HANDLING COMMANDS

CONT	RUN
LIST	SAVE
LOAD	VERIFY
NEW	

CONT
Format: CONT

This command is used in direct mode to restart a program which was halted by either a STOP or END statement encountered during program execution, or by the RUN/STOP key being pressed. The program will then restart from the next program statement. Used with strategically placed STOP commands CONT is most useful when debugging or examining a program. After a STOP, variables or strings can be inspected by PRINTing their current values on the screen. When the examination is complete the program is restarted with CONT.

However, if you change the program in any way or cause an error during the 'time-out' then the program will be unable to continue and the error message CAN'T CONTINUE will result. This will happen even if you inadvertently hit 'RETURN' and re-enter a pre-existing program line; as far as the CBM 64 is concerned a new line has been entered.

LIST

Format: LIST //N/–/M// (where N and M are program line numbers)

The LIST command is used to examine the BASIC program currently stored in memory.

Examples:

LIST or LIST0	will list the entire program.
LIST 300	will list line 300 of the current program.
LIST 300–500	will list lines 300 to 500 inclusive.
LIST –500	will list all program lines up to and including line 500.
LIST 500–	will list all program lines from 500 up.

The LIST command will normally cause the program to be listed onto the screen (the screen scrolling can be slowed by holding the CTRL key down). However, by using the CMD command to change the current output device to something other than the screen, a program LISTing can be directed to printer, disk or tape.

The LISTed form of a program is a sequence (SEQ) of ASCII codes, which is not the way that the CBM 64 stores programs in memory or SAVEs them to disk or tape, but rather the way in which human beings can read programs.

It should be noted that LIST, END and STOP are unique in that after these statements are executed in a program control reverts to direct mode, that is the computer stops runnning the program and comes back with a 'READY' which is its way of saying 'OK, what next?'. Unlike END or STOP, after executing LIST the program cannot be resumed using CONT. A LIST operation can be halted at any time by pressing the RUN/STOP key.

LOAD

Format: LOAD /"PROGNAME"/, <Device number>/, 1///

Here the device number specifies whether the LOAD is from cassette = 1, or disk = 8 or 9.

The LOAD command is used to load into the microcomputer's memory a previously saved program (PRG) file. If no device number is given the LOAD will be from cassette. When LOADing programs from cassette the file name can be omitted, in which case the next program on the tape will be LOADed. If LOAD is used from within a BASIC program the named program will be loaded and RUN (see Chapter 7 for further details of LOAD from within a BASIC program).

Examples:

LOAD	will load the next program from tape.
LOAD"PROGNAME"	will search the tape until the program with the name PROGNAME is encountered and will then store this into memory.
LOAD"PROGNAME",1	ditto.
LOAD"PROGNAME",1,1	will load PROGNAME from tape back into the part of memory from which it was originally saved, this is particularly useful when loading back a previously saved machine code program.
LOAD"PROGNAME",8	will load PROGNAME from disk (1541).
LOAD"0:PROGNAME",8	will load PROGNAME from a 1541 disk drive, or from drive 0 of a dual disk drive (4040 or 8050/8250).

LOAD"PROGNAME",8,1   will load **PROGNAME** from disk back into the part of memory from which it was originally saved, this is particularly useful when loading back a previously saved machine code program.

NEW
Format: NEW

Effectively erases the current BASIC program in memory and prepares the machine for a new program. In fact no large blocks of memory are actually erased, since NEW relies on resetting pointers. Because of this it is possible to recover a program which has been NEWed (provided another program has not been entered, of course), although the values of any variables created by RUNning the program will be lost since NEW contains a CLR — more about this later. Note that NEW will not affect a machine code program located in memory.

RUN
Format: RUN /LN/   (where LN is a program line number)

Executes a BASIC program in memory, but performs CLR so any pre-existing variable values are lost. The line number is optional.

Examples:
RUN   will begin execution of the program.
RUN 500   will begin execution of the program from line 500 (but beware the auto CLR).

SAVE
Format: SAVE /"PROGNAME"/,<Device number >/,2///

'Saves' the current BASIC program to an output device, usually cassette or disk, a file name is always required unless the SAVE is to cassette. If no device number is given the default value 1 is assumed and the SAVE will be to cassette. The effect of SAVE is to copy a consecutive block of RAM to the specified device. From BASIC the RAM block saved is always the BASIC program area as determined by the 'start of BASIC' and 'end of program' markers. The (PRG) file created consists of compressed BASIC text in the form of keyword tokens complete with other information integral to the program.

Examples:
SAVE"PROGNAME"   will initiate a save of the current program to tape under the name PROGNAME.
SAVE"PROGNAME",1,2   will save to tape with an 'end of tape' marker at the end of the file.
SAVE"PROGNAME",8   will save to disk.
SAVE"0:PROGNAME",8   this will cause the program to be saved to drive 0 when using a dual disk drive, it will have no adverse effect if a single disk drive is used.
SAVE"1:PROGNAME",8   will save to drive 1 when using a dual disk drive but will, not surprisingly, fail if used on a single disk drive such as 1540 or 1541.

VERIFY
Format: VERIFY /"PROGNAME"/,<Device number >/,1///

Compares a previously SAVEd program with the program currently in memory. The syntax is the same as LOAD. In fact VERIFY does a byte by byte comparison of a previously saved RAM block, a PRG file on tape or disk. If they are not identical a VERIFY ERROR results. (Note. Under some circumstances a VERIFY ERROR does not necessarily mean that a genuine error has occurred, refer to the discussion of link addresses in Chapter 4 for further details.) VERIFY is normally used on BASIC programs but it need not be so, using the 'secondary address' of 1 any PRG file can be verified, for example a machine code program previously saved from a machine language monitor can be LOADed and VERIFYed from BASIC in this way.

Examples

VERIFY	will compare memory with the next program on tape.
VERIFY"PROGNAME"	will search the tape until a program called PROGNAME is encountered and will then compare this with current memory.
VERIFY"PROGNAME",8	will compare memory with the program called PROGNAME on disk.
VERIFY"PROGNAME",8,1	will find PROGNAME on disk and note the RAM block from which PROGNAME was originally SAVEd; a byte by byte comparison will then be made with the same area of memory.

BASIC PROGRAM STATEMENTS

CLR	ON . . . GOTO	RETURN
DATA	IF . . . THEN	SPC(
DEFFN and FN	LET	ST
DIM	NEXT	STOP
END	PEEK	SYS
FOR . . . TO . . . STEP	POKE	TAB(
FRE	POS	TI
GOSUB	READ	TI$
ON . . . GOSUB	REM	USR
GOTO	RESTORE	WAIT

CLR
Format: CLR

'Clear' effectively erases all BASIC variables (integer, floating point and strings) currently in memory, leaving the BASIC program intact. Like NEW, CLR works by re-initializing the variable table which the operating system sets up when variables are encountered. The variable table pointers in decimal addresses 45 to 52 are reset according to whatever values are found in the 'end of program' and 'top of memory' pointers. CLR performs several other functions: it RESTOREs the DATA statement pointers, 'forgets' all FOR . . . NEXT and GOSUB . . . RETURN references, and aborts all OPEN files without properly CLOSEing them.

   IMPORTANT NOTE. CLOSE all logical files before performing CLR.

   The CLR command is most commonly used when lowering the 'top of memory' pointers to protect a block of RAM from being overwritten by BASIC.

Example:

POKE55,255:POKE56,127:CLR

This will lower the 'top of memory' (that is where the user BASIC part of memory ends) to 32767 thereby protecting memory from 32768 upwards from being used by BASIC. The 8K from 32768 up is a convenient place to locate an alternate screen and color buffer, leaving 2K of memory for Sprite data (it is *not* a convenient place to put your own character set). Examination of the 'bottom of strings' pointers (strings build down from the top of memory), decimal addresses 51 and 52, after entering the above commands will show that PEEK(51)=255 and PEEK(52)=127; thus CLR resets these pointers in accordance with the new 'top of memory'. If the values of previously defined numeric variables or arrays are needed by the program then CLR can be avoided when lowering the top of memory by resetting the pointers in addresses 51 and 52 using POKE; of course dynamic strings will be lost since these build from the top of memory downwards.

DATA, READ and RESTORE
We take three commands together.

Format: DATA d1/,d2,d3, . . .,dn/ (where d1,d2, . . . are numbers or strings)
Format: READ x/,y, . . .,z/   (where x,y, . . .,z are BASIC variables)
Format: RESTORE

DATA statements are used to store constant values of variables needed by a program. They store data which will normally be required sequentially in the order given in the DATA statements. String variables need not be inside quotes unless they contain a space, colon, comma or shifted characters. Two commas with nothing between them will either be read as zero or an empty string. A superfluous comma is therefore something to be avoided. Examples of situations where DATA statements can be usefully applied are: a machine code program which is to be POKEd byte by byte into memory, values of oscillator POKEs for a music program, graphics data to set up Sprites, or strings for messages. Once inserted into the program DATA statements are assigned to variables using READ, this command 'reads' the next DATA item from wherever it is located in the program. If the next item of DATA happens to be a number and you are trying to READ it as a string with, say, READX$ a syntax error will result. It is good practice to collect all DATA statements together in one block either at the beginning or at the end of a program.

READ uses two sets of pointers: the last program line number from which a DATA item was read is pointed to by the contents of addresses decimal 63 and 64, thus

Last line number = PEEK(63)+256*PEEK(64)

This can be useful in debugging a program with a large number of DATA statements. For example if one note of a long tune is wrong the program line number of the current DATA item can be PRINTed on the screen as the tune is played. The other pointer is contained in addresses decimal 65 and 66. This points to the address in memory of the next DATA item. Note that one pointer lags behind the other, as it were.

Address of next DATA item = PEEK(65)+256*PEEK(66)

The command RESTORE sets the next data statement pointers back to the first DATA item.

Examples:

```
1000  DATA "STRING",100,3.145
1010  READ A$,I%,X:REM NOW A$="STRING", I%=100, X=3.145
1000  DATA3:REM NUMBER OF NUMBERS-NN
1010  DATA100,1.25,300
1020  DATA3:REM NUMBER OF STRINGS-NS
1030  DATA"THESE","ARE","STRINGS"
1040  READNN
1050  FORI=1TONN
1060  READX(I):PRINTX(I)
1070  NEXT
1080  READNS
1090  FORI=1TONS
1100  READX$(I):PRINTX$(I)
1110  NEXT
1120  RESTORE:REM CAN NOW REREAD DATA FROM START
```

DEFFN

Format: DEFFN NM(X) = < BASIC numeric formula >

Here NM is any two-character function name, X is the variable, and the formula on the right can be any numeric BASIC expression which may or may not involve X. As with ordinary variable names more than two symbols can be used but only the first two will be recognized. 'Define function' is a convenient way to define any numeric standard BASIC formula which will be used in many places in a program. The definition can include other functions already defined using DEFFN. Having executed DEFFN once the function NM( ) can be called at any point in the program using FN, e.g. Y=FNNM(4). String functions cannot be defined in this way.

The action of Y=FNNM(5), say, is as follows; any previous value of X is stored elsewhere, X is then assigned the value 5 and the right-hand side of the expression in DEFFN is evaluated in the normal way, finally the original value is reassigned to X. Thus although the variable X is used in the evaluation of FN its value remains unchanged.

Examples:

```
1000  DEFFN NM(R)=3.14159*(R*R)
1010  FORR=1TO10
1030  AREA=FNNM(R):PRINTAREA
1040  NEXT
```

A useful function to define is the endearingly named DEEK, a double byte PEEK, e.g.

```
1000  DEFFN DEEK(X)=PEEK(X)+256*PEEK(X+1)
1010  PRINT FNDEEK(55):REM TOP OF BASIC
```

As with variable names only the first two characters of the defined function name will be recognized, e.g. FNDEEK( ) will not be distinguished from FNDECK( ) or FNDEAD( ).

DIM
Format: DIMa1(A,B,. . .,C)/a2(D,E,. . .,F),. . .,an(L,M,. . .,N)/

Here a1,a2,...,an are array names. The restrictions on array names are the same as those for ordinary variables, namely several characters may be used but only the first two are significant. Arrays can be of any data type for example; integer $X\%(I)$, floating point $X(I)$, or string array $X\$(I)$. The numbers A,B,...N are positive integer values which define the size of the array, e.g. the first array can contain $(A+1)*\ldots*(C+1)$ elements since the range for the subscripts is 0 to A, 0 to B, ..., 0 to C. The maximum value of any A,B,...,N is 32767, and the maximum number of subscripts or 'dimensions' for any array is 255.

The purpose of the DIM statement is to reserve memory for a large number of variables which are subscripted in an orderly fashion. Any particular array can only be DIMensioned *once* during program execution. The default size of an undimensioned array is 10 for each subscript; if the program encounters a larger subscript value than this it will give a BAD SUBSCRIPT ERROR. Arrays can be DIMensioned using a computed variable so that the memory reserved is appropriate to the purpose. Generally it is a good idea to DIMension all arrays near the start of the program. Preferably do this after all variables have been given their initial values, since arrays are stored above variables and if a new variable is encountered all arrays will be moved up (by the operating system) to accommodate it.

Examples:

        1000 DIM AR(100),IN%(20),TT$(40)
        1010 DIM AF(A,B,C),IK%(10,15,7),SS$(U,V)

Large arrays use up memory at an alarming rate, specifically:

        5 bytes for the array name
        2 bytes for each subscript or dimension
        2 bytes per element for integer variables
        5 bytes per element for floating point variables
        1 byte for each character of any string variable

Example

        DIM AR(7000) is O.K. on the CBM 64 but
        DIM AR(8000) gives an OUT OF MEMORY ERROR.

END
Format: END

When encountered whilst a program is running END causes the program to cease execution. If there are GOSUBs after the main body of program text, END should be placed as the last line of the main program to prevent the first GOSUB being inadvertently entered. Otherwise END can be placed anywhere in the program. Both END and STOP are commonly used in the debugging phase of program development (execution can be continued using CONT).

When debugging is complete the ENDing of a program can involve quite a lot of tidying up, to leave the user with a clean machine. For example, the top of memory may have been lowered, in which case it behoves the programmer to put it back again before terminating. (Note. RUN/STOP

+ RESTORE keys will not do this.) There may be other things which need to be restored to their original state. A really spectacular way to tidy up the machine in one move is with SYS64738, which executes a warm start and NEWs the program! However, CLOSE all open files first.

FOR . . . TO . . ./STEP and NEXT

We treat these commands together since every FOR . . . TO . . . must have a NEXT to come home to.

Format: FOR V = F TO L /STEP S/
Format: NEXT/V,W, . . .,Z/

Here V is the FOR loop variable or counter, which must be floating point. F is the first value of the variable, L is the last value and S is the value by which V is incremented each time through the loop, if STEP S is omitted it is assumed that S=1. The STEP variable can take any floating point value, positive or negative, but of course should follow the direction of F to L.

The purpose of a FOR loop is to permit repetitive execution of BASIC code lying between FOR and NEXT. A FOR loop is always executed at least once. Upon reaching NEXT the value of the loop counter is incremented and compared with the value specified by TO, if the loop counter is greater than L program execution proceeds to the instruction which follows NEXT.

Examples:
This example puts a green capital A in every location on the screen.

```
1000  SC=1024:CO=55296:REM SCREEN/COL BASE IN MEM
1010  FORI=0TO999:REM BEGIN LOOP (STEP=1)
1020  POKESC+I,1  :REM SCREEN CODE OF A
1030  POKECO+I,5  :REM COLOR CODE GREEN
1040  NEXT        :REM IF I<=999 GO BACK AGAIN
1050  END         :REM EXIT LOOP I=1000 NOW
```

FOR loops can be empty as in

```
1000  FORI=1TO500:NEXT:REM DELAY
```

FOR loops are a very powerful programming tool and very easy to use but there are a number of points to watch.

It is permitted to 'nest' FOR loops, that is put one inside another

```
1000  FORI=1TO10STEP.5
1010  PRINTI
1020  FORJ=1TO10
1030  PRINTJ
1040  NEXTJ:NEXTI
```

Entry into a new FOR loop makes housekeeping demands on the system, and there is a limit to how many nested FOR loops BASIC can cope with. This limit depends on what other activities are going on in the program but in any event the maximum is nine nested loops.

IMPORTANT NOTE. Nested FOR loops should always use different names for their loop counters.

When entering a new FOR loop the operating system checks that no current FOR loop has the same variable name. If it finds one this and all inner loops are aborted and replaced by the new one, havoc then ensues.

The syntax of NEXT permits a number of variations, thus in the last example line 1040 could be replaced by

    1040 NEXT:NEXT or 1040 NEXTJ,I

The first NEXT in 1040 pairs with FORJ..., the second NEXT pairs with FORI.... If no variable name follows NEXT then the operating system assumes that the NEXT pairs with the last FOR loop entered. If a variable name follows NEXT it *must* pair with the last FOR loop entered or a syntax error will result. It is probably best to put in the variable names during program development, this makes the program easier to follow, and remove them at the final stage if speed or memory are of primary importance.

IMPORTANT NOTE. Don't jump out of a FOR loop without going through its paired NEXT.

Example:
This is bad code:

```
1000  FORI=1TO10
1010  PRINTI:IFRND(0)<.5THEN1030
1020  NEXT
1030  REM PROG CONTINUES HERE BUT WE MAY STILL HAVE A LIVE LOOP
```

BASIC won't actually give you a syntax error if you do this, but nevertheless don't. It is the classic example of bad programming and can cause very weird bugs in a long program. (For later reference: the reason is that 18 unwanted bytes are left on the stack if a FOR loop is aborted without going through its NEXT; this can be bad news!) If you need to exit a FOR loop before the TO limit is reached there is an easy way to do it.

Example:

```
1000  FORI=0TO12345
1010  PRINTI*I
1020  GETA$:REM COLLECT ANY KEY PRESS
1030  IFA$<>" "THENI=12345:GOTO1060
1050  PRINT"O'K' BUT I'M BORED"
1060  NEXT
1070  PRINT"THANK GOODNESS"
```

This program will print the squares of the natural numbers and an assertion of boredom until either 12345 is reached or any key is pressed. In either case the loop is exited tidily.

Although it is permitted to change the value of the loop counter during execution of the loop, any changes in the other loop parameters such as the STEP value will not be acted upon unless the loop is re-entered at some subsequent time during program execution.

FRE
Format: FRE(<Dummy variable>)

Amongst other things this command is supposed to return the number of bytes free in the user BASIC program space, e.g. PRINT FRE(0), which is a measure of how much memory you have left to spare. In fact if there are more than 32767 bytes free, FRE(0) comes back with a negative value! Undoubtedly a legacy from the days when BASIC2 machines had at most 32K of user memory. However, this is no great problem since

PRINT FRE(0)−(FRE(0)<0)*65536

will give the correct value. (The expression FRE(0)<0 returns −1 if the inequality is true and zero otherwise.)

FRE first rationalizes dynamic string storage, which is a way of saying that it tidies up the storage of all the strings created by the program so far. The length of a string can change (e.g. A$=A$+CHR$(13)), and if it becomes longer a new place in memory may be required in which to store it. This process leaves gaps scattered about in string memory and the first thing FRE(0) does is to arrange that all the (variable) strings build down from the top of memory, with no gaps: aptly called a 'Garbage collect'. Another thing which may trigger a garbage collect is if execution of the next instruction would cause an out of memory error. The OUT OF MEMORY ERROR is only generated if even a garbage collect didn't create enough space to proceed. If the program generates a lot of changing strings, an involuntary garbage collect can be rather unnerving; the program may appear to have crashed for several tens of seconds and then suddenly start running again. Indeed, there is an example in 'Programming the PET/CBM' where a one-line program triggers an 83-minute garbage collect! With BASIC4 this problem has been substantially eliminated. If garbage collects are unavoidable it is best to produce them in a controlled fashion: pointers can be manipulated and memory freed-up, the pointers can then be reset. Frequent small garbage collects are much better than the occasional very long one. Where real time I/O is involved, such as running an RS 232 device from BASIC there are other ways round this problem.

The number of bytes free can be evaluated directly in BASIC by computing the difference between the 'bottom of strings', pointer at decimal addresses 51 and 52, and the 'top of arrays', pointer at decimal addresses 49 and 50.

Example:

```
1000  BS=PEEK(51)+256*PEEK(52):REM BOTTOM OF STRINGS
1010  TA=PEEK(49)+256*PEEK(50):REM TOP OF ARRAYS
1020  BYTES=BS−TA
1030  PRINT"BYTES FREE"BYTES
```

An OUT OF MEMORY ERROR is not necessarily caused by BYTES FREE being insufficient. It can happen in a (badly written) BASIC program which has inadvertently made unreasonable demands on the 'stack' (a special area of memory used by the 6510 microprocessor to queue jobs), for example by generating a recursive structure like:

```
1000  GOSUB1000
```

BASIC is not a recursive language and cannot be expected to cope with constructions of this type (technically the error should be STACK OVERFLOW ERROR, but this is not an error message in BASIC V2).

GOSUB and RETURN
Format: GOSUB < Line number >

Any long program is liable to have lines which are needed many times during a complete RUN. Rather than having to enter the same routine at many places in the program it makes sense and saves memory if the routine is entered once only and then called by the main part of the program whenever necessary. The GOSUB command is used for exactly this purpose. Following GOSUB the program proceeds to execute the BASIC code beginning at the specified line number, continuing until RETURN is encountered. The command RETURN causes program execution to continue with the first instruction following the original GOSUB call. Like FOR ... TO, which must have its NEXT, GOSUB must have its corresponding RETURN.

IMPORTANT NOTE. Never jump out of a GOSUB without going through RETURN.

Examples:
The following sketch is typical of the kind of construction frequently used.

```
1000  REM***MAIN LOOP***
1010  GETA$:IFA$=" "THEN1010
1020  IFA$="W"THENGOSUB4000  :REM WRITE FILE
1030  IFA$="R"THENGOSUB5000  :REM READ FILE
1040  IFA$="E"THENGOSUB6000  :REM EDIT FILE
1050  IFA$="Q"THEN1070        :REM TERMINATE
1060  GOTO1010:REM LOOP BACK
1070  END:REM USUALLY SOME TIDYING UP REQUIRED
. . . .
4000  REM**WRITE FILE**
4010  GOSUB7000:REM GET FILE NAME
. . .           (Code to write file to tape or disk)
4100  RETURN
5000  REM**READ FILE**
5010  GOSUB7000:REM GET FILE NAME
. . .           (Code to read file from tape or disk)
5100  RETURN
. . .           (Maybe another GOSUB)
7000  REM**GET FILE NAME**
. . .           (Code to input file name)
7100  RETURN
```

Thus it is perfectly OK to have GOSUBs which call other GOSUBs, nested GOSUBs. In the interests of clarity it is a good idea to put 'level 1' GOSUBs (that is, GOSUBs only called from the main body of the program) after the main body of the program, 'level 2' GOSUBs (those called by level 1 GOSUBs) after all the level 1 GOSUBs, and so on. Sometimes, where speed is vital GOSUBs are put before the main body of the program. In such cases the first program line can be a GOTO which jumps over all the GOSUBs.

As each GOSUB is entered the operating system has to remember the address to come back to when RETURN is encountered. Like FOR ... NEXT loops there is a limit on the level to which GOSUBs can be nested. The precise limit will depend on what other activities are going on in the program, but in any event the maximum is 23 nested GOSUBs.

GOSUB can also be used in direct mode, after STOP for example, to resume program execution without losing pre-existing variable values. When the appropriate RETURN is encountered no error is generated and control returns to direct mode.

If it is necessary to conditionally exit a GOSUB the 'structured' way to do it is illustrated below:

```
1000  GOSUB4000:IFEN<>0THEN ... (take action)
....
4000  REM**READ ERROR CHANNEL**
4010  INPUT#1,EN,EM$,ET,ES :REM READ DISK CMD/CHL
4020  IFEN=0THEN4070      :REM EN=0 MEANS NO ERROR
4030  PRINTEN:PRINTEM$     :REM PRINT ERR NB AND MESS
4040  PRINT"TRACK"ET:PRINT"SECTOR"ES
4050  PRINT"PRESS SPACE TO CONT"
4060  GETA$:IFCHR$(A$)<>CHR$(32)THEN4060
4070  RETURN
```

Generally it is a good idea to have just one RETURN for each GOSUB and to put it on a single line at the end of the subroutine. Thus line 4020 above could just as well be

```
4020  IFEN=0THENRETURN
```

but when this kind of exit occurs frequently the code becomes harder to debug and to edit. For this reason the original construction is to be preferred.

BASIC V2 does not support a computed GOSUB, that is a construction of the form GOSUB <Integer variable>, where the variable evaluates to a line number, but in extreme cases one can create a statement of the form GOSUB0000 and, having computed the correct ASC codes and addresses, POKE the line number in—to replace the zeros. Code of this type can be a very efficient way to branch to the correct GOSUB, but it suffers the considerable disadvantage of being dependent on the precise location of the characters 0000 (or whatever) in memory; any changes in the program prior to the GOSUB call will change these addresses. Incidentally the same technique can be used to provide a computed GOTO. Where there are only around 100 possible GOSUBs which may be selected several applications of the following command are probably to be preferred.

ON ... GOSUB
Format: ON V GOSUB<Line number>,<Line number>, ...

Branches to a selected GOSUB according to the value of a variable, in this case V. The variable must evaluate to a number in the range 0 to 255. If V=1 then the branch will be to the GOSUB specified by the first line number, if V=2 the second line number, and so on. If V=0 or V is greater than the number of line numbers specified, no error is generated and program execution proceeds to the next program statement. In this way ON ... GOSUBs which will not fit onto one line can be turned into multiple ON ... GOSUB statements. If V<0 then an ILLEGAL QUANTITY ERROR is generated.

Examples:

Suppose it is necessary to branch to one of 10 GOSUBs, and V takes computed values in the range 1 to 10. This can be accomplished by the following construction.

```
100  IF (V<1ORV>10) THENPRINT"ERROR V="V:STOP:REM ERROR TRAP
200  ONV    GOSUB1000,2000,3000,4000,5000
300  V=V−5:IFV<0THENV=0
400  ONVGOSUB6000,7000,8000,9000,10000
```

Many other variations are possible, for example the GOSUB to be selected may depend on two or more parameters, in which case the line

```
1000  ON V1 GOSUB2000,3000,4000,5000
```

could call GOSUBs, each of the form

```
2000  REM**SELECT ONE OF SEVERAL ALTERNATIVES WHEN V1=1**
2010  ON V2 GOSUB6100,6200,6300,6400
2020  RETURN:REM GO BACK TO 1000+ AFTER ALTERNATIVE
```

GOTO

Format: GOTO<Line number>

Performs a jump to any line in a program. Simultaneously one of the most powerful and dangerous of BASIC commands. A program with GOTOs all over the place is murderously difficult to debug or alter, and very difficult to read. One situation where it is reasonable to use several GOTOs is in forcing conditional exits from a GOSUB to pass through a single RETURN, similarly for a FOR . . . NEXT loop. Apart from situations like this, where the price paid to preserve global structure is a loss of local structure, GOTO should be very rarely needed in a well composed program. For a computed GOTO see the remarks following GOSUB.

When GOTO is encountered the operating system has to search through memory to find the target line. A comparison is made between the hi-byte of the current line number and the hi-byte of the target line number. If the target line number is greater (by this test) then the search will proceed from the current line upwards, otherwise the search will proceed from the start of the program. Thus if speed is important the target line number should either be near the beginning of the program or at least 256 larger than the current line number.

ON . . . GOTO

Format: ON V GOTO <Line number>,<Line number>, . . .

A way of implementing a conditional GOTO, similar to ON . . . GOSUB.

IF . . . THEN

Format: IF<BASIC statements>THEN<Line number>
        IF<BASIC statements>GOTO<Line number>   (slightly faster)
        IF<BASIC statements>THEN<BASIC statements>

This statement enables a program to make conditional branches or to execute code on the remainder of the program line. The main thing to grasp is that if <BASIC statements> evaluates as *true* (−1) then *program execution continues along the same line,* but if <BASIC statements>

evaluates as *false* (0) *program execution jumps to the next line.* In the interests of consistency it is probably better to stick to the IF ... THEN construction. Note that the corresponding THEN *must* be on the same line as IF.

Examples:

      1000 GETA$:IFA$=" "THEN1000

This is a standard line to leave a program looping until any key is pressed. Here is a line which loops until either 'Y' or 'N' is pressed.

      1000 GETA$:IFA$<>"Y"ANDA$<>"N"THEN1000

For examples of typical 'branch on condition' constructions see GOSUB.

It is permitted to have multiple IF ... THEN statements on the same line but remember that the first IF statement which fails to be true will cause the program to jump to the next line.

      1000 IFX<10THEN2000:IFY<0THENPRINT"Y NEGATIVE":GOTO2000
      1010 ....:REM LINE 1000 IS WRONG

This is an example of an incorrect construction. The second IF statement is never tested; because if the first IF statement fails program execution continues with line 1010, otherwise control branches to line 2000. Possibly the programmer intended

      1000 IFX<10THENIFY<0THENPRINT"Y NEGATIVE":GOTO2000
      1010 IFX<10THEN2000:REM BAD CODE BUT WILL WORK

Although this construction is legal it is ugly, time-consuming, and in this case easily avoided with

      1000 IF(X<10ANDY<0)THENPRINT"Y NEGATIVE"
      1010 IFX<10THEN2000:REM BETTER

LET
Format: LET<BASIC variable>=<BASIC expression>

A statement of variable assignment. LETX=10 is the same as X=10 in BASIC. Thus LET is the only word of BASIC which is totally redundant.

PEEK
Format: PEEK(<Numeric formula>)

The numeric formula must evaluate to a number in the range 0 to 65535, i.e. any valid address, Like many BASIC keywords which require an integral parameter PEEK will accept a non-integer parameter and round it down to the nearest integer. PEEK(<Address>) returns the content of the address specified, a number in the range 0 to 255.

Example:

      1000 SC=1024:REM BASE ADDRESS OF SCREEN MEMORY
      1010 FORI=0TO999   :REM COPY ENTIRE SCREEN
      1030 POKE8192+I,PEEK(SC+I) :REM MEMORY TO 8192 UPWARDS
      1040 NEXT

This example also serves to illustrate the next keyword.

POKE
Format: POKE<Numeric formula 1>,<Numeric formula 2>

The first numeric formula must evaluate to a number in the range 0 to 65535, i.e. any valid address. The second formula must evaluate to a number in the range 0 to 255, a byte, POKE <Address>,<Byte> places the given byte into the given address. On the CBM 64 any POKE is effective, even where the 6510 (the main processor) normally sees ROM, but the effect cannot always be observed with PEEK – the RAM at that address may not be enabled, in which case PEEK would read the ROM byte. POKEing about at random is quite likely to provoke a crash but used with care POKE is one of the most powerful of the BASIC keywords. Indeed, without POKE it would be impossible to use many of the more exciting features of the CBM 64. Notice PEEK takes brackets but POKE does not. Common uses of POKE are: putting graphics data into Sprites, moving sprites about the screen, and playing a tune, or inserting a machine code program into memory, from DATA statements.

Examples:
In direct mode the following POKEs will move the 'bottom of memory', i.e. the beginning of the user BASIC program area (normally 2048), to 8192 (=32*256).

POKE32*256,0:POKE44,32:NEW

Here decimal addresses 43 and 44 contain the pointers to the bottom of memory and 8192 is the new start of memory, which must contain a zero.

Another example of the use of POKE was given in the section on FOR...NEXT loops. We shall see many examples in the following chapters.

POS
Format: POS(<Dummy variable>)

One of the less useful BASIC keywords, POS returns the position of the cursor on the current logical screen line, this will be a number in the range 0 to 79. The distinction between a screen line and a *logical screen line* is as follows. A normal CBM 64 screen has 40 columns, but the operating system (not the video chip) can handle an 80-column screen. If, for example, when entering a program line it over-runs into a second 40-column line, the two screen lines are 'linked' and treated as one logical screen line. Consequently if POS returns with a value in the range 40 to 79 it means the cursor is on the second of a linked pair of screen lines. In practice this makes POS slightly less useful in screen handling on the CBM 64 than on an 80-column machine.

Example:
1000 X=POS(0):X=X−40*INT(X/40):PRINTX

will PRINT the screen column occupied by the cursor at the time POS was called.

REM
Format: REM

This is the only aid which BASIC offers towards making programs self-documenting. A REM inserted on any program line will cause everything else on the line to be ignored. Since most programs on the CBM 64 are unlikely to genuinely run out of memory it is a good idea to liberally sprinkle your programs with comments, this will make life far easier later on when the program comes to be modified or extended (but will slightly reduce the speed of execution).

It is an excellent idea to begin every GOSUB with a REM describing the function of the subroutine, and to make every target of a GOTO a REM. More generally use the REM statement at any point where the flow of program control changes or the actual code is obscure.

SPC(
Format: SPC(<Numeric formula>)

The numeric formula must evaluate to a number in the range 0 to 255. The general idea of PRINTSPC(N) is that it PRINTs N spaces, starting from the current cursor position. In actual fact it is not quite as simple as that. When PRINTing on the screen SPC(N) does not normally produce N spaces, but instead N cursor rights: the distinction only becomes apparent if you want to erase something which happens to be in one of those N spaces (see TAB(for a way around this problem). When SPC(is used in a PRINT# to a tape or disk file, genuine spaces (CHR$(32)) are sent. With CBM printers when using SPC(, if a 'space' is printed as the last character on the line a carriage return and line feed will automatically occur. No further 'spaces' will be printed on the next line.

Note that since the keyword is SPC(, the extra space in

SPC (X)

will cause it to be treated as an array SP(X).

Example:
1000 PRINTCHR$(147)"LEFT"CHR$(19)SPC(10)"RIGHT"

will clear the screen, print the word 'LEFT' in the top left and then go back to the beginning of the same line and print 10 'spaces' followed by the word 'RIGHT'. Note the first word is not erased.

STATUS
Format: ST

ST is a floating point variable name (which in fact takes integer values) that is used by the operating system. ST gives the user information describing the success or failure of the last Input/Output operation. The meaning of the different values of ST is given in the table below.

ST value	Cassette read data file GET# or INPUT#	Cassette read program file LOAD or VERIFY	Serial Bus R/W
1	—	—	Time out write
2	—	—	Time out read
4	Short block	Short block	—
8	Long block	Long block	—
16	Unrecoverable read error	Any mismatch	—
32	Checksum error	Checksum error	—
64	End of file	Null character	End or identify
−128	End of tape	End of tape	Device not present

The value of ST is reset after every I/O operation, excluding PRINT, so it should be read immediately after the relevant PRINT# or GET#/INPUT# and stored for later processing if required.

Example:
To read any file (PRG or SEQ) on tape byte by byte we can use the following program. Try it on two short files, one sequential (SEQ) and one a program (PRG) file. Hold down any key to keep reading and hit the 'RETURN' key to END the program. Observe how the end of a program file differs from the end of a sequential file by watching the value of ST. In a sequential file a single CHR$(0) will cause ST to take the value 64, whereas the end of a program file is signaled by two successive values of CHR$(0) and so ST must be 64 twice in succession.

```
1000  OPEN1,1,0,"FILENAME"
1010  GET#1,A$:ZZ=ST
1020  IFA$="" THENA$=CHR$(0)
1030  PRINTASC(A$),ZZ
1040  GETC$:IFC$="" THEN1040:REM WAIT FOR KEY PRESS
1050  IFC$=CHR$(13)THENCLOSE1:END
1060  GOTO1010
```

There are three points to note about this program. The first is that if a null character is read we replace it by CHR$(0). This is because ASC("") gives a syntax error. Secondly when reading a sequential (SEQ) file a null character, CHR$(0), will set ST to 64 and signify the end of the file. However, in a program (PRG) file created by saving a BASIC program, one null character merely signifies the end of a program line and two null characters in succession signal the end of the file.

STOP
Format: STOP

When encountered whilst a program is running, STOP causes the program to cease execution and the message BREAK IN LINE XXXX, where XXXX is the number of the program line which contains the STOP, to be printed on the screen. STOP is very similar to END and differs only in that END does not print a BREAK message. Like END, STOP is most useful when debugging a program, since after examining the values of variables program execution can be continued using CONT, GOSUB or GOTO (RUN will lose the current values of all variables).

Example:
```
1000  IFX<0THENPRINT"ERROR X NEGATIVE":STOP
```

SYS

Format: SYS<Numeric formula>
The numeric formula must evaluate to a number in the range 0 to 65535, i.e. any valid address. SYS<Address> causes the 6510 microprocessor to begin execution of a machine code program starting at the given address. The machine code program will continue to run until a corresponding RTS (return from subroutine) is encountered. At this point control is handed back to BASIC and program execution continues with the first statement following the original SYS call. Thus the effect of SYS is precisely analogous to GOSUB, except that the subroutine called is in machine code. Of course if there is no machine code present at the address SYSd then the computer is almost certain to crash, so SYSing around at random is liable to be a fruitless activity!

Examples:
In direct mode SYS64738 will initialize the machine, as if from power up, resetting all pointers. This can be useful in certain circumstances. Any BASIC program in memory will be lost (as with NEW) but apart from the cassette buffer most RAM is not actually cleared, so that a machine code program should be left intact.

In discussing FOR...NEXT loops we gave an example which filled the screen with green 'A's. The following program first POKEs the appropriate machine code into memory and then performs a similar routine, only this time in machine code. The gain in speed is quite remarkable. Note that for simplicity the machine language routine actually writes to 1024 consecutive screen and color locations (any sprite pointers would be lost).

```
1000 REM*SYS EXAMPLE-FILL SCREEN A'S*
1010 DATA169,0,133,251,169,4,133,252
1020 DATA169,1,32,87,3,169,0,133,251
1030 DATA169,216,133,252,169,5,32,87,3
1040 DATA96,160,0,162,0,145,251,200,208
1050 DATA251,230,252,232,224,4,208,244
1060 DATA96
1070 DATA5985:REM*CHECKSUM*
1080 REM*INSERT M/C IN CASS BUFFER*
1090 CC=0:FORI=0TO43
1200 READX:POKE828+I,X:CC=CC+X
1210 NEXT
1220 IFCC<>5985THENPRINT"DATA STATEMENT ERROR":STO
P
1230 SYS828:REM FILL SCREEN GREEN A'S
1240 END
```

TAB(
Format: TAB(<Numeric formula>)

Here the numeric formula must evaluate to a number in the range 0 to 255. If N exceeds the current cursor position (as indicated by POS) the effect of TAB(N) is to PRINT cursor rights up to the Nth position from the start of the current logical screen line. TAB( ) should only be used with PRINT, it has no effect if used with PRINT#. The principal use of TAB(is to facilitate PRINTing a column of data which is aligned on the left, known as 'left justification'. TAB(N) is identical with SPC(X) where X=N−(current cursor position).

Using knowledge of the zero page, in this case address 19, both TAB(and SPC(can be made to PRINT genuine spaces if required as the following example shows. However, if this technique is used care should be taken to restore the contents of address 19 to 0, otherwise some I/O operations may be disturbed.

Example:
```
1000  POKE19,1:REM NORMALLY ZERO
1010  PRINTCHR$(147):REM CLEAR/HOME
1020  FORI=0TO39:PRINT"A";:NEXT
1040  PRINTCHR$(19):REM HOME AGAIN
1050  PRINT"**"TAB(10)"**"SPC(10)"**"
1060  POKE19,0:END
```

Swapping the TAB(and SPC(commands in line 1050 will illustrate the difference between the two functions.

TIME

Format: TI

TI is a floating point variable name (which in fact takes integer values three bytes wide) that is used by the operating system. It is the time in *jiffys* (1/60 second) since the CBM 64 was powered up. The variable TI is reset to zero every 24 hours. TIME is most useful in measuring the time taken by some routine or in creating delays. Note that since the 'jiffy clock' is turned off during tape I/O it will not generally be precisely accurate. (For really accurate timing, with alarm clock facilities, the 6526 'Time of Day' clock should be used.) The three bytes of the jiffy clock are stored in addresses 160 to 162 (High,middle,low); although TI cannot be reset by a variable assignment (e.g. TI=0 gives a SYNTAX ERROR) TI$="000000" will reset both TI and TI$. Of course there is nothing to prevent us resetting the clock by POKEing directly to these locations.

Examples:
A typical delay for a measured amount of time would be

```
1000  T=TI:REM TAKE CURRENT TIME
1010  IFTI−T<60THEN1010:REM ONE SECOND DELAY
```

There is one pitfall in using this kind of delay loop, it is known as the 'midnight loop' and happens to addicts who leave their machine on for more than 24 hours. If line 1000 is executed fractionally before 'midnight', so that T is very large, and line 1010 is executed after 'midnight', so that TI is now very small, then line 1010 will take about 24 hours to execute − time to get some sleep!

The following code demonstrates the jiffy clock addresses; it is of curiosity value only since TI$="000000" has the same effect.

```
1000  REM*RESET JIFFY CLOCK BY POKES*
1010  PRINTCHR$(147)
1020  PRINTPEEK(160),PEEK(161),PEEK(162)
1030  GETA$:IFA$=" "THEN1010
1040  POKE160,0:POKE161,0:POKE 162,0
1050  REM TI AND TI$ NOW BOTH RESET TO ZERO
1060  GOTO1010
```

TIME$

Format: TI$

TI$ is TI in hours minutes and seconds formatted as a string of length six. Since TI$ is computed from the jiffy clock it is subject to the same limitations of accuracy as TI. Timing loops based on TI or TI$ may be subject to variation.

USR
Format: USR(<Numeric formula>)

The numeric formula can take any floating point value. USR(X) is designed to pass a floating point variable to a user written machine code routine and return with the result, which might be another floating point value. In general USR can be used to call any machine code routine, but is most appropriate where the routine takes a floating point variable as a parameter.

The action of the BASIC statement A=USR(X) is as follows. Firstly the value of X is placed in Floating Point Accumulator number 1, decimal addresses 97 through 101. (The precise way in which floating point variables are stored will be discussed in a later chapter, but at present this is not really relevant.) Secondly USR needs a JMP instruction to tell it where the machine code routine begins. To accomplish this it is necessary to take the following steps before calling USR: POKE784,76:POKE785,L:POKE786,H. Here 76 is the op-code for JMP, L is the lo-byte of the start of the machine code and H is the hi-byte. The 6510 microprocessor will now begin execution of the machine code starting at address 256*H+L. If the purpose of the code is to return to BASIC with a floating point value then the programmer must arrange to place this, in the correct format, in floating point accumulator number 1 before performing the relevant RTS. In our example A=USR(X), the value in the floating point accumulator will then be assigned to the variable A. The various machine code subroutines, available within the system, which can be used to manipulate floating point values will be discussed in the relevant machine code section.

Because it is far easier to perform floating point computations in BASIC than in machine code, the USR function is very rarely used in the manner for which it was designed. One example which would demonstrate USR very nicely would be a routine which given an angle X, rotates a high resolution screen through X radians about the centre point (a very slow process in BASIC). For this kind of graphics routine it would not be necessary to return a value in the floating point accumulator.

Example:
In this example the machine code routine is located at the start of the cassette buffer and is totally trivial in that it just performs an RTS (return from subroutine), leaving the value in the floating point accumulator unchanged.

```
1000  REM*USR EXAMPLE-TRIVIAL*
1010  X=3.14159
1020  POKE784,76:POKE785,60:POKE786,3
1030  REM 3*256+60=828
1040  POKE828,96:REM RTS IN MACHINE CODE
1050  A=USR(X):PRINTA
```

WAIT
Format: WAIT<Address>,A/,B/

Here 'Address' can be any number in the range 0 to 65535, A and B must be in the range 0 to 255. If the optional parameter B is not present it is assumed to be zero. WAIT causes program execution to halt until one or more bits at the specified address take values determined by the parameters A and B. The RUN/STOP key is not tested so it takes a RUN/STOP+RESTORE to halt an ill-judged WAIT. WAIT is designed for handling certain kinds of I/O from BASIC. It is very rarely used in conventional BASIC programs, probably because the manner in which A and B determine the bit pattern which will cause the WAIT to end is somewhat tortuous.

Before explaining the way in which A and B determine the bit pattern being WAITed for we must first explain what an 'Exclusive Or', abbreviated to EOR, does. In English (x EOR y) means either x or y but not both. Thus the 'bit table' of EOR is

	EOR	y 0	1
x	0	0	1
	1	1	0

The condition which determines the end of a WAIT is: *for any one of the eight bits*

If (<content of address> EOR B)AND(A)<>0 the WAIT ends.
If (<content of address> EOR B)AND(A) =0 the WAIT continues.

What this means in practice is that we can WAIT for any one of several bits in the given address to become either 1 or 0, at our choice, and if any one of these events happens the WAIT is ended. Assuming we know which bits we need to look at, the trick is to figure out the correct values for A and B.

Examples:

In the first example we are WAITing for bit 6 of address 203 to become zero. On the CBM 64 this means a key has been pressed (since 203 contains a value less than 64 if some key is pressed and 64 if no key is being pressed). Because the response is so fast, it is necessary to put a delay loop at the start of the program in order to give you time to take your finger off the 'RETURN' key after entering RUN!

```
1000  REM*WAIT– FOR KEY PRESS*
1010  FORI=0TO20:NEXT:REM DELAY
1020  WAIT 203,64,64:REM WAITS UNTIL BIT 6 IS ZERO
1030  PRINT"NOW":END
```

Here a zero in bit 6 of address 203 gives (0EOR1)AND1=1 and the WAIT ends, otherwise (1EOR1)AND1=0 and the WAIT continues.

```
1000  REM*WAIT– FOR NO KEY PRESS*
1010  REM*HOLD DOWN 'RETURN' KEY*
1020  REM* AFTER 'RUN' TO TEST*
1030  WAIT203,64: REM WAITS UNTIL BIT 6 IS ONE
1040  PRINT"NOW":END
```

In this example B defaults to zero. A one in bit 6 of address 203 gives (1EOR0)AND1=1 and the WAIT ends, otherwise (0EOR0)AND1=0 and the WAIT continues.

These two examples show how to test for either a zero (first example) in a given bit position, or a one (second example). To WAIT until any one of several bits in the address take assigned values (0 or 1) is just a matter of putting together the separate bit patterns for A and B.

ARITHMETIC FUNCTIONS

ABS	EXP	RND	SQR
ATN	INT	SGN	TAN
COS	LOG	SIN	

ABS
Format: ABS(<Numeric formula>)

The numeric formula can evaluate to any floating point value. For X >0 we have ABS(X)=X and ABS(−X)=X, the 'absolute value' of X simply 'forgets' the sign of X. If X=0 then ABS(X)=0.

Thus the absolute value of any number is always positive or zero. For example ABS(1.4) is 1.4 and ABS(−1.4) is also 1.4. A mathematically equivalent formula for ABS(X) is X*SGN(X), but this involves a multiplication which is far slower than just 'forgetting' any minus sign.

The function can be used to measure approximate equality, as in IF ABS(X−Y)<.01 THEN ..., or as an alternative measure of distance as in

$$AN=ABS(X1-X2)+ABS(Y1-Y2)$$

This is faster than

$$DI=SQR((X1-X2)*(X1-X2)+(Y1-Y2)*(Y1-Y2))$$

and for many purposes just as good.

ATN
Format: ATN(<Numeric formula>)

The numeric formula can evaluate to any floating point value. ATN(X) returns the angle (measured in radians) whose tangent is X, i.e. if Y=ATN(X) then X=TAN(Y). In other words ATN is the inverse function of TAN. Since TAN is not a one to one function it does not have a true inverse function. To overcome this only the branch of TAN between −pi/2 to +pi/2 is considered, so that values of ATN(X) will always lie strictly in this range.

ATN is useful in trigonometric calculations and is the only inverse trig function immediately available in BASIC, although of course any of the others can be computed by appropriate formulae, e.g.

ARCSIN(X) is ATN(X/SQR(1−X*X))   defined for ABS(X)<1,
ARCCOS(X) is pi/2−ATN(X/SQR(1−X*X)) defined for ABS(X)<1.

COS
Format: COS(<Numeric formula>)

The numeric formula can evaluate to any floating point value. The expression COS(X), where X is assumed to be in radians, returns the cosine of the angle X. If the angle X is measured in degrees then COS(pi*X/180) will give the correct cosine, since 2*pi radians equals 360 degrees.

In terms of a right-angled triangle, the cosine is defined as adj/hyp in Fig. 1. More generally cosine and sine can be defined by power series

$$COS(X)=1-X\uparrow2/2!+X\uparrow4/4!-X\uparrow6/6!-\ldots$$
$$SIN(X)=X-X\uparrow3/3!+X\uparrow5/5!-X\uparrow7/7!+\ldots$$

Here N!=1*2*3*...*N is the factorial function. The algorithms for evaluating trigonometric functions are usually based on some power series expansion.

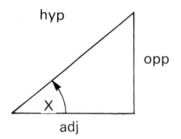

$$COS(X)=adj/hyp$$
$$SIN(X)=opp/hyp$$

Pythagoras's theorem is equivalent to

$$COS(X)*COS(X)+SIN(X)*SIN(X)=1$$

Fig. 1 – Trigonometry.

EXP
Format: EXP(<Numeric formula>)

The numeric formula can evaluate to any floating point value. The exponential function is funda-mental throughout scientific and mathematical calculation. It is characterized by being the only (smooth) function whose value at zero is 1 and whose rate of change is itself. It can also be defined in terms of the power series

$$EXP(X)=1+X+X\uparrow2/2!+X\uparrow3/3!+X\uparrow4/4!+\ldots$$

a formula not unrelated to the series for COS(X) and SIN(X). Note that EXP(1)=2.718 .... This number, normally denoted by e, is the base of natural logarithms.

Mathematically important properties of the exponential function are that EXP(X) is positive, strictly increasing, and

$$EXP(A+B)=EXP(A)*EXP(B)   \text{for any real A,B.}$$

These facts lead to the basic properties of logarithms.

Example:

The exponential function is apt to occur in any situation involving rates of growth or decay. The following program computes the net sum resulting when $1000 is invested for 10 years at 7% annually compounded continuously.

```
1000 I=1000 :REM INITIAL SUM
1010 R=.07   :REM RATE OF GROWTH
1020 T=10    :REM TIME PERIOD
1030 X=I*EXP(T*R):PRINTX
```

This gives a value of $2013.75 in contrast to the value $1967.15 obtained by compounding the same interest rate once annually. This is because in the exponential model the growth is continuous, whereas in the more conventional actuarial model annual interest is added once yearly, i.e. in discrete steps. Exponential growth models are more suited to biological or physical systems than to finance.

INT
Format: INT(<Numeric formula>)

The numeric formula can evaluate to any floating point value. The function INT(X), the 'integer part' of X, returns the greatest integer less than X. Thus INT(2.7) is 2, INT(-2.2) is -3. The resulting integer need not be in the range -32768 to $+32767$. In CBM BASIC V2, if X is in the range -32768 to $+32767$, the same effect can be achieved by putting X%=X, but in other BASICs this won't always work.

Note that INT(X) is not the 'nearest integer to X'. If a nearest integer function is required it can be defined as INT(X+0.5) for X positive or negative. This function is sometimes useful when 'rounding off'. For example the CBM 64 will compute the value of $2.23-2.18$ as .04999 . . . etc. This could cause difficulties in an accounting program which treated the two figures after the decimal point as representing the cents. The following technique, suggested by Jim Butterfield, illustrates one solution to this problem, namely turning all amounts into cents.

```
1000  INPUT"AMOUNT";A
1010  A=INT(A*100+.5)
1020  PRINT"THE AMOUNT IS"A/100
```

LOG
Format: LOG(<Numeric formula>)

The numeric formula must evaluate to a strictly positive value. The logarithmic function, LOG(X) for X>0, returns the logarithm, to base $e=2.718 \ldots$, of X. Because the exponential function is strictly increasing it has a well-defined inverse function and this function is LOG, i.e. if Y=EXP(X) the X=LOG(Y). Since e=EXP(1) it follows LOG(e)=1. To convert the logarithm to another base, b>0 say, we only need to divide by LOG(b). For example

Logarithm to base 10 of X = LOG(X)/LOG(10).

The formula EXP(A+B)=EXP(A)*EXP(B) leads to the most useful property of logarithms

LOG(X*Y)=LOG(X)+LOG(Y) for X,Y>0

This formula enables a multiplication to be accomplished by means of an addition provided a set of logarithm tables is available. It is also the basis of the slide rule. Of course the advent of the microcomputer has made log-tables and slide rules somewhat unnecessary.

According to Raeto West the evaluation of LOG in BASIC 2 is probably based on summing four terms of the series

LOG((1+X)/(1−X)) = 2*(X+X↑3/3+X↑5/5+X↑7/7+ . . .) for ABS(X)<1.

RND

Format: RND(<Numeric formula>)

The numeric formula can be any floating point variable, but only the sign (positive, negative or zero) is relevant. The function RND(X) is used for generating 'random' numbers. RND(X) will generate a number in the range 0 to 1, excluding 0 and 1. On power up, decimal addresses 139 to 143 contain a constant floating point number called a *seed*. Each call to RND(X), with X>0, takes the number stored in 139 to 143, uses it to compute the next number in a pseudo-random sequence, and stores the result in 139 to 143. Thus for X>0 the last number generated by RND(X) is used to generate the next number and the resulting sequence will be the same every time. This can be useful when testing a program. The pseudo-random sequence generated by a fixed seed has a square distribution, i.e. the probability that a number will fall in any given subinterval of 0 to 1 depends only on the length of the subinterval (in fact this probability *is* the length of the sub-interval) and not on its position.

RND(0) has a different effect. In this case the contents of addresses 139 to 143 are not used to compute the next number. Instead values from the free running jiffy clock are used. This means that the first use of RND(0) will generate a fairly random seed value. Subsequent calls to RND(X) with X>0 will then generate a new pseudo-random sequence. However, if the program loops periodically and RND(0) is used every time, then the numbers generated will bear a strong correla-tion with the jiffy clock, i.e. time, and may not appear random.

Finally if X<0 then RND(X) will cause a new seed to be used. The particular value placed in 139 to 143 will depend on the current contents of the floating point accumulator. Again, if the program is looping this could cause a non-random effect.

All in all, if the sequence is required to be as unpredictable as possible (whilst retaining a square distribution) the best approach is probably to set an initial random seed value, using RND(0), and then on all subsequent calls use RND(X) with X>0.

Examples of the use of RND are to be found in shuffling a deck of cards or in Monte Carlo simulations of a large number of random events.

Examples:

To generate a random integer N in the range A to B, inclusive, we can use the formula

$$N = A + INT((B+1-A)*RND(1))$$

A simpler and faster way to generate a random integer in the range 0 to 255 is to use the SID chip white noise generator. The following program illustrates this.

```
1000  REM WHITE NOISE RANDOM GENERATOR
1010  SID=54272:REM SID CHIP BASE ADDRESS
1020  POKESID+24,POKESID+24,128:REM OSC3 AUDIO OFF
1030  POKESID+14,255:REM FREQ LO-BYTE
1040  POKESID+15,255:REM FREQ HI-BYTE
1050  POKESID+18,POKESID+18,129:REM SELECT NOISE AND GATE
1060  FORI=1TO10:REM NOW READ 10 RANDOM NBRS
1070  PRINTPEEK(SID+27)
1080  NEXT
```

SGN

Format: SGN(<Numeric formula>)

The numeric formula can evaluate to any floating point value. The 'sign' function returns the following values

$$SGN(X) = \ \ 1 \text{ if } X>0$$
$$SGN(X) = \ \ 0 \text{ if } X=0$$
$$SGN(X) = -1 \text{ if } X<0$$

For X<>0 SGN(X) is therefore equivalent to X/ABS(X). The sign function is probably most useful for avoiding multiple IF...THEN statements where the branch depends on the sign of some number.

Example:

This example serves to illustrate both RND and SGN. Here RND is used to move a purple reverse field space around the screen. This point represents a quarry, which starts in the centre of the screen and moves two cells in a randomly selected direction. A white asterisk represents a pursuer and moves one cell on each move towards the quarry.

```
1000 REM CHASE
1010 SC=1024:CO=55296:REM SCREEN AND COL BASE
1020 PRINTCHR$(147):REM CLEAR SCREEN
1030 XQ=20:YQ=12:REM QUARRY IN CENTRE
1040 XP=0:YP=0:REM PURSUER IN TOP LEFT
1050 ZQ=40*YQ+XQ:REM QUARRY
1060 POKESC+ZQ,160:POKECO+ZQ,4:REM PURPLE QUARRY
1070 ZP=40*YP+XP:REM PURSUER
1080 POKESC+ZP,42:POKECO+ZP,1:REM WHITE PURSUER
1090 IF(XP=XQ)AND(YP=YQ)THENEND
1100 DY=1:IFRND(1)<.5THENDY=-1
1110 DX=1:IFRND(1)<.5THENDX=-1
1120 YQ=YQ+2*DY:IFYQ<0THENYQ=0
1130 IFYQ>24THENYQ=24
1140 XQ=XQ+2*DX:IFXQ<0THENXQ=0
1150 IFXQ>39THENXQ=39
1160 YP=YP+SGN(YQ-YP):XP=XP+SGN(XQ-XP)
1170 GOTO1050
```

SIN

Format: SIN(<Numeric formula>)

The numeric formula can evaluate to any floating point value. The expression SIN(X), where X is assumed to be in radians, returns the sine of the angle X. If the angle X is measured in degrees then SIN(pi*X/180) will give the correct sine, since 2*pi radians equals 360 degrees. Refer to the section on COS for further information on trigonometric functions.

SQR

Format: SQR(<Numeric formula>)

The numeric formula must evaluate to a non-negative number. The function SQR(X) returns the positive square root of X, i.e. the unique number Y>=0 such that Y*Y=X. The square root function is mathematically equivalent to X↑.5 but this takes roughly 5% longer to evaluate in BASIC.

TAN

Format: TAN(<Numeric formula>)

The numeric formula can evaluate to any floating point value not equal to an odd multiple of pi/2. TAN(X), where X is in radians, returns the tangent of the angle X. In terms of right-angled triangles this is the ratio opposite/adjacent (see Fig. 1). As X approaches pi/2 (90 degrees) this ratio becomes infinite, which explains why the TAN of any odd multiple of pi/2 is undefined.

STRING FUNCTIONS

ASC	LEN	VAL
CHR$	MID$	
LEFT$ and RIGHT$	STR$	

Detailed examples of PRINT formatting and string handling are given in Chapter 1 so in this section we shall merely describe the syntax of these BASIC keywords.

ASC

Format: ASC(A$)

Here A$ can be any string of length >0 and ASC(A$) will return the Commodore ASCII code for the first character of A$. This is an integer in the range 0 to 255: a table in the appendices shows the ASC code for each character. The null string N$="" is an example of a string of length zero; ASC(N$) will give an ILLEGAL QUANTITY ERROR. For this reason the following program lines are often used when processing strings into numbers.

```
1000  GET#1,A$:IFA$=" "THENA$=CHR$(0)
1010  X=ASC(A$)
```

Note that ASC(CHR$(0)) is zero and does not give an error message since CHR$(0) is a string of length 1. In general ASC(CHR$(N)) is N for any integer N in the range 0 to 255. Thus for single characters ASC is the inverse function of CHR$.

The ability to assign a unique number to each character is necessary in a variety of string handling procedures. Examples are sorting, enciphering or simply POKEing a file name into RAM to be picked up by a machine code subroutine as in

```
1000  INPUT"FILENAME";A$
1010  FORN=1TOLEN(A$)
1020  POKEBASE+N,ASC(MID$(A$,N,1))
1030  NEXT
```

CHR$

Format: CHR$(<Numeric expression>)

The numeric expression must evaluate to a number in the range 0 to 255. The CHR$ function takes a number, treats it as an ASC code, and returns with the corresponding character.

The characters with ASC codes 0 to 31 and 128 to 160 are reserved for printer control or screen control characters, for example CHR$(147) is the familiar reverse field heart 'CLR/HOME' character. The CHR$ function also enables us to PRINT characters which would otherwise pose problems, for example PRINTCHR$(34) will print a quote mark.

LEFT$

Format LEFT$(<String expression>, <Numeric formula>)

Here the string expression must evaluate to a valid string and the numeric formula should evaluate to an integer in the range 0 to 255. LEFT$(A$,N) returns with a string which consists of the N leftmost characters of A$. If N=0 the null string is returned. If N is greater than the length of A$ the whole of A$ is returned and no error is generated.

Examples:

LEFT$("ABC",4)	is "ABC"
LEFT$("ABC",0)	is " "
LEFT$(" ",1)	is " "
LEFT$("ABC"+"DEF",4)	is "ABCD"
LEFT$("A B"+"CDE",4)	is "A BC"

RIGHT$

Format: RIGHT$(<String expression>,<Numeric expression>)

Again the string expression must evaluate to a valid string and the numeric formula to a number in the range 0 to 255. RIGHT$(A$,N) returns with a string which consists of the N rightmost characters of A$. If N=0 the null string is returned. If N is greater than the length of A$ the whole of A$ is returned and no error is generated.

Examples:

RIGHT$("ABC",4)	is "ABC"
RIGHT$("ABC",0)	is " "
RIGHT$(" ",1)	is " "
RIGHT$("ABC"+"DEF",4)	is "CDEF"
RIGHT$("ABC"+" DE",4)	is "C DE"

LEN

Format: LEN(<String expression >)

LEN(S$) returns the length of S$, i.e. the number of characters in the string, an integer in the range 0 to 255. This is a useful function in many kinds of string manipulations.

Examples:

LEN("ABC"+"DEF")	is 6
LEN(" ")	is 0

```
1000  REM COUNT NUMBER OF 'I'S IN A$
1010  COUNT=0
1020  FORN=1TOLEN(A$)
1030  IFMID$(A$,N,1)="I"THENCOUNT=COUNT+1
1040  NEXT
```

MID$

Format: MID$(<String expr.>,<Numeric form. 1>/,<Numeric form. 2>/)

Numeric formula 1 should evaluate to an integer in the range 1 to 255; 0 will give an ILLEGAL QUANTITY ERROR. Numeric formula 2 should evaluate to an integer in the range 0 to 255. Since the second numeric formula is optional there are essentially two forms of MID$. The first MID$(A$,M,N) returns a substring of A$ which consists of N characters starting from the Mth character of A$. Thus MID$("ABCDE",3,2) is "CD". If M is greater than the length of A$, or N is zero, no error is generated and the function returns the null string. If A$ has fewer than N characters, starting from the Mth, the whole of the rest of the string is returned.

The second form is MID$(A$,M). This function extracts all characters in A$ starting from the Mth. Thus MID$("ABCDE",4) is "DE". If A$ has fewer than M characters no error is generated and the null string is returned.

Example:

If a program is to perform a large number of different GOSUBs according to which key is pressed there are several ways of selecting the correct GOSUB quickly. The following example illustrates one way. Here the key presses which trigger a subroutine are stored in a string KP$.MID$ is used to scan through KP$ in an attempt to find a match for whatever key has been pressed. This might seem an odd way to do it, using an array is another possibility, but it is surprisingly fast.

```
1000  KP$="FPADSRYI1234":REM 12 CHARS
1010  GETA$:IFA$=" "THEN1010
1020  KEY=0
1030  FORI=1TOLEN(KP$)
1040  IFA$<>MID$(KP$,I,1)THENNEXT:GOTO1010:REM NOT FOUND
1050   KEY=I:I=LEN(KP$):NEXT: REM FOUND–SO END FOR LOOP AND CONT
1060  ONKEY    GOSUB1100,1200,1300,1400,1500,1600
1070  KEY=KEY–6:IFKEY<0THENKEY=0
1080  ONKEYGOSUB1700,1800,1900,2000,2100,2200
1090  GOTO1010:REM GO BACK FOR NEXT KEY
```

STR$

Format: STR$(<Numeric formula>)

The numeric formula can evaluate to any floating point value. This function converts a number into its equivalent string representation, for example STR$(32.2) is " 32.2". The resulting string cannot be treated as a number, for example it cannot be multiplied, but can be manipulated like any other string.

STR$(X), where X is non-negative, will produce a string with a leading space. If X<0 this space is occupied by a minus sign, e.g. STR$(−32.2) is "−32.2"

The STR$ function is useful when formatting numerical output, for example it can be used to introduce trailing zeros. But there are some pitfalls. STR$ (0.0005) is " 5E−04" not " .0005" as one might expect.

Examples:

```
PRINTSTR$(2E+04):REM GIVES 20000

1000  INPUT"NUMBER";N
1010  N$=MID$(STR$(N),2): REM STRIP MINUS SGN OR SPACE
1020  PRINTN$
```

VAL
Format: VAL(<String expression>)

Roughly speaking VAL is the inverse function of STR$. VAL(<String>) converts the string into a numerical equivalent, where this can be sensibly done. VAL ignores spaces, accepts one occurrence only of '−' or '+' as prefixes and the decimal point. If the first non-blank character of the string is not '+', '−', '.', or some digit the value zero is returned. String conversion is terminated when any non-digits, except '.', 'E+', or 'E−' are found.

VAL is useful when using the INPUT statement. In the last example (above), if a non-numeric character is entered, the error message REDO FROM START is generated, since only numeric input was expected. This can ruin a carefully set up screen display and is avoided in the first example below.

Examples:

```
1000  INPUT"NUMBER";A$:N=VAL(A$)
1010  IFN=0THENPRINTCHR$(147)"TRY AGAIN":GOTO1000
1020  PRINTN:REM ZERO 'CANNOT' BE INPUT IN THIS WAY

PRINTVAL("   +    123")    :REM RESULT IS     123
PRINTVAL("   −    123")    :REM RESULT IS    −123
PRINTVAL("+−123")          :REM RESULT IS     0
PRINTVAL("123.456")        :REM RESULT IS     123.456
PRINTVAL("2E4")            :REM RESULT IS     20000
PRINTVAL("20000000000")    :REM RESULT IS     2E+10
```

LOGICAL OPERATORS

AND   NOT   OR

The logical operators are an extremely useful part of the BASIC language. They enable quite complex 'branch on condition' instructions to be expressed very easily. In addition the logical operators can be used as tools to read or alter any particular bit (i.e. binary zero or one) of a byte. Correct use of the logical operators along these lines requires an understanding of the binary notation for representing numbers − this material, with numerous examples, is covered in Chapter 1. The following brief descriptions are confined mainly to syntactical rules.

AND

Format: <Expression>AND<Expression>

The BASIC expressions must either be numeric, or logical propositions. When AND is evaluated both types are converted into 2-byte integers. Hence numeric values must lie in the range -32768 to $+32767$. If the expression is a logical proposition it will have a 'truth' value. For some curious reason in CBM BASIC V2 true$=-1$ and false$=0$. Conversely integer expressions are evaluated as 'true' logical propositions if non-zero and 'false' if zero. Thus the line

    1000 IFXTHEN5000:REM SAME AS IFX<>0THEN . . .

will cause program execution to branch whenever X is not zero.

First use: When used with logical propositions the effect of AND is what one might guess from its normal English usage. For example in the line

    1000 IF(X=10)AND(Y=100)THEN5000

program execution will branch to line 5000 only if $X=10$ and $Y=100$, if either condition is false the branch to 5000 will not occur. In a similar way we can utilize more complex statements with several conditions to be tested

    1000 IF(X=10)AND(A$<>"N")AND(Y=100)THEN5000

causes program execution to branch to line 5000 only if all of the propositions '$X=10$', 'A$ is not the string "N"', and '$Y=100$' are true.

Each logical proposition is assigned one of two values 0 (false) or -1 (true) and the function AND is evaluated according to the 'truth table'

AND	0	-1
0	0	0
-1	0	-1

NOTE. AND is symmetric

e.g. (-1)AND(0) is (0)AND(-1)

Second use: When used with integer values XANDY performs a bit by bit comparison across 16 bits, returning a two-byte integer whose Kth bit $(0<=K<=15)$ is 1 if the Kth bits of X and Y are both 1, and zero otherwise. Here are some examples

        63AND16 is 16
        17AND7 is 1
        17680AND567 is 16
        -32768AND32767 is 0

Although this may seem rather obscure at first sight, in practice, as we shall see in Chapter 1, the bit matching property of AND is exceedingly useful.

NOT

Format: NOT<Expression>

The BASIC expression may be either an integer or a logical proposition. When acting on an integer the effect of NOT is to flip each bit in the two-byte representation, i.e. bits which are zero are flipped to ones and viceversa. This is known as taking the 'ones complement' of the original 16 bits. Because of the manner in which integers in the range −32768 to +32767 are represented using 16 bits, the action of NOTX is equivalent to −(X+1). Thus if X=0 then NOTX is −1, and if X=−1 then NOTX is 0. The effect of NOT on a logical proposition is therefore to convert true to false and viceversa. Rather like the double negative in English grammar the use of NOT is generally best avoided.

Examples:

        1000 IFNOT(X=10)THEN5000:REM BRANCH IF X<>10

        1000 IFNOT((X=10)AND(Y=100))THEN5000:REM BRANCH IF X<>10 OR
              Y<>100

In untangling more mind-bending examples of such expressions it is helpful to use the De Morgan laws:

        P=NOT(NOTP)
        NOT(PANDQ)=(NOTP)OR(NOTQ)
        NOT(PORQ)=(NOTP)AND(NOTQ)

OR
Format: <Expression>OR<Expression>

As with AND the BASIC expressions must either be numeric, or logical propositions. When OR is evaluated both types are converted into 2-byte integers. Hence numeric values must lie in the range −32768 to +32767. As before, a logical proposition will be given the value of 0 or −1. The truth table for OR is as follows.

OR	0	−1
0	0	−1
−1	−1	−1

Note: OR is symmetric
        e.g. (−1)OR(0) is (0)OR(−1)

First use: When used with logical propositions the effect of OR is what one might guess from its normal English usage. For example in the line

        1000 IF(X=10)OR(Y=100)THEN5000

program execution will branch to line 5000 if either X=10, or Y=100, or both.

Second use: When used with integer values XORY performs a bit by bit comparison across 16 bits, returning a two-byte integer whose Kth bit (0<=K<=15) is 1 if the Kth bit of X is 1, or the Kth bit of Y is 1, or both, and zero otherwise. Here are some examples

        630R16 is 63
        170R7 is 23
        17680OR567 is 18231
        −327680OR32767 is −1

The exclusive or, EOR, was discussed in connection with WAIT. Although this command is not implemented in BASIC, it can be constructed from the other logical operators. Thus

A EOR B = ((NOTA)ANDB)OR((NOTB)ANDA)

INPUT/OUTPUT STATEMENTS

CLOSE	GET and GET#	OPEN
CMD	INPUT and INPUT#	PRINT and PRINT#

These are the BASIC keywords used to control the flow of information to and from peripheral devices. In general terms there are three main steps in communicating with a peripheral device. Firstly a logical file, i.e. channel of information flow, must be OPENed. Secondly information is sent using CMD or PRINT#, or received using INPUT# or GET#, and finally the logical file must be CLOSEd.

The most familiar I/O statement is of course PRINT. This is also one of the most complex subroutines of the operating system. PRINT normally directs output to the screen (device number 3) but using CMD, PRINT statements can be directed to other devices. The INPUT and GET statements obtain information from the keyboard (device number 0).

The words 'read' and 'write' are used to describe the direction in which data flows during an I/O operation. The CBM 64 is regarded as the 'central figure' so that data which comes from a peripheral device to the microcomputer is read (in), whereas data sent from the CBM 64 to a peripheral is written (out).

Summary of I/O keywords

PRINT	Output to the screen.
GET and INPUT	Input from the keyboard.
OPEN	Setup channel for output or input.
CMD	Change output device.
PRINT#	Send data through previously OPENed channel.
GET#	Input one character through OPENed channel.
INPUT#	Input data through previously OPENed channel.
CLOSE	Close down previously OPENed channel.

Peripheral devices may either send data to the CBM 64 ('talk'), receive data from the CBM 64 ('listen') or do both. In any particular I/O operation the CBM 64 has to know which device it is supposed to communicate with. To make this possible each peripheral has a device number. The following is a table of the standard Commodore device numbers.

Commodore device numbers

Device number	Device	Function	Model/Type
0	Keyboard	Talk	-----
1	Cassette	Talk and Listen	C2N
2	RS232	Either	Modem/Printer/Other (User port)
3	Screen	Listen	Monitor of TV
4 (or 5)	Printer	Listen	1515,1525/6, MPS 801 serial IEEE
6	Plotter	Listen	1520 serial IEEE
7	Not assigned	-----	Serial IEEE
8 (or 9)	Disk drive	Talk and Listen	1541 serial IEEE
10 to 255	Not assigned	-----	Serial IEEE

When manipulating files on tape or disk it is necessary to be aware of the file type. There are two main types of file applicable to tape or disk, these are the *program* file (PRG) and the *sequential* file (SEQ). In addition there are a number of more advanced file types used in disk handling. For the present it is enough to understand the distinction between program files and sequential files. A PRG file is normally created by the SAVE command and consists of some preliminary information (the header) followed by an exact copy of the BASIC program in RAM. Normally a PRG file is 'read' by simply LOADing back into the CBM 64. However, it is possible to read or even (on disk) to write a PRG file on a byte-by-byte basis using GET# and PRINT#. An example of a program which can read a PRG file byte by byte is given in the section on ST. An SEQ file is normally a data file created by a combination of the OPEN, PRINT# and CLOSE keywords and consisting of ASC codes. This file type is usually used to store text and/or numerical data.

The following is a complete list of Commodore file types.

Commodore file types

Type	Device	Comment
DEL	Disk only	A warning signal: a file which was not properly CLOSEd has been scratched under peculiar circumstances (e.g. full disk).
SEQ	Disk or tape	Standard data file.
PRG	Disk or tape	RAM image (usually BASIC or M/C program).
USR	Disk only	Alternative type of SEQ file (roughly).
REL	Disk only	Relative access file.

CLOSE
Format: CLOSE <Numeric formula>

The numeric formula should evaluate to an integer in the range 1 to 255, this number should correspond to a previously OPENed logical file number. CLOSE<Logical file number> is used to close a previously OPENed logical file when processing (reading or writing) of the file is complete. CLOSEing a logical file which has not been OPENed does not generate an error message. If the file was used to write data it *must* be CLOSEd or the data may be lost. (Where data has been written to disk and the file not properly CLOSEd, even if this data is not lost, future data consigned to the disk will sooner or later become corrupted.) When using tape or disk the CLOSE statement writes any non-full buffers to the device and generates the correct 'end of file' marker.

WARNING. An unCLOSEd file on disk will appear in the directory with an asterisk against the file type. DO NOT Scratch such files; use Validate.

CLOSE also deletes the CBM 64's internal record that a logical file is currently OPEN. There is a limit to the number of OPEN files, at most 10 at any one time with at most 5 of these OPEN to IEEE or serial bus devices; it is therefore good practice to CLOSE a file as soon as it is no longer required. There is one exception to this: CLOSEing a file which has been OPENed to a disk drive command channel (typically OPEN15,8,15) will also CLOSE all other OPEN files. This can have some very puzzling consequences if one is not aware of the problem. It follows that CLOSEing down the command channel to a disk drive should be left until other files have already been CLOSEd.

The number of currently OPEN files is stored in decimal address 152 and a table of information about active files (logical file numbers, device numbers and secondary addresses) is kept at decimal addresses 601 and 630. If a program crashes, owing to a SYNTAX ERROR for example, and is then edited before any OPEN files have been CLOSEd, it can happen that the contents of 152 are reset to zero leaving the table intact. Under these circumstances any OPEN files can be CLOSEd by first POKEing 152 with the number of OPEN files and then CLOSEing the files in the normal way.

When data has been sent to a file using CMD it will be necessary to send a null character before CLOSEing the file. This is because CMD leaves the output device still 'listening' (it hasn't been told to 'un-listen'!).

Examples:
To LIST a program to the printer

OPEN5,4:CMD5,"PROGNAME":LIST followed by PRINT#5:CLOSE5

Normal usage:

CLOSE1
CLOSEL   (L a previously OPENed logical file number)
CLOSE4*(I+J)   is syntactically correct but rarely used.

CMD

Format: CMD<Numeric formula>/,<String>/

The numeric formula should evaluate to an integer in the range 1 to 255 and this number should correspond to a previously OPENed logical file number. This keyword causes the current output device, normally the screen (device 3), to become the specified device. OPEN1,<Device number>: CMD1 has the effect of causing the specified device to listen, and hence to receive any subsequent

PRINTed data, until such time as it is told to un-listen. In addition CMD has the capability to output a string to the device. This second feature is quite useful for titling program LISTings (see above example).

Any system error will cause the output device to revert to the screen. In this event the device will still be listening, so a null character should be sent (e.g. PRINT#1, " "). In practice reversion to the screen is a frequent and somewhat unpredictable occurrence; for example GET used in a program can cause this problem. The CMD statement has the air of a slightly dubious fudge to enable programs with a large number of PRINT statements to send output to devices other than the screen. Unfortunately it won't always work. If a program is liable to be used to send data to a device other than the screen it is better to OPEN a logical file with a variable device number (which can be assigned as required) and then use PRINT# rather than PRINT.

Despite minor bugs CMD is a very useful command, mostly when directing an ASC program LISTing to printer, tape or disk. Text file LISTings of this type can be useful in several contexts, for example for incorporating a program into a word processor file. Jim Butterfield has published a number of ingenious programs based on this idea.

Example:
To LIST a program to disk

>   OPEN1,8,2,"0:PROGNAME,S,W":CMD1:LIST
>   Followed by PRINT#1;:CLOSE1

GET
Format: GET<Variable>/,<Variable>, . . . <Variable>/

The statements GETA$ or GETX read a single keypress from the keyboard buffer. If no key has been pressed then the null character or zero will be returned and program execution will continue. When numeric data is specified, as in GETX, only the number keys are acceptable, other keypresses will give a SYNTAX ERROR and halt program execution (or EXTRA IGNORED with ',' or ':'). For this reason it is better to always GET a string and then, if required, process it into a number using VAL.

Example:

>   1000 GETJUNK$:IFJUNK$<>" "THEN1000:REM KEYBOARD BUFFER NOW
>   EMPTY
>   1010 PRINT"IS THIS CORRECT ? (Y/N)"
>   1020 GETA$:IFA$<>"Y"ANDA$<>"N"THEN 1020

In these example lines the keyboard buffer is first emptied of spurious characters; possibly a key was pressed twice earlier in the program. A message is PRINTed on the screen and the program will loop on line 1020 until either 'Y' or 'N' is pressed.

GET#
Format: GET#<Numeric formula>,<Variable>/,<Variable>, . . . <Variable>/

The numeric formula should evaluate to an integer in the range 1 to 255, a logical file number.

The action of GET#<Logical file number> is identical to GET except that the character requested is input from a previously OPENed logical file. Indeed, GET is a subset of GET# and has the
same keyword token.

An unexpected feature of GET# is that it is possible to OPEN a logical file to device number
3 and GET# (or INPUT#) characters from the 'screen'. Obviously the TV screen is not itself an
input device, but the screen memory in the CBM 64 can be used as a very large buffer. When one
thinks about it this is the way that the Commodore screen editor works. The second example
below illustrates this. As each character is read the (invisible) cursor moves along one space and at
the end of each logical screen line a carriage return is appended. 'This method does not detect
reverse field charcters, will not always read a POKEd screen correctly and causes the screen to
scroll as the last character is read. Still, it makes a fast screen dump for a PRINTed normal-text
screen.

Examples:
The following program reads a sequential file from tape and prints it to the screen.

```
1000  PRINTCHR$(147);
1010  OPEN1,1,1,"FILENAME"
1020  PRINTCHR$(147);
1030  GET#1,A$:ZZ=ST
1040  PRINTA$
1050  IFZZ=64THENCLOSE1:END
1060  GOTO1030
```

Note that each time the operating system fills the cassette buffer the screen blanks, when the
buffer is full the screen display returns and program execution resumes. The GET# here is actually
a GET# from the filled cassette buffer. Screen blanking was forced upon Commodore because of
a technical problem caused by the VIC chip. Since the cassette unit is not an intelligent peripheral
it was not possible to cure the problem in that case. However, the 1540 disk drive was upgraded
to a 1541 by replacing its ROM, thereby curing the problem as far as the disk drive is concerned.

The second example dumps screen text to a printer.

```
1000  REM**SIMPLE TEXT DUMP**
1010  REM**SCREEN TO PRINTER*
1020  REM********************
1030  PRINTCHR$(19);:REM CURSOR TO START OF SCREEN
1040  OPEN1,3:REM OPEN TO SCREEN
1050  OPEN4,4:REM OPEN TO PRINTER
1060  FORSL=0TO999
1070  GET#1,A$:PRINT#4,A$;
1080  NEXT
1090  PRINT#4:CLOSE4:CLOSE1
```

INPUT
Format: INPUT/"PROMPT";/<Variable>/,<Variable>, . . .,<Variable>/

This statement provides a simple means whereby a program can input data consisting of more than a single character. The optional 'PROMPT' can, of course, be any literal string of length up to 38 (with longer prompts the prompt string is INPUT as part of the data), and is used to indicate the type of response expected. INPUT provides a flashing cursor, echoes keypresses to the screen, and accepts data from the keyboard until 'RETURN' is pressed. Data is input from the initial position of the cursor on the current logical screen line. In practice this limits the maximum length of the input string to 79 characters if no prompt is used. If the cursor runs off the end of the current logical screen line before 'RETURN' is pressed the INPUT buffer wraps back to its initial position, all keypresses so far are lost, and data is read in from the start of the next logical screen line.

INPUT with no prompt string will PRINT a single question mark at the current cursor position, this can be suppressed with POKE19,1 (see remarks under TAB).

If no data is entered and the 'RETURN' key is pressed the INPUT variable will be assigned its previous value (unlike the early PETs where this caused the program to crash!).

If two or more variables are to be received (as in INPUTX,A$) when typed in they must be separated by a comma. Thus 123.456,TESTING followed by the 'RETURN' key would in this case assign the values X=123.456 and A$="TESTING" to the variables. This makes it impossible to read commas as part of an INPUT string. If the INPUT statement is expecting two variables and only one is given before 'RETURN' is pressed then '??' is displayed, indicating that more data is expected. If too many variables are entered then the message EXTRA IGNORED will be displayed. Generally it is probably best to get only one piece of information on each INPUT statement.

When INPUT is expecting a numeric variable and a string is entered the message REDO FROM START will be displayed; unlike GET the program won't actually crash.

In addition to ',' the character ':' cannot be INPUT directly. If it is required to INPUT a literal string this can be done by preceding it by a quote mark; quotes in the middle of a string will generate a FILE DATA ERROR.

Because of these snags INPUT is not often used in professional programs, where data is normally carefully validated before it is accepted and where programs are not expected to generate nasty messages all over the screen simply because an unfamiliar user pressed the wrong key. Still, it provides a simple way for the user familiar with its limitations to enter data.

Finally, INPUT cannot be used in direct mode. The INPUT buffer is the same block of memory used to process direct mode commands.

Examples:

    1000INPUT"DATE–DA,MO,YR (E.G. 01,12,83)";D,M,Y:REM NOT
        RECOMMENDED
    1000INPUT"NUMBER";A$:N=VAL(A$):REM RECOMMENDED

INPUT#

Format: INPUT#<Numeric form.>,<Varbl.>/,<Varbl.>, . . . <Varbl.>/

The numeric formula should evaluate to an integer in the range 1 to 255, corresponding to a previously OPENed logical file number. The action of INPUT#<Logical file number> is similar to INPUT except that the data requested is input from a previously OPENed logical file. Unlike INPUT, however, there is no prompt string, and no problem with cursor positions and logical screen lines. INPUT# assumes the variable being read is finished when it reads CHR$(13) (which corresponds to the 'RETURN' key), a comma, a semicolon, or a colon. INPUT# will read strings up to 80 characters long (including a terminator) after which a STRING TOO LONG error is generated.

For examples of INPUT# see the next section.

OPEN

Format: OPEN<Numeric form.>,/<Numeric form.>/,<Numeric form.>/,<String>///

The numeric formulae should evaluate so that this translates as

OPEN<Logical file nb.>/,<Device number>/,<Secondary address>/,<String>///

The action of the OPEN statement is to prepare a channel of communication with a peripheral device, i.e. to OPEN a logical file. The logical file number must be an integer in the range 1 to 255. For output files a logical file number in the range 128 to 255 will cause a line feed to follow all carriage returns sent to the file; for most peripherals this is not wanted. Normally, therefore, a logical file number should be in the range 1 to 127, but is otherwise arbitrary.

Up to 10 logical files may be OPEN at any one time, with at most 5 of these to IEEE or serial bus devices.

The default device number is 1, the Cassette, and the simplest OPEN statement which does something concrete is OPEN1. This is equivalent to OPEN1,1,0, " " and reads the next header on tape into the cassette buffer (where it can be PEEKed).

The next parameter taken by the OPEN statement is the 'secondary address' (the primary or first address is the device number). The secondary address is not arbitrary, it determines the manner in which the selected device is expected to respond. This means we need to know how any particular device will respond to different secondary addresses. The following table is not comprehensive, so you should always refer to the peripheral manual for a complete description of its modes of operation (unfortunately these manuals are not always easy to read, but they are tending to get better!). On the CBM 64 the default value of the secondary address is 111 if you forget to code it − be warned!

When a file is OPENed to cassette a default secondary address of 0 (a read file) is assumed unless otherwise specified.

The final optional parameter in the OPEN statement is the string. Normally this will be a file name, possibly with other information which will determine the manner in which the peripheral will respond. With a file OPENed to a disk drive command channel quite complex commands may be sent in this string.

Examples:

OPEN1,1,0,"FILENAME"	Cass read
OPEN1,1,1,"FILENAME"	Cass create/write
OPEN1,1,2,"FILENAME"	Cass create/write with 'end of tape' mark
OPEN1,0	Keyboard input
OPEN1,3	Screen input/output
OPEN1,4	Printer output
OPEN1,4,7	Printer output in Lower/Upper-case (1515/25)
OPEN1,2,0,CHR$(10)	Open channel to RS232 device

OPEN1,8,2,"FILENAME,S,R"	Disk SEQ file read
OPEN1,8,2,"FILENAME,S,W"	Disk SEQ file create/write
OPEN1,8,2,"FILENAME,P,R"	Disk PRG file read
OPEN1,8,2,"FILENAME,P,W"	Disk PRG file create/write
OPEN1,8,2,"FLNME,L,"+CHR$(21)	Disk REL file create-each record 20 chars +C/R
OPEN1,8,2,"FILENAME,U,R"	Disk USR file read
OPEN1,8,2,"FILENAME,U,W"	Disk USR file create/write
OPEN1,8,15"I0"	Open disk command channel and initialize disk
OPEN1,8,4,"#"	Open channel to any available disk buffer

Common secondary addresses

Device	Effect
C2N Cassette (Device number 1)	
Secondary address 0	Read file
1	Write file
2	Write file with 'end of tape' on CLOSE
1515,1525(GP 100VC), MPS 801 Printer (Device number 4/5)	
Secondary address 0	Upper-case/Graphics
7	Lower-case/Upper-case
1520 Plotter (Device number 6)	
Secondary address 0	Print ASCII data
1	Plot X,Y data
2	Select color
3	Select character size
4	Character rotate
5	Select scribe line mode
6	Upper/Lower case shift mode
7	Reset printer and clear buffer
1541 Disk drive (Device number 8)	
Secondary address 0	Directory read
1	Directory write
15	Command channel

In this program a sequential file is OPENed to tape, 10 test strings preceded by a number are written to the file which is then read back.

```
1000 PRINTCHR$(147)
1010 OPEN1,1,1,"TEST":REM OPEN FOR CREATE/WRITE
1020 FORI=1TO10
```

```
1030  INPUT"TEST STRING";A$
1040  PRINT#1,I;CHR$(13);A$;CHR$(13);:REM WRITE
1050  NEXT
1060  CLOSE1
1070  PRINTCHR$(147)"NOW REWIND TAPE"
1080  PRINT"PRESS RETURN WHEN READY"
1090  GETC$:IFC$<>CHR$(13)THEN1090
1100  PRINT"OK"
1110  OPEN1,1,0,"TEST":REM OPEN FOR READ
1120  FORI=1TO10
1130  INPUT#1,X,A$:REM READ
1140  ZZ=ST
1150  PRINT"LINE"X:PRINTA$
1160  IF(ZZ<>0ANDZZ<>64)THENPRINT"ERROR ST IS"ZZ:I=10
1170  NEXT
1180  CLOSE1:END
```

The next example illustrates the power of a disk drive, which can read and write to several files 'simultaneously'. Of course this is not possible on tape. The program has been modified from an example given by Raeto West and actually does something very useful — it 'merges' two program files on disk. It is not very fast and is not a true merge, in that the first program must have lower line numbers than the second program and effectively a concatenation of the two program files is formed (see Chapter 3 for further comments on link addresses). Still for all that it is very simple and it works. Machine code programs which perform a true interlacing merge of two programs are available in various utility packages, for example POWER by Brad Templeton and Jim Butterfield.

```
1000 REM**DISK PRG FILES**
1010 REM**  AUTO MERGE  **
1020 REM********************
1030 INPUT"FIRST PROG NAME";FP$
1040 INPUT"SECND PROG NAME";SP$
1050 INPUT"MERGE PROG NAME";MP$
1060 OPEN15,8,15,"I0":GOSUB1240
1070 OPEN2,8,2,"0:"+FP$+",P,R":GOSUB1240
1080 OPEN3,8,3,"0:"+MP$+",P,W":GOSUB1240
1090 GET#2,X$
1100 Y$=X$:GET#2,X$:IFST<>0THEN1140
1110 IFY$=""THENY$=CHR$(0)
1120 PRINT#3,Y$;
1130 GOTO1100
1140 CLOSE2
1150 OPEN4,8,4,"0:"+SP$+",P,R":GOSUB1240
1160 GET#4,Y$:GET#4,Y$
1170 GET#4,Y$:IFST<>0THEN1210
```

```
1180 IFY$=""THENY$=CHR$(0)
1190 PRINT#3,Y$;
1200 GOTO1170
1210 PRINT#3,CHR$(0);
1220 CLOSE3:CLOSE4:CLOSE15
1230 END
1240 REM**DISK ERROR CHECK**
1250 INPUT#15,EN,EM$,ET,ES
1260 IFEN=0THENRETURN
1270 PRINTEN,EM$
1280 PRINT"TRACK"ET:PRINT"SECTOR"ES
1290 CLOSE3:CLOSE15:END
```

PRINT

Format: PRINT followed by any one or more of

  (i) a literal string or string expression,
  (ii) a numeric variable or numeric formula,
  (iii) SPC(or TAB(expressions,

separated by

  (i) nothing at all,
  (ii) a comma, or
  (iii) a semicolon.

The PRINT statement is the most versatile of all the BASIC keywords. The principal function of PRINT is to display messages and the results of computation or data processing on the screen. However, in skillful hands PRINT can be used to generate quite fast moving and complex graphics displays; it becomes almost a language of its own.

Let us examine the effect of PRINT in easy stages.

Firstly, every PRINT statement is followed by a carriage return and a line feed, i.e. the cursor moves to the start of the next line, unless steps are taken to prevent this. Thus PRINT on its own (effectively PRINT 'Nothing') simply moves the cursor to the start of the next line. If there is no 'next line', which means the cursor is already on the bottom line of the screen, then the whole screen scrolls up one line and the cursor is positioned at the start of the bottom line.

PRINT <Literal string>
Example: PRINT"ABC"

This has the effect of PRINTing the string, starting from the current cursor position, character by character onto the screen. The string may include cursor control or color control characters. PRINT will interpret these quite 'literally'. If it encounters a cursor down character in a string PRINT will obediently move the cursor down one cell. By including control characters in literal strings dramatic visual effects can be produced. At the very simplest level PRINTing a literal string is used to display text messages on the screen. PRINT"HELP! !"

PRINT <String expression>
Example: PRINTLEFT$(CD$,8)LEFT$(CR$,4)A$

Here we start to see how expressions to be PRINTed can quite easily begin to look rather complicated; any syntactical combination of the string handling keywords is covered by 'PRINT<String expression>'. In the example given the intent is quite simple; it is to position the cursor in row 7 column 4 and then print the string A$. Here CD$ consists of a string of cursor downs (preceded by the 'home' character) and CR$ a string of cursor rights. Notice that we do not have to concatenate LEFT$(CD$,8) with LEFT(CR$,4), as in LEFT$(CD$,8) +LEFT$(CR$,4). PRINT is clever enough to know that the first string followed by the second string is the only reasonable interpretation of what is required: it can cope as well with an expression like PRINTAB instead of PRINTA$+B$.

PRINT <Numeric variable>
Example: PRINTX

This has the effect of PRINTing the current value of the numeric variable X, beginning at the current cursor position. If the value can be expressed without using floating point notation then it will be PRINTed normally, otherwise floating point notation will be used. When numbers are PRINTed they are either preceded by a space or a minus sign. Since numbers are of unpredictable length and are PRINTed from left to right, right justification, rounding off, or formatting about a decimal point all require action on the part of the programmer. Numbers can be turned into strings using STR$ and then chopped about with the string handling commands. (Warning. This can have unexpected effects if the number is so large, or so small, as to require exponential floating point notation!)

PRINT <Numeric formula>
Example: PRINT 16.777*EXP(LOG(440)+(N−45)*LOG(2)/12)

Here the result of evaluating the numerical formula would be PRINTed as a number, starting from the current cursor position. Again we see how PRINT is able to handle very complex expressions. In program mode there is little point in consigning such involved numeric expressions to a PRINT statement. We may as well work out the value, assign it to a variable and then PRINT the value of the variable. However, in direct mode this facility enables the CBM 64 to perform as a very versatile calculator.

We may also use SPC or TAB at any suitable point in a PRINT statement to format any of the preceding types of output.

Example:
                    PRINTSPC(4)XTAB(14)"YEARS INTO THE QUEST"

In this example, 4 cursor rights are PRINTed followed by the value of X, a TAB across to the 14th column (counting from zero) and finally the text message.

Finally several of the preceding types of output can appear in a single PRINT statement each separated from the others by nothing at all, a comma or a semicolon. If nothing separates two items then PRINT will just plow on and PRINT the next item from the current cursor position.

To understand the effect of a comma we must imagine that the 80-column logical screen is divided into 8 print zones of 10 characters each. The effect of a comma after one of the preceding types of output is to move the cursor from its current position to the start of the next print zone.

If a PRINT statement is terminated by a semicolon the cursor will remain in its final position; no carriage return and line feed will be PRINTed. This can be very useful. To fully understand the effect of this we must note that the 'final position' after PRINTing some characters is the next unprinted screen cell. Thus if we PRINT 40 characters onto a line (starting at the beginning of the line) at the end of this the cursor is on the beginning of the next screen line. If no semicolon is used then a carriage return and line feed will take place and the cursor will now be on the start of a line two lines below our starting point. Effectively a gap of one line is created in the output PRINTed on the screen. If, however, a semicolon is used at the end of the PRINT statement then no carriage return and line feed will take place and the cursor will be resting immediately below its initial position. Finally it should be mentioned that, even if a semicolon is used, if you PRINT to the final screen location (bottom right) then of course the whole screen will scroll up and the top line is lost.

The best way to learn the subtleties of PRINT is to experiment yourself, but you will find many examples in the chapters which follow.

PRINT#

Format: PRINT#<Numeric formula>,<anything legal in PRINT>

The numeric formula should evaluate to a number in the range 1 to 255 and this should correspond to a previously OPENed logical file number. After the comma anything legal in PRINT is syntactically correct except that TAB(and commas should be avoided.

The function of PRINT# is to send numeric or string data to a previously OPENed logical file. The logical file could have been OPENed to the screen but is more likely to have been OPENed to a cassette, printer or disk drive.

PRINT# is the mirror image of INPUT#. The first writes data out to a peripheral, the second reads it back into the CBM 64. Because the primary purpose of PRINT# is different from that of PRINT complex statements of the kind common in PRINT should be avoided. Complex PRINT# statements are liable to send data out in a form wasteful of space on disk or tape and, what is far worse, difficult to read back. The rule should be: (i) evaluate the data you wish to send and (ii) send it as simply as possible.

Many of the complexities of the PRINT statement arise because we want output to the screen to appear in a well formatted presentation, it must be easy to grasp at a glance. These considerations do not apply to PRINT# to tape or disk, although of course care must be taken to format output to a printer if the result is to be easily legible. In writing to tape or disk we must regard the output as a continuous data stream. Unnecessary spaces, such as appear in PRINT when the comma is used, are in this context just a nuisance. Hence the comma should be avoided in PRINT# when writing to tape or disk. Each data item should be separated from the next in the data stream by a valid separating character. These are a comma,[†] a semicolon (PRINT#1,A$; ";";B$), or a carriage return without line feed (PRINT#1,A$;CHR$(13);B$). A line feed, CHR$(10),

[†]Note. Sending a comma in the data stream is not the same as using a comma in the PRINT# statement. Consider the statement PRINT#1,A$,B$ as against PRINT#1,A$;",";B$. It is the first of these which is bad news and may cause problems when read back, not the second.

automatically follows a carriage return unless it is supressed by a semi-colon. This unwanted character will take up unnecessary space and may be read as a null character by an unfortunate INPUT# which happens to encounter it. The best approach in writing files to tape or disk is to separate every data item with a CHR$(13) using semicolons. Even so it is necessary to read the data back in the 'type-order' that it was written, e.g. it is no good to use INPUT#1,X, a numeric data type, if the next item in the record is a string. The best rule is to read the data back using the same format for INPUT# that was used in the PRINT# which wrote the record. Care should be taken to terminate each string sent with a CHR$(13), otherwise INPUT#1,A$ will go on reading characters until the input buffer is full and a STRING TOO LONG ERROR will cause the program (which reads the data back) to crash. This problem can be avoided using GET#, but GET# is slower.

Example:
This example writes 10 mixed records in a sequential file to disk.

```
1000  R$=CHR$(13):PRINTCHR$(147)
1010  OPEN15,8,15:GOSUB5000
1020  OPEN2,8,2,"TEST,S,W":GOSUB5000
1030  FORI=1TO10
1040  INPUT"NAME";NM$
1050  INPUT"ADDRESS";AD$
1060  INPUT"DEBT";DB$
1070  PRINT#2,NM$;R$;AD$;R$;DB$;R$;:GOSUB5000
1080  NEXT:CLOSE2
1090  PRINTCHR$(147)"READING BACK"
1100  OPEN2,8,2,"TEST,S,R":GOSUB5000
1110  FORI=1TO10
1120  INPUT#2,NM$,AD$,DB$:ZZ=ST:GOSUB5000
1130  PRINTNM$:PRINTAD$:PRINTDB$
1140  IF(ZZ<>0ANDZZ<>64)THENPRINT"ERROR ST IS"ZZ:I=10
1150  NEXT
1160  CLOSE2:CLOSE15:END
5000  REM**DISK ERROR CHECK**
5010  INOUT#15,EN,EM$,ET,ES
5020  IFEN=0THEN5050:REM EXIT
5030  PRINT"ERROR NUMBER"EN
5040  PRINTEM$:PRINT"TRACK"ET:PRINT"SECTOR"ES
5050  RETURN
```

1

Some BASIC tools

INTRODUCTION

This chapter deals with a number of techniques designed to make BASIC programming easier. A well-written program should be easy to follow, easy to debug and, most important, easy to extend or modify. These aims are not difficult to achieve, provided certain simple principles are understood and used consistently. One of the first pieces of computer lore, well known to all would-be programmers, is that 'computers eat time'. This is just as true of professional programming projects; see for example *The Mythical Man Month* by F. Brooks (Addison Wesley, 1982). After reading this chapter you may be able to spend more time enjoying your programs than struggling to get them working.

The way in which a program PRINTs information onto the screen is a good example of how the right set of techniques, used from the beginning, can make a program very easy to modify. Since PRINTing to the screen is the standard way for a program to communicate with the user we first look at some useful ways to format PRINT statements and to handle strings.

Another, more fundamental, property which makes a program easy to read and modify is its 'structure'. The term 'structured program' has a precise meaning which we shall explain, but in general terms it means that the program has been written as a series of simple blocks, each having a clearly defined function and, as far as possible, being independent of the other 'blocks' of the program. Modifying a program written in this way is often simply a matter of adding a new block or removing a block and replacing it by another. For this reason the second topic covered in this chapter is that of structuring programs and the correct use of such keywords as FOR...TO... NEXT, GOTO, and GOSUB...RETURN in structures.

Finally we deal with some important aspects of BASIC which you will need to follow later sections of the book. These include: relational operators, the binary representation of numbers, and logical operators as a means of reading or writing single bits (binary zeros or ones). This will enable you to use PEEK and POKE with the kind of precision needed when playing with the VIC or SID chip. Understanding binary and hexadecimal notation will also prepare the way towards starting on machine code.

FORMATTING PRINTs AND STRING HANDLING

The main problem where a lot of PRINT statements occur at different points in a program is that, unless you take steps to prevent it, the position of each message on the screen is liable to depend on what messages have already been PRINTed. This is not so bad if messages are always PRINTed in the same order, but of course most programs have many optional paths along which control may flow. The screen may scroll on one path and not on another. Pretty soon the screen will look a mess and you can easily spend hours getting it to look right for all possible routes through the program. Now suppose you want to change the program by adding a new subroutine, or something like that. Before you know it you are having to sort out the PRINT statements all over again, only this time it is worse: the program is longer and the number of different paths through it has multiplied! Now the great thing is that with a little care and the right approach all this agony can be avoided.

The first rule is that unless you need it, for some special reason, never let the screen scroll. This means that with careful housekeeping you always know exactly where every message is on the current screen display. The second rule is to erase a message, and only that message, when it is no longer needed. Here is a simple subroutine which will make these objectives very easy to attain. Early in the program you need the following lines

```
1000  AC$=" ":DW$=CHR$(19):SP$=" "
1010  FORI=1TO39:AC$=AC$+CHR$(29)'NEXT:REM ACROSS STRING
1020  FORI=1TO24:DW$=DW$+CHR$(17):NEXT:REM HOME+DOWN STRING
1040  FORI=1TO40:SP$=SP$+CHR$(32):NEXT:REM SPACE STRING
1050  X=FRE(0):REM FORCE GARBAGE COLLECT
```

This has the effect of defining three strings for later use: a string of 39 cursor rights, a string which consists of a 'home' followed by 24 cursor downs, and finally a string of 40 spaces. These will be needed for a short subroutine we are about to construct. Note the use of the plus sign here; if you haven't come across it before it may be puzzling. The effect of '+' when used with two strings is to create a new string consisting of the first string followed by the second, e.g. "ABC"+ "CD" is the string "ABCCD". This is known as *concatenating* two strings. Of course, unlike plus for numbers, it is not generally true that A$+B$ is the same as B$+A$. Finally, because systematically increasing the length of a string, as these FOR loops do, creates a lot of 'garbage' in high memory, we use FRE to force a garbage collect, so that string memory is clean before the main body of the program is begun. These lines take just over half a second to RUN.

Now that our three strings are defined we can use the following GOSUB at any point in the program

```
5000  REM** POSITION CURSOR ROW R/COL C **
5010  PRINTLEFT$(DW$,R+1)LEFT$(AC$,C);
5020  RETURN
```

Counting the top left corner of the screen as row zero, column zero and bottom right as row 24, column 39 this GOSUB can position the cursor at any specified point on the screen. We can then either PRINT a message or, by using SP$, erase a message.

Add these lines to the main program.

```
1060  PRINTCHR$(147):REM CLEAR SCREEN
1070  M$="MESSAGE"
1080  R=10:C=10:GOSUB5000:PRINTM$:REM DISPLAY MESSAGE
1090  GETC$:IFC$=" "THEN1090:REM WAIT FOR KEY PRESS
1100  R=10:C=10:GOSUB5000:PRINTLEFT$(SP$,LEN(M$)):REM WIPE M$
1110  END
```

Now if you try the whole program the effect of the GOSUB should be clear. We have exact control over printing and erasing messages on the screen. If this technique is used throughout a program it makes moving PRINT statements about within the program relatively simple, since the position of the message is independent of any other PRINT statement and under immediate control.

To prevent the screen from scrolling we must remember two things: any PRINT to the bottom row of the screen must (a) end in a semicolon and (b) avoid the last character cell.

Another, quite different technique for sending messages to the screen is to scroll them from right to left across a single screen row. This is quite a useful way to send a long message without disturbing the graphics display. The effect is like the fluorescent 'ticker-tape' displays in Times Square. One disadvantage of this method is that an inattentive user might miss the message entirely! (A sound prompt could help here.)

Try the following program.

```
1000  PRINTCHR$(147)
1010  SP$=" ":FORI=1TO40:SP$=SP$+CHR$(32):NEXT
1020  P$=CHR$(19):FORI=1TO10:P$=P$+CHR$(17):NEXT
1030  M$="MESSAGE ALERT":GOSUB5000
1040  M$="HERE IS A WAY TO SCROLL MESSAGES":GOSUB5000
1050  M$="MESSAGE ENDS":GOSUB5000
1060  END
5000  REM** SCROLL MESSAGE M$ **
5010  Z$=SP$+M$+SP$
5020  FORN=1 TOLEN(Z$)-38
5030  PRINTP$CHR$(18)CHR$(156)MID$(Z$,N,40)CHR$(146)CHR$(154);
5040  FORI=0TO10:NEXT:REM DELAY
5050  NEXTN
5060  PRINTP$+SP$;:REM WIPE MESSAGE
5070  RETURN
```

Formatting PRINTed data on the screen can pose some interesting problems. Two common examples are right-justifying a column of integers or justifying numbers about a decimal point. In both cases the simplest approach is to turn the numbers into strings, using STR$, and then to manipulate the strings using the string handling commands.

Example. Right-justifying a column of integers.

```
1000  PRINTCHR$(147):REM CLEAR SCREEN
1010  FORN=1TO20
1020  X%=INT(32767*RND(1)):REM RANDOM INTEGER
1030  PRINTSPC(7)RIGHT$("       "+STR$(X%),6):REM 4 SPACES
1040  NEXT
```

The explanation is as follows. Suppose X%=2 then

"   "+STR$(2) is "   2"   (4 spaces + "   2"),

whereas if X%=32766 we have

"   "+STR$(32766) is "   32766".

Now if RIGHT$(,6) is used on both of these, with the first PRINTed above the second, the result is

        2
32766

as required.

We have said that every BASIC keyword has a unique meaning. This is not strictly true, although it is true if the context of the keyword is taken into account. An example is the plus sign, which can be used to add numbers or, as we have seen, to concatenate strings. Another example is the 'less than' sign, '<'. Again this can be used with numbers, as in IFX<YTHEN..., or with strings, e.g. IFA$<B$THEN.... How can one string be 'less than' another? The answer lies in the fact that every character has an ASC code. For example it is true that "A"<"B" because ASC("A") is 65 and ASC("B") is 66. Strings longer than a single character are compared by successive comparison of ASC codes, thus "AAA"<"AAB". This is useful on two counts. Firstly it enables us to compare two strings and see if they are equal or not equal. Secondly, since the ASC codes for alphabetic characters run sequentially up from 65 it means that alphabetic strings are ordered just as they would be in a dictionary (the word is 'lexicographically'). This can be useful in various text-handling procedures. For example, sorting words into alphabetical order becomes equivalent to sorting numbers into order, although there is a problem with upper/lower case.

STRUCTURING PROGRAMS

You may be interested to know that something like 90% of professional programming time is spent updating or modifying existing programs. This strikes us as an absurd state of affairs; just think of all the programs that never get written.

The reasons are not hard to see. Updating an earlier program, generally written by someone who is no longer available, need not be time consuming but often is because of (a) poor documentation, (b) lack of ordered program structure. Lack of structure usually involves one major flaw in programming technique: over-use of GOTO.

The GOTO statement is simultaneously the most powerful and most dangerous of all BASIC keywords. If GOTO is not strictly necessary, avoid it. If a program reeks of GOTOs it is wrong. To put it another way, if the program is sensibly ordered GOTO should rarely be needed. With GOTO hiding in every other line, debugging or modifying a program can become like wrestling with an octopus; every time you think you have things under control there is this nasty wet feeling around your throat!

Structured programming attempts to prevent numerous jumps in program control of the kind which occur when GOTO is encountered by building the program from three simple kinds of module. Any program can be assembled out of the following three types of module.

1. A linear sequence of steps executed consecutively: S1, S2, S3, etc., where S1, S2, S3 may be single instructions or an entire program.
2. A conditional structure of the type 'if C then S1 otherwise S2'. Here S1 is executed if C is true and S2 if C is false.
3. A loop structure of the type 'do S until C', where S is an instruction or sequence of instructions and C is a looping condition which is tested after each completion of the loop. Note that this has the effect of guaranteeing that the loop is always executed at least once. A special case of this structure is the FOR loop of BASIC, in which the condition tested is whether the loop counter has exceeded a preset value. (The inflexibility of this type of repeat—until structure is one of the major weaknesses of BASIC.)

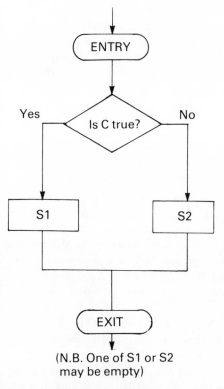

Fig. 1.1 – Flow chart of the 'If–then–otherwise' structure.

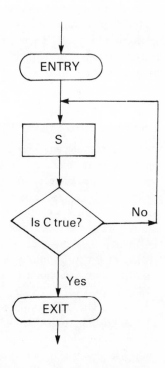

Fig. 1.2 – Flow chart of the 'Repeat–until' structure.

A glance at Figs. 1.1 and 1.2 will show immediately that both conditional and loop structures have a *single entry* and a *single exit*.

We can characterize the principal features of structured programming as being:

I. Only the three basic structures, and possibly a small number of auxiliary structures, are necessary.
II. Structures may be nested to any level of complexity so that any structure can, in turn, contain any of the structures.
III. Each structure has only a *single* entry and a *single* exit.

The advantages of structured programming are that: the sequence of operations is easy to trace, which allows easy testing and debugging; the structures can easily be made into modules; the structured version of a program is partly self-documenting and generally easy to read, and consequently structured programs are easy to document.

The disadvantages are that: structured programs are sometimes slower and can use more memory than unstructured programs; the three basic structures are not always efficient or convenient for a given implementation. Structured programs consider only the sequence of program operations, not the real-time flow of data, and therefore structures may handle data awkwardly. In future systems it may be that improvements in hardware design will help to overcome these difficulties, see 'Combining data flow and control flow computing' by P. Rautenbach, *Computer Journal,* 1982.

Still, the CBM 64 has more than adequate memory for most applications and the fact remains that if even a moderate proportion of existing programs were properly structured an enormous saving would result. To put it simply, no doubt over-simply, the occasional GOTO may be perfectly placed and acceptable, but we should like to register the plea that Frankenstein be given a monopoly in creating monsters.

IMPLEMENTING STRUCTURES IN BASIC

As a programming language BASIC has many virtues. It has a clear notation, simple syntax, an easy operating environment, and wide availability. However, BASIC has a number of limitations: to name but one, there is no natural way to implement the 'If—then—otherwise' or 'Repeat—until' structures. Of course it is no great problem to contrive the effect of these structures in BASIC, most of the time we do it without even noticing, but it is worth realizing that it is a contrived effort to achieve these results and it shouldn't be! There are modified forms of BASIC, notably COMAL, where these deficiences have been rectified. Anyone who feels that we are being over-critical of BASIC should seek the opportunity to try a COMAL system. In this context you may find the book *Structured Programming with COMAL,* by R. Atherton (Ellis Horwood, Chichester, 1982), helpful.

In the UK, a Commodore-approved extension to BASIC, called Simons' BASIC, which adds 114 commands to BASIC V2, is available. In addition to special graphics and sound commands this cartridge adds structured programming commands which largely obviate the need for GOTOs and GOSUBs in a BASIC program. For example, the PROC command is used to label each subroutine, equivalent to 'Paragraph naming' in COBOL. The structure of FOR . . . NEXT loops is also changed. The REPEAT . . . UNTIL command allows a procedure to be executed a defined number of times and LOOP...EXIT IF...END LOOP provides multiple condition testing within a loop. The command IF...THEN...ELSE is also implemented. Of course programs written in Simons' BASIC can only be RUN with the cartridge in place and so lack portability, but this add-on certainly removes most of the structural problems of BASIC V2.

However, in due course other languages such as PASCAL and LOGO will become more widely available in home computer implementations. When they do it seems probable that the days of BASIC as an almost universal microcomputer language will be numbered. Both LOGO and PASCAL implementations can be expected for the CBM 64 and both languages have the advantage of being recursive and naturally structured.

Let us first consider the 'If–then–otherwise' structure, also known as IF...THEN...ELSE. This can be implemented in BASIC V2 as illustrated in the following example.

```
1000  S=RND(1)
1010  IFNOT(S<.5)THEN1050:REM OTHERWISE
1020  REM IF TRUE
1030  PRINT"CONDITION 'S<.5' TRUE"
1040  GOTO1070:REM SKIP TO END
1050  REM OTHERWISE
1060  PRINT"CONDITION 'S<.5' FALSE"
1070  END
```

Here the simple PRINT statements of 1030 and 1060 could in some real application be many lines of code, in which case a cumbersome construction of this type is forced upon us and GOTO is unavoidable. In the example given we could use the following code.

```
1000  S=RND(1)
1010  IFS<.5THENPRINT"CONDITION 'S<.5' TRUE"
1020  IFS>=.5THENPRINT"CONDITION 'S<.5' FALSE"
1030  END
```

However, it is not possible to effect such simplifications where both branches of the program flow contain more than one line of BASIC statements.

Now consider the 'Repeat–until' structure. Here are some ways of implementing this in BASIC.

First method. Essentially the archetypal repeat–until structure of BASIC. The following uses GOTO in the form of THEN<Line number>.

```
1000  S=RND(0):N=1
1010  REM REPEAT
1020  PRINT"DONE"N:N=N+1
1030  S=RND(1):IFS<.5THEN1010
1040  REM UNTIL S>=.5
1050  END
```

We may wish to perform a 'Repeat–until' structure a maximum number of times say 100. This means there are two conditions which must cause an exit from the structure, say either S>=.5 or N=101. There are two possible ways to handle this.

Other methods

```
1000  S=RND(0):N=1
1010  REM REPEAT
1020  PRINT"DONE"N:N=N+1
1030  S=RND(1):IF(S<.5)AND(N<101)THEN1010
1040  REM UNTIL S>=.5 OR N=101
1050  END
```

Note here that because the counter N is incremented before the condition is tested, its value upon exit is 101 although 'DONE' has been printed 100 times.

```
1000  FORN=1TO100
1010  PRINT"DONE"N:S=RND(1)
1020  IF(S>=.5)THENN=100:REM FORCE EXIT
1030  NEXT
1040  END
```

The last example (above) shows that in many instances the 'Repeat–until' structure can be constructed from a FOR loop, provided the loop is exited correctly. Note that the action of NEXT is to increment N before testing if N>100, thus once more N=101 upon exit.

By inserting the line

```
1025 N=N-1
```

we can ensure that the loop is never exited until S>=.5. Since S>=.5 could be any condition whatsoever, this shows that any repeat–until structure can be constructed from a FOR loop (albeit somewhat tortuously).

It is often desirable to repeat a set of instructions at various points within the same program. When this is the case a subroutine should be created, using GOSUB and RETURN. One of the features which makes a structured program easily modified is the principle that each structure should have just one entry point and one point of exit. When writing subroutines it is a good idea to avoid multiple entry points and exit through a single RETURN statement. To avoid multiple entry points you can make each entry a distinct subroutine with its own RETURN. These subroutines can call their common part as another subroutine. Programs written in this way often achieve far greater clarity of presentation.

PEEK( ), binary, bytes and POKE

The memory of the CBM 64 consists of 65536 ($2\uparrow64$) 'cells'. So that each cell can be identified it is given a number which is called its address; valid addresses lie in the range 0 to 65535. The command PEEK(<Address>) enables us to look at the contents of any cell given its address. For example the command

```
PRINTPEEK(65535)
```

should return the value 255 (65535 is an address in ROM at the very top of memory).

Each address contains a number in the range 0 to 255. Why 255, you may ask? The answer to this question lies in the way that computers count. Human beings count in multiples of 10, thus 64035 really means

$$6*(10\uparrow4)+4*(10\uparrow3)+0*(10\uparrow2) +3*(10\uparrow1)+5$$

(by convention $10\uparrow0$ is 1). In this way we can represent any number using only the digits 0,1,2,3, 4,5,6,7,8,9. Notice that 9 is one less than the magic number 10. We say that human beings do arithmetic to *base* 10. Now in reality there is nothing magic about 10, any other whole number greater than one could serve just as well as the base for an arithmetic. In fact computers do arithmetic to base 2. Thus the number 129, which in human terms means

$$1*(10\uparrow2)+2*(10\uparrow1)+9$$

is remembered by the computer as

$$1*(2\uparrow7)+0*(2\uparrow6)+0*(2\uparrow5)+0*(2\uparrow4)+0*(2\uparrow3)+0*(2\uparrow2)+0*(2\uparrow1)+1$$

or more briefly as 10000001. Notice we are still talking about the same number, namely 129, but the representation of that number is different. Think of 10000001 as a synonym for 129.

Since computers do arithmetic to base 2 they need only use the digits 0,1. A switch is either on or off, a pulse is either present or absent. It is easy to see why base 2 makes sense for computers. Arithmetic to base 2 is, for obvious reasons, called *binary* arithmetic, and the digits 0, 1 are called *bits*.

Let us return to the question: why does each address contain a number in the range 0 to 255? The answer is quite simple: each memory cell contains exactly 8 bits. Therefore the biggest binary number which can live at any address is 11111111, that is

$$1*(2\uparrow7)+1*(2\uparrow6)+1*(2\uparrow5)+1*(2\uparrow4)+1*(2\uparrow3)+1*(2\uparrow2)+1*(2\uparrow1)+1$$

or in human terms $128+64+32+16+8+4+2+1=255$. Eight bits equals one *byte,* the contents of any address. On power-up the CBM 64 displays the message 38911 BYTES FREE which tells the user that there is this number of bytes in the user BASIC program area available for his use.

Because any valid address lies in the range 0 to 65535 and $256*256=65536$ it is possible to express an address using two bytes, a Hi-byte and a Lo-byte. For example suppose the address is 8193 then

Hi-byte $=INT(8193/256)=32$
Lo-byte $=8193-(Hi\text{-}byte)*256=1$

We may think of the memory of the CBM 64 as 256 pages each page containing 256 bytes, the Hi-byte of an address being its page number. Page zero starts at address zero and ends at address 255. This page is used exclusively by the operating system because it can be accessed more rapidly in 6510 machine code than any other part of memory. Page one starts at address 256 and ends at 511: the 6510 requires a block of RAM at these addresses to act as special high-speed, short-term memory called the processor *stack*. Since there are $256*256=2\uparrow16$ addresses in total this means there are 256 pages altogether. The Lo-byte of an address may be thought of as the position of the address on its page in memory.

The following program will display the decimal contents and equivalent binary bit pattern of any valid address.

```
1000 REM** BIT PATTERNS **
1010 REM*********************
1020 DW$="
1030 AC$="
1040 PRINTCHR$(147):R=20:C=4:GOSUB1210:PRINT"'SPAC
     E BAR' FOR NEW ADDRESS"
1050 R=21:C=10:GOSUB1210:PRINT"NULL INPUT TO END"
1060 PRINTLEFT$(DW$,2):A$="":INPUT"ADDRESS";A$:A=V
     AL(A$)
1070 IFA$=""THENPRINTCHR$(147):END
1080 IFA<0ORA>65535THENPRINTCHR$(147):GOTO1040
1090 HI=INT(A/256):LO=A-256*HI
1100 R=5:C=5:GOSUB1210:PRINT"ADDRESS  LO-BYTE  HI-
     BYTE"
1110 R=7:C=4:GOSUB1210:PRINTATAB(15)LOTAB(24)HI
1120 R=10:C=4:GOSUB1210:PRINT"CONTENTS"SPC(8)"BIT
     PATTERN"
1130 R=11:C=23:GOSUB1210:PRINT"76543210"
1140 P=PEEK(A):R=12:C=6:GOSUB1210:PRINT"       ":GOSU
     B1210:PRINTP
1150 FORI=7TO0STEP-1
1160 BIT=(PAND(2↑I))/(2↑I)
1170 PRINTLEFT$(DW$,13)SPC(29-I)RIGHT$(STR$(BIT),1
     )
1180 NEXT
1190 GETC$:IFC$=CHR$(32)THEN1040
1200 GOTO1140
1210 REM**POSITION CURSOR**
1220 PRINTLEFT$(DW$,R+1)LEFT$(AC$,C);
1230 RETURN
```

If this seems a bit tame the next program is a kind of souped-up magical version of the same idea. In this program the whole of any selected page in memory (interpreted as screen codes) is displayed on the top part of the screen in virtually real-time, regardless of what else may be going on. This is accomplished by a machine code subroutine which can continue to run even if the BASIC program is ENDed and another program entered. The machine code lives in the cassette buffer.

```
1000 REM*******64 HYPER PEEK*********
1010 REM*DISPLAY ANY PAGE OF MEMORY*
1020 REM*ON TOP HALF OF C64  SCREEN*
1030 REM*  IN 'REAL' SHARED TIME    *
1040 REM*****************************
1050 REM
1060 REM    M/C DATA STATEMENTS
1070 REM    (IRQ WEDGE $033C UP)
1080 REM
1090 D$="                           "
1100 N=0:PRINTCHR$(147):GOSUB1250
1110 PRINTLEFT$(D$,22)SPC(8)"+/- INC/DEC PAGE NUMB
ER"
1120 PRINTLEFT$(D$,23)SPC(8)"HIT"CHR$(18)"RETURN"C
HR$(146)"TO STOP PROGRAM"
1130 PRINTLEFT$(D$,24)SPC(11)CHR$(18)"F1"CHR$(146)
"FOR TIME SHARING";
1140 POKE650,128:REM REPEAT ALL KEYS
1150 SYS829
1160 N=PEEK(828):REM PAGE NUMBER
1170 PRINTLEFT$(D$,21)SPC(15)CHR$(18)"PAGE
"NCHR$(142)
1180 GETA$:IFA$=""THEN1180
1190 IFA$="+"THENN=N+1:IFN>255THENN=0
1200 IFA$="-"THENN=N-1:IFN<0THENN=255
1210 IFA$=CHR$(13)THEN1240
1220 IFA$=CHR$(133)THENEND
1230 POKE828,N:GOTO1160
1240 POKE650,0:SYS847:PRINTCHR$(147):END
1250 REM******INSERT M/C DATA*********
1260 DATA0,120,169,92,141,20,3,169,3
1270 DATA141,21,3,169,0,141,60,3,88,96
1280 DATA120,169,49,141,20,3,169,234
1290 DATA141,21,3,88,96,169,0,133,251
1300 DATA173,60,3,133,252,162,0,160,0
1310 DATA177,251,9,128,157,0,4,169,1
1320 DATA157,0,216,232,200,208,240,76
1330 DATA49,234
1340 DATA6697:REM*CHECKSUM*
1350 CC=0
1360 FORI=0TO63:READX:CC=CC+X:POKE828+I,X:NEXT
1370 READX:IFCC<>XTHENPRINT"DATA STATEMENT ERROR":
STOP
1380 RETURN
```

You can use this program in many interesting ways. With the aid of a memory map wander about in CBM 64 memory and watch what is going on. Here is an example of what you can do.

Example. Watch an array being filled as it happens. First LOAD and RUN HYPERPEEK then select Page 9 using the '+' or '−' keys. Exit HYPERPEEK with the 'F1' key. Page 9 will continue to be displayed. Now enter NEW and type in the following short program.

```
1000  PRINTCHR$(147):DIMA%(20,5)
1010  D$=CHR$(19)
1020  FORL=1TO10:D$=D$+CHR$(17):NEXTL
1030  FORJ=1TO5
1040  FORD=1TO10
1050  FORI=1TO20
1060  A%(I,J)=5*D+J−20
1070  PRINTD$SPC(11)"A%(";RIGHT$(STR$(I),2);
1080  PRINTRIGHT$(STR$(J),2);")=";A%(I,J)
1090  NEXT
2000  NEXTD
2010  NEXTJ
```

When this program is RUN you will see the array being initialized and the D loop filling each consecutive block of 40 memory locations. Each block corresponds to 20 integers (remember − 2 bytes each) as the I loop varies for fixed J. When the D loop has changed a block 10 times, J is incremented by one and the next block varied. The entire array occupies around 200 bytes on Page 9 of memory, so you should be able to watch the whole array being filled in real-time.[†] Remember that the content of each byte of the array is interpreted by HYPERPEEK as a screen code. Note that between each varying block there is a space of two bytes. Why is this, certainly there are no gaps in the array itself? (Hint: what is the first index to an array element?)

Another example you may care to try is to use HYPERPEEK to display Page 159, at the top of BASIC memory, and write a little program that slowly builds a dynamic string. With care you will be able to watch the string build up and then see a garbage collect as it happens.

As we know memory in the CBM 64 may be of two types RAM or ROM. In normal operation large blocks of high memory in the CBM 64 act as ROM, Read Only Memory. This ROM memory contains such things as information on the shape of characters and the BASIC Interpreter which runs BASIC. When using BASIC we can hardly manage without these ROM areas of memory. However, the CBM 64 has the ability to 'change' any ROM into RAM under software control. Of course ROM cannot really be changed into RAM − what happens is that a different kind of memory is switched in, or enabled, at the same block of addresses. We shall go into this in detail in Chapter 3. All we need to know for the present is that every ROM address has a RAM address lying 'underneath' and that this RAM can be revealed by suitable commands.

Assuming the address we are looking at corresponds to RAM the contents can be set to whatever we want, some number in the range 0 to 255 of course, by means of POKE. For example try

POKE1024,1:POKE55296,2

†It may be necessary to use smaller line numbers and compact the program to see the *whole* array.

A red 'A' should appear in the top left-hand corner of the screen. Here we put the number 1, the screen code for A, in address 1024 and the number 2, the color code for red, in address 55296. It happens that 1024 is the first location in the block of memory devoted to the screen display, and 55296 the first location of the corresponding block of memory devoted to the color display. Notice PEEK( ) takes brackets but POKE does not.

What happens if we POKE to ROM? With most microcomputers the answer would be 'nothing', POKEing to ROM is generally considered to be a rather pointless activity! However, with the CBM 64 this is not true. When you POKE to ROM the byte POKEd 'falls through' into the under-lying RAM. It is there sure enough, but you can't read it back with PEEK unless the ROM is flipped out and replaced by RAM.

Plainly PEEK and POKE are fairly fundamental keywords. The first gives us the ability to read any part of the CBM 64's memory and the second gives us the power to alter the contents of any address provided that this is possible.

LOGICAL OPERATORS AND BINARY MASKS

Apart from arithmetic and string manipulations the CBM 64 can also perform logical operations. Like everything else the CBM 64 does, logical operations are expressed in terms of zeros and ones.

The logical operators are AND, OR and NOT. Although we have never found much reason to use NOT, the operators AND and OR are extremely useful; they enable the microcomputer to take quite complex decisions on the basis of several numeric or string parameters. For example

IFX<10ORY>9ANDA$<>"B"THEN1000

In this case program execution will jump to line 1000 if the condition is met; that is if the com-pound logical statement is true, otherwise program execution will continue on the next line.

Try the following program

```
1000 X=10
1010 PRINT(X<10)
```

When RUN it should print 0. This is because X<10 is false. If you now change line 100 to X=9 the program will print −1 because then X<10 is true.

NOTE: False=0, True=−1.

Now try ANDing and ORing various combinations of −1 and 0. The results can be summarized in two little tables.

AND	0	−1		OR	0	−1
0	0	0		0	0	−1
−1	0	−1		−1	−1	−1

Note both operations are symmetric, e.g. 0AND−1 is the same as −1AND0. We can interpret these 'truth tables', as they are called, along the following lines. If you take a proposition which is false (0) AND a proposition which is true (−1) the result is a proposition which is false, that is 0AND −1 is 0.

In the line

$$IFX<10ORY>9ANDA\$<>\text{"B"}THEN1000$$

each relational operator X<10, Y>9 and A\$<>"B" returns the value of 0 or −1 according to whether it is true or false. Thus if X=9, Y=10 and A\$="A" we get the values −1, −1, −1 for these operations. To decide the truth or falsity of the compound logical proposition the operating system merely works out

$$(-1OR-1)AND-1 \qquad (=-1)$$

using the truth tables given above.

However, this is only half the story on logical operators. It is pretty neat being able to base decisions on the outcome of a compound logical proposition, but AND and OR have another equally important yet quite different application. Try the following program.

```
1000 X=32767:Y=1024
1010 PRINT(XANDY),(XORY)
```

When RUN it should print

    1024   32767

Here X and Y can be integer values in the range −32768 to +32767, other values will give a SYNTAX ERROR. Integers in this range can be represented by a 16-bit binary number as in Table 1.1. Note, incidentally, that negative integers have their top bit set. We can interpret this as follows. With 16 bits we can represent any integer in the range 0 to 65535 $((2\uparrow16)-1)$. We actually represent positive and negative integers in the range −32768 to 32767 using the top bit to signify a negative number. It is as if half of the interval 0 to 65535, the right-hand half, had been picked up bodily and translated to the other side of the origin. This picture leads to the following BASIC code to compute an integer from the contents of ADR and ADR+1, where ADR is the address in memory where the integer is stored (see Table 1.1). At this point only the fact that 32768 is subtracted if the sign bit is set should be noted.

Table 1.1 — How positive and negative integers are stored.

Integer	Bit pattern as stored in two addresses															
	ADR								ADR+1							
	15	14	13	12	11	10	9	8	7	6	5	4	3	2	1	0
. . .																
−3	1	1	1	1	1	1	1	1	1	1	1	1	1	1	0	1
−2	1	1	1	1	1	1	1	1	1	1	1	1	1	1	1	0
−1	1	1	1	1	1	1	1	1	1	1	1	1	1	1	1	1
0	0	0	0	0	0	0	0	0	0	0	0	0	0	0	0	0
1	0	0	0	0	0	0	0	0	0	0	0	0	0	0	0	1
2	0	0	0	0	0	0	0	0	0	0	0	0	0	0	1	0
3	0	0	0	0	0	0	0	0	0	0	0	0	0	0	1	1
. . .																

Remark: NOTX=−(X+1).

```
1090 HI=PEEK(ADR):LO=PEEK(ADR+1)
1110 SIGNBIT=((HIAND128)/128)
1120 VAR=LO+256*(HIAND127)—32768*SIGNBIT
```

Returning to our discussion of how AND and OR work in the program:

```
1000 X=32767:Y=1024
1010 PRINT(XANDY),(XORY)
```

The explanation is that AND and OR are actually matching the bit patterns of X and Y in two different ways. If we look at the bit patterns of the two numbers this should become apparent.

	15	14	13	12	11	10	9	8	7	6	5	4	3	2	1	0
32767	0	1	1	1	1	1	1	1	1	1	1	1	1	1	1	1
1024	0	0	0	0	0	1	0	0	0	0	0	0	0	0	0	0

In the case of AND if both of the corresponding bits are 1 we get a 1, otherwise we get a 0. Similarly for OR if either or both of corresponding bits is a 1 we get a 1, otherwise we get a 0. When we use AND in this way we can think of one of the variables as a 'mask' against which the other variable is matched.

Examples:

```
  63AND16=16       1 1 1 1 1 1 AND 0 1 0 0 0 0 = 0 1 0 0 0 0
  17AND7 = 1       0 1 0 0 0 1 AND 0 0 0 1 1 1 = 0 0 0 0 0 1
  63OR16 =63       1 1 1 1 1 1  OR 0 1 0 0 0 0 = 1 1 1 1 1 1
  17OR7  =23       0 1 0 0 0 1  OR 0 0 0 1 1 1 = 0 1 0 1 1 1
  −1AND8  = 8      1 1 1 1 1 1 1 1 1 1 1 1 1 1 1 1 AND 1 0 0 0 = 1 0 0 0
−32768OR8 =−32760 1 0 0 0 0 0 0 0 0 0 0 0 0 0 0 0  OR 1 0 0 0 =
                  1 0 0 0 0 0 0 0 0 0 0 0 1 0 0 0
```

    XAND7 = The remainder when X is divided by 8.

    XAND15 = The remainder when X is divided by 16.

XAND255 = The Lo-byte of X (but only if 0<X<32768).

If you managed to get this far relax, the nasty part is over and we now come to the useful part. When discussing PEEK( ) and POKE we concluded that these were both fairly fundamental commands. In the BIT PATTERN program we were able to view the bit pattern in any address in the CBM 64's memory. Notice how the Ith bit of P is obtained in line 1160 of the program.

If PAND($2\uparrow I$)=$2\uparrow I$ then the Ith bit is 1,
If PAND($2\uparrow I$)=0   then the Ith bit is 0.

Either way the Ith bit of P is given by

BIT=(PAND($2\uparrow I$))/($2\uparrow I$)

This tells us how to look at any particular bit of any byte in the entire CBM 64 memory. But it does even more than that, it changes POKE from a hammer which knocks bytes in, to a scalpel which can insert or excise any bit of any byte of memory provided the byte is not in ROM.

Examples:
(a) To set the Ith bit of address A to 1, without changing any other bit

       POKEA,PEEK(A)OR(2↑I)

(b) To set the Ith bit of address A to 0, without changing any other bit

       POKEA,PEEK(A)AND(255−(2↑I))

(c) To change the Ith bit of address A whatever its value, without changing any other bit.

       B=1−(PEEK(A)AND(2↑I))/(2↑I):POKEA,PEEK(A)AND(255−(2↑I))OR(B*(2↑I))

HEXADECIMAL NOTATION

We have seen how zeros and ones can be used to represent an integer in binary notation (base 2). With a little practice one is soon able to convert integers in the range 0 to 255 from decimal to binary or vice versa. However, when the number of zeros and ones in the binary representation exceeds 8, rapid conversion is less easy. Apart from the more conventional decimal notation (base 10) there is another representation of numbers which is useful when working with computers or microcomputers. This is the *hexadecimal* notation (base 16). Indeed when working in Assembler or Machine code the hexadecimal representation is indispensable. In case base 16 sounds heavy going it is perhaps worth remarking that hexadecimal numbers are no harder to grasp than binary numbers.

    To begin with let us see how to count to 15 in hexadecimal.

Decimal	Hexadecimal	Binary (4 bits)
0	0	0 0 0 0
1	1	0 0 0 1
2	2	0 0 1 0
3	3	0 0 1 1
4	4	0 1 0 0
5	5	0 1 0 1
6	6	0 1 1 0
7	7	0 1 1 1
8	8	1 0 0 0
9	9	1 0 0 1
10	A	1 0 1 0
11	B	1 0 1 1
12	C	1 1 0 0
13	D	1 1 0 1
14	E	1 1 1 0
15	F	1 1 1 1

When 9 is reached we have run out of conventional single digits with which to represent the number. Therefore to base 16 we need to invent 6 more single-digit symbols, and the first 6 letters of the alphabet are normally used. A number greater than 15 can be expressed in hexadecimal using only the symbols 0,1,2,3,4,5,6,7,8,9,A,B,C,D,E,F.

Example:

Decimal $249 = 2*(10\uparrow2) + 4*(10\uparrow1) + 9$ (powers of 10)

Decimal $249 = 1*(2\uparrow7) + 1*(2\uparrow6) + 1*(2\uparrow5) + 1*(2\uparrow4) +$
                    $1*(2\uparrow3) + 0*(2\uparrow2) + 0*(2\uparrow1) + 1$ (powers of 2)

Decimal $249 = 15*(16\uparrow1) + 9 = F*(16\uparrow1) + 9$ (powers of 16)

Hence

249 in binary is   1   1   1   1   1   0   0   1

249 in hexadecimal is   F   9

Similarly

         250 in hexadecimal is FA
         251 in hexadecimal is FB
         252 in hexadecimal is FC
         253 in hexadecimal is FD
         254 in hexadecimal is FE
         255 in hexadecimal is FF

Notice how easy it is to convert from hexadecimal to binary. Each block of 4 binary bits corresponds to one hexadecimal symbol and this is still true for numbers greater than 255. Thus

Binary   1   1   1   1   1   1   1   0

is the same as

Hexadecimal   F   E

Binary   1   0   1   0   1   0   0   1   1   0   1   1   0   1   1   1

is the same as

Hexadecimal   A   9   B   7

Viewed in this way hexadecimal is no more than a shorthand method of writing binary.

Example:
To convert hexadecimal A9B7 to decimal we write

         $A9B7 = A*(16\uparrow3) + 9*(16\uparrow2) + B*(16\uparrow1) + 7$

             $= 10*(16\uparrow3) + 9*(16\uparrow2) + 11*(16\uparrow1) + 7$

             $= 43447$ (decimal)

    Now it can happen that a hexadecimal representation looks just like a decimal representation; for example, is 1234 the decimal number 1234 or the hexadecimal number 1234 ($=$ decimal 4660)? To avoid this kind of confusion it is customary to prefix any hexadecimal representation with a $ sign, for example hexadecimal A9B7 is written as $A9B7 and hexadecimal 1234 is written as $1234.

Converting from decimal to hexadecimal is not quite as straightforward as the other way round, although it is not difficult. However, computers are supposed to take the pain out of computation, so here is a little program which will convert either way. It will be useful when studying later chapters.

To convert a hex number to decimal, just enter the $ sign followed by four characters. If no $ sign is entered the program assumes you want to convert from decimal to hex. To end the program just enter a $ sign followed by the 'RETURN' key.

```
1000 REM***HEX/DEC CONVERSION***
1010 D$="▓▓▓▓▓▓▓▓▓▓▓▓▓▓▓▓▓▓▓▓▓▓▓▓▓":REM CURSOR HOM
E+24 DOWN
1020 SP$="                                        "
:REM 40 SPACES
1030 PRINTCHR$(147)LEFT$(D$,5)LEFT$(SP$,12)"INPUT
NUMBER"
1040 PRINTLEFT$(D$,8)LEFT$(SP$,6)"PRECEED HEX NUMB
ERS BY '$'"
1050 PRINTLEFT$(D$,20)LEFT$(SP$,6)"END PROGRAM WIT
H '$' SIGN"
1060 PRINTLEFT$(D$,10)LEFT$(SP$,40)
1070 PRINTLEFT$(D$,10)LEFT$(SP$,10);
1080 INPUT"NUMBER";A$
1090 IFA$="$"THENPRINTCHR$(147):END
1100 IFLEN(A$)>5THEN1060
1110 IFLEFT$(A$,1)="$"THENGOSUB1170:IFD=-1THEN1060

1120 IFLEFT$(A$,1)<>"$"THENGOSUB1250:IFD=-1THEN106
0
1130 PRINTLEFT$(D$,14)LEFT$(SP$,40)
1140 PRINTLEFT$(D$,14)LEFT$(SP$,10)HX$
1150 PRINTLEFT$(D$,14)TAB(20)D
1160 GOTO1060
1170 REM***HEX TO DECIMAL***
1180 HX$=RIGHT$("000"+MID$(A$,2),4):D=0
1190 FORL=1TO4:NB=ASC(HX$)
1200 NB=NB-48+(NB>64)*7:HX$=MID$(HX$,2)
1210 IFNB<0ORNB>15THEND=-1:GOTO1240
1220 D=16*D+NB
1230 NEXT:HX$=A$
1240 RETURN
1250 REM***DEC TO HEXADECIMAL****
1260 D=VAL(A$)
1270 IFD<0ORD>65535THEND=-1:GOTO1330
1280 D=D/4096:HX$=""
```

```
1290  FORL=1TO4:NB=INT(D)
1300  HX$=HX$+CHR$(48+NB-(NB>9)*7)
1310  D=16*(D-NB)
1320  NEXT:HX$="$"+HX$:D=VAL(A$)
1330  RETURN
```

2

Manipulating data

INTRODUCTION

The CBM 64 is a powerful tool for manipulating data. Large amounts of data are often best stored in a systematic fashion, by means of arrays or other kinds of tables. In this chapter we study the question of data storage by means of arrays. Simple techniques of array manipulation are illustrated by means of a card shuffle.

To save searching through a long list, an array can frequently be used to speed up data access. When an array is used like this it is called a translation array. We discuss this trade-off between memory and speed and give examples of translation arrays. Another technique useful in handling arrays is division with remainder, a simple but powerful idea which is explained fully.

These methods are illustrated by a BLACKJACK program. Apart from illustration, the development of the card shuffle and display routines will enable you to write card games of your own; all you have to do is program the rules and the computer's decisions. Getting a computer to make reasonable decisions is, in many card games, far harder than it might first appear. To illustrate this we have programmed the CBM 64 to play GINRUMMY; you will find the program in the Appendices. It uses the same shuffle and card display routines as BLACKJACK, and enables the CBM 64 to play a reasonably good (and fair!) game of Gin.

Following the BLACKJACK program we return to the subject of data handling methods. Our first example is the 'binary search', finding a particular entry from a previously ordered list, which leads to a discussion of sorting methods. The theory of sorts deserves a book of its own. Our first sorting program, the Insertion sort, uses a very natural method, but is also very slow. A great deal of ingenuity has been applied to find less time-consuming methods and there is a large body of theory. Still, even the Insertion sort can have useful applications and we give as an example the program INDEX PREP which enables a book Index to be prepared easily. INDEX PREP sorts upper-case strings into alphabetical order as they are entered, builds a list of page numbers for each entry and can save the resulting index to disk and/or print it to screen or printer. We next give a version of C. A. R. Hoare's Quicksort which in most situations provides a practical fast sort.

Finally we shall look at the way the CBM 64 stores variables or strings. This is a useful thing to understand if you need to swap variables between BASIC and a machine code subroutine, but it is also a good example of the way memory can be used to create tables of information.

WHAT ARE ARRAYS?

The concept of an array is quite simple. We can picture an array A(I) (0<=I<=N) as a sequence of boxes into which we can place data.

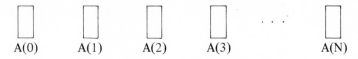

$$A(0) \qquad A(1) \qquad A(2) \qquad A(3) \qquad \cdots \qquad A(N)$$

The statement DIMA(N) creates this array.

For a floating point array a typical element might be A(I) and each box would be 5 bytes of memory. For an integer array, typical element A%(I), each box would be 2 bytes of memory. Every element of an array is, in effect, a separate variable which can be specified by means of its subscript.

Of course an array can be set up to use more than one subscript. For example a typical element of the two-dimensional array might be A(I,J). Still, the principle remains the same: a host of variables is created under one collective heading, using the DIM statement, and each individual variable is subsequently accessed by means of its unique subscript or subscripts.

We can also define string arrays; a typical element of such an array might be A$(I). In this case A$(I) could be any string of length up to 255. For example if we have 100 short messages these can be put in DATA statements, READ into an array and then when we need to PRINT the Ith message it is only necessary to PRINTA$(I).

ARRAYS IN PRACTICE-SHUFFLES

Our first example of using arrays is in shuffling a deck of cards. As we shall see this can be done in several ways; the program below gives three methods.

Each card in a standard deck is identified by an integer in the range 1 to 52. We therefore dimension an array D%( ), with DIMD%(52), in which to store the cards. The array is first filled with the numbers 1 to 52. The shuffle proceeds as follows. To begin with a random integer A, in the range 1 to 52, is selected and the Ath element of the array D%( ) is placed in a temporary variable TEMP. Next every element up to the (A−1)th is moved one position to the right and TEMP is then inserted as the first array element. Next time around a random integer A, in the range 2 to 52, is selected and the Ath element of the array is stored in TEMP. Every element from the second to the (A−1)th is then moved one to the right and TEMP inserted as the second element. The process continues until all 52 elements are exhausted. Note that the routine correctly handles the case A=1 and the extreme case A=I=1.

In the second method an identical procedure is applied to a sequence of consecutive addresses in the cassette buffer. This is a substantial block of memory which is normally free during program execution. (Of course if the cassette is used whilst a program is RUNning any data in the cassette buffer will be lost.) Thus the array D%( ) is replaced by addresses 828 to 828+52 and D%(J)= D%(J−1) is replaced by POKE828+J,PEEK(828+J−1). Still, the principle of the shuffle is just the same.

In both the first and second method the shuffle is rather slow. The reason for this is that moving every element of a big block of the array one to the right each time we go round the loop is very time-consuming. The third method of performing a shuffle avoids this problem by exploiting the string handling functions. First a string D$ of length 52 is set up, with the Ith character of the string being CHR$(I). The string D$ replaces the array D%( ) and holds the deck of cards. The effect of the main loop in both previous shuffles is to lift the Ath element out of the array and place it at the beginning. Using the string D$, rather than the array D%( ), we can accomplish this in one move with

$$D\$=MID\$(D\$,A,I)+LEFT\$(D\$,A-1)+RIGHT\$(D\$,52-A)$$

No FOR loop is needed.

```
1000 REM**THREE KINDS OF SHUFFLE**
1010 PRINTCHR$(147):DIMD%(52)
1020 PRINT"USING ARRAYS IT TAKES..."
1030 T=TI:REM TAKE TIME
1040 FORI=1TO52:D%(I)=I:NEXT:REM SETUP
1050 FORI=1TO52:A=I+INT((53-I)*RND(1))
1060 TMP=D%(A)
1070 FORJ=ATOISTEP-1:D%(J)=D%(J-1):NEXT
1080 D%(I)=TMP:NEXTI
1090 PRINT(TI-T)/60"SECS"
1100 PRINT:PRINT
1110 PRINT"USING PEEK/POKE IT TAKES..."
1120 T=TI:REM TAKE TIME
1130 FORI=1TO52:POKE828+I,I:NEXT
1140 FORI=1TO52:A=I+INT((53-I)*RND(1))
1150 TMP=PEEK(828+A)
1160 FORJ=ATOISTEP-1
1170 POKE828+J,PEEK(828+J-1):NEXT
1180 POKE828+I,TMP:NEXTI
1190 PRINT(TI-T)/60"SECS"
1200 PRINT:PRINT
1210 PRINT"USING STRINGS IT TAKES..."
1220 T=TI:REM TAKE TIME
1230 D$="":FORI=1TO52:D$=D$+CHR$(I):NEXT
1240 FORI=1TO52:A=I+INT((53-I)*RND(1))
1250 D$=MID$(D$,A,1)+LEFT$(D$,A-1)+RIGHT$(D$,52-A)
```

```
1260 NEXT
1270 PRINT(TI-T)/60"SECS"
1280 END
```

When the program is RUN we find that the first shuffle takes around 8 seconds, the second around 12 seconds and the third about 2 seconds. If the program is RUN several times another interesting point emerges, namely, in all cases the time taken varies from RUN to RUN: we leave you to work out why this is so.

ARRAYS IN PRACTICE-TRANSLATION ARRAYS

Another use of arrays is to impose order on an otherwise disordered set of data. For example, if we wished to use the QWERTYUIOP@*↑ line of keys on the keyboard to play musical notes in ascending frequency we should be faced with several problems. The first problem is to 'translate' the keypress (or the ASCII code of the keypress) into a frequency which can be POKEd into an oscillator. The main difficulty here is that in each pair of numbers (ASCcode, Frequency) the second bears no simple mathematical relationship to the first. Finally, to add to our problems, if the notes are to be played in 'real time' then the right value for the oscillator POKE needs to be immediately available. The solution to this kind of problem is to use an array created by DATA statements. The ASCII code can then be used as an index to an array of frequency values.

Example
```
1000  REM TRANSLATION ARRAY EXAMPLE
1010  DATA 81,87,69,82,84,89     :REM ASC QWERTY
1020  DATA 85,73,79,80,64,42,94  :REM ASC UIOP@*↑
1030  REM NOW SET UP TRANSLATION ARRAY
1040  DIMTR(53):REM MAX-MIN+1=94-42+1=53
1050  FORI=1TO13
1060  READ CODE: OFFSET=CODE-41
1070  TR(OFFSET)=I:REM USE NUMBERS 1 TO 13 AS 'FREQUENCIES'
1080 NEXT
1090  REM NOW TEST TRANSLATION ARRAY
2000  GETA$:IFA$=" "THEN2000
2010  OFFSET=ASC(A$)-41
2030  IF(OFFSET<1OROFFSET>53)THEN2000:REM ARRAY BOUNDS
2040  IFTR(OFFSET)=0THEN2000:REM NOT INTERESTED
2050  PRINTTR(OFFSET):REM COULD BE POKE FREQUENCY
2060  GOTO2000:REM NEXT KEYPRESS
```

In this example we have substituted the numbers 1 to 13 for frequencies. If required, frequency values could be assigned to TR( ) from another array constructed from a second set of DATA statements. Note that the values in the array which have not been assigned will be zero and this fact is used in line 2040 to field keypresses which we are not interested in. The net effect of the program is to PRINT the numbers 1 to 13 when the keys QWERTYUIOP@*↑ are pressed.

Note the trade-off in memory against time. By using a translation array we can produce an immediate response to a valid keypress and ignore all others, but the price paid is the use of an array of size 53 (of course in practice we could make this an integer array).

This example should serve to illustrate the idea of a translation array. No doubt you can soon think up some applications of your own.

DIVISION WITH REMAINDER

The characteristic feature of a one-dimensional array is that it is a block of data which is organized so that any individual piece of data can be accessed by a single parameter. In this sense all three methods of storing the numbers 1 to 52 in SHUFFLES could be said to use 'arrays'.

Another example of an array in this more general sense is the area of memory devoted to the screen display. Normally this area of memory begins at $SC=1024$ and extends to $SC+999$, a total of 1000 possible screen locations. Each of these 1000 addresses contains a byte which is the screen code of the corresponding character displayed on the screen. Addresses SC to $SC+39$ contain the first row of the screen display, $SC+40$ to $SC+79$ the second row, and so on for all 25 rows. Thus if we index the screen row by Y, $0<=Y<=24$, and the column by X, $0<=X<=39$, the address in screen memory of character cell (X,Y) is $SC+SL$ where

$$SL=40*Y+X \qquad (0<=X<=39).$$

Here SL lies in the range 0 to 999.

Conversely we may pose the question: given a screen location SL, $0<=SL<=999$, how do we find the corresponding row and column, i.e. the corresponding values of Y and X? Notice that there are many solutions of the equation $SL=40*Y+X$ in integers Y,X. For example if $SL=147$ we have

$$147=40*5-53=40*4-13=3*40+27=2*40+67, \text{etc.}$$

Nevertheless only one of these representations, namely $147=3*40+27$, corresponds to a value of X in the range 0 to 39. For any integer SL there is a unique representation $SL=40*Y+X$, in multiples of 40 plus a remainder in the range 0 to 39. We can find X and Y with the following BASIC code

$$Y=INT(SL/40):X=SL-40*Y$$

There is a very useful general principle at work here. If we want to express any integer N in multiples of a positive integer M, plus a remainder X in the range 0 to $M-1$, that is

$$N=M*Y+X \qquad (0<=X<=M-1)$$

then this can be done in only one way and the BASIC code

$$Y=INT(N/M):X=N-M*Y$$

will do it. The idea goes back to Euclid who used it to devise a method of finding the highest common factor of N and M. (Note that if an integer divides N and M it must also divide X, which is smaller than M.)

Example

An integer N in the range 0 to 65535 can be expressed as a 16-bit binary number which we can consider as being made up of two bytes, a Hi-byte and a Lo-byte. Remember a byte is 8 bits. A single byte represents an integer in the range 0 to 255 and 256*256=65536. Therefore to find the Hi-byte and the Lo-byte of N we should work in multiples of 256. Applying division with remainder we have

$$\text{Hi-byte} = \text{INT}(N/256) : \text{Lo-byte} = N - 256*(\text{Hi-byte})$$

This is a result which we shall use many times when finding an address.

The technique of division with remainder finds many applications in computing since it enables us to label the data in an array in more than one way. For example, in the case of the screen memory: given SL we can find the corresponding row and column, or conversely given the row and column we can readily compute SL. Another example is in dealing with a high resolution screen where we need to work in multiples of 8.

DISPLAYING CARDS

In the first part of this chapter, three routines for shuffling cards were discussed. We can now turn our attention to displaying all 52 cards of a standard deck. In the program a card is represented by a number CD in the range 1 to 52. To display a card we first need to know its suit and value. Each suit contains 13 cards so we can assign the value of CD as

1 to 13 Spades	,CH%(0)=65, S%=0,
14 to 26 Hearts	,CH%(1)=83, S%=1,
27 to 39 Clubs	,CH%(2)=88, S%=2,
40 to 52 Diamonds	,CH%(3)=90, S%=3,

where the array CH%( ) contains the screen code for the spade symbol, heart symbol, etc. and S% denotes the suit.

Given a value CD we would like to know the suit and value of the card. It seems sensible to assign the values 1,2,3,4,...,13 to the cards Ace,Two,King respectively. We can compute the suit S% and the value V using division with remainder, but there is a slight snag since remainders which are 0 should really be 13 to give a King. Taking this into account we have

$$S\% = \text{INT}(CD/13) : V = CD - 13*S\% : \text{IF} V = 0 \text{ THEN} V = 13 : S\% = S\% - 1$$

where the IF statement is a 'fix' to take care of the fact that for multiples of 13 both the value and the suit would otherwise be incorrect.

Having found the suit and value we next consider the steps which are needed to display the card. The first decision to be taken is, how many cards might we want to display simultaneously? Given the size of the CBM 64 screen and requirement that each card displayed should be of reasonable size, the number 8 was chosen for the maximum number of cards to be displayed at any one time.

The position of a card on the screen is therefore specified by a position indicator PI which takes values in the range 1 to 8. The numbers CD and PI must be specified before the CARD GOSUB is called.

From PI we can compute the offset DD% of the top left corner of the card from the base SC of screen memory, see Fig. 2.1. To find DD% we give each card a 'row' RW% and a 'column' CM%. Since we are working in multiples of 4 these are computed by division with remainder as

$$RW\% = INT((PI-)/4):CM\% = PI-1-4*RW\%$$

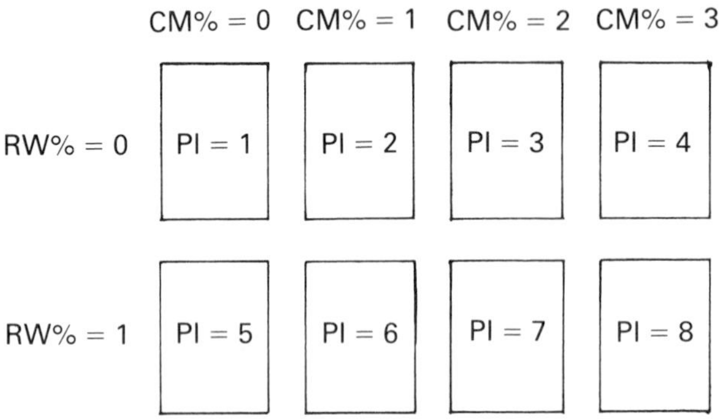

	CM% = 0	CM% = 1	CM% = 2	CM% = 3
RW% = 0	PI = 1	PI = 2	PI = 3	PI = 4
RW% = 1	PI = 5	PI = 6	PI = 7	PI = 8

Fig. 2.1 – The eight card positions.

The top left corner of the first card position corresponds to screen location 45 and the difference between successive top left corners in the same row is 6. Finally, the offset between corresponding screen locations from one row to the next is 360. This gives

$$DD\% = 45 + 6*CM\% + 360*RW\%$$

As a safeguard against the possibility that the CARD GOSUB might be called with a value of PI greater than 8 we AND the number RW% with 1, which effectively wraps the hypothetical card position 9 back to overprint position 1. Defensive programming requires that one should never POKE to an address outside the area of memory intended, and the CARD GOSUB will involve a lot of POKEs! So our final formula for DD% is

$$DD\% = 45 + 6*CM\% + 360*(RW\% AND1)$$

If the base of the screen memory is SC and that of color memory is CO then the top left corner of card position PI corresponds to screen address B and color address C, where

$$B = SC + DD\%:C = CO + DD\%$$

Having decided where in memory the top left corner of the card to be displayed is actually located we can now proceed to display first the card frame then the pattern. The pattern will be determined by S% and V. A program which tests the whole CARD GOSUB is listed below.

```
10 REM**TEST CARD GOSUB**
20 DIMCH%(3):CH%(0)=65:CH%(1)=83:CH%(2)=88:CH%(3)=
90:REM SUIT CHARS
30 SC=1024:REM BASE OF SCREEN MEM
40 CO=55296:REM BASE OF COL MEM
50 POKE53281,1:REM WHITE BACKGROUND
60 POKE53280,5:REM GREEN BORDER
70 PI=1:REM FIRST POSITION
80 FORCD=1TO52
90 PI=1:REM FIRST POSITION
100 PRINTCHR$(147):GOSUB1740
110 GETA$:IFA$=""THEN110
120 NEXT
130 END
1740 REM**CARD GOSUB**
1750 S%=INT(CD/13):V=CD-13*S%:IFV=0THENV=13:S%=S%-
1:REM SUIT & VALUE
1760 RW%=INT((PI-1)/4):CM%=PI-1-4*RW%:DD%=45+6*CM%
+360*(RW%AND1):REMFRAME OFFSET
1770 B=SC+DD%:C=CO+DD%
1780 REM*CARD FRAME*
1790 POKEB,85:POKEB+1,64:POKEB+2,64:POKEB+3,64:POK
EB+4,73 :REM TOP
1800 POKEC,13:POKEC+1,13:POKEC+2,13:POKEC+3,13:POK
EC+4,13:REM COLS
1810 POKEB+40,93:POKEB+80,93:POKEB+120,93:POKEB+16
0,93:POKEB+200,93  :REM LEFT
1820 POKEC+40,13:POKEC+80,13:POKEC+120,13:POKEC+16
0,13:POKEC+200,13:REM COLS
1830 POKEB+44,93:POKEB+84,93:POKEB+124,93:POKEB+16
4,93:POKEB+204,93:REM RIGHT
1840 POKEC+44,13:POKEC+84,13:POKEC+124,13:POKEC+16
4,13:POKEC+204,13:REM COLS
1850 POKEB+240,74:POKEB+241,64:POKEB+242,64:POKEB+
243,64:POKEB+244,75:REM BOT
1860 POKEC+240,13:POKEC+241,13:POKEC+242,13:POKEC+
243,13:POKEC+244,13:REM COLS
1870 IFZ%=DP-2ANDPI=2THEN2040:REM DOWN CARD
1880 REM*PATTERN*
1890 A=CH%(S%):CC=2*(S%AND1):REM CHAR&COL
1900 ONVGOTO1910,1920,1930,1940,1950,1960,1970,198
0,1990,2000,2010,2020,2030
1910 GOSUB2070:POKEB+41,1:POKEC+41,0:GOTO2040:REM
ACE
```

Listing continued next page

```
1920 GOSUB2080:GOTO2040:REM TWO
1930 GOSUB2080:GOSUB2070:GOTO2040:REM THREE
1940 GOSUB2090:GOTO2040:REM FOUR
1950 GOSUB2090:GOSUB2070:GOTO2040:REM FIVE
1960 GOSUB2090:GOSUB2110:GOTO2040:REM SIX
1970 GOSUB2090:GOSUB2110:GOSUB2070:GOTO2040:REM SE
VEN
1980 GOSUB2090:GOSUB2110:GOSUB2080:GOTO2040:REM EI
GHT
1990 GOSUB2090:GOSUB2120:GOSUB2070:GOTO2040:REM NI
NE
2000 GOSUB2090:GOSUB2120:GOSUB2080:GOTO2040:REM TE
N
2010 GOSUB2070:POKEB+41,10:POKEC+41,0:GOTO2040:REM
 JACK
2020 GOSUB2070:POKEB+41,17:POKEC+41,0:GOTO2040:REM
 QUEEN
2030 GOSUB2070:POKEB+41,11:POKEC+41,0:GOTO2040:REM
 KING
2040 IFV>10THENV=10
2050 RETURN
2060 REM**PATTERN BUILDING BLOCKS**
2070 POKEB+122,A:POKEC+122,CC:RETURN
2080 POKEB+82,A:POKEB+162,A:POKEC+82,CC:POKEC+162,
CC:RETURN
2090 POKEB+41,A:POKEB+43,A:POKEB+201,A:POKEB+203,A

2100 POKEC+41,CC:POKEC+43,CC:POKEC+201,CC:POKEC+20
3,CC:RETURN
2110 POKEB+121,A:POKEB+123,A:POKEC+121,CC:POKEC+12
3,CC:RETURN
2120 POKEB+81,A:POKEB+83,A:POKEB+161,A:POKEB+163,A

2130 POKEC+81,CC:POKEC+83,CC:POKEC+161,CC:POKEC+16
3,CC:RETURN
```

In displaying the frame we have the option of using FOR loops for the two horizontal lines and for the two vertical lines or, alternatively simply POKEing every screen and color location individually. In fact the second alternative is adopted, because although using FOR loops saves approximately 200 bytes of program space the resulting routine is rather slow.

After setting up the card frame in lines 1780 to 1860 (ignore line 1870 for the present) we next have to insert the pattern. For this we need the suit symbol from CH%(S%) and the color (black=0, red=2), which can be computed from S%; both are set in line 1890. The subsequent pattern is now determined by the value of V. In line 1900 V is used to select one of 13 pattern display subroutines. Thus line 1910 displays an Ace, line 1920 displays a Two, and so on until line 2030 which displays a King. Rather than using 13 blocks of POKE statements, one block for each pattern, these routines call upon just 5 such pattern-building blocks from which all number cards can be assembled. The court cards, including the Ace, are essentially a modified One (line 2070). A Five, for example, is an overlay of a One (line 2070) and a Four (line 2090).

Having assembled the CARD DISPLAY routine the next and, with any luck, final step is to test it before incorporating it as a single GOSUB in a longer card game program.

BLACKJACK

Now that the card-shuffle and card-display routines are available it becomes possible to construct a program to play a card game. The game selected is Blackjack (Pontoon), being reasonably simple and quite well known.

A schematic for Blackjack is given in Figure 2.2; this relates to lines 1130 to 1670 of the program. The key variable is DP, the deck pointer, which normally points to the next card in the deck D%( ). Before any cards have been dealt DP is set equal to 1 in line 1180. In lines 1190 to 1260 four cards are dealt, alternately to the player and computer, and displayed on the screen. The second computer card is displayed 'face down' (decided by line 1870). The player's cards are stored in an array P%( ) and the computer's cards in an array C%( ). The variable P is used to juggle the card positions so that the player's cards are displayed in positions 5 and 6, whilst the computer's cards are displayed in positions 1 and 2. Since DP has been selected as the FOR loop counter in this routine, when line 1260 is reached DP has been incremented from its initial value by 4, which is correct since 4 cards have been dealt. For the remainder of the current game DP will always be incremented by 1 whenever a card is dealt, consequently DP will always point to the next available card.

Note that in line 2040 after a court card has been displayed its value V is set to 10, so that V can be used for scoring. The player can always decide the value of an Ace, after it has been displayed (lines 1290 and 1360).

```
1000 REM***BLACKJACK64***
1010 DIMD%(52),P%(2),C%(2),CH%(3):CH%(0)=65:CH%(1)
=83:CH%(2)=88:CH%(3)=90
1020 SC=1024:CO=55296:POKE53281,1:POKE53280,5
1030 D$="                                  ":W$="
                                  "
1040 PRINTCHR$(14)"        "SPC(15)"|LACKJACK":PRIN
T:PRINTSPC(18)"BY":PRINT
1050 PRINTSPC(13)"_IDGE  *YSTEMS"
1060 PRINT"      -O YOU WANT _IVE CARD TRICKS ( |/)
..?"
1070 GETC$:IFC$<>"Y"ANDC$<>"N"THEN1070
1080 IFC$="Y"THENFV=1
1090 P$=LEFT$(D$,13):REM SCROLL POSN
```

Listing continued next page

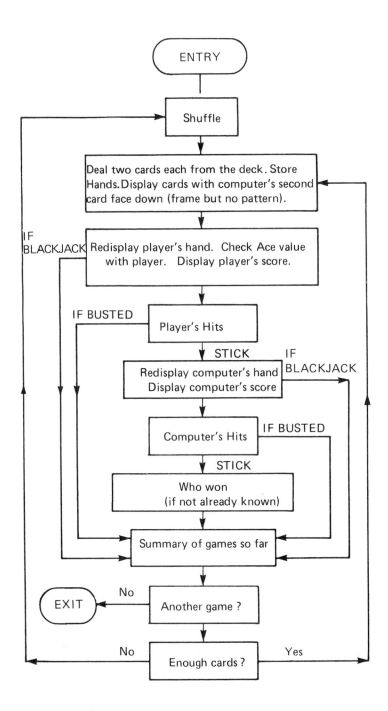

Fig. 2.2 – Schematic for BLACKJACK64

```
1100 M$="|RAIN THE SIZE OF A PLANET AND THEY WANT
ME TO PLAY BLACKJACK"
1110 GOSUB2160
1120 M$="、 WON'T ENJOY IT...."::GOSUB2160
1130 REM*SHUFFLE*
1140 PRINT"        WAIT WHILE I SHUFFLE THE CARD
S":XX=RND(0):REM NEW SEED
1150 DK$="":FORI=1TO52:DK$=DK$+CHR$(I):NEXT
1160 FORI=1TO52:A=I+INT((53-I)*RND(1))
1170 DK$=MID$(DK$,A,1)+LEFT$(DK$,A-1)+RIGHT$(DK$,5
2-A)
1180 D%(I)=ASC(MID$(DK$,1,1)):NEXTI:DP=1:PC=0:XX=F
RE(0):REM FREE STRINGS
1190 REM*TWO CARDS EACH*
1200 P=1:Z%=DP:PRINT""CHR$(142)
1210 PRINTLEFT$(D$,15)SPC(23)"PLAYER":PRINTLEFT$(D
$,6)SPC(23)"COMPUTER"
1220 FORDP=Z%TOZ%+2 STEP2
1230 P%(P)=D%(DP):CD=P%(P):PI=P+4:GOSUB1740:REM PL
AYER
1240 C%(P)=D%(DP+1):CD=C%(P):PI=P:GOSUB1740:REM CO
MP
1250 P=P+1:NEXTDP
1260 PRINTD$:PRINTSPC(12)"PRESS ANY KEY":GETB$:IFB
$=""THEN1260
1270 REM*PLAYER'S HAND*
1280 PRINT"":V1=0:FORPI=1TO2:CD=P%(PI):GOSUB1740:
REM CARD
1290 IFV=1THENGOSUB1720:REM I/P ACE
1300 V1=V1+V:NEXTPI:GOSUB1680
1310 IFV1=21THENGOSUB2150:M$="YOU GOT BLACKJACK!":
PW=PW+1:GOTO1590
1320 REM*PLAYER'S HITS*
1330 PRINTD$:PRINT"    HIT..(Y/N)?":GETB$:IFB$<>"Y
"ANDB$<>"N"THEN1330
1340 PRINTD$:PRINTW$:IFB$="N"THEN1420:REM STICK
1350 CD=D%(DP):DP=DP+1:GOSUB1740:PI=PI+1:REM CARD
1360 IFV=1THENGOSUB1720:REMI/P ACE
1370 V1=V1+V:GOSUB1680
1380 IFV1>21THENGOSUB2150:M$="YOU'RE BUSTED...!!!"
:CW=CW+1:GOTO1590
1390 IFFV=1ANDPI=6THENGOSUB2150:M$="YOU GOT A FIVE
 CARD TRICK":PW=PW+1:GOTO1590
1400 IFV1=21THENGOSUB2150:GOTO1420:REM 21
```

Listing continued next page

```
1410 GOTO1320
1420 REM*COMP'S HAND*
1430 PRINT"⬛":V2=0:FORPI=1TO2:CD=C%(PI):GOSUB1740:
REM CARD
1440 IFV=1ANDV2<11THENV=11
1450 V2=V2+V:NEXTPI:GOSUB1700
1460 IFV2=21THENGOSUB2150:M$="COMPUTER GOT..BLACKJ
ACK!":CW=CW+1:GOTO1590
1470 REM*COMP'S HITS*
1480 IFV2>V1OR(V2=V1ANDV2>16)THENGOSUB2150:GOTO155
0:REM STICK
1490 CD=D%(DP):DP=DP+1:GOSUB1740:PI=PI+1:REM CARD
1500 IFV=1ANDV2<11THENV=11:REM ACE
1510 V2=V2+V:GOSUB1700
1520 IFV2>21THENGOSUB2150:M$="COMPUTER BUST..YOU W
IN":PW=PW+1:GOTO1590
1530 IFFV=1ANDPI=6THENGOSUB2150:M$="I GOT A FIVE C
ARD TRICK !!!":CW=CW+1:GOTO1590
1540 GOTO1470
1550 REM*WHO WON*
1560 IFV1>V2THENM$="WELL DONE..YOU WON":PW=PW+1
1570 IFV1=V2THENM$="STAND OFF"
1580 IFV1<V2THENM$="TOUGH..COMPUTER WON":CW=CW+1
1590 REM*SUMMARY*
1600 PRINT"⬛⬛⬛⬛⬛⬛"SPC(9)"COMPUTER   WINS..";CW:PR
INTSPC(9)"YOUR       WINS..";PW
1610 GOSUB2170:REM SCROLL M$
1620 PRINTD$"       CONTINUE ....⬛SPACE⬛":PRINT
1630 PRINT"       END        ....⬛ F-1 ⬛"
1640 GETB$:IFB$=""THEN1640
1650 IFB$=CHR$(133)THENPRINT"⬛":POKE53280,14:POKE5
3281,6:END
1660 IFDP<40THEN1190:REM DEAL
1670 PRINT"⬛":GOTO1130
1680 PRINTD$+"YOUR SCORE IS";V1" ";:GOSUB2230
1690 PRINT" POINTS COUNT    ⬛⬛⬛⬛⬛";PC:RETURN
1700 PRINTD$+"COMP SCORE IS";V2" ";:GOSUB2230
1710 PRINT" POINTS COUNT    ⬛⬛⬛⬛⬛";PC:RETURN
1720 PRINTD$:PRINTSPC(4);:INPUT"ACE=⬛⬛⬛⬛⬛⬛⬛⬛";B$:V=
VAL(B$):IFV<>1ANDV<>11THEN1720
1730 PRINTD$:PRINTW$:RETURN
1740 REM**CARD GOSUB**
1750 S%=INT(CD/13):V=CD-13*S%:IFV=0THENV=13:S%=S%-
1:REM SUIT & VALUE
```

```
1760 RW%=INT((PI-1)/4):CM%=PI-1-4*RW%:DD%=45+6*CM%
+360*(RW%AND1):REMFRAME OFFSET
1770 B=SC+DD%:C=CO+DD%
1780 REM*CARD FRAME*
1790 POKEB,85:POKEB+1,64:POKEB+2,64:POKEB+3,64:POK
EB+4,73 :REM TOP
1800 POKEC,13:POKEC+1,13:POKEC+2,13:POKEC+3,13:POK
EC+4,13:REM COLS
1810 POKEB+40,93:POKEB+80,93:POKEB+120,93:POKEB+16
0,93:POKEB+200,93 :REM LEFT
1820 POKEC+40,13:POKEC+80,13:POKEC+120,13:POKEC+16
0,13:POKEC+200,13:REM COLS
1830 POKEB+44,93:POKEB+84,93:POKEB+124,93:POKEB+16
4,93:POKEB+204,93:REM RIGHT
1840 POKEC+44,13:POKEC+84,13:POKEC+124,13:POKEC+16
4,13:POKEC+204,13:REM COLS
1850 POKEB+240,74:POKEB+241,64:POKEB+242,64:POKEB+
243,64:POKEB+244,75:REM BOT
1860 POKEC+240,13:POKEC+241,13:POKEC+242,13:POKEC+
243,13:POKEC+244,13:REM COLS
1870 IFZ%=DP-2ANDPI=2THEN2040:REM DOWN CARD
1880 REM*PATTERN*
1890 A=CH%(S%):CC=2*(S%AND1):REM CHAR&COL.
1900 ONVGOTO1910,1920,1930,1940,1950,1960,1970,198
0,1990,2000,2010,2020,2030
1910 GOSUB2070:POKEB+41,1:POKEC+41,0:GOTO2040:REM
ACE
1920 GOSUB2080:GOTO2040:REM TWO
1930 GOSUB2080:GOSUB2070:GOTO2040:REM THREE
1940 GOSUB2090:GOTO2040:REM FOUR
1950 GOSUB2090:GOSUB2070:GOTO2040:REM FIVE
1960 GOSUB2090:GOSUB2110:GOTO2040:REM SIX
1970 GOSUB2090:GOSUB2110:GOSUB2070:GOTO2040:REM SE
VEN
1980 GOSUB2090:GOSUB2110:GOSUB2080:GOTO2040:REM EI
GHT
1990 GOSUB2090:GOSUB2120:GOSUB2070:GOTO2040:REM NI
NE
2000 GOSUB2090:GOSUB2120:GOSUB2080:GOTO2040:REM TE
N
2010 GOSUB2070:POKEB+41,10:POKEC+41,0:GOTO2040:REM
 JACK
2020 GOSUB2070:POKEB+41,17:POKEC+41,0:GOTO2040:REM
 QUEEN
```

Listing continued next page

```
2030 GOSUB2070:POKEB+41,11:POKEC+41,0:GOTO2040:REM
     KING
2040 IFV>10THENV=10
2050 RETURN
2060 REM**PATTERN BUILDING BLOCKS**
2070 POKEB+122,A:POKEC+122,CC:RETURN
2080 POKEB+82,A:POKEB+162,A:POKEC+82,CC:POKEC+162,
CC:RETURN
2090 POKEB+41,A:POKEB+43,A:POKEB+201,A:POKEB+203,A
2100 POKEC+41,CC:POKEC+43,CC:POKEC+201,CC:POKEC+20
3,CC:RETURN
2110 POKEB+121,A:POKEB+123,A:POKEC+121,CC:POKEC+12
3,CC:RETURN
2120 POKEB+81,A:POKEB+83,A:POKEB+161,A:POKEB+163,A
2130 POKEC+81,CC:POKEC+83,CC:POKEC+161,CC:POKEC+16
3,CC:RETURN
2140 REM**DELAY**
2150 FORI=0TO2000:NEXT:RETURN
2160 REM**SCROLL MESSAGE**
2170 Z$=W$+M$+W$
2180 FORN=1TOLEN(Z$)-38
2190 PRINTP$CHR$(18)CHR$(156)MID$(Z$,N,40)CHR$(146
)CHR$(154);
2200 FORM=0TO10:NEXT:REM DELAY
2210 NEXT:PRINTP$+W$;:REM WIPE
2220 RETURN
2230 REM*******ADJUST POINTS COUNT******
2240 REM*COUNT HIGH-LESS HIGHS IN DECK*
2250 REM*COUNT LOW -MORE HIGHS IN DECK*
2260 IFV<>10RV<>11THENPC=PC+V-7
2270 RETURN
```

A BINARY SEARCH OF AN ORDERED LIST

Suppose we have an array of numeric or string data which is already sorted into some order. If the array is numeric it may be ordered in increasing size; a string array will probably be ordered alphabetically. Consider the problem of finding a known entry (if it is present) or determining that it is absent. The simplest approach would be to examine each element of the array in turn until the correct entry is located. Indeed if the array were not already ordered, this sequential examination would be the only sure way to proceed. For an array of size N sequential examination requires a maximum of N comparisons. However, since the array data is ordered in some way, there is a much faster method, known as 'binary search'. A binary search of an ordered array of N elements takes at most $INT(LOG(N)/LOG(2))+1$ comparisons, far faster than a sequential search.

The idea of the binary search is very simple. Suppose we wish to search an array of floating point numbers, which are stored in numerically increasing order with respect to the array index. To determine if the number X is present in the array with index 1 to N we compare X with the middle of the array, say index INT$((1+N)/2)$. If X is less than the middle element then we know that, if it is present at all, it must be in the first half of the array. If X is greater than the middle element then it must be in the last half of the array. Of course if X happens to be equal to the middle element then our search is ended. Suppose we find that X must be in the first half. Then we just go through the same process again using the first half of the array. In this way the array index range we have to search is halved on every iteration, a technique known as 'divide and conquer'. Plainly a procedure of this type would be most easily implemented as a procedure which calls itself, i.e. as a recursive procedure. However, BASIC does not cope well with recursive procedures so the following program BINARY SEARCH uses GOTO to emulate recursion.

Example:

This program illustrates the binary search by constructing an ordered array and then locating any specified element. The routine is very fast even for very large arrays. If some element occurs more than once then we could easily arrange to continue the search; however, this program stops searching when it finds one occurrence.

```
1000 REM*BINARY SEARCH OF ORDERED *
1010 REM*ARRAY FOR ONE OCCURENCE   *
1020 REM*****************************
1030 REM*    CREATE TEST ARRAY     *
1040 INPUT"ARRAY SIZE N(1TO7000)";N
1050 DIMAR(N)
1060 FORI=1TON:AR(I)=10*I:NEXT
1070 REM*    WHAT TO LOOK FOR ?    *
1080 INPUT"SEARCH FOR (10TO10*N)";X
1090 REM*****************************
1100 REM*   PERFORM BINARY SEARCH  *
1110 L=1:R=N
1120 M=INT((L+R)/2)
1130 IFX=AR(M)THENPRINT"FOUND AT"M:END
1140 IFX<AR(M)THENR=M-1
1150 IFX>AR(M)THENL=M+1
1160 IFL=MORR=MTHENPRINT"NOT FOUND":END
1170 GOTO1120
```

SORTING METHODS

The binary search is very fast but it does presuppose that the data is already ordered. An obvious next question is: how can we efficiently order a disordered array? This question is very much bigger than it looks!

The process of ordering a disordered set of data is known as 'sorting', and a routine which does this is called a 'sort'. It is important to distinguish two different kinds of sorting problem. The first, the easier of the two, is when there is sufficient memory in the microcomputer to store all the data, for example in an array. This is the kind of sort we shall discuss. The second type of sort is when the data to be sorted is of such a size that it cannot all be read into the computer at one fell swoop, for example the data might be stored in several sequential files. The reader who needs a sort of this type should consult *Algorithms + Data Structures = Programs* by N. Wirth (an 'algorithm' is just a procedure for achieving some computational goal) or *Fundamentals of Computer Algorithms* by E. Horowitz and S. Sahni. Both are excellent books and we strongly recommend them to anyone who wishes to know more about sorts, in particular (or algorithms in general), than we are able to cover in this book.

There are many different algorithms for sorting data held within memory, usually as an array. These divide into two types:

(i) A second array of the same size is created and data is transferred from the first into the second in such a way that the second array contains an ordered copy of the data contained in the first array. Sorts of this type can be quite useful and are easy to program. However, they suffer the considerable disadvantage of doubling the memory requirement to sort a given set of data. In many applications this is not an option, since the program designer will probably want to get in as much data as possible.

(ii) The data is sorted using the array in which it is stored. This is harder to accomplish quickly. However, it is the type of sort which we shall discuss.

The simplest type of sort is the Insertion sort, see Fig. 2.3.

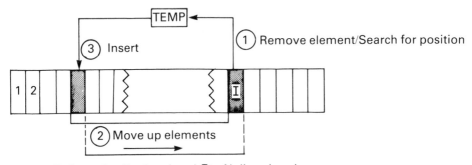

Before : 1 to I − 1 ordered, I to N disordered
After   : 1 to I ordered, I + 1 to N disordered

Fig. 2.3 – The Insertion sort.

The Insertion sort applied to sort a numeric array A(I) for I=1 to N can be paraphrased as:

FOR I=2 TO N
    TEMP=A(I)
    IF TEMP<A(I−1)THEN (i) Search for position in A(1),...,A(I−1)'
                     (ii) Move everything from insertion position onward one to the right.
NEXT I

At each stage when (i) is reached the array A(1),...,A(I−1) is already ordered, so we can perform a binary search to find a correct insertion point. To perform the insertion (ii) is very reminiscent of the 'SHUFFLES' routine.

```
1000 REM*SORT ARRAY WITH POSSIBLY *
1010 REM*    EQUAL ELEMENTS INTO   *
1020 REM*      INCREASING ORDER     *
1030 REM****************************
1040 REM* INPUT ARRAY DIMENSION    *
1050 INPUT"ARRAY SIZE N(2TO7000)";N
1060 REM*   INITIALISE TEST ARRAY  *
1070 DIMAR(N)
1080 FORI=1TON:AR(I)=N*RND(1):NEXT
1090 REM***** BEGIN SORTING *******
1100 PRINT"START SORT":T=TI
1110 FORI=2TON:NE=I-1
1120 IFAR(I)>AR(NE)THEN1200
1130 V=AR(I)
1140 GOSUB1240:REM SEARCH FOR POSITION
1150 REM*    MOVE ELEMENTS RIGHT   *
1160 FORJ=ITOASTEP-1
1170 AR(J)=AR(J-1)
1180 NEXT
1190 AR(A)=V:REM INSERT
1200 NEXTI:SEC=(TI-T)/60
1210 FORI=0TON:PRINTAR(I):NEXT
1220 PRINT"SORT COMPLETED IN"SEC"SECS"
1230 END
1240 REM****************************
1250 REM*   PERFORM BINARY SEARCH  *
1260 REM*       ON ORDERED LIST    *
1270 A=1:B=NE
1280 M=INT((A+B)/2)
1290 IFV=AR(M)THENPRINT"PRESENT AT"M:NI=1:GOTO1340
1300 IFV<AR(M)THENB=M-1
1310 IFV>AR(M)THENA=M+1
1320 IFA=MORB=MTHENNI=0:GOTO1340
1330 GOTO1280
1340 RETURN
```

An Insertion sort of this type, which uses a binary search for position, can be expected to take at most N*LOG(N) comparisons and at most 0.5*N*N moves (approximately). The time-consuming aspect of this method is therefore the number of moves required. It is not surprising that the binary insertion sort works best when the data is nearly ordered, less well when the data is randomly ordered and worst when the data is inversely ordered.

In the process of designing a program it pays to consider whether to sort the data as it is entered: large sorts can be very time-consuming. Our next program INDEX PREP illustrates this approach, using a binary search to locate the position of insertion and then moving array elements up to create space.

This program can cope with an Index of over 1000 entries. It sorts upper-case entries into alphabetical order in a string array IN$( ) and stores the associated page numbers in another string array PG$( ). A partial Index can be 'Saved', as a sequential file, to disk and 'Loaded' back for later extension. The 'save' and 'load' routines can easily be modified for tape. Screen displays are minimal in order to keep the program length down, but these could readily be made more attractive and helpful. Note that, if no further entry is required, entering a null string will get you to the main menu. A facility has been included to delete an entry.

A simple modification of this program could be used as an address list or telephone directory. To accomplish this it is only necessary to add a routine which calls the binary search GOSUB to find the entry you wish to display.

```
1000 REM*CREATE ALPHABETIC INDEX  *
1010 REM* SAVE/LOAD OR PRINT IT   *
1020 REM*****************************
1030 REM*    ARRAY PARAMETERS      *
1040 REM*    NEW OR OLD INDEX      *
1050 NE=0:R$=CHR$(13)
1060 DW$="                        "
1070 PRINTCHR$(147)"NEW/OLD INDEX (N/O)"
1080 GETA$:IFA$<>"N"ANDA$<>"O"THEN1080
1090 IFA$="N"THEN1290:REM SKIP LOAD
1100 REM*******LOAD OLD INDEX*******
1110 PRINTCHR$(147)CHR$(18)"LOAD MODE"
1120 OPEN15,8,15,"I0"
1130 GOSUB2350:IFEN<>0THEN1260
1140 OPEN1,8,2,"0:INDEX,SEQ,R"
1150 GOSUB2350:IFEN<>0THEN1250
1160 INPUT#1,N:REM MAX SIZE OF INDEX
1170 GOSUB2350:IFEN<>0THEN1250
1180 DIM IN$(N),PG$(N)
1190 INPUT#1,NE:REM NUMBER OF ENTRIES
1200 GOSUB2350:IFEN<>0THEN1250
1210 FORI=1TONE
1220 INPUT#1,IN$(I),PG$(I)
1230 GOSUB2350:IFEN<>0THENI=NE:GOTO1250
1240 NEXT
1250 CLOSE1
1260 CLOSE15:PRINTCHR$(147)
```

```
1270 IFEN<>0THENRUN:REM RESTART PROG
1280 GOTO1320:REM SKIP SETUP
1290 REM*********SETUP NEW INDEX******
1300 INPUT"MAX INDEX SIZE";N
1310 DIM IN$(N),PG$(N)
1320 REM***  ASSEMBLE INDEX  ****
1330 IFNE=NTHEN1560:REM INDEX FULL
1340 REM*INPUT ENTRY TO BE INSERTED*
1350 INPUT"TEXT OF NEW ENTRY";V$
1360 IFV$=""THEN1560:REM MENU
1370 GOSUB1890:REM SEARCH FOR POSITION
1380 IFNI=1THENA=M:GOSUB1980:GOTO1490:REM DON'T IN
SERT TEXT BUT DO PAGE NBR
1390 IFA=NE+1THENIN$(NE+1)=V$:GOTO1470
1400 REM*** MOVE ELEMENTS RIGHT****
1410 FORJ=NE+1TOA+1STEP-1
1420 IN$(J)=IN$(J-1):PG$(J)=PG$(J-1)
1430 NEXT
1440 REM***PERFORM INSERTIONS****
1450 IN$(A)=V$:REM INSERT NEW TEXT
1460 PG$(A)="":REM NEW NULL STRING
1470 GOSUB1980:REM INSERT PAGE NBR
1480 NE=NE+1:IFNE=NTHENPRINT"INDEX FULL":GOTO1560
1490 V$="":REM RESET INPUT STRING
1500 PRINTCHR$(147)
1510 XX=FRE(0)-(FRE(0)<0)*65536
1520 PRINTDW$CHR$(18)"BYTES FREE "XX
1530 PRINTCHR$(18)"NUMBER OF ENTRIES "NE
1540 PRINTCHR$(18)"MAX SIZE THIS INDEX "NCHR$(19)
1550 GOTO1320:REM NEXT ENTRY
1560 REM*********MENU OPTIONS********
1570 PRINTCHR$(147)
1580 IFNE=NTHENPRINT"INDEX FULL"
1590 PRINT"SAVE   (S)"
1600 PRINT"PRINT (P)"
1610 PRINT"CONT   (C/R)"
1620 PRINT"DELETE ENTRY (D)"
1630 PRINT"QUIT   (Q)"
1640 GETC$:IFC$<>"S"ANDC$<>"P"ANDC$<>"Q"ANDC$<>CHR
$(13)ANDC$<>"D"THEN1640
1650 IFC$="S"THENGOSUB2020:REM SAVE
1660 IFC$="P"THENGOSUB2200:REM PRINT
1670 IFC$=CHR$(13)ANDNE<NTHENPRINTCHR$(147):GOTO13
20
```

Listing continued next page

```
1680 IFC$="D"THENGOSUB1720:REM DELETE
1690 IFC$="Q"THENEND
1700 GOTO1560:REM NEXT OPERATION
1710 REM*********GOSUBS**************
1720 REM********DELETE ENTRY*********
1730 REM*INPUT ENTRY TO BE DELETED*
1740 PRINTCHR$(147)CHR$(18)"DELETE MODE":PRINT
1750 INPUT"TEXT OF ENTRY TO KILL";V$
1760 IFV$=""THEN1880:REM EXIT
1770 GOSUB1890:REM SEARCH FOR POSITION
1780 IFNI=0THENPRINT"NOT FOUND":GOTO1860:REM EXIT
1790 IFM=NETHEN1840:REM EXIT
1800 REM*** MOVE ELEMENTS LEFT****
1810 FORJ=M+1TONE
1820 IN$(J-1)=IN$(J):PG$(J-1)=PG$(J)
1830 NEXT
1840 NE=NE-1:REM DECREMENT NBR ENTRS
1850 PRINT"ENTRY DELETED"
1860 FORL=0TO1000:NEXT:REM DELAY
1870 V$="":REM RESET INPUT STRING
1880 RETURN
1890 REM***PERFORM BINARY SEARCH***
1900 A=1:B=NE
1910 M=INT((A+B)/2)
1920 IFV$=IN$(M)THENPRINT"PRESENT AT"M:NI=1:GOTO19
70
1930 IFV$<IN$(M)THENB=M-1
1940 IFV$>IN$(M)THENA=M+1
1950 IFA=MORB=MTHEN:NI=0:GOTO1970:REM INSERT AT M
1960 GOTO1910:REM CONTINUE SEARCH
1970 RETURN
1980 REM***ADD NEW PAGE NUMBER***
1990 PN$="":INPUT"PAGE NUMBER";PN$
2000 PG$(A)=PG$(A)+PN$+" "
2010 RETURN
2020 REM*********SAVE    INDEX********
2030 PRINTCHR$(147)CHR$(18)"SAVE MODE"
2040 OPEN15,8,15,"I0"
2050 GOSUB2350:IFEN<>0THEN2180
2060 PRINT#15,"S0:INDEX"
2070 OPEN1,8,2,"0:INDEX,SEQ,W"
2080 GOSUB2350:IFEN<>0THEN2170
2090 PRINT#1,N;R$;:REM MAX INDEX SIZE
2100 GOSUB2350:IFEN<>0THEN2170
```

```
2110 PRINT#1,NE;R$;:REM NUMBER OF ENTRS
2120 GOSUB2350:IFEN<>0THEN2170
2130 FORI=1TONE
2140 PRINT#1,IN$(I);R$;PG$(I);R$;
2150 GOSUB2350:IFEN<>0THENI=NE:GOTO2160
2160 NEXT
2170 PRINT#1:CLOSE1
2180 CLOSE15
2190 RETURN
2200 REM****PRINT INDEX****
2210 PRINTCHR$(147)CHR$(18)"PRINT MODE":PRINT
2220 PRINT"TO SCREEN/PRINTER (S/P)?"
2230 GETC$:IFC$<>"S"ANDC$<>"P"THEN2230
2240 IFC$="S"THENDV=3
2250 IFC$="P"THENDV=4
2260 OPEN4,DV:PRINT#4,CHR$(13)
2270 PRINT#4,"INDEX"CHR$(13)
2280 FORI=1TONE
2290 PRINT#4,IN$(I),PG$(I)
2300 NEXT
2310 PRINT#4:CLOSE4
2320 PRINTCHR$(18)"SPACE TO CONT"
2330 GETC$:IFC$<>CHR$(32)THEN2330
2340 RETURN
2350 REM********DISK ERROR CHECK******
2360 INPUT#15,EN,EM$,ET,ES
2370 IFEN=0THENRETURN
2380 PRINTCHR$(18)"DISK ERROR"
2390 PRINT"ERROR NUMBER"EN
2400 PRINTEM$
2410 PRINT"TRACK"ET:PRINT"SECTOR"ES
2420 PRINTCHR$(18)"SPACE TO CONT"
2430 GETC$:IFC$<>CHR$(32)THEN2430
2440 RETURN
```

Of course sorting the data as it is entered is not helpful if the program may be required to sort the data into some other order. Thus the problem of finding a fast, suitable sort cannot always be avoided. The sort popular in many computing books is the Bubble sort. Just why this should be so we are not sure, since the Bubble sort gives the worst performance in just about all cases! Instead we give as a good all-round sort program Quicksort. Normally Quicksort will require of the order N*LOG(N) comparisons and moves. However, in the unlikely event of the worst case situation being encountered, this could degenerate to order N*N.

```
1000 REM*** QUICKSORT   ***
1010 REM* A SORT DEVISED BY*
1020 REM*   C.A.R. HOARE   *
1030 REM***********************
1040 REM* SORT ANY NUMERIC *
1050 REM*     ARRAY        *
1060 REM***********************
1070 INPUT"NO OF NUMBERS(>1)";N
1080 DIMAR(N),ST(2*LOG(N)+1,1)
1090 FORI=1TON:AR(I)=I*RND(0):NEXT
1100 T=TI:REM TAKE TIME
1110 SP=1:REM STACK POINTER
1120 ST(1,0)=1:REM INITIALISE LEFT
1130 ST(1,1)=N:REM INITIALISE RIGHT
1140 REM** MAIN LOOP **
1150 REM** PULL STACK**
1160 LEFT=ST(SP,0):RIGHT=ST(SP,1):SP=SP-1
1170 J=LEFT:K=RIGHT:COMP=AR((J+K)/2)
1180 IFAR(J)<COMPTHENJ=J+1:GOTO1180
1190 IFAR(K)>COMPTHENK=K-1:GOTO1190
1200 IFJ<=KTHENGOSUB1300:GOTO1180
1210 REM**PUSH STACK**
1220 IFJ<RIGHTTHENSP=SP+1:ST(SP,0)=J:ST(SP,1)=RIGH
T
1230 RIGHT=K
1240 IFLEFT<RIGHTTHEN1170
1250 IFSP>0THEN1150
1260 REM **END OF SORT**
1270 PRINT"SORTED IN"(TI-T)/60"SECS":STOP
1280 FORI=1TON:PRINTAR(I):NEXT
1290 END
1300 REM***SWAP***
1310 TEMP=AR(J):AR(J)=AR(K):AR(K)=TEMP
1320 J=J+1:K=K-1
1330 RETURN
```

Again we have used GOTO (and a pseudo-stack) to simulate recursion. Quicksort is based on the observation that exchanges should preferably be made over large distances in order to be most effective. The algorithm scans from the left of the current interval until an element with AR(J) >COMP is found, and then scans from the right until an element A(K)<COMP is found. Next the two elements are exchanged and the process of 'scan and swap' is continued until the two scans meet somewhere in the middle. At this point the array is now partitioned into a left part with elements less than COMP and a right part with elements greater than COMP. After partitioning the

array the same process is applied to both partitions and then to partitions of partitions until the entire array is sorted. After each step, two partitioning tasks arise. Only one of them can be attacked directly by the next iteration; the other is pushed onto the pseudo-stack to be dealt with later. Each partition request is represented as a left and right index, specifying the bounds of the partition to be further partitioned. In our program left intervals are partitioned immediately and right intervals are pushed onto the pseudo-stack. When all moves left are complete the top right interval is pulled off the stack and partitioned. This process is continued until no further stack requests are present. Theory tells us the maximum size of the stack required, and the stack array is dimensional accordingly.

ANATOMY OF A BASIC PROGRAM: MAIN POINTERS

The material in this and the next section is not often relevant to the writing of BASIC programs. However, we want to start you thinking about how the operating system actually gets things done, and this information may help you to write better BASIC, or BASIC which RUNs faster. On a first read through this chapter you may prefer to skip these two sections and come back to them later as the need arises. When interfacing machine code subroutines with BASIC a detailed knowledge of how a BASIC program keeps track of its variables can be very useful.

When a program line is first typed in it is transferred by the operating system from the keyboard to the screen memory. After the 'RETURN' key is depressed the operating system compresses the text of the program line, coding it as a sequence of BASIC keyword codes. A table of these codes can be found in the Appendices. The compressed text is then stored in that area of memory allotted as the user BASIC program space. The start of the BASIC program area is pointed to by the contents of decimal addresses 43 and 44, i.e.

$$\text{Start address of BASIC program} = \text{PEEK}(43) + 256*\text{PEEK}(44)$$

This is known as the 'bottom of memory' or TXTTAB, a slightly confusing term since the true bottom of memory is of course address zero. Normally the contents of addresses 43 and 44 are 1 and 8 respectively, which means that the bottom of memory is decimal address 2049 and the BASIC program is built up in memory from this address.

The 'top of memory', or MEMSIZ, is the end of the BASIC program area of memory. This is pointed to by the contents of decimal addresses 55 and 56, i.e.

$$\text{End address of BASIC program area} = \text{PEEK}(55) + 256*\text{PEEK}(56)$$

Normally the contents of addresses 55 and 56 are 0 and 160 respectively so that the user BASIC part of memory ends at decimal address 40960. This should not be confused with the end of the BASIC program, which in most cases will be a lot lower in memory.

When a program is RUNning the whole of the user BASIC program area above the program is potentially usable by the operating system, as memory space in which to store the values of the variables (integer, floating point, arrays and strings) needed during program execution. Whether the whole area is in fact used depends on how many variables the program actually needs.

This allocation of storage is a dynamic process. When the program is RUN as each variable is encountered the operating system reserves memory in which to store its name and current value. The organization of the different variables in memory is as follows.

Memory map for variables/arrays/dynamic strings.

Start of BASIC (bottom of memory)	PEEK(43)+256*PEEK(44)	Static
. . . . BASIC program	. . . .	Static
Start of variables/End of program + 1	PEEK(45)+256*PEEK(46)	Static
Start of arrays/End of variables + 1	PEEK(47)+256*PEEK(48)	Dynamic
Lower limit of strings/End of arrays + 1	PEEK(49)+256*PEEK(50)	Dynamic
Current bottom of strings	PEEK(51)+256*PEEK(52)	Dynamic
Top of memory	PEEK(55)+256*PEEK(56)	Static

Fig. 2.4 should serve to clarify the picture.

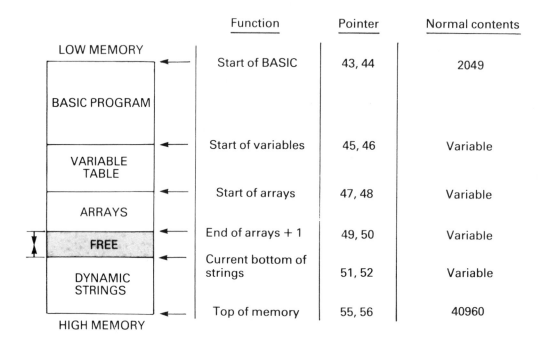

Fig. 2.4 — A BASIC program in memory.

HOW VARIABLES AND STRINGS ARE STORED

Integer variables, floating point variables and pointers for the location of string variables are stored in a variable table which builds up in memory from the end of the BASIC program. Arrays are built above the other variables. When a new variable is encountered during program execution the operating system shifts the entire array storage area up 7 bytes in memory to create space to accommodate the new variable. This is one reason why in a long program it is advisable to initialize the values of all numeric and string variables before DIMensioning any arrays.

The storage of strings is necessarily more complicated than that of other variables. Integer or floating point variables both require a fixed number of bytes (namely 7), but a string may need up to 255 bytes. The operating system copes with this complication by only storing the length of the string and a pointer to the address of the start of the string, rather than its actual value, in the table which begins after the BASIC program. If a string is defined in the program, e.g. A$="ABC-DEF", then this pointer will be to the first byte of the string within the BASIC program area. Such a string is called a 'static' string. If and when the program alters the value of a string variable it becomes a 'dynamic' string. The values of dynamic strings are built down from the top of memory and the pointer in the variable table altered accordingly. In this way each entry in the variable table is held to a constant 7 bytes.

Format of variables in the variable table.

Integer variables

	Byte	Contents	
	0	First character of variable name	(ASCII code plus 128)
	1	Second character of variable name	(ASCII code plus 128)
	2	High order byte of signed integer	(see Chapter 1)
	3	Low order byte of integer	(see Chapter 1)
	4	0—Not used	
	5	0—Not used	
	6	0—Not used	

Floating point variables

	Byte	Contents	
	0	First character of variable name	(ASCII code)
	1	Second character of variable name	(ASCII code)
P0	2	Binary exponent plus 128	
D1	3	Sign bit and Mantissa 1	
D2	4	Mantissa 2	
D3	5	Mantissa 3	
D4	6	Mantissa 4	

String variables

Byte	Contents	
0	First character of variable name	(ASCII code)
1	Second character of variable name	(ASCII code plus 128)
2	Number of characters	
3	Lo-byte of address where string is stored	
4	Hi-byte of address where string is stored	
5	0—Not used	
6	0—Not used	

Format of variables in the variable table (cont.)

Function definition (DEFFN)

Byte	Contents	
0	First character of function name	(ASCII code plus 128)
1	Second character of function name	(ASCII code)
2	Lo-byte, pointer to address following DEFFN '='	
3	Hi-byte, pointer to address following DEFFN '='	
4	Lo-byte, pointer to variable exponent byte	
5	Hi-byte, pointer to variable exponent byte	
6	0–Not used	

Note that the operating system determines the data-type of a variable by the pattern of 128s added to the ASCII codes of the variable name.

The following programs illustrate how variables can be located in memory and translated back into their usual format. The key to each of these programs is the fact that immediately after a variable has been used in BASIC the contents of decimal addresses 71 ($47) and 72 ($48) point to the address in memory of the start of the variable. We have to be quick to recover this information since location 71 ($47) is also used by the operating system when evaluating some numerical expressions. For this reason the programs for finding an integer and string variable both immediately POKE the contents of 71 and 72 into harmless locations in the cassette buffer before proceeding. This technique could also be used for a floating point variable. However, for a floating point variable there is a neater method based on the fact that when DEFFN is used to define a function of X then X is used (but its original value left unchanged) whenever FN is called, regardless of whether X appears on the right-hand side of the function definition.

```
1000 REM**FIND AN INTEGER IN MEMORY**
1010 X%=3456
1020 REM**MAKE X% CURRENT VARIABLE**
1030 X%=X%
1040 REM**SAVE POINTER TO VAR TABLE**
1050 POKE828,PEEK(71):POKE829,PEEK(72)
1060 REM**ADDRESS IN VAR TABLE**
1070 ADR=PEEK(828)+256*PEEK(829)
1080 REM**LOOK AT ENTRY IN VAR TABLE**
1090 LO=PEEK(ADR+1):HI=PEEK(ADR)
1100 REM**COMPUTE RESULT**
1110 SIGNBIT=(HIAND128)/128
1120 VAR=LO+256*(HIAND127)-32768*SIGNBIT
1130 PRINT VAR
```

```
1000 REM**FIND A FPVAR IN MEMORY**
1010 DEF FNADR(X)=PEEK(71)+256*PEEK(72)
1020 ADD=FNADR(0) :REM ALWAYS RETURNS ADDRESS OF X
1030 X=-3.14159
1040 REM**CONVERT FROM BASE 2 TO DECIMAL
1050 POWERTWO=2↑(PEEK(ADD)-129)
1060 SIGN=(-1)↑((PEEK(AD+1)AND128)/128)
1070 REM*FRACTION PART IS 31 BITS WIDE*
1080 D1=PEEK(ADD+1)AND127 :REM 7 BITS
1090 D2=PEEK(ADD+2) :REM 8 BITS
1100 D3=PEEK(ADD+3) :D4=PEEK(ADD+4)
1110 REM**GULP!**
1120 FRACT=2↑(-7)*D1+2↑(-15)*D2+2↑(-23)*D3+2↑(-31)
*D4
1130 MANT=1+FRACT
1140 VAR=SIGN*POWERTWO*MANT
1150 PRINTVAR
```

```
1000 REM**FIND A STRING IN MEMORY**
1010 X$="ABCDEF"
1020 REM**MAKE X$ CURRENT VARIABLE**
1030 X$=X$+""
1040 REM**SAVE POINTER TO VAR TABLE**
1050 POKE828,PEEK(71) :POKE829,PEEK(72)
1060 REM**ADDRESS IN VAR TABLE**
1070 ADR=PEEK(828)+256*PEEK(829)
1080 REM**LOOK AT ENTRY IN VAR TABLE**
1090 LS=PEEK(ADR) :REM LENGHT OF STRING
1100 SA=PEEK(ADR+1)+256*PEEK(ADR+2)
1110 REM SA IS START ADDR OF STRING
1120 REM**NOW READ STRING**
1130 FORI=SATOSA+LS
1140 VAR$=VAR$+CHR$(PEEK(I))
1150 NEXT
1160 PRINTVAR$
```

HOW ARRAYS ARE STORED

When a DIM statement is executed memory is reserved for the array. This consists of an array header plus the number of bytes needed for element storage.

Format of array header

Byte	Contents	
0	First character in array name	(ASCII code plus data-type code if any)
1	Second character in array name	(ASCII code plus data-type code if any)
2	Lo-byte, number of bytes in array: points to next array	
3	Hi-byte, number of bytes in array: points to next array	
4	Number of dimensions of array	
5	Lo-byte, number of elements (inc. 0th) for last subscript specified	
6	Hi-byte, number of elements (inc. 0th) for last subscript specified	
7	Lo-byte, number of elements (inc. 0th) for penultimate subscript	
8	Hi-byte, number of elements (inc. 0th) for penultimate subscript	
. . .	. . .	

Continuing to byte $2*N+4$, where N is the number of subscripts

. . .   . . .

$2*N+5$ Start of array data

We next consider how array data is stored for the three different data types.

Format of variables as stored in an array

Integer variables

Byte	Contents
0	High order byte of signed integer (see Chapter 1)
1	Low order byte of signed integer (see Chapter 1)

Floating point variables

Byte	Contents
0	Binary exponent plus 128
1	Sign bit and Mantissa 1
2	Mantissa 2
3	Mantissa 3
4	Mantissa 4

String variables

Byte	Contents
0	Number of characters
1	Lo-byte of address where string is stored
2	Hi-byte of address where string is stored

One last piece of information is required if we should need to compute where in memory the value of a particular array element is stored. We have to know the order in which the operating system stores array elements. The variables (or Pointers) of an array with typical element A(I,J,K) are enumerated first by I, then by J and finally by K. Thus the array defined by DIM A(1,2) has the elements stored in the order

A(0,0),A(1,0),A(0,1),A(1,1),A(0,2),A(1,2).

To see how this actually works in practice use the example given following the program HYPER-PEEK in Chapter 1.

The same techniques of recovery used for integer and string variables can be used to read the contents of arrays directly from memory, and we leave this as an exercise for the reader. However, beware of creating new variables in the process of reading the array from memory, since if you do this the whole array will move up!

3

Memory management

INTRODUCTION

Up to this point we have mainly concentrated on developing BASIC programming without bothering too much about what was actually happening within the CBM 64. A more detailed knowledge of how the CBM 64 stores and executes a BASIC program will enable us to do many new things, e.g. to store more than one BASIC program in memory simultaneously. Indeed the function of the main example program in this chapter 'DATASTATE' is to create another BASIC program, consisting of DATA statements, elsewhere in memory. The program so created can then be edited and SAVEd in the usual way.

Mainly we propose to discuss how the combination of BASIC and the 6510 microprocessor 'sees' the standard memory configuration, but the 6510 is a very versatile microprocessor with the ability to 'bank' in and out different blocks of memory. Even from BASIC there are times when we may need to do this. For example when copying the standard characters from ROM down into RAM, where we can then modify them to produce our own personalized character set. These memory-swapping capabilities of the 6510 are also of great significance to the designer of machine code programs. It is possible for the machine code programmer to dispense with the two principal components of the operating system, the BASIC Interpreter and the Kernal, and run a bare machine with 60K of RAM and 4K of I/O addresses. This is an extreme example, since by dispensing with the Kernal the programmer would have to write all his own I/O driving routines, without which the machine would be totally unable to communicate. Still, it serves to illustrate the enormous range of applications which are technically possible. For this reason we shall discuss the memory configurations which are available, if one is prepared to swap out the Interpreter or the Kernal, towards the end of the chapter.

The first thing to understand about the CBM 64 is that it has 64K of RAM and 20K of ROM, a total of 84K. However, under no circumstances can the 6510 microprocessor address all this memory at once. At any one time the 6510 can only see 64K of memory. An example of a block of memory which under normal circumstances the 6510 cannot see is the character matrix ROM. This 4K block of memory contains all the information necessary to display standard upper-case, lower-case or graphics characters in normal or reversed field. However, the 6510 does not normally need to see the character matrix since the job of displaying characters on the screen is assigned to the VIC-II chip. The 6566/9 video chip scans the screen memory to determine the required characters and then acquires the necessary information from the character matrix. Thus the VIC-II chip and the 6510 microprocessor see different memory maps, each according to its need. The VIC-II chip is discussed extensively in Chapters 5 and 6.

We begin by examining the standard configuration of the CBM 64.

BASIC AND THE STANDARD MEMORY MAP

We should first know in broad terms how the memory of the CBM 64 is divided into blocks each allotted to a specific purpose, that is where in memory different kinds of data are stored.

We recall that a 'bit' is a binary 1 or 0. The 6510 has a 16-bit address bus, essentially 16 parallel wires which can be set either 'high' (5 volts) or 'low' (0 volts). This enables the 6510 to access any one of $2\uparrow16$ memory locations, numbered from 0 to $(2\uparrow16)-1$, i.e. 65535 decimal or $FFFF. The content of each location consist of an 8-bit binary number, a *byte*, whose value will lie in the range 0 to $(2\uparrow8)-1$, i.e. 255 decimal or $FF.

A memory location may be: RAM, random access memory, the contents of which can be changed for example by use of POKE; or ROM, read only memory, the contents of which cannot be changed. Examples of locations on the CBM 64 which are ROM are 40960–49151 ($A000–$BFFF), which contains the BASIC Interpreter, and 57344–65535 ($E000–$FFFF) which contains the Kernal. 'Beneath' these two 8K blocks is 16K of RAM which the 6510 does not normally see, although a POKE to these addresses will 'drop through' to the underlying RAM and can be read back by swapping out the ROM (of course, if you swap out the BASIC ROM you won't be able to read the underlying RAM using PEEK!). The shaded portion of Fig. 3.1 shows what the 6510 normally sees.

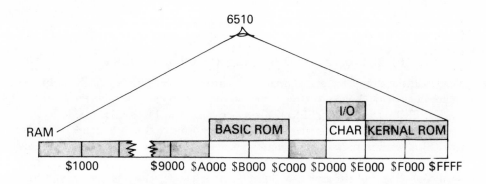

Fig. 3.1 – What the 6510 normally sees.

Note that in the range 53284–57343 ($D000–$DFFF) the memory is not stacked two deep, as with the Interpreter and Kernal, but is in fact three deep! Normally the 6510 sees the top level which is where the 6526 I/O chips live (after all a microprocessor is pretty useless without I/O) but it is possible to 'bank out' the 4K of I/O and read the character ROM, which in turn can be banked out to reveal the underlying RAM. Now we can see how a chip with a 16-bit address bus can cope with 84K of memory.

Together the BASIC Interpreter and the Kernal comprise the normal operating system of the CBM 64. Although they live in ROM these machine code programs, for that is what they are, require the use of memory locations whose contents can be varied, that is RAM rather than ROM, just as any BASIC program needs memory for its variables. To this end the block of RAM 0–1023 ($0000–$03FF) is reserved for use by the operating system. A detailed knowledge of what the contents of these locations mean and the effect of changing them can be of considerable use to the programmer. A list containing a brief explanation of the contents of each of these locations is given in the Appendices.

IMPORTANT NOTE. Because any address consists of 16 bits it requires the contents of two memory locations in order to specify a given address. On the CBM 64 these are always stored in Lo-byte, Hi-byte order.

Example:
Suppose the address is 8193 then

$$\text{Hi-byte} \;\; = \text{INT}(8193/256) = 32 \qquad (\text{page})$$
$$\text{Lo-byte} \;\; = 8193 - 256*(\text{Hi-byte}) = 1 \qquad (\text{position})$$

We may think of the Lo-byte as representing the position of the address in question on its page; and the Hi-byte as the 'page number'. Both Lo and Hi-bytes can take decimal values in the range 0–255 ($00 to $FF).

To see how this works in practice and how useful the memory map of the first 1K block can be, we take a specific example in the following section.

RAISING THE BOTTOM AND LOWERING THE TOP OF MEMORY

We saw, at the end of Chapter 2, that the 'start of user BASIC' is pointed to by the contents of decimal addresses 43 and 44. If you turn on the CBM 64 and examine the contents of 43 and 44 using PEEK you will find PEEK(43) = 1, Lo-byte, and PEEK(44) = 8, Hi-byte. This specifies position 1 on page 8 as the start address of user BASIC; that is 8*256+1=2049. In fact, user BASIC really starts at 2048 but, since the operating system requires the first byte always to be 0, it is said to start at 2049.

Because 43 and 44 are RAM locations it is possible for the programmer to change their contents and thereby alter the start address of user BASIC, the so called 'bottom of memory'. Lowering the bottom of memory may cause problems, since the screen memory normally lives from 1024 to 2047; but if we were to raise the bottom of memory, then the area between 2048 and the new bottom of memory would not be used by the operating system (it would be ours!).

To raise the bottom of memory by two pages to 2560 we should enter as one line in command

POKE2560,0:POKE44,10:NEW

The first POKE is required to guarantee that the operating system will find a 0 at the new start location, the second resets the pointer (effectively moving the start of user BASIC) and NEW is used as a quick way to reset all the other pointers in 45 to 56 (discussed at the end of the last chapter).

If we use FRE(0) to find how many bytes are free, we should find this number reflects the fact that 512 bytes have been stolen from BASIC. Any program which was previously contained, as compressed text, in pages 8 and 9 is now protected, except from a direct POKE to an address in this area, and cannot be LISTed or RUN, since as far as the operating system is concerned this block of memory no longer exists. We can now enter new programs, which may even have the same line numbers as the protected program, and RUN them in the normal way. Having done this we can delete these other programs by entering NEW and recover our original program by POKE44, 8:CLR to lower the bottom of memory, and LIST.

If it is desired to raise or lower the bottom of memory from within a program the use of NEW as a quick way to reset the variable pointers is obviously unacceptable, since one or other program will be lost (we are assuming that there are now two programs in memory!). In this case all the pointers have to be reset with their own separate POKEs.

In order for a BASIC program to RUN effectively the base of the variable table must be above the end of the BASIC program in memory. The action of CLR includes resetting all the pointers in 45–50 to point to the byte following the end of the program currently in memory. RUN contains CLR as a subroutine, so at RUN time the system ensures that the variable table is in what it thinks is the right place. There is one interesting exception to this. A LOAD from within a program causes a second program to be loaded and RUN, but the variable table pointers are not reset. This is deliberate, since if the start of the variable table lies above the second program it can use the variable values computed by the first program, i.e. share variables. If the second program is shorter than the first this causes no problems, but if it is longer then variables cannot be shared and the second program should immediately reset the pointers with appropriate POKEs.

To lower the top of memory by one page we simply enter the command

POKE56,159:POKE51,0:POKE52,159

We recall that 51 and 52 are the pointers to the bottom of active space for dynamic string storage (which builds down). By changing the top of memory we have changed the base address of the start of dynamic strings, BASIC will therefore lose sight of them. Thus we reset the pointers in 51 and 52 and are ready for new dynamic strings. Other variables are still available to BASIC, however, and in some situations this fact can be exploited. If we wanted to reset all variables then it would suffice to

POKE56,159:CLR

Again use of FRE(0) should verify that BASIC has lost 256 bytes.

Table 3.1 — Large-scale memory map for normal configuration

| 6510 view | Address | | VIC-II view |
	Decimal	Hex	
	0	0000	←————Base of normal 16K window
O/S RAM			
	1023	03FF	
Screen RAM (Video matrix)	1024	0400	Screen RAM (Video matrix)
	2039	07F7	
Sprite pointers	2040	07F8	Sprite pointer
	2047	07FF	
User BASIC	2048	0800	
	4096	1000	Start of Character ROM image
program area	8191	1FFF	End of Character ROM image
	16383	3FFF	←————End of normal 16K window
	40959	9FFF	
BASIC Interpreter ROM	40960	A000	
	49151	BFFF	
4K of free RAM	49152	C000	
	53247	CFFF	
VIC-II chip (6566/9)	53248	D000	←————(Actual start of Character matrix ROM; in fact not seen here by either chip).
	53295	D02E	
VIC Images	53296	D02F	
	54271	D3FF	

Table 3.1 — Large-scale memory map for normal configuration

6510 view	Address		VIC-II view
	Decimal	Hex	
SID chip (6581)	54272	D400	
	54300	D41C	
SID Images	54301	D41D	
	55295	D7FF	
Color RAM	55296	D800	Color RAM
	56295	DBE7	
Not used	56296	DBE8	
	56319	DBFF	
CIA #1 (6526)	56320	DC00	
	56335	DC0F	
CIA #1 Images	56336	DC10	
	56575	DCFF	
CIA #2 (6526)	56576	DD00	
	56591	DD0F	
CIA #2 Images	56592	DD10	
	56831	DDFF	
Reserved for future I/O	56832	DE00	
	57343	DFFF	←————(Actual end Char ROM)
Kernal ROM	57344	E000	
	65535	FFFF	

NORMAL CONFIGURATION LARGE-SCALE MEMORY MAP

The exact configuration adopted by the CBM 64 varies according to the presence or absence of additional ROM. On power-up the 6510 microprocessor begins execution of a program whose start address is stored in 65532 and 65535, in fact PEEK(65532)+256*PEEK(65533)=64738 which is the address in question. You can check this by entering SYS64738, which will initialize the CBM 64 as if from a cold start. Almost the first function of this program is to check if ROM is present in the 8K-expansion block beginning at 32768 ($8000), it does this by searching for a specific string of five bytes from 32770 to 32774 ($8002 to $8006). The first three bytes must be the CBM ASCII code for 'CBM' with bit 7 set in each letter. The remaining two bytes must be the digits '80' in CBM ASCII. If this test is successful then program control jumps to whatever address is stored in 32768 ($8000) and 32769 ($8001). This is the technique used by commercial ROM-based games, for example, to provide an auto-start on power-up. If the test is unsuccessful the normal initialization proceeds.

The memory map in Table 3.1 shows the normal configuration for the 6510 and separately for the VIC-II chip. We shall see later how to change each microprocessor's view of memory, but for the time being let's stay with the normal map.

One of the most remarkable things about this memory map is that the VIC-II chip, which shares the same data and address lines with the 6510, 'sees' a Character matrix image at 4069–8191 ($1000–$1FFF) whereas in fact the Character matrix is located at 53248–55295 ($D000–$D7FF). Just how this comes about we shall explore later, but it is also important to grasp that, using control registers on the 6510, both the 6510 view and the VIC-II view can be changed.

ANATOMY OF A BASIC PROGRAM: LINK ADDRESSES

In this section we complete the picture of exactly how a BASIC program is stored as compressed text in memory.

If we enter a simple program such as

```
1000  PRINT"AJJ"
1010  END
```

in the normal way, this will be stored as a sequence of CBM 64 BASIC keyword codes building up from the bottom of memory, normally 2048. A table of these codes is given in the Appendices.

We can examine this sequence directly by entering the one line command

```
FOR I=0TO19:PRINTPEEK(2048+I);:NEXT
```

(which is not itself a program line). When the 'RETURN' key is pressed the CBM 64 will respond with

```
 0   12   8   232   3   153   34   65   74   74
34    0  18     8  242     3   128    0    0    0
```

These numbers are Interpreted as follows:

Address	Contents	Interpretation
2048	0	BASIC begins with a 0
2049	12	Link address, Lo-byte ⎫ Points to start address of
2050	8	Link address, Hi-byte ⎭ next program line (2060)
2051	232	Program line number, Lo-byte
2052	3	Program line number, Hi-byte
2053	153	PRINT
2054	34	"
2055	65	A
2056	74	J
2057	74	J
2058	34	"
2059	0	End of line
2060	18	Link address, Lo-byte ⎫ Points to start address of
2061	8	Link address, Hi-byte ⎭ next program line (2066)
2062	242	Program line number, Lo-byte
2063	3	Program line number, Hi-byte
2064	128	END
2065	0	End of line
2066	0	Return to
2067	0	direct mode

Whilst a program is RUNning the line number being executed is stored in addresses 57 ($39) and 58 ($3A). If the contents of these two locations is 0 then a direct mode of operation is indicated. Thus the link address attached to the last line of the program, stored in 2060 and 2061, points not to another link address, as in a normal program line, but to two 0 bytes in 2066 and 2067. These two 0 bytes indicate a return to direct mode. Of course execution of END at any point in a program will also cause a return to direct mode.

Example:
A program which rewrites itself the first time it is RUN.

```
1000 PRINT"AJJ"
1010 POKE2055,67:POKE2056,66:POKE2057,77
1020 END
```

If you RUN this program and then LIST it, you should obtain

```
1000 PRINT"CBM"
1010 POKE2055,67:POKE2056,66:POKE2057,77
1020 END
```

Of course 67, 66 and 77 are the keyword codes for C, B and M respectively (for characters these are just the CBM ASC codes).

Within a program line any 0 is stored as 48, the ASC code for "0", the actual number 0 is reserved as an end of line or program marker.

Example:
A program which counts the number of times it has been RUN.

```
1000  REM0
1010  N=PEEK(2054)
1020  PRINTN-47:N=N+1
1030  IFN=256THENN=48
1040  POKE2054,N
```

The address for the 0 after the REM is 2054, the 0 being stored as 48. Line 1030 simply ensures that when N reaches 256 its value is wrapped back to 0 so that an ILLEGAL QUANTITY error does not occur in 1010. Thus the program will count the number of times it has been RUN up to 208, after which it will start counting again from one. It is a simple exercise to extend the count.

Although the zero end bytes mark the end of a program as far as LIST is concerned they do not control the end-of-file markers used by SAVE or LOAD.

Example:
A program which when LOADed from tape or disk will not LIST or RUN until it has been 'unlocked'.

We begin by entering

```
1000  REM ANY COMMENT
1010  FORI=0TO10
1020  PRINT"CBM 64"
1030  NEXT
1040  END
```

Before SAVEing the program we determine the correct link address in 2049 and 2050

PRINTPEEK(2049),PEEK(2050)

which gives

19   8

Next

POKE2049,0:POKE2050,0

The program will now neither LIST nor RUN. Finally SAVE the program to disk or tape.

Upon LOADing the program will again neither LIST nor RUN, because the zero end bytes have been preserved, but can be 'unlocked' by the command

POKE2049,19:POKE2050,8

When a program is SAVEd an image of the whole block of RAM is written out to disk or tape, this includes the link addresses. When a program is reloaded on a VIC-20 or CBM 64 (but not on earlier Commodore PETs) the link addresses are rebuilt. This was obviously necessary on the VIC-20 (whose bottom of memory alters with additional plug-in RAM) to enable a program written and SAVEd with one bottom of memory to be LOADed and RUN with a different bottom of memory. This is an excellent feature, since it enables BASIC programs written on other Commodore machines to be transferred to the CBM 64. There is, however, a small price to be paid for this sleight-of-hand. The action of VERIFY is to perform a byte by byte comparison between a program in RAM and the corresponding PRG file on disk or tape. If any corresponding bytes differ a VERIFY error is generated. Hence a program SAVEd from one bottom of memory will, if LOADed back with a different bottom of memory, always produce an error when VERIFYed: because the new link addresses differ from the old ones.

Knowing the precise format of a BASIC program in memory allows us to do many useful things. Many CBM 64 users will be familiar with utility programs which include a renumbering facility for BASIC programs. Apart from their speed, which results from the fact that they are machine language programs, there is nothing mysterious about the manner in which such facilities work. The next example demonstrates the principle from BASIC.

Example:
This program extravagantly called RENUMBER, is supposed to be LOADed above another, original, program. RENUMBER tracks through the original program by following the link addresses to find those bytes which describe program line numbers and then changes them appropriately. Of course a serious renumbering facility would also change all GOTOs and GOSUBs, which RE-NUMBER does not do. Still, it is easy to see how a more elaborate routine could actually scan through each original program line, searching for the keyword codes for GOTO, GOSUB and other variations of these commands. If such a keyword is encountered then the current line number and target line number can be kept so that later the correct target line number can be substituted.

```
1000 REM***********RENUMBER**************************
1010 S=2049:REM START OF BASIC
1020 REM*******************************************
1030 REM*RAISE MEMBOT BYOND PROG TO BE RENUMBERED*
1040 REM*BY:- POKE?*256,0:POKE44,?:NEW            *
1050 REM*THEN LOAD AND RUN THIS PROGRAM.          *
1060 REM*FINALLY LOWER MEMBOT WITH                *
1070 REM*POKE44,8:CLR                             *
1080 REM*WILL NOT RENUMBER GOTOS GOSUBS ETC.      *
1090 REM*******************************************
1100 PRINTCHR$(147)"RENUMBER"
1110 INPUT"FROM,INTERVAL";X$,Y$
1120 REM**NO SAFTETY CHECKS ONLY A DEMO**
1130 X=VAL(X$):Y=VAL(Y$)
1140 K=S+1:REM FIRST LINK ADDRESS LO
1150 NL=PEEK(K)+256*PEEK(K+1):REM NEXT LINK ADDRESS
1160 IFNL=0THENEND:REM TWO ZERO BYTES
1170 HL=INT(X/256):LL=X-256*HL:REM HI/LO NEW LINE NUMBER
1180 REM**INSERT NEW LINE NUMBER**
1190 POKEK+2,LL:POKEK+3,HL
1200 X=X+Y:REM INCREMENT LINE NUMBER
1210 K=NL:REM MOVE POINTER TO NEXT LINK
1220 GOTO1150
```

Our next program puts together all we have learnt about pointers and link addresses. DATA-STATE has been written for use with a disk drive, but can easily be modified for use with tape by eliminating the disk drive handling routines, and making the device number 1. The object of the program is to translate the contents of a block of RAM into DATA statements. The output of DATASTATE is another BASIC program which lives higher in memory. The program created consists of a set of DATA statements together with a checksum. The idea is to take the hard work out of translating Sprite data, a machine code program, or any other kind of data, into a set of DATA statements. When DATASTATE first starts to RUN it checks that it is located at the normal start of BASIC. If it is not correctly located it resets BASIC and reloads itself; remember LOAD from within a program contains an autoRUN. Next DATASTATE asks which block of RAM you wish to turn into DATA statements. The start and end addresses can be entered in decimal or hex. Lastly before beginning to do the job DATASTATE asks where in memory you wish the output progam to live. This is so that you can ensure the program created does not overwrite the block of RAM you are trying to save. The start of the new program must be above page 32 in order to give DATASTATE room to RUN. When DATASTATE has written the new program it will display a message to that effect. When any key is pressed the bottom of BASIC is moved up to the start of the new program and it is LISTed on the screen. It may now be edited and SAVEd in the normal way. Finally the CBM 64 should be normalized with SYS64738.

```
100 REM***********DATASTATE**************
102 REM**THIS PROGRAM SCANS A GIVEN***
104 REM**BLOCK OF MEMORY AND CREATES**
106 REM**A PROGRAM OF DATASTATEMENTS**
108 REM**FROM   THE   SPECIFIED   DATA **
110 REM*******************************
112 IFPEEK(44)=8THEN130
114 PRINTCHR$(147)CHR$(17)
116 PRINTSPC(7)"  BASIC IS SET AT WRONG PAGE"
118 PRINTSPC(3)" THERE WILL BE A SHORT DELAY WHILE
"
120 PRINTSPC(3)" BASIC IS RESET & PROGRAM RE-LOADE
D"
122 PRINTSPC(14)"            HIT ANY KEY ";
124 POKE45,0:POKE46,31:POKE47,0:POKE48,31:POKE49,0
:POKE50,31:REM RESET VAR PTRS
126 GETA$:IFA$=""THEN126
128 POKE2048,0:POKE44,8:LOAD"0:DATASTATE",8:REM RE
SET BASIC AND RELOAD
130 POKE55,255:POKE56,32:CLR:REM LOWER MEMTOP
132 D$="                          ":REM CURSOR HO
ME+26DOWN
134 R$="                                        ":R
EM CURSOR 40RIGHT
136 SP$="                                        " "
```

```
REM 40 SPACES
138 PRINTCHR$(147)CHR$(17)
140 PRINTSPC(13)"▓▓BASIC UNLOADER▓▓"
142 PRINTSPC(6)"▓▓▓PLEASE ENTER ADDRESSES IN HEX▓"
144 PRINTSPC(6)"▓▓PRECEDED BY A $ OR IN DECIMAL.▓"
146 PRINTSPC(10)"▓▓E.G. $C123 OR 49443▓"
148 PRINTLEFT$(D$,11)
150 PRINTSPC(3)"▓MACHINE CODE START ADDRESS
        ";:INPUTA$
152 IFLEN(A$)>5THEN148
154 IFLEFT$(A$,1)="$"THENGOSUB288:SA=Z1:GOTO158
156 SA=VAL(A$)
158 IFSA>65535ORSA<0THEN148
160 PRINTLEFT$(D$,13)
162 PRINTSPC(5)"MACHINE CODE END ADDRESS
    ";:INPUTA$
164 IFLEN(A$)>5THEN160
166 IFLEFT$(A$,1)="$"THENGOSUB288:EA=Z1:GOTO170
168 EA=VAL(A$)
170 IFEA>65535OREA<0THEN160
172 IFEA>SA THEN 184
174 PRINTSPC(4)"▓▓START ADDRESS MUST BE LESS THAN"
:PRINTSPC(14)"END ADDRESS"
176 PRINTLEFT$(D$,24)
178 PRINTSPC(14)"▓▓HIT ANY KEY▓";
180 GETA$:IFA$=""THEN180
182 GOTO138
184 PRINTLEFT$(D$,15)
186 PRINTSPC(1)"OUTPUT TO PAGE ($HEX OR DEC)
        ";:INPUTA$
188 IFLEN(A$)>3THEN184
190 IFLEFT$(A$,1)="$"THENGOSUB288:BA=Z1:GOTO194
192 BA=VAL(A$)
194 IFBA>32ANDBA<136THEN212
196 PRINTSPC(3)"▓PAGE VALUE MUST BE GREATER THAN
32"
198 PRINTSPC(11)"AND LESS THAN 136"
200 PRINTLEFT$(D$,24)
202 PRINTSPC(14)"▓▓HIT ANY KEY▓";
204 GETA$:IFA$=""THEN204
206 PRINTLEFT$(D$,19)SP$
208 PRINTLEFT$(D$,20)SP$
210 PRINTLEFT$(D$,24):PRINTSP$;:GOTO184
212 REM*****************************************
```

Listing continued next page

```
214 REM*                                  *
216 REM*         DO  CONVERSION           *
218 REM*                                  *
220 REM**********************************
222 PRINT"█████████████";:PRINTSPC(12)"██CONVERTING
 CODE"
224 PRINTSPC(12)"█ADDRESS - "
226 GOSUB308:REM* SETUP FOR CONVERT*
228 FORI=SATOEA:REM***MAIN LOOP***
230 PRINTLEFT$(D$,14)LEFT$(R$,21);I
232 REM*GET BYTE AND DITCH SPACE*
234 BT=PEEK(I):CT=CT+BT:BT$=MID$(STR$(BT),2):BL=LE
N(BT$)
236 REM*PARSE BYTE AND STORE ASC CODES*
238 FORJ=1TOBL
240 AC%(J)=ASC(MID$(BT$,J,1))
242 NEXT
244 IFLL+BL>31THENGOSUB346:REM CREATE NEW PROGRAM
LINE
246 REM*INSERT DATA ITEM INTO LINE*
248 FORJ=1TOBL:BB=AC%(J):GOSUB366:NEXT
250 REM*INSERT COMMA AFTER ITEM*
252 BB=CC:GOSUB366:REM COMMA
254 NEXTI:REM***MAIN LOOP ENDS****
256 PRINTLEFT$(D$,17);
258 PRINT"█  YOU MAY EDIT OR SAVE DATA AS NORMAL."
260 PRINTSPC(7)"NOTE: BASIC IS AT PAGE";BA
262 PRINTSPC(6)"SYS64738 TO RESET TO PAGE 8"
264 PRINTSPC(11)"█AFTER█ SAVING DATA."
266 GOSUB428:REM*END OF BASIC*
268 PRINTLEFT$(D$,24):PRINTSPC(14)"█HIT ANY KEY██"
;
270 GETA$:IFA$=""THEN270
272 PRINT"█"
274 POKE55,0:POKE56,160:REM RAISE MEMTOP
276 POKE50,BE+2:POKE48,BE+1:POKE44,BA:POKE46,BE+1:
CLR:LIST
278 REM********************************
280 REM*****GOSUBS START HERE*********
282 REM********************************
284 REM**********************************
286 REM*                                  *
288 REM*   HEX STRING TO DECIMAL NUM    *
290 REM*                                  *
```

```
292 REM*****************************
294 Z1=0:HX$=RIGHT$("000"+MID$(A$,2),4)
296 FORZ=1TO4:HC=ASC(HX$)
298 HC=HC-48+(HC>64)*7:HX$=MID$(HX$,2)
300 IFHC<0ORHC>15THENZ1=-1:Z=4:GOTO304
302 Z1=16*Z1+HC
304 NEXT
306 RETURN
308 REM*****************************
310 REM*                          *
312 REM*SETUP VARS FOR CREATE BASIC  *
314 REM*                          *
316 REM*****************************
318 BS=BA*256:REM*BASIC START ADDRESS*
320 POKEBS,0:REM*'0'FOR BASIC START*
322 LA=BS+1:REM*LINK ADDRESS*
324 LN=BS+3:REM*LINE MUNBER*
326 LS=BS+5:REM*LINE STARTS*
328 LL=0:REM*LENGTH OF CURRENT LINE*
330 VL=100:VH=0:REM*CURRENT LINE NUMBER*
332 AL=1:AH=BA:REM*LAST LINK ADDR VALS*
334 DA=131:REM*KEYWORD TOKEN FOR 'DATA'*
336 CT=0:REM CHECKSUM
338 CC=44:REM* ASCII FOR ','*
340 EL=0:REM*END OF LINE MARKER*
342 GOSUB422:REM*LINE NO & 'DATA'*
344 RETURN
346 REM*****************************
348 REM*                          *
350 REM*    CREATE NEW BASIC LINE   *
352 REM*                          *
354 REM*****************************
356 LL=LL-1:REM DEC PTR TO LOSE ','
358 BB=EL:GOSUB366:REM*END OF LINE*
360 GOSUB384:REM*UPDATE LINK ADDR*
362 GOSUB404:REM*LINE NO & 'DATA'*
364 RETURN
366 REM*****************************
368 REM*                          *
370 REM*OUTPUT BYTE                *
372 REM*                          *
374 REM*****************************
376 PA=LS+LL:REM*ADDR TO POKE*
378 POKEPA,BB:REM*POKE BYTE*
```

Listing continued next page

```
380 LL=LL+1
382 RETURN
384 REM************************************
386 REM*                                  *
388 REM*   UPDATE LINK ADDRESSES          *
390 REM*                                  *
392 REM************************************
394 REM
396 AL=AL+LL+4:IFAL>255THENAL=AL-256:AH=AH+1
398 POKELA,AL:POKELA+1,AH
400 LA=LA+LL+4:REM*NEW LINK POINTER*
402 RETURN
404 REM************************************
406 REM*                                  *
408 REM*   NEW LINE NO & DATA TOKEN       *
410 REM*                                  *
412 REM************************************
414 REM
416 LN=LN+LL+4:REM*NEW LINE NO*
418 VL=VL+10:IFVL>255THENVL=VL-256:VH=VH+1:REM*NEW
    LINE NO VAL*
420 LS=LS+LL+4:REM*NEW LINE STARTS*
422 POKELN,VL:POKELN+1,VH
424 LL=0:BB=DA:GOSUB366:REM*'DATA'*
426 RETURN
428 REM************************************
430 REM*                                  *
432 REM*      END OF CREATING BASIC       *
434 REM*                                  *
436 REM************************************
438 REM40 GOSUB346:REM* END OF LINE*
442 CT$=MID$(STR$(CT),2):CL=LEN(CT$)
444 FORJ=1TOCL:BB=ASC(MID$(CT$,J,1)):GOSUB366:NEXT
    :REM*CHECKSUM VALUE*
446 BB=58:GOSUB366:BB=143:GOSUB366:REM*':REM'*
448 CM$="*CHECKSUM*":CL=LEN(CM$)
450 FORJ=1TOCL:BB=ASC(MID$(CM$,J,1)):GOSUB366:NEXT
    :REM*'CHECKSUM'*
452 BB=EL:GOSUB366:REM*END OF LINE*
454 GOSUB384:REM*DO LAST LINK ADDR*
456 GOSUB366:GOSUB366:REM*'00' FOR END OF BASIC*
458 BE=LS+LL:BE=INT(BE/256)+1:REM*NEW BEGINNING OF
    VARS*
460 RETURN
```

```
99 REM**GINRUMMY UPDATES 05/03/84**
100 CHANGED 41 TO 37 IN LINE 3815
101 CHANGED 2445 TO 2420 IN LINE 2330
102 CHANGED V>0 TO V>=0 IN LINE 4100
103 CHANGED 3830 TO 3835 IN LINE 3820
104 DELETED GOTO IN LINE 3825
105 DELETED LINE 3830
106 LINE 3850 NOW READS GOTO3900
107 DELETED GOTO3900 IN LINE 3840
108 CHANGED 3885 TO 3875 IN LINE 3865
109 DELETED LINE 3045
110 DELETED LINE 2810
111 DELETED LINE 4530
112 CHANGED 4530 TO 4535 IN LINE 4520
113 CHANGED 41 TO 37 IN LINE 3765
114 CHANGED 37 TO 41 IN LINE 3870
115 LINE 2645 NOW READS IF<PK>=PO>AND<DT$="k")THENUK$="Y"
116 CHANGED V2=0 TO 4630 IN LINE 4615
117 CHANGED V2=12 TO 4645 IN LINE 4630
999 REM**ADDED NEW LINES AS FOLLOWS**
1981 IFCN-1<3THENGOSUB515:GOTO1973
3847 IF<RU<S>4)OR<RD<S>=3)THENV4=V:GOSUB4175:GOSUB4055
3876 VL=V+1:IFVL>12THEN3880
3877 IF<CA2<S,VL)AND5)<>5THEN3880
3878 IF<CA2<S,VL)AND41)=41THENJ=J+1
3879 VL=VL+1:IFVL<13THEN3877
READY.
```

On page 122 (DATASTATE) amend to
LINE) 438 REM
LINE) 440 GOSUB346: REM *END OF LINE*

THE 6510 MEMORY MAPPING CAPABILITIES

The aim of this section is to describe the way in which the standard memory map of the 6510 can be radically varied. These controls provide for a large range of exciting future possibilities for the CBM 64.

Firstly we look at those alterations to the memory map which are purely software controlled. At the very bottom of memory the 6510 has two important registers.

Address 0 is a so-called data-direction-register (DDR) for an I/O port at Address 1. Each bit set to a 1 means the corresponding bit of Address 1 is treated as an Output. A 0 bit in Address 0 means the corresponding bit of Address 1 is treated as an Input. The normal setup of these addresses is

Addresses 0 and 1

Address 0 (DDR)			*Address 1* (I/O Port)	
Bit	Contents	Function	Name	Function
0	1	Output	LORAM	Control $A000–$BFFF (BASIC or RAM)
1	1	Output	HIRAM	Control $E000–$FFFF (KERNAL or RAM)
2	1	Output	CHAREN	Control $D000–$DFFF (I/O or CM ROM)
3	1	Output	CASS WRT	Cassette write line
4	0	Input	CASS SNS	Cassette switch sense
5	1	Output	CASS MTR	Cassette motor on/off
6	0	X	—	Not known (multiplexed pinout?)
7	0	X	—	Not known (multiplexed pinout?)

In fact five control lines are provided to select various memory maps for the 6510. Three of these (LORAM,HIRAM and CHAREN) provided by the I/O port contained in the 6510 microprocessor are under software control. The remaining two lines (GAME and EXROM) are pinouts on the Expansion port.

LORAM Address 1 Bit 0

This line can be thought of as a switch to bank out the 8K BASIC ROM. Typically LORAM is programmed high for normal BASIC operation. If LORAM is programmed low, the BASIC ROM will disappear from memory and be replaced by 8K of RAM from $A000–$BFFF. Of course flipping out BASIC is not such a good idea unless (a) you have replaced it by another operating system or (b) are running a pure machine language program. We can demonstrate LORAM with the following program.

```
1000  REM**TEST LORAM**
1010  FOR I=40960TO49152:REM $A000–$BFFF
1020  POKEI,PEEK(I):REM COPY BASIC ROM TO RAM
1030  NEXT
1040  REM**NOW FLIP TO BASIC IN RAM**
```

```
1050  POKE1,PEEK(1)AND254:REM BIT 0 NOW 0
1060  REM**NOW RUNNING BASIC IN RAM**
1070  FORI=0TO10
1080  PRINT"I'M IN RAM TIDDILYROM"
1090  NEXT
1100  REM**NOW FLIP BACK TO BASIC IN ROM**
1110  POKE1,PEEK(1)OR1
1120  END
```

HIRAM Address 1 Bit 1

This line can be thought of as a switch to bank out the 8K KERNAL ROM. Typically HIRAM is programmed high for normal BASIC operation. If HIRAM is programmed low, the KERNAL ROM will disappear from memory and be replaced by 8K of RAM from $E000–$FFFF. Since many BASIC operations use KERNAL routines, banking out the KERNAL is liable to bring matters to a grinding halt. Once again we could copy the KERNAL down into RAM before flipping.

> To bank out the KERNAL: POKE1,PEEK(1)AND253
> To bank in the KERNAL: POKE1,PEEK(1)OR2

CHAREN Address 1 Bit 2

This is used to bank the 4K Character Matrix ROM in or out of the 6510 address space ($D000–$DFFF). When CHAREN is set to 1, as is normal, the 6526 devices (CIAs) appear in the microprocessor address space, and the Character ROM is not accessible. When CHAREN is cleared to 0 the Character ROM appears in the 6510 address space and the I/O devices are not accessible.

About the only time you might want the 6510 to see the Character ROM is when copying the character set down into RAM prior to using redefined user characters. This copying process requires some care. Every 1/60 second one of the CIA 6526 timers generates an Interrupt and triggers the keyscan routine. Because this Interrupt line is hard wired, the Interrupt will occur even when the CIA 6526s are no longer accessible to the 6510. If the 6510 attempts a keyscan when no CIA is visible the result is a mess. Hence before copying or flipping CHAREN it is first necessary to turn off the timer.

```
1000  REM**COPY DOWN CHARACTER SET**
1010  POKE56,32:CLR:REM LOWER MEMTOP
1020  POKE56334,PEEK(56334)AND254:REM TURN OFF IRQ TIMER
1030  POKE1,PEEK(1)AND251:REM BIT2 NOW 0/CHAREN=0
1040  REM**NOW PERFORM COPY**
1050  FORI=0TO4096
1060  POKE8192+I,PEEK(53248+I)
1070  NEXT
1080  REM**COPY COMPLETE**
1090  POKE1,PEEK(1)OR4:REM BIT 2 NOW1/CHAREN=1
1100  POKE56334,PEEK(56334)OR1:REM TURN ON IRQ TIMER
1110  END
```

On its own this routine will not produce any observable effect since (a) all we did was to copy characters down and (b) the VIC-II chip is still seeing the original Character ROM; We leave the VIC-II chip controls until Chapter 5. Still, for fun you may like to edit in the following lines

```
1110  REM**NOW CHANGE CM POINTER**
1120  POKE53272,(PEEK(53272)AND240)OR8:REM CM AT 8192
1130  REM**JUST TO MAKE THE POINT**
1140  CM=8192
1150  FORI=0TO7:AR(U)=PEEK(CM+8+I):NEXT:REM STORE CHAR 'A'
1160  FORI=0TO7:POKECM+8+I,AR(7-I):NEXT:REM  TURN  ALL  A'S  UPSIDE
      DOWN
1170  PRINT"AABBCCAA"
```

Plugging into the Expansion port gives access to 44 lines on the main board. These include all main control lines for the 6510, the 8-bit data bus and the 16-bit address bus. This port is used for plug-in Cartridges of amazing variety, from games to the long-promised CP/M.

Two memory control lines provided by the Extension port are Pins 8 and 9, GAME and EXROM.

GAME Pin 8 on the Expansion port

When brought low this line causes the CBM 64 memory map to 'collapse' into the memory map of the Commodore ULTIMAX video game unit. However, this line also interacts with the other control lines to produce various memory configurations. On an ULTIMAX game cartridge this line would be pulled low, indicating to the CBM 64 that a GAME cartridge is being used. Thus the CBM 64 is downwards compatible with the ULTIMAX. When no cartridge is installed, or when a cartridge other than a game is used this line is held high.

EXROM Pin 9 on the Expansion port

This line is used to bank the 8K of RAM from $8000−$9FFF out of the 6510's address space and replace it with up to 8K of ROM in a plug-in cartridge. This line is normally held high but would be pulled low in a BASIC 'expansion' cartridge such as the Programmer's Aid. In order for an expansion cartridge to perform an auto-start on power-up the necessary bytes must appear in $8000−$8006 (described earlier in this chapter).

4

Sound on the Commodore 64

INTRODUCTION

An exciting feature of the CBM 64 is its very sophisticated sound-generating capability. This is accomplished by a dedicated 6581 microprocessor called a Sound Interface Device, or SID. The SID chip is virtually a sound synthesizer in its own right.

Sound from the 64 is normally taken from the RF socket straight through to the TV. However, the sound output can also be connected, via the audio/video socket, to a hi-fi system for high quality playback or recording. In addition to the creation of complex sounds under software control the SID chip can also accept input from an external audio signal. Such signals may be from other SID chips or, for example, an electric guitar. The external audio signal can then be mixed with the audio output from the SID chip and processed through its filters. (Caution: incorrect connection of external lines can seriously damage your CBM 64; consult the Appendices for correct pinouts and levels before attempting any external connects.)

Programming sound on the CBM 64 is achieved through prolific use of POKE. If we set SID=54272, the base address of the SID chip, then the adresses SID to SID+28 control the SID chip and hence all sound on the CBM 64. In the sections which follow we shall describe each control register's function and finish with a program, '64-SYN'. Together these will enable you to experiment at your leisure. At best we can only begin to explore the world of possibilities that the SID chip opens up. For those who require an in-depth study of sound on the CBM 64, Commodore have promised a book entitled *Making Music on Your Commodore Computer*.

Before plunging into the intricacies of the SID chip we first review some basic facts about the nature of sound and musical notes.

SOUND AND MUSIC

Sound reaches our ears in the form of periodic variations of air pressure. Our ear-drums are incredibly sensitive. Under favourable conditions a sound wave of such feeble intensity that the air is displaced through only a ten-thousand-millionth part of an inch will send a signal to the brain. The change of pressure produced by such a sound wave is less than a ten-thousandth-millionth part of the normal atmospheric pressure.

The number of vibrations per second is called the *frequency*, or pitch, of the sound. The volume, or intensity, of a sound is determined by the amount of energy it transmits. In a musical note, or pure tone, this intensity is directly related to the amplitude, or maximum displacement of each air molecule (see Fig. 4.1). We can think of any sound as being composed of pure tones of differing frequencies and amplitudes.

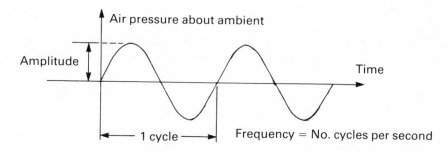

Fig. 4.1 – A pure sine wave.

The lower limit of human hearing is around 15 cycles per second (or 15 Hertz); tones below the lower limit affect the ear but they give noisy effects and not distinct pitches. A pure tone whose frequency is 100 Hz sounds low to the ear, a bass note. In 1939 an international conference standardized the A above middle C at 440 Hz. A note whose frequency is 3000 Hz sounds high to our ears, a treble note. Normal human hearing has an upper limit of about 20,000 Hz, although with advancing years the upper limit decreases: few people over 60 years of age can hear tones above 8000 Hz.

If we *double* the frequency of a tone then we raise its pitch *one octave*. So normal human hearing spans a range of around 10.5 octaves. The three tone oscillators of the SID chip span a range of around 8 octaves, 0–4000 Hz.

The ear can readily distinguish between the same pitch of note played on different instruments. This is because no instrument produces a perfectly pure tone. Each instrument has a unique timbre by which we recognize it. This comes about as follows. Any musical note is made up of pure tones having respectively 1, 2, 3, etc. times the frequency of the fundamental note. These associated tones are called the *natural harmonics* of the fundamental note. Helmholtz was the first to show that the timbre of a musical note is determined by the proportions in which the various natural harmonics are heard. The fact that a bowed string on a violin has a fuller, more brilliant and richer tone than the plucked string arises from the different mixes of natural harmonics. Body vibrations of the instrument are also critical. For example the body vibrations of a first-class Stradivarius are fairly evenly distributed between 3200 and 5200 Hz. In other violins the frequencies are usually lower and less evenly distributed.

Plainly with only three oscillators at our disposal we could not hope to imitate different instruments by adding harmonics of the fundamental. In fact the CBM 64 has no facility to generate a pure tone. Fortunately there is another factor to be considered. What is mainly important to the ear is the overall effect of the waveform, the graph of amplitude against time for one complete note. To some extent the same effect or timbre can be achieved by controlling the *envelope* (or outer shape) of the sound wave, see Fig. 4.2. The SID chip provides very detailed control of this envelope. Independently from controlling the envelope we can alter the harmonic content by using four different kinds of generic wave form as follows:

(1) *Sawtooth wave.* Here all harmonics are present, the Nth harmonic has intensity proportional to $1/N$
(2) *Triangular wave.* This contains only odd harmonics. For odd N the Nth harmonic has intensity proportional to $1/(N \uparrow 2)$.
(3) *Rectangular wave.* A square wave has odd harmonics proportional to $1/N$. By changing the pulse width we can get a variety of rectangular waves each having its own harmonic mix.
(4) *White noise.* A random mixture of frequencies, mostly used for special effects.

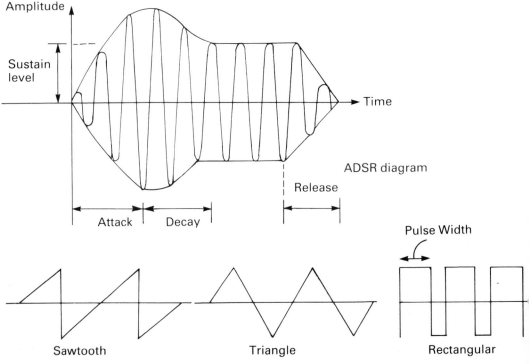

Fig. 4.2 — Waveforms.

The harmonic content of a sound can also be altered by filtering. As we shall see the SID chip offers three kinds of filter. By using careful combinations of filters you can get just about any harmonic content you want.

ENVELOPE CONTROL

Figure 4.2 shows the general shape of a musical note with emphasis on those factors which the SID chip allows us to control. Collectively known as ADSR these factors are:

(1) *Attack*. The rise time of a note.
(2) *Decay*. The time taken for the note to fall to a steady amplitude.
(3) *Sustain level*. The volume of the steady amplitude.
(4) *Release*. The time taken for the volume of the note to fall from the sustain level to zero.

Typical ADSR characteristics are

	Violin				Piano/Harpsichord		
	Time	POKE			Time	POKE
A	500 ms	10		A	2 ms	0
D	300 ms	8		D	750 ms	9
S		10		S		0
R	750 ms	9		R	6 ms	0

To produce a sound on the CBM 64 we have to take a minimum of six steps, namely:

Step 1.   Turn on the volume with

    POKE SID+24,15

Step 2.   Select ADSR. For example

    POKE SID+5,9   :REM ATTACK/DECAY VOICE 1 A=0,D=9
    POKE SID+6,0   :REM SUSTAIN/RELEASE VOICE 1 S=0,R=0

Step 3.   Select the frequency for each oscillator. For example

    POKE SID+1,25 :REM HI-BYTE FREQ VOICE 1
    POKE SID,0   :REM LO-BYTE FREQ VOICE 1

Step 4.   Select the desired waveform for each oscillator. For example

    POKE SID+4,33 :REM SELECT SAWTOOTH FOR VOICE 1

At this point the sound begins to play, we have opened the 'Gate' as the saying goes.

Step 5.   A delay loop whilst the note plays at the sustain level.

Step 6.   The waveform must be released, for example

    POKE SID+4,32 :REM RELEASE SAWTOOTH VOICE 1

The simplest way to program the CBM 64 to play a tune is to set initial values of ADSR, and construct a FOR loop which READs frequency HI/LO bytes from DATA statements. By inserting zeros in the DATA statements the tempo can be varied for different voices whilst keeping the delay constant. There are many examples of programs of this type freely available (see Jim Butterfield's 'Dixie' for example) so we shall not go into details.

SID READY-RECKONER (Courtesy Elizabeth Coley)

As many of the sound functions are controlled by only one or two bits of the 8-bit register it is necessary to POKE the register with a value that will change the required bits and leave the remainder unaffected. This would normally be achieved by PEEKing the register value and performing logical (AND/OR) operations on it to set or clear the required bits. Unfortunately, SID to SID+24 are write only regiaters so a copy of the contents of each register must be maintained (in 64-SYN this is done using arrays) that can be PEEKed instead. This could be located at 49152 to 49152+24 and represented by CPY to CPY+24. When sound editing is complete for a register the current value in the CPY location can be POKEd into the appropriate SID register with POKE-SID+X,PEEK(CPY+X). Statements may be used in programs exactly as given.

Variables

SID	= 54272		AT = Attack Time	$(0-15)$
CPY	= 49152		DT = Decay Time	$(0-15)$
FLO	= Frequency Lo-Byte	$(0-255)$	SL = Sustain Level	$(0-15)$
FHI	= Frequency Hi-byte	$(0-255)$	RT = Release Time	$(0-15)$
PLW	= Pulse Width Lo-Byte	$(0-255)$	CO = Filter Cutoff	$(0-2047)$
PHW	= Pulse Width Hi-Byte	$(0-15)$	FR = Filter Resonance	$(0-15)$
VOL	= Master volume	$(0-15)$		

The Frequency number   = Freq(Hz)*0.0609594583(NTSC) or Freq(Hz)*0.0587254763(PAL)

The Pulse Width number   = PW(%)*40.95

VOICE 1

Set FLO	– POKECPY,FLO
Set FHI	– POKECPY+1,FHI
Set PLW	– POKECPY+2,PLW
Set PHW	– POKECPY+3,PHW
Select Noise	– POKECPY+4,(PEEK(CPY+4)AND15)OR128
Select Pulse	– POKECPY+4,(PEEK(CPY+4)AND15)OR64
Select Sawtooth	– POKECPY+4,(PEEK(CPY+4)AND15)OR32
Select Triangle	– POKECPY+4,(PEEK(CPY+4)AND15)OR16
Deselect all waveforms	– POKECPY+4 PEEK(CPY+4)AND15
Select Test	– POKECPY+4,PEEK(CPY+4)OR8
Deselect Test	– POKECPY+4,PEEK(CPY+4)AND247
Ring Mod. 01 with 03 – on	– POKECPY+4,PEEK(CPY+4)OR4
– off	– POKECPY+4,PEEK(CPY+4)AND251
Sync 01 to 03 – on	– POKECPY+4,PEEK(CPY+4)OR2
– off	– POKECPY+4,PEEK(CPY+4)AND253
Envelope Gen. – gate	– POKECPY+4,PEEK(CPY+4)OR1
– ungate	– POKECPY+4,PEEK(CPY+4)AND254
Set AT	– POKECPY+5,(PEEK(CPY+5)AND15)OR(AT*16)
Set DT	– POKECPY+5,(PEEK(CPY+5)AND240)ORDT
Set SL	– POKECPY+6,(PEEK(CPY+6)AND15)OR(SL*16)
Set RT	– POKECPY+6,(PEEK(CPY+6)AND240)ORRT

VOICE 2
As Voice 1 replacing CPY+n with CPY+n+7

VOICE 3
As Voice 1 replacing CPY+n with CPY+n+14

N.B. Voice 2 Sync. and Ring Mod. as voice 1. Voice 3 Sync. and Ring Mod. as voice 2.

General

Set CO 3 Least sig. bits	—	POKECPY+21,COAND7
Set CO 8 Most sig bits	—	POKECPY+22,INT(CO/8)
Set FR	—	POKECPY+23,(PEEK(CPY+23)AND15)ORFR*16)
Filter ext. input	— yes	POKECPY+23,(PEEK(CPY+23)OR8
	— no	POKECPY+23,PEEK(CPY+23)AND247
Filter Osc. 3	— yes	POKECPY+23,PEEK(CPY+23)OR4
	— no	POKECPY+23,PEEK(CPY+23)AND251
Filter Osc. 2	— yes	POKECPY+23,PEEK(CPY+23)OR2
	— no	POKECPY+23,PEEK(CPY+23)AND253
Filter Osc. 1	— yes	POKECPY+23,PEEK(CPY+23)OR1
	— no	POKECPY+23,PEEK(CPY+23)AND254
Osc. 3	— on	POKECPY+24,PEEK(CPY+24)OR128
	— off	POKECPY+24,PEEK(CPY+24)AND127
High Pass	— on	POKECPY+24,PEEK(CPY+24)OR64
	— off	POKECPY+24,PEEK(CPY+24)AND191
Band Pass	— on	POKECPY+24,PEEK(CPY+24)OR32
	— off	POKECPY+24,PEEK(CPY+24)AND223
Low Pass	— on	POKECPY+24,PEEK(CPY+24)OR16
	— off	POKECPY+24,PEEK(CPY+24)AND239
Set VOL	—	POKECPY+24,(PEEK(CPY+24)AND240)ORVOL
Potentiometer X co-ord	—	PEEK(SID+25)
Y co-ord	—	PEEK(SID+26)
Osc. 3 output (digitized)	—	PEEK(SID+27)
Env. 3 output (digitized)	—	PEEK(SID+28)

The statements above are most useful when the characteristics of sounds have to change during a program. If the registers are set only once in a short program it is unnecessary to go to such lengths to protect them. But, if you wish to RUN a program which changes values and RUN it again it would be wise to be careful.

THE SID CONTROL REGISTERS

There are 29 eight-bit registers on the SID chip which control the production of sound. These registers are either READ only or WRITE only as shown in the table below, and the location of these registers is between 54272 and 55295 ($D400–$D7FF).

Table 4.1 – SID Register map.

	A4	A3	A2	A1	A0	REG # (HEX)	D7	D6	D5	D4	D3	D2	D1	D0	REG NAME	REG TYPE
			ADDRESS							DATA					**Voice 1**	
0	0	0	0	0	0	00	F_7	F_6	F_5	F_4	F_3	F_2	F_1	F_0	FREQ LO	WRITE-ONLY
1	0	0	0	0	1	01	F_{15}	F_{14}	F_{13}	F_{12}	F_{11}	F_{10}	F_9	F_8	FREQ HI	WRITE-ONLY
2	0	0	0	1	0	02	PW_7	PW_6	PW_5	PW_4	PW_3	PW_2	PW_1	PW_0	PW LO	WRITE-ONLY
3	0	0	0	1	1	03	—	—	—	—	PW_{11}	PW_{10}	PW_9	PW_8	PW HI	WRITE-ONLY
4	0	0	1	0	0	04	NOISE	⊓⊔	⋀	⊿	TEST	RING MOD	SYNC	GATE	CONTROL REG	WRITE-ONLY
5	0	0	1	0	1	05	ATK_3	ATK_2	ATK_1	ATK_0	DCY_3	DCY_2	DCY_1	DCY_0	ATTACK/DECAY	WRITE-ONLY
6	0	0	1	1	0	06	STN_3	STN_2	STN_1	STN_0	RLS_3	RLS_2	RLS_1	RLS_0	SUSTAIN/RELEASE	WRITE-ONLY
															Voice 2	
7	0	0	1	1	1	07	F_7	F_6	F_5	F_4	F_3	F_2	F_1	F_0	FREQ LO	WRITE-ONLY
8	0	1	0	0	0	08	F_{15}	F_{14}	F_{13}	F_{12}	F_{11}	F_{10}	F_9	F_8	FREQ HI	WRITE-ONLY
9	0	1	0	0	1	09	PW_7	PW_6	PW_5	PW_4	PW_3	PW_2	PW_1	PW_0	PW LO	WRITE-ONLY
10	0	1	0	1	0	0A	—	—	—	—	PW_{11}	PW_{10}	PW_9	PW_8	PW HI	WRITE-ONLY
11	0	1	0	1	1	0B	NOISE	⊓⊔	⋀	⊿	TEST	RING MOD	SYNC	GATE	CONTROL REG	WRITE-ONLY
12	0	1	1	0	0	0C	ATK_3	ATK_2	ATK_1	ATK_0	DCY_3	DCY_2	DCY_1	DCY_0	ATTACK/DECAY	WRITE-ONLY
13	0	1	1	0	1	0D	STN_3	STN_2	STN_1	STN_0	RLS_3	RLS_2	RLS_1	RLS_0	SUSTAIN/RELEASE	WRITE-ONLY
															Voice 3	
14	0	1	1	1	0	0E	F_7	F_6	F_5	F_4	F_3	F_2	F_1	F_0	FREQ LO	WRITE-ONLY
15	0	1	1	1	1	0F	F_{15}	F_{14}	F_{13}	F_{12}	F_{11}	F_{10}	F_9	F_8	FREQ HI	WRITE-ONLY
16	1	0	0	0	0	10	PW_7	PW_6	PW_5	PW_4	PW_3	PW_2	PW_1	PW_0	PW LO	WRITE-ONLY
17	1	0	0	0	1	11	—	—	—	—	PW_{11}	PW_{10}	PW_9	PW_8	PW HI	WRITE-ONLY
18	1	0	0	1	0	12	NOISE	⊓⊔	⋀	⊿	TEST	RING MOD	SYNC	GATE	CONTROL REG	WRITE-ONLY
19	1	0	0	1	1	13	ATK_3	ATK_2	ATK_1	ATK_0	DCY_3	DCY_2	DCY_1	DCY_0	ATTACK/DECAY	WRITE-ONLY
20	1	0	1	0	0	14	STN_3	STN_2	STN_1	STN_0	RLS_3	RLS_2	RLS_1	RLS_0	SUSTAIN/RELEASE	WRITE-ONLY
															Filter	
21	1	0	1	0	1	15	—	—	—	—	—	FC_2	FC_1	FC_0	FC LO	WRITE-ONLY
22	1	0	1	1	0	16	FC_{10}	FC_9	FC_8	FC_7	FC_6	FC_5	FC_4	FC_3	FC HI	WRITE-ONLY
23	1	0	1	1	1	17	RES_3	RES_2	RES_1	RES_0	FILTEX	FILT 3	FILT 2	FILT 1	RES/FILT	WRITE-ONLY
24	1	1	0	0	0	18	3 OFF	HP	BP	LP	VOL_3	VOL_2	VOL_1	VOL_0	MODE/VOL	WRITE-ONLY
															Misc.	
25	1	1	0	0	1	19	PX_7	PX_6	PX_5	PX_4	PX_3	PX_2	PX_1	PX_0	POT X	READ-ONLY
26	1	1	0	1	0	1A	PY_7	PY_6	PY_5	PY_4	PY_3	PY_2	PY_1	PY_0	POT Y	READ-ONLY
27	1	1	0	1	1	1B	O_7	O_6	O_5	O_4	O_3	O_2	O_1	O_0	OSC3/RANDOM	READ-ONLY
28	1	1	1	0	0	1C	E_7	E_6	E_5	E_4	E_3	E_2	E_1	E_0	ENV3	READ-ONLY

Register descriptions
VOICE 1
Register No. 00,01 Address 54272,54273 $D400,$D401

Function FREQ LO/FREQ HI

This pair of registers form a 16-bit number, Fn, which controls the frequency of Oscillator 1. The actual output frequency can be calculated as follows:

$$\text{Fout} = \text{Fn} * \text{Fclk}/16777216 \text{ Hz}$$

where Fclk is a frequency of the system clock. In the case of the CBM 64 the Flck frequency is 1.022730 (U.S–NTSC) or 0.985250 (Europe – PAL) MHz, and so the output frequency is given by:

$$Fout = Fn * 0.0609594583 \text{ (NTSC) or } Fn * 0.0587254763 \text{ (PAL)}$$

Register No. 02.03 Address 54274,54275 Hex $D402,$D403

Function PW LO/PW HI

Together these registers form a 12-bit number (bits 4–7 of register 03 are not used) which controls the Pulse Width (duty cycle) of the Pulse Waveform on Oscillator 1. To put that in simpler terms think of a square wave like this-:

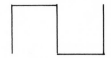

The value of the wave is high for 50% of the time, therefore it has a Pulse Width of 50%. If the wave had a Pulse Width of 100% it would be high all of the time, and if it had a Pulse Width of 0% then it would be low all of the time. The actual Pulse Width is calculated as follows:

$$PWout = PWn/40.95 \%$$

Thus a value of PWn = 0 or PWn = 4095 will produce a constant DC output, while a value of PWn = 2048 will produce a square wave.

Register No. 04 Address 54276 $D404

Function control register

The control register contains eight control bits each of which select various options on Oscillator 1.

Bit 0 – GATE: The GATE bit controls the Envelope Generator for Oscillator 1. When this bit is set to a one, The Envelope Generator is triggered (GATEd) and the Attack/Decay/Sustain part of the cycle starts. Once the GATE bit is reset to zero the release part of the cycle will start. If the GATE bit is reset before the A/D/S part of the cycle is complete then the Release stage will start from whatever value the volume has reached. Since the GATE bit controls the Envelope Generator which in turn controls the volume of the Oscillator, the GATE bit must be set to get any audible sound out of the Oscillator.

Bit 1 – SYNC: When the SYNC bit is set the fundamental frequency (i.e. the frequency set in registers 00 and 01 as opposed to any harmonics) of Oscillator 1 is synchronized to that of Oscillator 3. When the frequency of Oscillator 1 is then varied it will produce a range of harmonics derived from the fundamental frequency of Oscillator 3. In order to SYNC the Oscillators, the frequency of Oscillator 3 must be set to some value other than zero, and preferably less than that of Oscillator 1. No parameters of Oscillator 3 other than the frequency will affect SYNC.

Bit 2 – RING MOD: When the RING MOD bit is set the Triangle waveform of Oscillator 1 is replaced by a RING Modulated combination of Oscillators 1 and 3. If the frequency of Oscillator 1 is then varied a range of non-harmonic sounds are produced. These sounds may be used to create gong or bell sounds, or used in special effects. In order to produce a RING MODulated sound the frequency of Oscillator 3 must be any value other than zero. No parameters of Oscillator 3 other than the frequency will affect RING MODulation.

Bit 3 – TEST: When the TEST bit is set Oscillator 1 is reset and locked to zero, the Noise waveform is turned off, and the Pulse waveform output is held at a DC level (Pulse Width = 0%). The Oscillator is released when the TEST bit is reset, and thus although this feature is normally used for testing, it can be used to synchronize Oscillator 1 to some external event.

Bit 4 – TRIANGLE: When this bit is set the TRIANGLE waveform of Oscillator 1 is selected. The TRIANGLE waveform has few harmonics and is a mellow, flute-like sound.

Bit 5 – SAWTOOTH: When this bit is set the SAWTOOTH waveform is selected. This is a rich, brassy sound with many harmonics.

Bit 6 – PULSE: This bit selects the Pulse waveform. The harmonics of this waveform can be varied by changing the Pulse Width. This allows generation of sounds which vary from a reedy, nasal pulse to a bright hollow square wave.

Bit 7 – NOISE: This bit selects the NOISE waveform. The sound produced can be varied from a low rumbling to a hissing white noise by altering the frequency of the Oscillator. NOISE is also useful in creating such sounds as explosions, wind and jet engines also cymbals and some drums may be produced.

Register 05 Address 54277 $D405

Function ATTACK/DECAY

Bits 4–7 of this register select which of the 16 possible ATTACK rates is used by the Envelope Generator. The ATTACK rate determines how quickly the volume of the Oscillator reaches its maximum after the GATE bit is set. The ATTACK rate varies from 2 ms to 8 s, and the values are given in Table 4.2 below.

Bits 0–3 of the register select 1 of the possible 16 DECAY rates of the Envelope Generator. The DECAY cycle follows the ATTACK cycle and determines how quickly the volume falls from the maximum level to the level selected by SUSTAIN. The DECAY values vary from 6 ms to 24 s, and are given in Table 4.2 below.

Register 06 Address 54278 $D406

Function SUSTAIN/RELEASE

Bits 4–7 of this register select which of the 16 possible SUSTAIN levels is used by the Envelope Generator. The SUSTAIN cycle follows the DECAY cycle, and the volume of Oscillator 1 will remain at the selected SUSTAIN level as long as the GATE bit is set. The sustain levels vary from 0 to 15 in equal steps, with a SUSTAIN level of 0 selecting zero volume and a SUSTAIN value of

15 selecting the maximum volume as reached by the ATTACK cycle. Thus a SUSTAIN value of 8 will cause the volume to be SUSTAINed at a value of one-half that of the maximum.

Bits 0–3 of the register select 1 of the possible 16 DECAY rates of the Envelope Generator. The RELEASE cycle follows the SUSTAIN cycle when the GATE bit is reset. The value of RE-LEASE determines how quickly the volume drops from the SUSTAIN level to zero. The RELEASE rates are identical to the DECAY rates. If, however, the GATE bit is reset before the ATTACK/DECAY/SUSTAIN cycle is complete, then the RELEASE rate will determine how quickly the volume drops from its current value to zero.

Table 4.2 — Envelope rates.

VALUE		ATTACK RATE	DECAY/RELEASE RATE
DEC	(HEX)	(Time/Cycle)	(Time/Cycle)
0	(0)	2 ms	6 ms
1	(1)	8 ms	24 ms
2	(2)	16 ms	48 ms
3	(3)	24 ms	72 ms
4	(4)	38 ms	114 ms
5	(5)	56 ms	168 ms
6	(6)	68 ms	204 ms
7	(7)	80 ms	240 ms
8	(8)	100 ms	300 ms
9	(9)	250 ms	750 ms
10	(A)	500 ms	1.5 s
11	(B)	800 ms	2.4 s
12	(C)	1 s	3 s
13	(D)	3 s	9 s
14	(E)	5 s	15 s
15	(F)	8 s	24 s

VOICE 2
Register No. 07,08 Address 54279,54280 $D407,$D408

　　　　Function FREQ LO/FREQ HI

As voice 1.

Register No. 09/10 Address 54281,54282 $D409,$D40A

　　　　Function PW LO/PW HI

As voice 1.

Register No. 11 Address 54283 $D40B

　　　　Function CONTROL REGISTER

As voice 1, except:
1. When selected, SYNC synchronizes Oscillator 2 with Oscillator 1.
2. When selected, RING MOD replaces the triangle waveform of Oscillator 2 with the RING MODulated combination of Oscillators 2 and 1.

Register No. 12 Address 54284 $D40C

       Function ATTACK/DECAY

As voice 1.

Register No. 13 Address 54285 $D40D

       Function SUSTAIN/RELEASE

As voice 1.

VOICE 3
Register No. 14,15 Address 54286,54287 $D40E,$D40F

       Function FREQ LO/FREQ HI

As voice 1.

Register No. 16/17 Address 54288,54289 $D410,$D411

       Function PW LO/PW HI

As voice 1.

Register No. 18 Address 54290 $D412

       Function CONTROL REGISTER

As voice 1, except:
1. When selected, SYNC synchronizes Oscillator 3 with Oscillator 2.
2. When selected, RING MOD replaces the triangle waveform of Oscillator 2 with the RING MODulated combination of Oscillators 3 and 2.

Register No. 19 Address 54291 $D413

       Function ATTACK/DECAY

As voice 1.

Register No. 20 Address 54292 $D414
       Function SUSTAIN/RELEASE

As voice 1.

FILTER
Register No. 21,22 Address 54293,54292 $D415,$D416

       Function FC LO/FC HI

This pair of registers form an 11-bit number (bits 3—7 of FC LO are not used) which linearly controls the Cutoff or Centre Frequency of the Filter. The Cutoff Frequency ranges from approximately 30 Hz to 12 kHz.

Register No. 23 Address 54295 $D416

> Function RES/FILT

Bits 4—7 of this register control the RESonance of the filter. The effect of RESonance is to emphasize the frequency components of the sound of the Cutoff Frequency of the Filter. This effect causes a sharper sound. There are 16 possible linear RESonance settings ranging from 0 to no RESonance to 15 for maximum RESonance.

Bits 0—3 determine what goes through the filter as follows:

Bit 0 — FILT 1: When this bit is set to a one, the output of Oscillator 1 will be passed through the filter and its harmonic content changed according to the filter settings. When reset to zero the output from Oscillator 1 goes directly to the audio output without being affected by the filter.

Bit 1 — FILT 2: Identical to FILT 1, except affects output of Oscillator 2.

Bit 2 — FILT 3: Identical to FILT 1, except affects output of Oscillator 3.

Bit 3 — FILTEX: Identical to FILT 1, except affects External Audio Input.

Register No. 24 Address 54296 $D418

> Function MODE/VOL

Bits 4—7 of this register select various options as follows:

Bit 4 — LP: When this bit is set, the *Low Pass* output of the filter is sent to the audio output. The effect of the Low Pass filter is to allow all frequencies below the Cutoff Frequency to pass through unaffected, whilst all frequencies above the Cutoff Frequency are attenuated at a rate of 12 dB/octave, i.e. frequencies within one octave above the Cutoff Frequency are reduced in volume by a factor of 4 (attenuation of 3dB halves the volume), frequencies 2 octaves above by a factor of 8 etc. This produces a full-bodied sound.

Bit 5 — BP: When this bit is set, the *Band Pass* output of the filter is sent to the audio output. The effect of the Band Pass filter is to attenuate all frequencies above and below the Cutoff Frequency by 6 dB/octave. This produces a thin, open sound.

Bit 6 — HP: When this bit is set, the *High Pass* output of the filter is sent to the audio output. The effect of the High Pass filter is to allow all frequencies above the Cutoff Frequency to pass through unaffected, whilst all frequencies below the Cutoff Frequency are attenuated at a rate of 12 dB/octave. This produces a tinny, buzzy sound.

Bit 7 — 3 OFF: When this bit is set, the output of Oscillator 3 is not sent to the audio output. By setting this bit and by setting FILT 3 = 0 the output of Oscillator 3 cannot reach the audio output, and may thus be used for modulation without any unwanted output.

It should be noted that the various filter modes may be used together, for example setting LP and HP will filter out frequencies around the Cutoff but allow those above and below to pass, having effectively the opposite effect to the Band Pass filter.

Bits 0–3: These bits select 1 of 16 possible Master Volume levels for the final audio output of the SID chip. The values range in linear steps from 0 (no output) to 15 (maximum volume).

MISCELLANEOUS
Register No. 25,26 Address 54297,54298 $D419,$D41A

> Function POTX/POTY

These registers contain the positions of potentiometers attached to pins 24 and 23 respectively. In the case of the CBM 64 these registers are used to read the values of the Potentiometer Joysticks (paddles).

Register No. 27 Address 54299 $D41B

> Function OSC 3/RANDOM

This register contains the top eight bits of the output of Oscillator 3. The distribution of the values found in this register directly reflect the waveform selected for Oscillator 3. If the Triangle waveform has been selected then the numbers will increment from 0 to 255 then decrement back to 0 again, the rate at which this happens will depend upon the frequency. If the Sawtooth waveform is selected then the numbers will count up from 0 to 255 then recommence from 0 again. If the Pulse waveform is selected then the values will be either 255 or 0, and the distribution will be determined by the Pulse Width. If the White noise waveform is selected then a series of random integers in the range 0 to 255 will appear. This register can therefore be used for generating random numbers in, for example, games where the speed of the PEEK basic keyword is an advantage over using RND. Other uses of this register are to read the values and write them back into other registers of the SID chip. For example, if Oscillator 3 is set to Sawtooth waveform and the values of this register are added to the Oscillator or Filter frequencies or to the Pulse Width of one of the Oscillators, a siren-like sound can be produced.

Register No. 28 Address 54300 $D41C

> Function ENV 3

This register is similar to OSC 3 except that it contains the output of the Oscillator 3 Envelope Generator. This output can be added to the Filter Frequency to produce harmonic envelopes and wah-wah effects. Adding this value to the frequency of an oscillator will produce a phasor effect. In order to get any output from this register the Envelope Generator must be GATEd.

GETTING FAMILIAR WITH THE SOUNDS

One of the failings of CBM 64 Basic (it does have a few!) is the fact that there are no BASIC commands which can be used for sound. It's PEEK and POKE time again.

In order to give you a chance to try out the CBM 64's sound facilities we have the program 64–SYN. This program sets up the 64 as a sound synthesizer, using the top two rows of keys as a two octave keyboard, which means you will have to turn your 64 around to play a tune on it, as shown in Fig. 4.3.

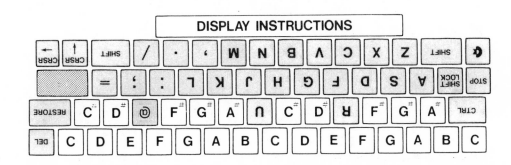

Fig. 4.3 – 64-SYN keyboard layout.

```
1000 REM***********64-SYN***************
1010 CLR
1020 KP$="FPADSRYI1234████VETLBHCU████"
1030 DN$=" █████████████████████████████"
1040 SID=13*4096+4*256:FV=SID+24:RF=SID+23
1050 HI=256:S4=16:C1=1:B7=255:CL=53280:POKECL,1:PO
KECL+1,1
1060 PRINT"█"SPC(17)"███64 SYN███":PRINTLEFT$(DN$,12)
SPC(12)"█D█ISK OR █T██PE ?"
1070 GETA$:IFA$=""THEN1070
1080 IFA$="T"THENDV=1
1090 IFA$="D"THENDV=8:OPEN15,8,15,"I0":GOSUB3750:I
FEN<>0THENRUN
1100 IFA$<>"D"ANDA$<>"T"THEN1070
1110 PRINT"█"LEFT$(DN$,13)SPC(12)"  PLEASE WAIT
"
1120 REM***INITIALISE VARS AND SID***
1130 FORI=0TO7:A(I)=2↑I:NEXT
1140 GOSUB3980:REM SETUP ARRAYS
1150 FORI=0TO28:POKESID+I,0:NEXT
1160 FORI=0TO2:N=SID+I*7
1170 FR(I)=0:PW(I)=0:SU(I)=0
1180 AT(I)=0:RE(I)=0:DE(I)=0
1190 NEXT
1200 FM=0:FR=0
```

Listing continued next page

```
1210 GOSUB1610:REM MAIN DISPLAY
1220 REM*******EDIT MODE****
1230 PRINT"■■■■■■■■■■■■■■■■■■■■■■■■■■■■■■■■■■■■EDI
T":POKE650,128:GETA$
1240 GOSUB3960:REM WAIT FOR KEYPRESS
1250 PRINT"■  ■■MODE:"A$"■■":N=SID+7*VO
1260 FORI=1TOLEN(KP$):IFA$<>MID$(KP$,I,C1)THENNEXT
:GOTO1310:REM NOT FOUND
1270 KEY=I:I=LEN(KP$):NEXT:REM FOUND KEY
1280 ONKEYGOTO1850,1920,2010,2080,2150,2220,2290,2
360,2430,2430,2430,2430
1290 ONKEY-12GOTO3030,3030,3030,2470,2540,2610,268
0,2750,2820,2890,2960,1330
1300 ONKEY-24GOTO3060,3390,1540,1010
1310 PRINT"■  ■■MODE:   ■■"
1320 GOTO1240:REM NEXT KEY
1330 REM*******PLAY SOUND*****
1340 GOSUB3810:REM SETUP FOR PLAY
1350 K=PEEK(197):IFK=64THEN1350
1360 IFK%(K)>22THEN1490
1370 IFK%(K)=22THENPOKEFV,0:GOTO1230:REM EXIT
1380 B=K%(K)+12*FR(0)
1390 POKESID,FL%(B):POKESID+1,FH%(B)
1400 B=K%(K)+12*FR(1)
1410 POKESID+7,FL%(B):POKESID+8,FH%(B)
1420 B=K%(K)+12*FR(2)
1430 POKESID+14,FL%(B):POKESID+15,FH%(B)
1440 POKESID+4,(CR(0))OR1
1450 POKESID+11,(CR(1))OR1
1460 POKESID+18,(CR(2))OR1
1470 K1=PEEK(197):IFK1=KTHEN1470
1480 IFK1<>64THENK=K1:GOTO1360
1490 POKESID+4,CR(0)
1500 POKESID+11,CR(1)
1510 POKESID+18,CR(2)
1520 GOTO1350:REM NEXT PLAY KEY
1530 REM***TERMINATE PROGRAM**
1540 PRINT"■"SPC(18)"■EXIT■"
1550 PRINT"■■■■■"SPC(8)"ARE YOU SURE N/CR OR Y ?"
1560 GOSUB3960:REM GET KEYPRESS
1570 IFA$<>"Y"THEN 1210
1580 IFDV=8THENCLOSE15
1590 POKECL,14:POKECL+1,6:FORI=0TO28:POKESID+I,0:N
EXT:PRINT"■■":END
```

```
1600 REM****'GOSUBS' START HERE******
1610 REM****MAIN   DISPLAY**********
1620 PRINT"▉ ▉MODE: ▉      ▉64 SYN▉
     ▉▉":PRINT""
1630 PRINTSPC(2)"▉+▉-▉ UP/DN/ON/OFF";
1640 PRINTTAB(24)"▉F7▉ EDIT/PLAY"
1650 PRINTSPC(2)"▉D▉ DIVIDE BY TWO";
1660 PRINTTAB(24)"▉F2▉ TO LOAD DATA"
1670 PRINTSPC(2)"▉M▉ MULTIPLY BY TWO";
1680 PRINTTAB(24)"▉F4▉ TO SAVE DATA"
1690 PRINTTAB(24)"▉F6▉ TO EXIT▉"
1700 PRINTSPC(2)"VOICE (▉F1▉,▉F3▉,▉F5▉):"VO+1
1710 PRINTSPC(12)"▉MASTER ▉V▉OLUME:"FMAND15
1720 PRINTSPC(2)"▉▉F▉REQ RNGE.     ▉P▉ULSE WIDTH
     ∧ ⌐ ⊓ *"
1730 FORI=0TO2:PRINTTAB(4)FR(I);TAB(19)PW(I);
1740 P=CR(I):PRINTTAB(32);:FORJ=4TO7:PRINT"▉";-((P
     ANDA(J))>0);:NEXT
1750 NEXT:PRINTTAB(32)"▉1▉2▉3▉4"
1760 PRINT:PRINT"  ▉A▉TK ▉D▉EC ▉S▉US ▉R▉LS S▉Y▉NC
     R▉NG   FIL▉ER"
1770 FORI=0TO2:PRINTTAB(3)T(I)TAB(7)DE(I)TAB(11)SU
     (I)TAB(15)RE(I)"▉"
1780 P=CR(I):PRINTTAB(20);
1790 FORJ=1TO2:PRINT-((PANDA(J))>0)"▉";:NEXT:PRIN
     T"  ";(FRANDA(I))/A(I):NEXT
1800 PRINT:PRINT"  R▉E▉SONANCE:"INT(FR/16);
1810 PRINTTAB(19)"▉L▉OW ▉B▉AND ▉H▉IGH ▉O▉UT3"
1820 PRINTTAB(20);:FORJ=4TO7:PRINT(FMANDA(J))/A(J)
     "▉";:NEXT
1830 PRINT:PRINT"  C▉U▉TOFF FREQUENCY:"CO;
1840 RETURN
1850 REM*******FREQUENCY
1860 GOSUB3960:REM GET KEYPRESS
1870 IFA$="+"ANDFR(VO)<4THENFR(VO)=FR(VO)+1:GOTO19
     00
1880 IFA$="-"ANDFR(VO)>0THENFR(VO)=FR(VO)-1:GOTO19
     00
1890 GOTO1250:STOP     REM EXIT
1900 GOSUB3940:PRINTSPC(4)"        ▉▉▉▉▉▉▉"FR(VO)
1910 GOTO1860:REM ANOTHER VALID KEY?
1920 REM******PULSE WIDTH
1930 GOSUB3960:REM GET KEYPRESS
1940 IFA$="+"THENPW(VO)=(PW(VO)+64)AND4095:GOTO199
```

Listing continued next page

```
0
1950 IFA$="M"THENPW(VO)=(PW(VO)*2)AND4095:GOTO1990
1960 IFA$="D"THENPW(VO)=INT(PW(VO)/2):GOTO1990
1970 IFA$="-"THENPW(VO)=(PW(VO)-64)AND4095:GOTO199
0
1980 GOTO1250:REM EXIT
1990 GOSUB3940:PRINTSPC(19)"        ▮▮▮▮▮▮▮▮"PW(VO)
2000 GOTO1930:REM ANOTHER VALID KEY?
2010 REM********ATTACK
2020 GOSUB3960:REM GET KEYPRESS
2030 IFA$="+"THENAT(VO)=(AT(VO)+1)AND15:GOTO2060
2040 IFA$="-"THENAT(VO)=(AT(VO)-1)AND15:GOTO2060
2050 GOTO1250:REM EXIT
2060 GOSUB3930:PRINT"        ▮▮▮▮"AT(VO)
2070 GOTO2020:REM ANOTHER VALID KEY?
2080 REM********DECAY
2090 GOSUB3960:REM GET KEYPRESS
2100 IFA$="+"THENDE(VO)=(DE(VO)+1)AND15:GOTO2130
2110 IFA$="-"THENDE(VO)=(DE(VO)-1)AND15:GOTO2130
2120 GOTO1250:REM EXIT
2130 GOSUB3930:PRINTSPC(7)"    ▮▮▮▮"DE(VO)
2140 GOTO2090:REM ANOTHER VALID KEY?
2150 REM********SUSTAIN
2160 GOSUB3960:REM GET KEYPRESS
2170 IFA$="+"THENSU(VO)=(SU(VO)+1)AND15:GOTO2200
2180 IFA$="-"THENSU(VO)=(SU(VO)-1)AND15:GOTO2200
2190 GOTO1250:REM EXIT
2200 GOSUB3930:PRINTSPC(11)"    ▮▮▮▮"SU(VO)
2210 GOTO2160:REM ANOTHER VALID KEY?
2220 REM********RELEASE
2230 GOSUB3960:REM GET KEYPRESS
2240 IFA$="+"THENRE(VO)=(RE(VO)+1)AND15:GOTO2270
2250 IFA$="-"THENRE(VO)=(RE(VO)-1)AND15:GOTO2270
2260 GOTO1250:REM EXIT
2270 GOSUB3930:PRINTSPC(15)"    ▮▮▮▮"RE(VO)
2280 GOTO2230:REM ANOTHER VALID KEY?
2290 REM********CONTROL REG/SYNC
2300 GOSUB3960:REM GET KEYPRESS
2310 IFA$="+"THENCR(VO)=(CR(VO))OR2:GOTO2340:REM S
YNC ON
2320 IFA$="-"THENCR(VO)=(CR(VO))AND253:GOTO2340:RE
M SYNC OFF
2330 GOTO1250:REM EXIT
2340 GOSUB3930:PRINTSPC(20);:PRINT(CR(VO)AND2)/2
```

```
2350 GOTO2300:REM ANOTHER VALID KEY?
2360 REM*********CONTROL REG/RING MOD
2370 GOSUB3960:REM GET KEYPRESS
2380 IFA$="+"THENCR(VO)=(CR(VO))OR4:GOTO2410:REM R
ING MOD ON
2390 IFA$="-"THENCR(VO)=(CR(VO))AND251:GOTO2410:RE
M RING MOD OFF
2400 GOTO1250:REM EXIT
2410 GOSUB3930:PRINTSPC(25);:PRINT(CR(VO)AND4)/4
2420 GOTO2370:REM ANOTHER VALID KEY?
2430 REM**********CONTROL REG/WAVEFORM
2440 CR(VO)=(CR(VO)AND7)ORA(VAL(A$)+3)
2450 GOSUB3940:PRINTSPC(31)" 0 0 0 0█████████"SPC(
(VAL(A$))*2)"1"
2460 GOTO1310:REM EXIT
2470 REM**********VOLUME
2480 GOSUB3960:REM GET KEYPRESS
2490 IFA$="+"THENFM=(FMAND240)+(((FMAND15)+1)AND15
):GOTO2520:REM UP
2500 IFA$="-"THENFM=(FMAND240)+(((FMAND15)-1)AND15
):GOTO2520:REM DOWN
2510 GOTO1250:REM EXIT
2520 PRINT"█"LEFT$(DN$,8)SPC(26)"   ████"FMAND15
2530 GOTO2480:REM ANOTHER VALID KEY?
2540 REM**********REASONANCE
2550 GOSUB3960:REM GET KEYPRESS
2560 IFA$="+"THENFR=(FRAND15)+(((FR/16)+1)AND15)*1
6:GOTO2590
2570 IFA$="-"THENFR=(FRAND15)+(((FR/16)-1)AND15)*1
6:GOTO2590
2580 GOTO1250:REM EXIT
2590 PRINT"█"LEFT$(DN$,21)SPC(12)"   ████"INT(FR/16
)
2600 GOTO2550:REM ANOTHER VALID KEY?
2610 REM**********FILTER ON/OFF
2620 GOSUB3960:REM GET KEYPRESS
2630 IFA$="+"THENFR=FROR(A(VO)):GOTO2660
2640 IFA$="-"THENFR=FRAND(255-A(VO)):GOTO2660
2650 GOTO1250:REM EXIT
2660 GOSUB3930:PRINTTAB(32)(FRANDA(VO))/A(VO)
2670 GOTO2620:REM ANOTHER VALID KEY?
2680 REM**********LOW PASS FILTER
2690 GOSUB3960:REM GET KEYPRESS
2700 IFA$="+"THENFM=FMORA(4):GOTO2730
```

Listing continued next page

```
2710 IFA$="-"THENFM=FMAND(255-A(4)):GOTO2730
2720 GOTO1250:REM EXIT
2730 PRINT"■"LEFT$(DN$,22)SPC(20)"  ▮▮▮";-((FMANDA(
4))>0)
2740 GOTO2690:REM ANOTHER VALID KEY?
2750 REM*********BAND PASS FILTER
2760 GOSUB3960:REM GET KEYPRESS
2770 IFA$="+"THENFM=FMORA(5):GOTO2800
2780 IFA$="-"THENFM=FMAND(255-A(5)):GOTO2800
2790 GOTO1250:REM EXIT
2800 PRINT"■"LEFT$(DN$,22)SPC(25)"  ▮▮▮";-((FMANDA(
5))>0)
2810 GOTO2760:REM ANOTHER VALID KEY?
2820 REM*********HIGH PASS FILTER
2830 GOSUB3960:REM GET KEYPRESS
2840 IFA$="+"THENFM=FMORA(6):GOTO2870
2850 IFA$="-"THENFM=FMAND(255-A(6)):GOTO2870
2860 GOTO1250:REM EXIT
2870 PRINT"■"LEFT$(DN$,22)SPC(30)"  ▮▮▮";-((FMANDA(
6))>0)
2880 GOTO2830:REM ANOTHER VALID KEY?
2890 REM*********CUT VOICE THREE
2900 GOSUB3960:REM GET KEYPRESS
2910 IFA$="+"THENFM=FMORA(7):GOTO2940
2920 IFA$="-"THENFM=FMAND(255-A(7)):GOTO2940
2930 GOTO1250:REM EXIT
2940 PRINT"■"LEFT$(DN$,22)SPC(35)"  ▮▮▮";-((FMANDA(
7))>0)
2950 GOTO2900:REM ANOTHER VALID KEY?
2960 REM*********CUTOFF FREQ FOR FILTERS
2970 GOSUB3960:REM GET KEYPRESS
2980 IFA$="+"THENCO=(CO+16)AND1023:GOTO3010
2990 IFA$="-"THENCO=(CO-16)AND1023:GOTO3010
3000 GOTO1250:REM EXIT
3010 PRINT"■"LEFT$(DN$,24)SPC(19)"      ▮▮▮▮▮"CO;
3020 GOTO2970:REM ANOTHER VALID KEY?
3030 REM*********CHANGE VOICE
3040 VO=KEY-13:PRINT"■"LEFT$(DN$,6)SPC(19)VO+1;
3050 GOTO1310:REM EXIT
3060 REM******LOAD*******
3070 POKE649,10:REM NORMALISE KYBD BUFF
3080 PRINT"◆"SPC(11)"▮▮LOAD▮ ▮MODE▮"
3090 PRINTSPC(7)"▮▮▮▮▮▮FILENAME ";:INPUTF$
3100 IFDV=1THEN3240:REM SKIP DISK RTNS
```

```
3110 OPEN2,8,2,F$+",S,R":GOSUB3750
3120 IFEN=0THEN3190:REM NO ERROR
3130 IFEN<>62THENFORDR=0TO5000:NEXT:GOTO3220
3140 CLOSE2:PRINTSPC(8)"██ANOTHER FILE CR/N OR Y ?
"
3150 GETR$:IFR$=""THEN3150
3160 IFR$="Y"THEN3080
3170 GOTO3220:REM TRY AGAIN
3180 REM***DISK
3190 PRINTSPC(9)"██LOADING "+F$
3200 GOSUB3280:GOSUB3750
3210 IFEN<>0THENFORI=0TO5000:NEXT
3220 POKE649,1:CLOSE2:GOTO3270
3230 REM***TAPE
3240 OPEN2,1,0,F$
3250 GOSUB3280:CLOSE2
3260 IFST<>0THENPRINTSPC(8)"██LOAD ERROR":GOTO3140
3270 GOTO1210:REM EXIT
3280 REM***READ DATA
3290 FORDR=0TO2
3300 INPUT#2,FR(DR):INPUT#2,PW(DR)
3310 INPUT#2,CR(DR):INPUT#2,AT(DR)
3320 INPUT#2,DE(DR):INPUT#2,SU(DR)
3330 INPUT#2,RE(DR)
3340 NEXT
3350 INPUT#2,FM
3360 INPUT#2,FR
3370 INPUT#2,CO
3380 RETURN
3390 REM********SAVE********
3400 POKE649,10:REM NORMALISE KYBD BUFF
3410 PRINT"J"SPC(11)"◤◢SAVE█ █MODE█"
3420 PRINTSPC(7)"██████FILENAME ";:INPUTF$
3430 IFDV=1THEN3580:REM SKIP DISK RTNS
3440 OPEN2,8,2,F$+",S,W":GOSUB3750
3450 IFEN=0THEN3530
3460 IFEN<>63THENFORI=0TO5000:NEXT:GOTO3560
3470 CLOSE2:PRINTSPC(7)"█OVERWRITE FILE CR/N OR Y
?"
3480 GETR$:IFR$=""THEN3480
3490 IFR$<>"Y"THEN3560
3500 PRINT#15,"S:"+F$
3510 GOTO3440
3520 REM***DISK
```

Listing continued next page

```
3530 PRINTSPC(9)"◣SAVING "+F$
3540 GOSUB3610:GOSUB3750
3550 IFEN<>0THENFORI=0TO5000:NEXT
3560 POKE649,1:CLOSE2:GOTO3600
3570 REM***TAPE
3580 OPEN2,1,1,F$
3590 GOSUB3610:CLOSE2
3600 GOTO1210:REM EXIT
3610 REM***WRITE DATA**
3620 FORDR=0TO2
3630 PRINT#2,FR(DR)
3640 PRINT#2,PW(DR)
3650 PRINT#2,CR(DR)
3660 PRINT#2,AT(DR)
3670 PRINT#2,DE(DR)
3680 PRINT#2,SU(DR)
3690 PRINT#2,RE(DR)
3700 NEXT
3710 PRINT#2,FM
3720 PRINT#2,FR
3730 PRINT#2,CO
3740 RETURN
3750 REM**DISK ERROR CHANNEL**
3760 INPUT#15,EN,EM$,ET,ES
3770 IFEN=0THEN3800
3780 PRINTSPC(11)"▨▨▨ERROR# ▬";EN:PRINTSPC(11)"▨";
EM$;"▬"
3790 PRINTSPC(11)"▨TRACK▬ ";ET:PRINTSPC(11)"▨SECTO
R ";ES
3800 RETURN
3810 REM*****SETUP FOR PLAY********
3820 PRINT"▨▮▮▮▮▮▮▮▮▮▮▮▮▮▮▮▮▮▮▮▮▮▮▮▮▮▮▮▮▮▮▮▮▮▮▮▨PLA
Y"
3830 POKE650,0:POKE649,1
3840 FORVP=0TO2:NN=SID+7*VP
3850 POKENN+5,AT(VP)*S4+DE(VP)
3860 POKENN+6,SU(VP)*S4+RE(VP)
3870 POKENN+2,PW(VP)ANDB7:POKENN+3,PW(VP)/HI
3880 NEXT
3890 POKERF,FR:POKEFY,FM
3900 POKESID+21,COAND7:POKESID+22,CO/8
3910 RETURN
3920 REM****
3930 PRINT"▨"LEFT$(DN$,16+VO):RETURN
```

```
3940 PRINT"■"LEFT$(DN$,10+VO):RETURN
3950 REM***WAIT FOR KEY PRESS***
3960 GETA$:IFA$=""THEN3960
3970 RETURN
3980 REM*SETUP ARRAYS**
3990 DIMK%(64),FH%(96),FL%(96)
4000 FORK=0TO96
4010 F=16.777*EXP(LOG(440)+(K-45)*LOG(2)/12)
4020 FH%(K)=INT(F/256)
4030 FL%(K)=F-256*FH%(K)
4040 NEXT
4050 REM***KEYS/NOTES-TRANSLATION ARRAY
4060 DATA62,59,9,8,14,17,16,22,19,25,24
4070 DATA30,33,32,39,35,41,46,43,49,48
4080 DATA54,3
4090 DATA727:REM*CHECKSUM*
4100 CC=0
4110 FORI=0TO64:K%(I)=23:NEXT
4120 FORI=0TO22:READK:K%(K)=I:CC=CC+K:NEXT
4130 READK:IFK<>CCTHENPRINT"CHECKSUM ERROR1":END
4140 RETURN
```

5

Graphics and the VIC-II chip

INTRODUCTION

The introduction of the Commodore 64 was quickly followed by numerous software packages designed to exploit the possibilities opened up by full-screen, high resolution color graphics. In this chapter our aim is to give you all the basic information necessary to write your own graphics software. This includes machine code routines, which can be run from BASIC, to efficiently Save and Load color graphics screens.

Applications of graphics include simulations of physical processes, anything from a nuclear reactor to orbital mechanics, the design of textile patterns, and three-dimensional representation of objects from different viewpoints. All of these are eminently practical projects for the CBM 64. However, if the software is written in BASIC one of the main limitations is speed. From BASIC the CBM 64 cannot be expected to match the incredible real time displays found in the best arcade games. For these effects it is necessary to use machine code programs. This may seem rather daunting but the principles used are identical and by the time you have read this book and acquired the necessary software tools (such as a machine language monitor and an Assembler Editor) you should be in a position to put together some real time graphics software. To help you on the way we give a machine code, hi-resolution PLOTSUB in a later chapter.

We begin by examining how the CBM 64 normally displays characters from ROM. This will lead into how to design your own RAM-based character set — *programmable characters* as they are called. Using programmable characters you can replace the entire character set, as displayed on the screen, by any set of characters you want, anything from space invaders to Anglo-Saxon runes! It is often overlooked that the Commodore's own extensive set of lo-resolution characters can be used to generate quite complex displays. To demonstrate this we have written a SCREEN EDITOR program which will allow you to create, Save and Load an entire lo-resolution screen in full color. By extracting the DATA statements for the machine code subroutines and incorporating them into your own BASIC programs these can then display numerous previously prepared screens without ever using a single PRINT statement. Why do work when the computer can do it for you! Incidentally, this program also shows you how to create an alternate screen on the CBM 64, in fact as many alternate screens as memory permits.

Altogether there are basically eight different screen graphic modes on the CBM 64. In low resolution graphics the character set may be in ROM or RAM and displayed in one of three possible modes: Standard mode, Multicolor mode or Extended Background color mode. Also there are two hi-resolution modes: Standard and Multicolor. In addition to these basic modes a number of other variations are possible: the screen can be set up to have 38 columns (as opposed to the normal 40 columns) and/or 24 rows (as opposed to 25). The last features are normally used in conjunction with smooth horizontal or vertical scrolling.

Following the SCREEN EDITOR program we turn to the topic of hi-resolution graphics on the CBM 64 and give a short BASIC program to illustrate the underlying principles.

Finally there is a complete list of the VIC-II chip registers and their functions. Sprites and animation using sprites are covered in Chapter 6.

THE VIC-II WINDOW

It is the function of the 6566/69 Video Interface (VIC-II) chip to generate the video display signal which is passed to the TV or to a TV monitor. To do this the VIC-II must be able to read data from RAM or ROM. This is accomplished by allowing the VIC-II access to some (but not all) lines on the address bus and all lines on the data bus. The process by which the VIC-II reads ROM or RAM shared with the 6510 is called Direct Memory Access (DMA). Ideally the VIC-II would be using the address or data lines at times when the 6510 does not need them, in which case the action of the two processors would be transparent to one another. Unfortunately the amount of data that the VIC-II must read in order to generate the video display is so large that there is not enough time available to operate in this way. Because of this the 6566/69 has a special control line, called the BA (Bus Available/not Available) line, which it can use to send a 'hold-off' signal to the 6510. This enables the VIC-II to reserve as much time as it needs to read ROM or RAM. The 6510 is quite unaware that it has been put onto 'hold'; when it is re-enabled it just carries on from where it left off. Apart from 'slowing up' the 6510 by as much as 15—20% the DMA's performed by the VIC-II have no effect on the internal working of the machine. However where real time I/O is concerned these unpredictable 'absences' of the 6510 may be a problem; the tape cassette is an example. In such cases it may be necessary to blank the screen (POKE53265,11) during the I/O and re-enable it (POKE53265,27) after the I/O is finished. Whether or not the VIC-II DMA is a problem during I/O will depend on the external device and the method used to communicate with it, in many instances screen blanking will not be necessary.

The VIC-II chip sees a different and far simpler memory map from the 6510. At any time the VIC-II can see one of four 16K blocks (or banks) of memory. We can think of this 16K block as the VIC-II *window* onto memory. The base address of this window can take one of four values under software control.

```
1000 REM**SELECT BANK FOR VIC WINDOW**
1010 POKE56578,PEEK(56578)OR3:REM  DDR CIA#2 BITS 0,1  TO OUTPUT
1020 WD=3:REM THIS SELECTS NORMAL WINDOW
1030 POKE56576,(PEEK(56576)AND252)ORWD:REM PORT A CIA #2 BITS 0,1
```

The relationship between WD and the corresponding base address of the VIC-II chip window is given in Table 5.1.

Table 5.1 – Setting the base address of the VIC-II window

Value of WD	Bank	Bits	Window start		Window end		ROM image
0	3	00	49152	$C000	65536	$FFFF	not visible
1	2	01	32768	$8000	49151	$BFFF	visible
2	1	10	16384	$4000	32767	$7FFF	not visible
3	0	11	0	$0000	16383	$3FFF	visible

In banks 0 and 2 the VIC-II will see the normal 4K character set from ROM (even though the true location of the character ROM is elsewhere). In bank 0 the ROM image will appear at addresses 4096–8191 ($1000–$1FFF), in bank 2 the ROM image appears at addresses 36864–40959 ($9000–$9FFF). Should we wish, we can make the VIC-II get its character data from RAM elsewhere in these windows but we should remember that at those addresses the standard character set will always be visible. In banks 1 and 3 the character ROM image will not be present, the VIC-II sees only pure RAM in these windows. This enables us to use either of these two windows for our own character set. In the case of the high window the character set should not be located in the range 55296–56295 ($D800–$DBE7) since (a) the VIC-II is using the area as color RAM and (b) the color RAM consists of nybbles (4 bits wide) rather than bytes (8 bits wide). Another complication using the high window is that to read from the underlying RAM the memory map of the 6510 must be changed, as was explained in Chapter 3. Thus using the high window is more complicated from the programming point of view but it has the advantage of not making any inroads whatsoever on RAM used by BASIC.

The base address of the current VIC-II window can be found with the following formula

$$WB = 16384*(3-(PEEK(56576)AND3))$$

WITHIN THE VIC-II WINDOW

Within the VIC-II window the 6566/69 chip expects to see the screen memory (i.e. video matrix), character matrix data and possibly sprite data. Just where in the window these various types of data are stored is largely up to the programmer (apart from the character ROM image). There are pointers in the VIC-II chip control registers which we can set to point to the start of screen memory and character matrix memory. The pointers for each of the eight sprites are tacked on to the end of the screen memory (and so must be moved around with the screen). Here are the details.

Locating the screen

The offset of the start of screen memory from the base of the current VIC-II window is controlled by the upper 4 bits of the VIC-II control register at address 53272 ($D018). Using these 4 bits we can place the screen at any one of sixteen 1K blocks within the window.

```
1000  REM**SELECT SCREEN OFFSET FROM BASE OF WINDOW**
1010  SRO=16:REM THIS SELECTS NORMAL SCREEN OFFSET
1020  POKE53272,(PEEK(53272)AND15)ORSRO
```

The relationship between SRO (Screen Offset) and the corresponding address offset from the base of the VIC-II window is given in Table 5.2.

Table 5.2 – Setting screen memory offset within the window

Value of SRO	Bits in 53272	Screen offset in memory		
0	0000XXXX	0	$0000	
16	0001XXXX	1024	$0400	(default)
32	0010XXXX	2048	$0300	
48	0011XXXX	3072	$0C00	
64	0100XXXX	4096	$1000	
80	0101XXXX	5120	$1400	
96	0110XXXX	6144	$1800	
112	0111XXXX	7168	$1C00	
128	1000XXXX	8192	$2000	
144	1001XXXX	9216	$2400	
160	1010XXXX	10240	$2800	
176	1011XXXX	11264	$2C00	
192	1100XXXX	12288	$3000	
208	1101XXXX	13312	$3400	
224	1110XXXX	14336	$3800	
240	1111XXXX	15360	$3C00	

The base address of the current screen in memory can be found using the formula

$$SC=16384*(3-(PEEK(56576)AND3))+64*(PEEK(53272)AND240)$$

which is the window base address plus the offset (SC=WB+Offset).

One problem with moving the screen about is that the color RAM does not move. So if we wish to have an alternate screen we must also reserve space for a color buffer and move the color information in and out of the buffer as appropriate. From BASIC this involves 1000 POKEs and so is rather slow. This is a situation where it is useful to have a machine code subroutine for copying a block of RAM from one part of memory to another. The program SCREEN EDITOR uses such a routine and a detailed explanation of this is given in a later chapter.

A further factor to consider when moving the screen about is that if you wish to PRINT to the new screen then it is necessary to tell the Operating System where the new screen is located. This is done by a POKE to decimal address 648 ($0288) which is a pointer that should contain the Hi-byte of the video matrix base address. If SC is computed as above then the following BASIC code will effect the required POKE

```
POKE648,INT(SC/256)
```

Locating the character matrix

The offset of the start of the character memory from the base of the current VIC-II window is controlled by bits 3, 2 and 1 of the VIC-II control register at address 53272 ($D018). Using these 3 bits we can place the 2K character matrix at any one of eight 2K blocks within the window. Although the character matrix is 4K wide the VIC-II chip normally only sees it in 2K blocks, Upper-case/Graphics or Lower-case/Upper-case.

```
1000 REM**SELECT CHARACTER MATRIX OFFSET FROM BASE OF WINDOW**
1010 CHO=4:REM THIS SELECTS NORMAL CM OFFSET
1020 POKE53272,(PEEK(53272)AND240)ORCHO
```

The relationship between CHO (Character memory Offset) and the corresponding address offset from the base of the VIC-II window is given in Table 5.3.

Table 5.3 — Setting 2K block character memory offset within the window

Value of CHO	Bits in 53272	Character memory offset		
0	XXXX000X	0	$0000	
2	XXXX001X	2048	$0800	
4	XXXX010X	4096	$1000	ROM image banks 0,2
6	XXXX011X	6144	$1800	ROM image banks 0,2
8	XXXX100X	8192	$2000	
10	XXXX101X	10240	$2800	
12	XXXX110X	12288	$3000	
14	XXXX111X	14336	$3800	

The base address of the current character memory can be found using the formula

$$CM=16384*(3-(PEEK(56576)AND3))+1024*(PEEK(53272)AND14)$$

which is the window base address plus the offset (CM=WB+Offset).

THE CONSTRUCTION OF CHARACTERS

To create user-defined graphics characters or to plot an individual pixel dot to a specified point on the screen, it helps a great deal to first understand how the standard characters are displayed.

As we know there are two distinct ways to put a character on the screen, we can use PRINT or simply POKE the appropriate screen code into the required address in the video matrix (and set the color). In either case, from the viewpoint of the VIC-II chip, the sequence of events which then takes place is the same. The screen code is read from the video matrix, multiplied by 8 and the resulting number is used as an offset, from the base address of the character matrix, to find the start address of the 8 bytes which describe the character in question.

Normally the base address of the ROM image, as seen by VIC-II, is 4096 ($1000), but the 6510 cannot see this image. If we wish to discover what VIC-II sees in character matrix the easiest way is to move the entire character set into RAM, as described at the end of Chapter 3. We can do this with the following BASIC code, which copies the character matrix into a 4K block of RAM beginning at 8192. After this process is complete the VIC-II is still seeing the ROM image but the copy we have created is visible to the 6510.

```
1000  REM**COPY DOWN CHARACTER SET**
1010  POKE56,32:CLR:REM LOWER MEMTOP
1020  POKE56334,PEEK(56334)AND254:REM TURN OFF IRQ TIMER
1030  POKE1,PEEK(1)AND251:REM BIT 2 NOW 0/CHAREN=0
1040  REM**NOW PERFORM COPY**
1050  FORI=0TO4095
1060  POKE8192+I,PEEK(53248+I)
1070  NEXT
1080  REM**COPY COMPLETE**
1090  POKE1,PEEK(1)OR4:REM BIT 2 NOW 1/CHAREN=1
1100  POKE56334,PEEK(56334)OR1:REM TURN ON IRQ TIMER
1110  END
```

If we now PEEK the first 16 addresses from 8192 upwards we can see how the first two characters are constructed, as in Table 5.4.

Table 5.4 – Character as stored in ROM.

Screen code	True decimal address	Contents	Bit pattern 76543210	Character row
0	53248	28	111	0
	53249	34	1 1	1
	53250	74	1 1 1	2
(Char @)	53251	86	1 1 11	3
	53252	76	1 11	4
	53253	32	1	5
	53254	30	1111	6
	53255	0		7
1	53256	24	11	0
	53257	36	1 1	1
	53258	66	1 1	2
(Char A)	53259	126	111111	3
	53260	66	1 1	4
	53261	66	1 1	5
	53262	66	1 1	6
	53263	0		7

If you study the bit patterns in Table 5.4 you will see exactly how an individual character is constructed. Each bit represents one of 64 pixel dots, if the bit is zero that pixel dot is not lit on the screen, if the bit is set to 1 then the pixel dot will be lit provided the color nybble associated with the character cell indicates a color distinct from the screen background color.

Screen codes take values in the range 0 to 255, therefore, since the screen code is used as an offset from the base of the character matrix, the total number of bytes for a single block of immediately accessible character matrix is 255*8, i.e. 2K. Unfortunately 256 characters are not enough to give all combinations of upper-case, lower-case, graphics and reversed field characters. To overcome this the character matrix is addressed in two 2K blocks, only one of which can be displayed by the VIC-II at a time. The first block gives the upper-case characters and graphics symbols. The second block consists of lower-case and upper-case characters plus some graphics symbols. When you use the SHIFT+CBM combination of keys (or PRINTCHR$(14) or POKE 53272,23) the effect is to switch to the second block in the character matrix. Then of course every character on the screen will change. The layout of the character matrix in ROM is given in Table 5.5.

Table 5.5 — ROM character matrix layout.

Decimal start true address	Contents		Screen codes	Keyboard entry
53248	Upper-case & Misc. Graphics/Graphics		0 − 63 64 − 127	No SHIFT SHIFT/CBM
54272	Upper-case & Misc. Graphics/Graphics	reverse field	128 − 191 192 − 255	No SHIFT SHIFT/CBM
55296	Lower-case & Misc. Upper-case/Graphics		0 − 63 64 − 127	No SHIFT SHIFT/CBM
56320	Lower-case & Misc. Upper-case/Graphics	reverse field	128 − 191 192 − 255	No SHIFT SHIFT/CBM

USER-DEFINED CHARACTERS

To put all the above into practice and create some new characters is now a simple matter. We take the program which copied down the character matrix and add one line which directs the VIC-II to obtain its character data from our copy rather than the usual ROM image.

Example:
```
1000  REM**COPY DOWN CHARACTER SET**
1010  POKE56,32:CLR:REM LOWER MEMTOP
1020  POKE56334,PEEK(56334)AND254:REM TURN OFF IRQ TIMER
1030  POKE1,PEEK(1)AND251:REM BIT 2 NOW 0/CHAREN=0
1040  REM**NOW PERFORM COPY**
```

```
1050  FORI=0TO4095
1060  POKE8192+I,PEEK(53248+I)
1070  NEXT
1080  REM**COPY COMPLETE**
1090  POKE1,PEEK(1)OR4:REM BIT 2 NOW1/CHAREN=1
1100  POKE56334,PEEK(56334)OR1:REM TURN ON IRQ TIMER
1110  REM**NOW CHANGE CM POINTER**
1120  POKE53272,(PEEK(53272)AND240)OR8:REM CM AT 8192
1130  REM**JUST TO MAKE THE POINT**
1140  CM=8192
1150  FORI=0TO7:AR(I)=PEEK(CM+8+I):NEXT:REM STORE CHAR 'A'
1160  FORI=0TO7:POKECM+8+I,AR(7-I):NEXT:REM  TURN  ALL  A'S  UPSIDE
      DOWN
1170  PRINT"AABBCCAA"
```

Notice that in this example we used the default VIC-II window, which simplified the process somewhat. In general when programming graphics we must take the following steps.

(1) Decide if user-defined characters or hi-resolution graphics are needed.
(2) Choose the best VIC-II window (don't forget the ROM image in blocks 0 and 2), i.e. the one which leaves as much space as possible for the program. If machine code subroutines are used then a good place to put these is in the $C000 block.
(3) Decide where in the window you are going to locate the character matrix, screen and sprite data (if any).
(4) If necessary copy the character matrix data from ROM to the area of RAM you have selected. Normally it won't be necessary to copy the entire character set (all 4K takes a while to copy from BASIC).
(5) Insert the new character matrix data by POKEing from DATA statements or in some other way.
(6) Reset the VIC window base address.
(7) Reset the character matrix offset pointer.
(8) Reset the screen matrix offset pointer (and pointer in 648 if necessary).
(9) Insert the sprite pointers at the end of the new screen memory.

We hasten to add that for many programs it will not be necessary to take all of these steps, but with great power goes great responsibility and it is as well to plan carefully!

In creating the DATA statements for the user-defined characters it is helpful to either write or obtain a Character Editor program. The function of a Character Editor is to take the pain out of producing the new character data. An enlarged picture of the character is displayed on the screen and edited until it is satisfactory. It can then be assigned to replace any desired normal character and the data (or the entire set of new character data) saved in some convenient way. To begin with it is probably a good idea to try writing your own Character Editor, this being the best way to ensure that the process is fully understood. Alternatively, there are a number of excellent programs available and these offer some sophisticated facilities which would be quite time-consuming to reproduce.

THE SCREEN EDITOR PROGRAM

This program demonstrates many of the principles described above. The idea is to be able to design a lo-resolution graphics screen in full color at one's leisure and then save it to be loaded back by a BASIC program whenever it is needed. In this way many different pictures can be displayed by a single BASIC program without using large numbers of PRINT statements.

The program has been written for use with a disk drive but can be easily modified for use with a tape cassette; the resulting program will be much shorter. To make this modification all references to disk routines (i.e. the subroutine which checks the disk drive error channel, the disk directory subroutine, all calls to these GOSUBs and any reference to logical file 15) and change the device number in the 'LOAD' and 'SAVE' subroutines from 8 to 1.

In order to function quickly and conveniently this program uses three machine language subroutines: Save, Load and Copy. The DATA statements for these subroutines are at the end of the program and should be extracted and incorporated in any BASIC program which wants to Load previously Saved screens.

When the alternate screen is in use the VIC-II window is set to 32768 and the character matrix pointers are left at their default values, since 32768 is the start of block 2 which contains a VIC-II character matrix ROM image. The Copy routine is used to swap the color matrix in and out of a color buffer located above the screen. This leaves 2K of free memory above the color buffer (before the ROM image) which could be used in an extended version of the program to hold sprite data. In this case the Save routine could be used to save the entire block of memory from the start of the screen to the end of the sprite data. This would enable an entire color screen together with 2K of sprite data to be reloaded in one painless move.

The program has been written so that '.S' is automatically added to the file name of any saved screens. This is to prevent any confusion with BASIC or machine code programs since the data is saved as a PRG file. On the book software disk there are two sample screens DRAGON and ABSTRACT; the file name of each is preceded by a space (which should be entered when Loading) to inset these files on the disk directory.

Another feature of this program which may be worth noting is that the 'STOP' key is disabled (but not RUN/STOP+RESTORE) and re-enabled upon exiting the program. It is very irritating to spend some time designing a screen only to lose it when the 'STOP' key is inadvertently pressed!

```
1000 REM**SCREEN EDITOR/DISK*****
1010 PRINTCHR$(147)
1020 POKE55,255:POKE56,127:POKE51,255:POKE52,127:C
LR:REM MEMTOP
1030 OPEN15,8,15,"I0":GOSUB3440:IFEN<>0THENCLOSE15
:STOP
1040 REM**SCREEN EDITOR SETUP**
1050 DIMC1%(32),C2%(32)
1060 FORI=0TO32:C1%(I)=0:NEXT
1070 DATA5,17,18,19,20,28,29,30,31
1080 FORI=1TO9
```

```
1090 READRR:C1%(RR)=I
1100 NEXT
1110 FORI=0TO32:C2%(I)=0:NEXT
1120 DATA1,5,9,10,16,17,18,19,21,22,23
1130 DATA24,25,26,27,28,29,30,31
1140 FORI=1TO19
1150 READRR:C2%(RR)=I
1160 NEXT
1170 REM*******************************
1180 GOSUB3580:REM SETUP M/C COPY
1190 GOSUB3900:REM SETUP M/C LOAD
1200 GOSUB4210:REM SETUP M/C SAVE
1210 POKE788,52:REM DISABLE STOP KEY
1220 GOSUB2410:REM MENU
1230 REM**MAIN LOOP**
1240 GETC$:IFC$=""THEN1240
1250 IFC$=CHR$(134)THENGOSUB1330:REM EDIT
1260 IFC$=CHR$(135)THENGOSUB2580:REM SAVE
1270 IFC$=CHR$(136)THENGOSUB2760:REM LOAD
1280 IFC$=CHR$(137)THENGOSUB2350:REM SCREEN COL
1290 IFC$=CHR$(138)THENGOSUB2380:REM BORDER COL
1300 IFC$=CHR$(139)THENGOSUB3070:REM DISK
1310 IFC$=CHR$(140)THENGOTO3350:REM END
1320 GOTO1240
1330 REM******SCREEN EDITOR SETUP*****
1340 GOSUB2190:REM TO ALTERNATE SCREEN
1350 SC=32768:CO=55296:RF=0
1360 FL=0:CC=(PEEK(53281)+1)AND15:PRINT"#";:SL=0
1370 CH=PEEK(SC+SL):RV=128-(CHAND128):POKESC+SL,(C
HAND127)ORRV
1380 CL=PEEK(CO+SL)AND15:POKECO+SL,CC
1390 REM*SED LOOP**
1400 GETA$:IFA$=""THEN1400
1410 W=ASC(A$):Z=(WAND224)/32
1420 POKESC+SL,CH:POKECO+SL,CL
1430 ONZ+1GOSUB1470,1630,1640,1650,1660,1940,1950
1440 IFFL=1THENGOSUB2010:RETURN
1450 GOTO1370
1460 REM*******************************
1470 REM*CONTROL1*
1480 ONC1%(W)GOSUB1500,1510,1530,1540,1550,1570,15
80,1600,1610
1490 RETURN
1500 CC=1:RETURN
```

Listing continued next page

```
1510 IFSL<960THENSL=SL+40
1520 RETURN
1530 RF=128:RETURN
1540 SL=0:RETURN
1550 IFSL>0THENSL=SL-1:POKESC+SL,32
1560 RETURN
1570 CC=2:RETURN
1580 IFSL<999THENSL=SL+1:RETURN
1590 RETURN
1600 CC=5:RETURN
1610 CC=6:RETURN
1620 REM*OTHERS*
1630 CD=W:GOSUB1960:RETURN
1640 CD=WAND31:GOSUB1960:RETURN
1650 CD=(WAND31)OR64:GOSUB1960:RETURN
1660 REM*CONTROL2*
1670 ZZ=C2%(W-128):IFZZ=0THEN1710
1680 ONZZGOSUB1720,1730,1740,1750,1760,1770,1790,1
800,1810,1820,1830
1690 ZZ=ZZ-11:IFZZ<0THENRETURN
1700 ONZZGOSUB1840,1850,1860,1870,1880,1890,1910,1
920
1710 RETURN
1720 CC=8:RETURN
1730 FL=1:RETURN
1740 GOSUB2350:RETURN
1750 GOSUB2380:RETURN
1760 CC=0:RETURN
1770 IFSL>39THENSL=SL-40
1780 RETURN
1790 RF=0:RETURN
1800 PRINTCHR$(147);:SL=0:RETURN
1810 CC=9:RETURN
1820 CC=10:RETURN
1830 CC=11:RETURN
1840 CC=12:RETURN
1850 CC=13:RETURN
1860 CC=14:RETURN
1870 CC=15:RETURN
1880 CC=4:RETURN
1890 IFSL>0THENSL=SL-1
1900 RETURN
1910 CC=7:RETURN
1920 CC=3:RETURN
```

```
1930 REM*LAST TWO*
1940 CD=(WAND31)OR96:GOSUB1960:RETURN
1950 CD=(WAND31)OR64:GOSUB1960:RETURN
1960 REM*DISPLAY*
1970 POKESC+SL,CDORRF:POKECO+SL,CC
1980 IFSL<999THENSL=SL+1
1990 RETURN
2000 REM*****************************
2010 REM**FLIPBACK TO NORMAL SCREEN**
2020 REM**SETUP TO GET COLOR**
2030 POKE49872,0:REM START LO (COL RAM)
2040 POKE49873,216:REM START HI (COL RAM)
2050 POKE49874,0:REM END LO (COL RAM)
2060 POKE49875,220:REM END HI (COL RAM)
2070 POKE49876,0:REM BUFFER LO
2080 POKE49877,132:REM BUFFER HI
2090 POKE49878,0:REM COPY NOT SWAP
2100 SYS49879:REM COPY COL INTO BUFFER
2110 REM* NOW GO TO NORMAL SCREEN *
2120 POKE56578,PEEK(56578)OR3:REM CIA #2 DDR TO OU
TPUT ON BITS 0 AND 1
2130 POKE56576,(PEEK(56576)AND252)OR3:REM SELECT B
ANK 0 AT $0000
2140 POKE53272,(PEEK(53272)AND15)OR16:REM SCREEN O
FFSET=1024 SO SC=1024
2150 POKE648,4:REM TELL O/S WHERE SCR
2160 PRINTCHR$(14)CHR$(154);
2170 GOSUB2410:REM DISPLAY MENU
2180 RETURN
2190 REM**FLIP TO ALTERNATE SCREEN**
2200 POKE56578,PEEK(56578)OR3:REM CIA #2 DDR TO OU
TPUT ON BITS 0 AND 1
2210 POKE56576,(PEEK(56576)AND252)OR1:REM SELECT B
ANK 2 AT $8000
2220 POKE53272,(PEEK(53272)AND15)OR0:REM SCREEN OF
FSET=0 SO SC=32768
2230 POKE648,128:REM TELL O/S WHERE SCR
2240 REM**NOW SETUP TO GET COLOR**
2250 POKE49872,0:REM BUFF START LO
2260 POKE49873,132:REM START BUFF HI
2270 POKE49874,0:REM END BUFF LO
2280 POKE49875,136:REM END BUFF HI
2290 POKE49876,0:REM COL RAM LO
2300 POKE49877,216:REM COL RAM HI
```

Listing continued next page

```
2310 POKE49878,0:REM COPY NOT SWAP
2320 SYS49879:REM COPY COL FROM BUFF
2330 PRINTCHR$(142)CHR$(154);
2340 RETURN
2350 REM**ROTATE SCREEN COL**
2360 POKE53281,(PEEK(53281)+1)AND15
2370 RETURN
2380 REM**ROTATE BORDER COL**
2390 POKE53280,(PEEK(53280)+1)AND15
2400 RETURN
2410 REM**DISPLAY MENU**
2420 PRINTCHR$(147):PRINTCHR$(156)CHR$(14)
2430 PRINTSPC(10)" &-IN 64 *CREEN "DITOR"
2440 PRINT:PRINTSPC(19)"BY"
2450 PRINT:PRINTSPC(14)"_IDGE *YSTEMS"CHR$(154)
2460 PRINT:PRINT:PRINT
2470 PRINTSPC(18)CHR$(18)"\ENU"CHR$(146)
2480 PRINT:PRINT:PRINT
2490 PRINTSPC(11)CHR$(18)"F1"CHR$(146)" -ALL THIS
PAGE."
2500 PRINTSPC(11)CHR$(18)"F2"CHR$(146)" _OTATE *CR
EEN -OLOR."
2510 PRINTSPC(11)CHR$(18)"F3"CHR$(146)" "DIT SCREE
N."
2520 PRINTSPC(11)CHR$(18)"F4"CHR$(146)" _OTATE !OR
DER -OLOR."
2530 PRINTSPC(11)CHR$(18)"F5"CHR$(146)" *AVE SCREE
N."
2540 PRINTSPC(11)CHR$(18)"F6"CHR$(146)" -ISK DIREC
TORY."
2550 PRINTSPC(11)CHR$(18)"F7"CHR$(146)" LOAD SCREE
N."
2560 PRINTSPC(11)CHR$(18)"F8"CHR$(146)" "ND PROGRA
M."
2570 RETURN
2580 REM*SAVE SCREEN*
2590 PRINTCHR$(147)CHR$(142)SPC(14)"&SAVE MODE":PR
INT
2600 GOSUB2900:IFEX=1THENEX=0:GOSUB2410:RETURN:REM
 NAME
2610 PRINT:PRINTSPC(11)"SAVING "+F$:PRINT
2620 POKE50128,0:REM SCR START LO
2630 POKE50129,128:REM SCR START HI
2640 POKE50130,0:REM END BUF LO
```

```
2650 POKE50131,136:REM END BUFF HI
2660 POKE50132,8:REM DEVICE NUMBER
2670 F$=F$:REM MAKE F$ CURRENT STR
2680 GOSUB3440:REM ERROR CHECK
2690 SYS50167:REM SAVE
2700 GOSUB3440:REM ERROR CHECK
2710 IFEN=0THENPRINTSPC(11)"SAVED "+F$
2720 PRINT:PRINTSPC(14)"F1 TO EXIT"
2730 GETCC$:IFCC$<>CHR$(133)THEN2730
2740 GOSUB2410
2750 RETURN
2760 REM*LOAD SCREEN*
2770 PRINTCHR$(147)CHR$(142)SPC(14)"LOAD MODE":PR
INT
2780 GOSUB2900:IFEX=1THENEX=0:GOSUB2410:RETURN:REM
 NAME
2790 PRINT:PRINTSPC(11)"LOADING "+F$:PRINT
2800 POKE49984,8:REM DEVICE NUMBER
2810 REM PRINT#15,"I0":REM INITIALISE DISK
2820 F$=F$:REM MAKE F$ CURRENT STR
2830 SYS50019:REM LOAD
2840 GOSUB3440:REM ERROR CHECK
2850 IFEN=0THENPRINTSPC(11)"LOADED "+F$
2860 PRINT:PRINTSPC(14)"F1 TO EXIT"
2870 GETCC$:IFCC$<>CHR$(133)THEN2870
2880 GOSUB2410
2890 RETURN
2900 REM*GET FILE NAME*
2910 PRINT"    "SPC(14)"F1 TO EXIT":PRINT
2920 PRINTSPC(6)" NAME LENGTH UP TO 14":PRINT
2930 PRINTSPC(6)" NAME?                "
2940 T$="":F$="":FORN=1TO14
2950 GETT$:IFT$=""THEN2950
2960 IFT$=CHR$(133)THENEX=1:RETURN
2970 IFT$=CHR$(13)THENN=14:GOTO3020
2980 IF(T$=CHR$(20)ANDN>1)THENN=N-2:F$=LEFT$(F$,N)
:PRINT"   ";:GOTO3020
2990 IFASC(T$)<32ORASC(T$)>127THEN2950
3000 F$=F$+T$
3010 PRINT"        "TAB(12)F$;
3020 NEXT:F$=F$+",S"
3030 PRINT:PRINT:PRINTSPC(14)"O.K. (Y/N)?"
3040 GETCC$:IFCC$<>"Y"ANDCC$<>"N"THEN3040
3050 IFCC$="N"THENPRINT"          "
```

Listing continued next page

```
                        " : GOTO2900
3060 RETURN
3070 REM*DIRECTORY*
3080 NN=0:PRINTCHR$(147)CHR$(142)SPC(14)"DIRECTOR
Y":PRINT
3090 PRINT#15,"I0":GOSUB3440:IFEN<>0THENGOSUB2410:
RETURN
3100 OPEN4,8,0,"$0"
3110 GET#4,AA$,BB$
3120 GET#4,AA$,BB$
3130 GET#4,AA$,BB$
3140 C1=0
3150 IFAA$<>""THENC1=ASC(AA$)
3160 IFBB$<>""THENC1=C1+ASC(BB$)*256
3170 PRINTSPC(10)CHR$(18)MID$(STR$(C1),2);TAB(13)C
HR$(146);
3180 GET#4,BB$:IFST<>0THEN3290
3190 IFBB$<>CHR$(34)THEN3180
3200 GET#4,BB$:IF BB$<>CHR$(34)THENPRINTBB$;:GOTO32
00
3210 GET#4,BB$:IFBB$=CHR$(32)THEN3210
3220 PRINTTAB(18);
3230 GET#4,BB$:IFBB$<>""THEN3230
3240 PRINT:NN=NN+1
3250 IFNN=19THENPRINT:PRINTSPC(12)"SPACE TO CONT
INUE";
3260 IFNN=19THENGETCC$:IFCC$<>CHR$(32)THEN3260
3270 IFNN=19THENPRINTCHR$(147)SPC(14)"DIRECTORY":
PRINT:NN=0
3280 IFST=0THEN3120
3290 PRINT" BLOCKS FREE"
3300 CLOSE4
3310 PRINT:PRINTSPC(14)"F1 TO EXIT";
3320 GETCC$:IFCC$<>CHR$(133)THEN3320
3330 GOSUB2410
3340 RETURN
3350 REM**TERMINATE**
3360 POKE53272,21:REM NORMALISE SC/CM
3370 POKE53280,14:REM NORMALISE BDR COL
3380 POKE53281,6:REM NORMALISE BACKGRD COL
3390 PRINTCHR$(147)CHR$(154)
3400 POKE55,0:POKE56,160:POKE51,0:POKE52,160:CLR:R
EM RESET MEMTOP
3410 CLOSE15
```

```
3420 POKE788,49:REM ENABLE STOP KEY
3430 END
3440 REM*ERROR CHANNEL**
3450 INPUT#15,EN,EM$,ET,ES
3460 IFEN=0THENRETURN
3470 SB=PEEK(53281)AND15
3480 POKE53281,1
3490 PRINT:PRINTSPC(14)"※※DISK ERROR※"
3500 PRINT:PRINTSPC(8)EM$:PRINT
3510 PRINTSPC(10)" ERROR NO"EN
3520 PRINTSPC(10)" TRACK"ET
3530 PRINTSPC(10)" SECTOR"ES
3540 PRINTSPC(11)"※SPACE※ TO CONTINUE"
3550 GETCC$:IFCC$<>CHR$(32)THEN3550
3560 POKE53281,SB:REM RESTORE SCR COL
3570 RETURN
3580 REM***M/C RAM SWAP OR COPY****
3590 REM** 49872 START ADDRESS LO**
3600 REM** 49873 START ADDRESS HI**
3610 REM** 49874 END   ADDRESS LO**
3620 REM** 49875 END   ADDRESS HI**
3630 REM** 49876 TO    ADDRESS LO**
3640 REM** 49877 TO    ADDRESS HI**
3650 REM** 49878 SWAP=1/COPY=0   **
3660 REM** TO USE POKE VALS THEN **
3670 REM**       SYS49879        **
3680 REM***************************
3690 DATA173,210,194,205,208,194,173
3700 DATA211,194,237,209,194,144,80,173
3710 DATA208,194,133,251,173,209,194
3720 DATA133,252,173,212,194,133,253
3730 DATA173,213,194,133,254,173,210
3740 DATA194,133,247,173,211,194,133
3750 DATA248,173,214,194,133,249,160,0
3760 DATA177,251,166,249,240,8,133,250
3770 DATA177,253,145,251,165,250,145
3780 DATA253,230,251,208,2,230,252,230
3790 DATA253,208,2,230,254,165,252,197
3800 DATA248,208,222,165,247,197,251,48
3810 DATA3,76,10,195,96
3820 DATA17560:REM*CHECKSUM*
3830 CC=0
3840 FORI=49879TO49973
3850 READX:CC=CC+X:POKEI,X
```

Listing continued next page

```
3860 NEXT
3870 READX:IFX<>CCTHENPRINT"CHECKSUM ERROR IN M/C
COPY":END
3880 PRINT"LOADED COPY OK"
3890 RETURN
3900 REM***** M/C LOAD ROUTINE ******
3910 REM** POKE49984,DEVICE NUMBER **
3920 REM** MOST RECENT STRING VAR  **
3930 REM** IS TAKEN TO BE FILE NAME**
3940 REM** E.G.-   A$="FILENAME"    **
3950 REM**THEN -   SYS50019         **
3960 REM*****************************
3970 DATA70,73,76,69,78,65,77,69,32,83
3980 DATA84,82,73,78,71,32,68,79,69,83
3990 DATA32,78,79,84,32,69,88,73,83,84
4000 DATA0,160,0,165,45,166,46,134,96
4010 DATA133,95,228,72,208,4,197,71,240
4020 DATA24,165,69,209,95,208,8,165,70
4030 DATA200,209,95,240,21,136,165,95
4040 DATA24,105,7,144,225,232,208,220
4050 DATA169,68,160,195,32,30,171,76
4060 DATA200,195,200,177,95,141,65,195
4070 DATA200,177,95,141,66,195,200,177
4080 DATA95,141,67,195,169,1,174,64,195
4090 DATA160,1,32,186,255,173,65,195
4100 DATA174,66,195,172,67,195,32,189
4110 DATA255,169,0,162,255,160,255,32
4120 DATA213,255,96
4130 DATA16042:REM*CHECKSUM*
4140 CC=0
4150 FORI=49988TO50120
4160 READX:CC=CC+X:POKEI,X
4170 NEXT
4180 READX:IFX<>CCTHENPRINT"CHECKSUM ERROR IN M/C
LOAD":END
4190 PRINT"LOADED LOAD OK"
4200 RETURN
4210 REM**** M/C SAVE ROUTINE *****
4220 REM** 50128 START ADDRESS LO**
4230 REM** 50129 START ADDRESS HI**
4240 REM** 50130 END   ADDRESS LO**
4250 REM** 50131 END   ADDRESS HI**
4260 REM** 50132 DEVICE NUMBER   **
4270 REM** MOST RECENT STRING VAR**
```

```
4280 REM** IS TAKEN AS FILENAME    **
4290 REM** E.G.- A$="FILENAME"      **
4300 REM**THEN - SYS50167           **
4310 REM****************************
4320 DATA70,73,76,69,78,65,77,69,32,83
4330 DATA84,82,73,78,71,32,68,79,69,83
4340 DATA32,78,79,84,32,69,88,73,83,84
4350 DATA0,160,0,165,45,166,46,134,96
4360 DATA133,95,228,72,208,4,197,71,240
4370 DATA24,165,69,209,95,208,8,165,70
4380 DATA200,209,95,240,21,136,165,95
4390 DATA24,105,7,144,225,232,208,220
4400 DATA169,216,160,195,32,30,171,76
4410 DATA104,196,200,177,95,141,213,195
4420 DATA200,177,95,141,214,195,200,177
4430 DATA95,141,215,195,173,208,195,133
4440 DATA251,173,209,195,133,252,169,1
4450 DATA174,212,195,160,1,32,186,255
4460 DATA173,213,195,174,214,195,172
4470 DATA215,195,32,189,255,169,251,174
4480 DATA210,195,172,211,195,32,216,255
4490 DATA96
4500 DATA19632:REM*CHECKSUM*
4510 CC=0
4520 FORI=50136TO50280
4530 READX:CC=CC+X:POKEI,X
4540 NEXT
4550 READX:IFX<>CCTHENPRINT"CHECKSUM ERROR IN SAVE
":END
4560 PRINT"LOADED SAVE OK"
4570 RETURN
```

MULTICOLOR MODE

In Multicolor mode it becomes possible to have four colors within a single character cell as opposed to two. There is a price to be paid, in that horizontal resolution is now in pairs of pixel dots rather than single pixels. Multicolor mode can be used in hi- or lo-resolution graphics, although the dot colors are determined slightly differently in Multicolor, hi-resolution graphics

Let us first design a character:

Row	Decimal value	Bit 7 6 5 4 3 2 1 0	Color 7–6	5–4	3–2	1–0
0	255	1 1 1 1 1 1 1 1	C	C	C	C
1	126	0 1 1 1 1 1 1 0	1	C	C	2
2	126	0 1 1 1 1 1 1 0	1	C	C	2
3	90	0 1 0 1 1 0 1 0	1	1	2	2
4	90	0 1 0 1 1 0 1 0	1	1	2	2
5	66	0 1 0 0 0 0 1 0	1	S	S	2
6	66	0 1 0 0 0 0 1 0	1	S	S	2
7	0	0 0 0 0 0 0 0 0	S	S	S	S

Each pair of pixel dots now becomes a single wide dot whose color is determined as follows:

Bit pattern	Color		Determined by
0 0	Screen background	(S)	53281 ($D021) Bits 0–4
0 1	Multicolor #1	(1)	53282 ($D022) Bits 0–4
1 0	Multicolor #2	(2)	53283 ($D023) Bits 0–4
1 1	Cursor color	(C)	Bits 0–3 of color RAM cell

```
POKE53270,PEEK(53270)OR16        Turns Multicolor ON.
POKE53270,PEEK(53270)AND239      Turns Multicolor OFF.
```

When Multicolor is on, if bit 4 of the associated color nybble is 1 the character is interpreted in Multicolor mode, with the lower three bits determining the color. Thus characters whose associated color nybbles lie in the range 0–7 are displayed normally. If the color code lies in the range 8–15 then the character will be displayed in Multicolor. This makes it possible to mix normal and Multicolor characters on the screen at the same time. Moreover by flipping the contents of addresses 53282 and 53283 we can instantaneously change every associated Multicolor pixel pair.

The following program demonstrates the Multicolor mode on the standard characters. You may observe that with standard characters the effects are rather unsatisfactory. This is because these characters were not designed with Multicolor mode in mind. The results are much more interesting if you use a combination of Multicolor mode and user-defined characters.

```
1000 REM**  MULTICOLOR DEMO  **
1010 REM**WITH STANDARD CHARS**
1020 REM**********************
1030 PRINTCHR$(147)SPC(10)"MULTICOLOR DEMO"
1040 PRINT:PRINT:CC=14:REM STANDARD CURSOR COLOR
1050 PRINT"HERE IS THE STANDARD ALPHABET:- "
1060 GOSUB1220:PRINT:PRINT
```

```
1070 PRINTSPC(4)"{F1} ROTATE SCREEN BACKGROUND COL
OR"
1080 PRINTSPC(4)"{F2} TOGGLE MULTICOLOR MODE ON/OF
F"
1090 PRINTSPC(4)"{F3} ROTATE CURSOR COLOR"
1100 PRINTSPC(4)"{F5} ROTATE MULTICOLOR #1"
1110 PRINTSPC(4)"{F7} ROTATE MULTICOLOR #2"
1120 REM**MAIN LOOP**
1130 GETA$:IFA$=""THEN1130
1140 IFA$=CHR$(133)THENGOSUB1270:REM SCREEN COLOR
1150 IFA$=CHR$(137)THENGOSUB1300:REM TOGGLE MULTIC
OLOR MODE
1160 IFA$=CHR$(134)THENGOSUB1350:REM ROTATE CURSOR
 COLOR
1170 IFA$=CHR$(135)THENGOSUB1380:REM ROTATE MULTIC
OL #1
1180 IFA$=CHR$(136)THENGOSUB1410:REM ROTATE MULTIC
OL #2
1190 GOSUB1220:REM REDISPLAY
1200 GOTO1120
1210 END
1220 REM**DISPLAY ALPHABET**
1230 POKE646,CC:REM SET CURSOR COL
1240 PRINTCHR$(19)"{reverse chars}";
1250 FORI=65TO90:PRINTCHR$(I);:NEXT
1260 RETURN
1270 REM**ROTATE SCREEN COLOR**
1280 POKE53281,(PEEK(53281)+1)AND15
1290 RETURN
1300 REM**TOGGLE MULTICOLOR MODE**
1310 BIT=(PEEK(53270)AND16)/16
1320 IFBIT=0THENPOKE53270,PEEK(53270)OR16:REM MULT
ICOLOR ON
1330 IFBIT=1THENPOKE53270,PEEK(53270)AND239:REM MU
LTICOL OFF
1340 RETURN
1350 REM**ROTATE CURSOR COLOR CC**
1360 CC=(CC+1)AND15:POKE646,CC
1370 RETURN
1380 REM**ROTATE MULTICOLOR #1**
1390 POKE53282,(PEEK(53282)+1)AND15
1400 RETURN
1410 REM**ROTATE MULTICOLOR #2**
1420 POKE53283,(PEEK(53283)+1)AND15
1430 RETURN
```

EXTENDED COLOR MODE

This mode gives the programmer control over the background color of the first 64 characters in the character matrix. The same character can appear on the screen with up to four different background colors, one of which is the screen background color. The remaining characters cannot be displayed in Extended color mode since bits 6 and 7 of the screen code are used to indirectly control the background color of the character. For example, the screen code for 'A' is 1 and that of a reverse field 'A' is 65. However, if we POKEd 65 to the screen in Extended color mode we should see not a reverse field 'A' but a normal 'A' with a background color determined by the contents of address 53282 ($D022). Similarly POKEing 129 to the screen would produce a normal 'A' but with a background color determined by the contents of address 53283 ($D023).

Extended color mode cannot be used in conjunction with Multicolor mode.

```
POKE53265,PEEK(53265)OR64      Turns Extended color mode ON.
POKE53265,PEEK(53265)AND191    Turns Extended color mode OFF.
```

The screen codes and color registers are related as follows:

Screen code	Bit 7	Bit 6	Background color register
0 − 63	0	0	53281 ($D021) − Screen background
64 − 127	0	1	53282 ($D022) − Extended col #1
128 − 191	1	0	53283 ($D023) − Extended col #2
192 − 255	1	1	53284 ($D024) − Extended col #3

The following program demonstrates Extended color mode.

```
1000 REM**EXTENDED COLOR DEMO**
1010 REM**WITH STANDARD CHARS**
1020 REM************************
1030 PRINTCHR$(147)SPC(5)"EXTENDED BACKGROUND COLO
R DEMO"
1040 PRINT
1050 CC=14:REM STANDARD CURSOR COLOR
1060 SC=1024:CO=55296:REM SCR/COL BASE
1070 A=3+4*40:B=A+40:C=B+40:D=C+40:REM DISPLAY OFF
SETS
1080 PRINT"HERE IS THE STANDARD ALPHABET:- "
1090 GOSUB1270:REM DISPLAY 4 ALPHABETS
1100 PRINT:PRINT:PRINT:PRINT:PRINT:PRINT
1110 PRINTSPC(4)"#F1# TOGGLE BACKGROUND COLOR MODE
"
1120 PRINTSPC(4)"#F2# ROTATE CURSOR COLOR"
1130 PRINTSPC(4)"#F3# ROTATE SCREEN BACKGROUND COL
OR"
1140 PRINTSPC(4)"#F4# ROTATE COLOR #1"
```

```
1150 PRINTSPC(4)"⬛F5⬛ ROTATE COLOR #2"
1160 PRINTSPC(4)"⬛F7⬛ ROTATE COLOR #3"
1170 REM**MAIN LOOP**
1180 GETA$:IFA$=""THEN1180
1190 IFA$=CHR$(133)THENGOSUB1350:REM TOGGLE MODE
1200 IFA$=CHR$(137)THENGOSUB1430:REM ROTATE CURSOR
  COL
1210 IFA$=CHR$(134)THENGOSUB1400:REM ROTATE SCREEN
  COL
1220 IFA$=CHR$(138)THENGOSUB1460:REM ROTATE COL #1
1230 IFA$=CHR$(135)THENGOSUB1490:REM ROTATE COL #2
1240 IFA$=CHR$(136)THENGOSUB1520:REM ROTATE COL #3
1250 GOTO1170
1260 END
1270 REM**DISPLAY ALPHABETS**
1280 FORI=1TO26
1290 POKESC+A+I,I:POKESC+B+I,I+64
1300 POKECO+A+I,CC:POKECO+B+I,CC
1310 POKESC+C+I,I+128:POKESC+D+I,I+192
1320 POKECO+C+I,CC:POKECO+D+I,CC
1330 NEXT
1340 RETURN
1350 REM**TOGGLE EXTENDED COL MODE**
1360 BIT=(PEEK(53265)AND64)/64
1370 IFBIT=0THENPOKE53265,PEEK(53265)OR64:REM EXTE
N BCKGRND COL ON
1380 IFBIT=1THENPOKE53265,PEEK(53265)AND191:REM EX
TEN BCKGRND COL OFF
1390 RETURN
1400 REM**ROTATE SCREEN COLOR**
1410 POKE53281,(PEEK(53281)+1)AND15
1420 RETURN
1430 REM**ROTATE CURSOR COLOR CC**
1440 CC=(CC+1)AND15:GOSUB1270
1450 RETURN
1460 REM**ROTATE MULTICOLOR #1**
1470 POKE53282,(PEEK(53282)+1)AND15
1480 RETURN
1490 REM**ROTATE MULTICOLOR #2**
1500 POKE53283,(PEEK(53283)+1)AND15
1510 RETURN
1520 REM**ROTATE MULTICOLOR #3**
1530 POKE53284,(PEEK(53284)+1)AND15
1540 RETURN
```

HI-RESOLUTION GRAPHICS

In hi-resolution graphics the object is to have a fixed area on the screen within which every pixel dot may be addressed independently. With user-defined graphics the characters are initially written into the RAM character matrix and subsequently moved about the screen as if they were normal characters. After the character matrix is generated it is normally left severely alone. With hi-resolution graphics exactly the reverse procedure is employed. A part, or the whole, of the character matrix memory is assigned 'positions' on the display, this is known as 'bit-mapping' the display. Pixel dots are then moved about the display by directly addressing the corresponding bit in the character matrix. Hence in hi-resolution graphics it is the contents of the character matrix memory which varies.

How is bit-mapping accomplished? One way to bit-map a quarter of the screen would be to POKE the screen codes 0–255 into specific screen memory locations, essentially producing hi-resolution graphics from programmable characters. If fewer codes were used there would be some left over which we could use for normal characters. In fact this is the way that bit-mapping worked on the VIC-20. On the CBM 64 the VIC-II chip provides us with a Hi-resolution Bit-map Mode. The effect of this is to display the contents of an entire 8K RAM character matrix on the whole of the CBM 64 screen.

POKE53265,PEEK(53265)OR32   To turn Bit-mapped mode ON.
POKE53265,PEEK(53265)AND223   To turn Bit-mapped mode OFF.

Before entering bit-map mode it is necessary to move to a RAM-based character matrix (using the method explained earlier) but it would be pointless to copy down a character set since the character matrix is going to be used for pixel dot data. By moving the base of the VIC-II window and setting the character matrix offset from the base of the window we can place the RAM character matrix, subject to limitations already covered, anywhere in memory. In the sample program given below the default VIC-II window has been used and the character matrix placed at 8192. If the character matrix is placed in the user BASIC program area the top of memory should be lowered to protect the pixel data.

When bit-map mode is entered an 8K character matrix is displayed as a 200 vertical by 320 horizontal set of pixel dots, each dot corresponding to a binary 0 or 1; a 1 if a dot is present and a 0 if it is absent. It is as if 'screen codes' from 0 to 999 were being displayed simultaneously in consecutive 'screen cells'. The 8×8 character cell corrresponding to 'screen code' zero is located in the top left corner of the display, and so on.

In fact each byte of the true screen memory is used to control the color of the corresponding 8×8 cell in the display. The top 4 bits of a byte in screen memory control the color of any pixel dot set to a 1, the lower 4 bits control the color of any dot set to 0. This means that on exiting bit-map mode the original screen display is not still present, the character codes have been replaced by hi-resolution color information.

Having bit-mapped the display the next problem is: given the screen coordinates of a pixel dot how can we set the corrresponding bit in the character matrix to a 1 and thereby plot the dot on the display?

The solution to this problem is summarized in Fig. 5.1. Here X,Y are the pixel dot coordinates on the hi-resolution display ($0<=X<=319$, $0<=Y<=199$). We first work out which 8×8 cell the dot lies in, say row U, column V where $0<=U<=24$ and $0<=V<=39$ (these are like screen cell coordinates only they are not really). Having found the right cell we can locate it in memory at address $CM+(40*U+V)*8$, where CM is the start of the 8K character matrix. This is because it is the $40*U+V$ th cell from the start of the display and each cell takes 8 bytes of memory. Now we need to know the row and column R,C of the pixel within the cell. The row R gives us the address of the right byte and C tells us which bit of the byte we have to change.

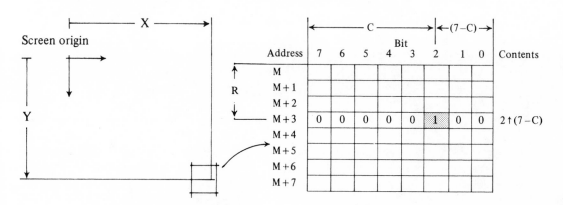

X,Y – pixel dot coordinates
$0 \leqslant X \leqslant 40*8-1 = 319$
$0 \leqslant Y \leqslant 25*8-1 = 199$
$U = INT(Y/8): V = INT(X/8)$
CM = character matrix start address.
$M = CM + (40*U+V)*8$: Address of first byte of character in character matrix.
$R = YAND7$: REM REMAINDER AFTER DIVISION BY 8
$C = XAND7$: REM REMAINDER AFTER DIVISION BY 8
Address of byte is $M+R$
To set the correct bit of this byte without disturbing any other bit.
POKE $M+R$, $(2\uparrow(7-C))$ OR PEEK$(M+R)$

U,V character cell row, column
pixel dot row, column within character cell

Fig. 5.1 – Which bit is the pixel dot.?

The following program illustrates the whole process.

```
1000 REM*************64HIRES***************
1010 REM********PLOT A SPIRAL**********
1020 REM
1030 REM FIRST SET UP HANDY ARRAY
1040 POKE56,32:CLR:REM LOWER MEMTOP
1050 FORI=0TO7:C%(I)=2↑(7-I):NEXT
1060 POKE53272,(PEEK(53272)AND240)OR8:REM CM AT 81
92
1070 CM=8192:SC=1024:REM SCREEN MEM ACTS AS COLOR
MEM IN HI-RES
```
Listing continued next page

```
1080 POKE53265,PEEK(53265)OR32:REM BITMAP MODE ON
1090 FORI=CMTOCM+7999:POKEI,0:NEXT:REM CLR CHAR MA
TRIX
1100 PC=2:REM RED PIXELS
1110 BC=1:REM WHITE BACKGROUND
1120 C=64*PC+BC
1130 FORI=SCTOSC+1023:POKEI,C:NEXT:REM PIXEL COL T
O CYAN/RED
1140 REM**PLOT AXES
1150 Y=99:FORX=0TO319:GOSUB1280:NEXT
1160 X=159:FORY=0TO199:GOSUB1280:NEXT
1170 REM**DRAW SPIRAL
1180 FORA=0TO10*πSTEPπ/80
1190 X=159+INT(90*EXP(-A/10)*COS(A+π/2))
1200 Y=99+INT(90*EXP(-A/10)*SIN(A+π/2))
1210 GOSUB1280
1220 NEXT
1230 GETA$:IFA$=""THEN1230
1240 POKE53272,(PEEK(53272)AND240)OR4:REM RESTORE
CM
1250 POKE53265,PEEK(53265)AND223:REM BITMAP MODE O
FF
1260 POKE56,160:CLR:REM RESET MEMTOP
1270 PRINTCHR$(147):END
1280 REM**PLOTSUB**
1290 U=INT(Y/8):V=INT(X/8)
1300 M=CM+(40*U+V)*8
1310 R=YAND7:C=XAND7
1320 POKEM+R,C%(C)ORPEEK(M+R)
1330 RETURN
```

Obviously one technique for generating hi-resolution screens is to write the mathematical routines to draw the picture, after all it is hardly practicable to draw in up to 64000 pixel dots one at a time! An even better way to create hi-resolution screens would be to point a video camera at something and digitalize the image. This need not be as expensive or as complicated as it sounds. Systems which do exactly this are available at very modest cost. You can give your CBM 64 hi-resolution vision for well under $1000. Fig. 5.2 is an example of what such a system can do. It is a hi-resolution digitalized image of one of the authors.

Fig. 5.2 – Antonia. Courtesy of Digithurst, Royston.

SPLIT SCREEN GRAPHICS AND INTERRUPTS

Interrupts occur when, in response to some predefined signal, a microprocessor ceases execution of its current program, stores such information as will be required to resume the program at a later time, and begins execution of another program at a previously defined address. The 6510 is capable of responding to a number of different types of interrupt. The signal which triggers an interrupt is simply one of the 6510 control lines being pulled high or low. There are two of these lines of particular interest to the machine language programmer: the NMI (Non-maskable interrupt) line and the IRQ (Interrupt request) line. Both are discussed in the chapters on machine code but one is of particular interest to us at present, namely the IRQ line.

There are several ways that an IRQ to the 6510 can be triggered. One is as follows. Within the VIC-II chip there is an interrupt flag register: register 25 at address 53273 ($D019). Bits in this register are set to 1 by VIC-II if certain events occur, for example if two sprites collide. There is another register, an interrupt enable register (number 26), which acts as a switch to the 6510 IRQ line. If corresponding bits in this register are set by the programmer then bits set in the interrupt flag register will trigger a 6510 IRQ.

We can arrange that one of the events which will trigger a 6510 IRQ is if the raster scan line count is equal to a predefined value. In this way we can change the display mode at any predetermined raster line. A routine which did this would have the following structure.

(1) Was the IRQ caused by the VIC-II chip? If not continue with normal IRQ. Was the VIC-II interrupt triggered by the raster flag? If not return from interrupt, or otherwise deal with it.
(2) On entering the raster interrupt code check if at the top, or half-way down the screen. Jump to (i), or (ii) accordingly.
  (i) Set up the next raster interrupt to occur halfway down the screen. Change mode to hi-resolution for top half. Return from interrupt.
  (ii) Set up the next raster interrupt to occur at the top of the screen. Change mode to lo-resolution for bottom half. Return from interrupt.

In this way we can arrange that the top half of the screen is displayed in bit-map mode (screen RAM as color codes) and the bottom half in normal lo-resolution mode (screen RAM as screen codes). To prevent screen flicker it is necessary to ensure that the interrupts occur at times when the raster beam is not on visible parts of the display.

A simpler way to get a small part of the screen to act as a hi-resolution window is to use programmable characters, as explained earlier, or sprites.

THE VIC-II CONTROL REGISTERS

There are 47 eight-bit registers on the VIC-II chip which control the screen display. These registers are shown in Table 5.6, and they are located between addresses 53248 and 54271 ($D000 – $D3FF). Many of these have been covered earlier in this chapter, those concerning sprites are covered in Chapter 6.

Register descriptions
Register No. 00,01 Address 53248,53249 $D000,$D001
  Function: Sprite 0 Position

These registers contain, respectively, the X and Y pixel co-ordinates of the position of sprite 0 ($0<=X<=319, 0<=Y<=199$). However, a single byte can only contain a value up to 255, and while this is sufficient for the Y co-ordinate it is not enough for the X co-ordinate. If each byte contained 9 bits instead of 8 there would be no problem, so to make up for this the lowest 8 bits of the 9-bit value are stored here and the 9th bit is in Register 16.

The next 14 registers serve the same purpose for the other seven sprites, but for ease of reference we will list them all.

Register No. 02,03 Address 53250,53251 $D002,$D003
  Function: Sprite 1 Position

Register No. 04,05 Address 52252,53253 $D004,$D005
  Function: Sprite 2 Position

Table 5.6 — The VIC-II control registers.

ADDRESS	DB7	DB6	DB5	DB4	DB3	DB2	DB1	DB0	DESCRIPTION
00 ($00)	M0X7	M0X6	M0X5	M0X4	M0X3	M0X2	M0X1	M0X0	MOB 0 X-position
01 ($01)	M0Y7	M0Y6	M0Y5	M0Y4	M0Y3	M0Y2	M0Y1	M0Y0	MOB 0 Y-position
02 ($02)	M1X7	M1X6	M1X5	M1X4	M1X3	M1X2	M1X1	M1X0	MOB 1 X-position
03 ($03)	M1Y7	M1Y6	M1Y5	M1Y4	M1Y3	M1Y2	M1Y1	M1Y0	MOB 1 Y-position
04 ($04)	M2X7	M2X6	M2X5	M2X4	M2X3	M2X2	M2X1	M2X0	MOB 2 X-position
05 ($05)	M2Y7	M2Y6	M2Y5	M2Y4	M2Y3	M2Y2	M2Y1	M2Y0	MOB 2 Y-position
06 ($06)	M3X7	M3X6	M3X5	M3X4	M3X3	M3X2	M3X1	M3X0	MOB 3 X-position
07 ($07)	M3Y7	M3Y6	M3Y5	M3Y4	M3Y3	M3Y2	M3Y1	M3Y0	MOB 3 Y-position
08 ($08)	M4X7	M4X6	M4X5	M4X4	M4X3	M4X2	M4X1	M4X0	MOB 4 X-position
09 ($09)	M4Y7	M4Y6	M4Y5	M4Y4	M4Y3	M4Y2	M4Y1	M4Y0	MOB 4 Y-position
10 ($0A)	M5X7	M5X6	M5X5	M5X4	M5X3	M5X2	M5X1	M5X0	MOB 5 X-position
11 ($0B)	M5Y7	M5Y6	M5Y5	M5Y4	M5Y3	M5Y2	M5Y1	M5Y0	MOB 5 Y-position
12 ($0C)	M6X7	M6X6	M6X5	M6X4	M6X3	M6X2	M6X1	M6X0	MOB 6 X-position
13 ($0D)	M6Y7	M6Y6	M6Y5	M6Y4	M6Y3	M6Y2	M6Y1	M6Y0	MOB 6 Y-position
14 ($0E)	M7X7	M7X6	M7X5	M7X4	M7X3	M7X2	M7X1	M7X0	MOB 7 X-position
15 ($0F)	M7Y7	M7Y6	M7Y5	M7Y4	M7Y3	M7Y2	M7Y1	M6Y0	MOB 7 Y-position
16 ($10)	M7X8	M6X8	M5X8	M4X8	M3X8	M2X8	M1X8	M0X8	MSB of X-position
17 ($11)	RC8	ECM	BMM	DEN	RSEL	Y2	Y1	Y0	See text
18 ($12)	RC7	RC6	RC5	RC4	RC3	RC2	RC1	RC0	Raster register
19 ($13)	LPX8	LPX7	LPX6	LPX5	LPX4	LPX3	LPX2	LPX1	Light Pen X
20 ($14)	LPY7	LPY6	LPY5	LPY4	LPY3	LPY2	LPY1	LPY0	Light Pen Y
21 ($15)	M7E	M6E	M5E	M4E	M3E	M2E	M1E	M0E	MOB Enable
22 ($16)	—	—	RES	MCM	CSEL	X2	X1	X0	See text
23 ($17)	M7YE	M6YE	M5YE	M4YE	M3YE	M2YE	M1YE	M0YE	MOB Y-expand
24 ($18)	VM13	VM12	VM11	VM10	CB13	CB12	CB11	—	Memory Pointers
25 ($19)	IRQ	—	—	—	ILP	IMMC	IMBC	IRST	Interrupt Register
26 ($1A)	—	—	—	—	ELP	EMMC	EMBC	ERST	Enable Interrupt
27 ($1B)	M7DP	M6DP	M5DP	M4DP	M3DP	M2DP	M1DP	M0DP	MOB-DATA Priority
28 ($1C)	M7MC	M6MC	M5MC	M4MC	M3MC	M2MC	M1MC	M0MC	MOB Multicolor Sel
29 ($1D)	M7XE	M6XE	M5XE	M4XE	M3XE	M2XE	M1XE	M0XE	MOB X-expand
30 ($1E)	M7M	M6M	M5M	M4M	M3M	M2M	M1M	M0M	MOB-MOB Collision
31 ($1F)	M7D	M6D	M5D	M4D	M3D	M2D	M1D	M0D	MOB-DATA Collision
32 ($20)	—	—	—	—	EC3	EC2	EC1	EC0	Exterior Color
33 ($21)	—	—	—	—	B0C3	B0C2	B0C1	B0C0	Bkgd #0 Color
34 ($22)	—	—	—	—	B1C3	B1C2	B1C1	B1C0	Bkgd #1 Color
35 ($23)	—	—	—	—	B2C3	B2C2	B2C1	B2C0	Bkgd #2 Color
36 ($24)	—	—	—	—	B3C3	B3C2	B3C1	B3C0	Bkgd #3 Color
37 ($25)	—	—	—	—	MM03	MM02	MM01	MM00	MOB Multicolor #0
38 ($26)	—	—	—	—	MM13	MM12	MM11	MM10	MOB Multicolor #1
39 ($27)	—	—	—	—	M0C3	M0C2	M0C1	M0C0	MOB 0 Color
40 ($28)	—	—	—	—	M1C3	M1C2	M1C1	M1C0	MOB 1 Color
41 ($29)	—	—	—	—	M2C3	M2C2	M2C1	M2C0	MOB 2 Color
42 ($2A)	—	—	—	—	M3C3	M3C2	M3C1	M3C0	MOB 3 Color
43 ($2B)	—	—	—	—	M4C3	M4C2	M4C1	M4C0	MOB 4 Color
44 ($2C)	—	—	—	—	M5C3	M5C2	M5C1	M5C0	MOB 5 Color
45 ($2D)	—	—	—	—	M6C3	M6C2	M6C1	M6C0	MOB 6 Color
46 ($2E)	—	—	—	—	M7C3	M7C2	M7C1	M7C0	MOB 7 Color

NOTE: A dash indicates a no connect. All no connects are read as a "1."

Register No. 06,07 Address 53254,53255 $D006,$D007
    Function: Sprite 3 Position

Register No. 08,09 Address 53256,53257 $D008,$D009
    Function: Sprite 4 Position

Register No. 10,11 Address 53258,53259 $D00A,$D00B
    Function: Sprite 5 Position

Register No. 12,13 Address 53260,53261 $D00C,$D00D
    Function: Sprite 6 Position

Register No. 14,15 Address 53262,53263 $D00E,$D00F
    Function: Sprite 7 Position

Register No. 16 Address 53264 $D010
    Function: Most Significant Bit X Co-ordinate

This register contains the additional 9th bit required to make up the value of the X co-ordinate of the 8 sprite positions. The bits are stored as follows:

        Bit 0 — Sprite 0
        Bit 1 — Sprite 1
        Bit 2 — Sprite 2
        Bit 3 — Sprite 3
        Bit 4 — Sprite 4
        Bit 5 — Sprite 5
        Bit 6 — Sprite 6
        Bit 7 — Sprite 7

Register No. 17 Address 53265 $D011
    Function: Control Register 1.

Various bits of this register control the display as follows:

Bits 0–2 – Y0,Y1,Y2
These bits control vertical scrolling when using a reduced screen height of 24 rows.

Bit 3 – RSEL
When this bit is set the height of the display screen is 25 rows, when cleared the height is reduced to 24 rows. In the latter mode smooth scrolling may be achieved in conjunction with bits 0–3 of this register.

Bit 4 – DEN
When the DEN bit is cleared the screen will blank, i.e. be filled with the border color. Whilst this seems fairly unexciting, screen blanking indirectly allows the 6510 processor to work more efficiently.

Bit 5 – BMM
When this bit is set the display changes from normal mode to bit-map mode. This feature is used to produce hi-resolution graphics.

Bit 6 — ECM
When the ECM bit is set the display is in Extended color mode. This allows each character to have one of sixteen foreground colors and one of four background colors. However, the character set is limited to only 64 characters.

Bit 7 — RC8
This bit is the 9th bit of the Raster Register (Register 18).

Register No. 18 Address 53266 $D012
   Function: Raster Register

This register has two functions. When read it gives bits 0–7 of the current raster scan position (bit 8 is in register 17). This is the actual spot on your TV screen that is being updated at that moment. When written to (including bit 8) the value input is stored and compared with the current raster position. When they are equal the raster interrupt bit is set in the interrupt register (Register 25), and if the interrupt is enabled will cause the video chip to interrupt the 6510.

Register No. 19,20 Address 53267,53268 $D013,$D014
   Function: Light Pen Co-ordinates

The registers give the X and Y pixel co-ordinates of the position of the light pen. Register 19 contains the X position and Register 20 the Y position. However, since 9 bits are needed to define all X co-ordinates on the screen, Register 19 contains the 8 most significant bits, which means that the X resolution is 2 horizontal dots. The Y register is accurate to one dot since a Y position can be defined in 8 bits.

Register No. 21 Address 53269 $D105
   Function: Sprite Enable

Each bit in this register determines whether a sprite is enabled (visible) or not. When a bit is set the sprite is enabled, when cleared it is disabled. Bits 0–7 control sprites 0–7 respectively.

Register No. 22 Address 53270 $D016
   Function: Control Register 2

Various bits of this register control the display as follows:

Bits 0–2 — X0,X1,X2
These bits control horizontal scrolling when using a reduced screen width of 38 columns.

Bit 3 — CSEL
When this bit is set, the width of the display screen is 40 columns; when cleared, the width is reduced to 38 columns. In the latter mode smooth scrolling may be achieved in conjunction with bits 0–3 of this register.

Bit 4 — MCM
When the MCM bit is set the display is in Multicolor mode. This allows each character to have two foreground colors and two background colors. However, horizontal character resolution is reduced.

Bit 5 – RES
This bit is normally set to one. If cleared, it is reputed to suspend all operations of the video chip; however the authors have been unable to achieve this effect.

Bit 6 and 7 –no connect
These bits are not connected, cannot be changed and will always read '1'.

Register No. 23 Address 53271 $D017;
    Function: Sprite Y – expand;

Each bit in this register determines whether a sprite is expanded in the vertical direction or not. When a bit is set the sprite is expanded, when cleared the sprite is normal size. Bits 0–7 control sprites 0–7 respectively.

Register No. 24 Address 53272 $D018
    Function: Memory pointers

Despite its rather drab title this is one of the most powerful registers for the graphics programmer, since it is this register which allows us to change the location of the video matrix and character memory.

Bit 0 – no connect

Bits 1–3 – CB11,CB12,CB13
These bits are bits 11 to 13 of the address of the character memory of the CBM 64.

Bits 4–7 – VM10,VM11,VM12,VM13
These bits are bits 10 to 13 of the address of the video matrix of the CBM 64.

Register No. 25 Address 53273 $D019
    Function: Interrupt Flag Register

There are four possible sources of an interrupt generated by the 6566/9. When any of these events occur the appropriate bit in this register is set.

Bit 0 – IRST
When a value is written to the raster register it is latched and compared with the current raster value. When they are equal this bit in the interrupt flag register is set.

Bit 1 – IMDC
When a sprite collides with a non-sprite character this bit is set.

Bit 2 – IMMC
When a sprite collides with another sprite this bit is set.

Bit 3 – ILP
This bit is set when the LP line to the video chip goes low. This will occur at the end of every frame. Note this line is also connected to joystick button B.

Bits 4–6 – no connect

Bit 7 – IRQ to 6510
When any bits 0–3 are set in this register, and their corresponding bits in the Interrupt Enable

Register (Register 26) is also set then the IRQ bit will be set to 1. When VIC-II pulls the IRQ line high, an interrupt to the 6510' is generated. An interrupt bit of the flag register will remain set until a '1' (really, a *one* not a zero) is written to that bit, at which point further interrupts may be received from that source.

Register No. 26 Address 53274 $D01A
     Function: Interrupt Enable Register

When an interrupt occurs, from one of the sources mentioned above, a bit is set in the Interrupt Flag Register. If the corresponding bit in this register is also set then the IRQ bit in register 25 will be set, and the VIC-II chip will interrupt the 6510 processor. The bits are as follows

Bit 0 – ERST
This bit enables interrupts from the raster scan as described above.

Bit 1 – EMDC
This bit enables interrupts caused by sprite data collisions.

Bit 2 – EMMC
This bit enables interrupts caused by sprite/data collisions.

Bit 3 – ELP
This bit enables interrupts from the LP line of the 6566/7.

Bits 4–7 – no connect

Register No. 27 Address 53275; $D01B
     Function: Sprite/Data Priority Register

Each bit in this register determines whether a sprite appears in front of or behind text and other data on the screen. When a bit is set the sprite appears behind the data, when cleared the sprite appears in front. Bits 0–7 control sprites 0–7 respectively.

Register No. 28 Address 53276 $D01C
     Function: Sprite Multicolor Select

Each bit in this register determines whether a sprite is displayed in normal or Multicolor mode. When a bit is set the sprite is in Multicolor mode, when cleared the sprite is displayed in normal mode. Bits 0–7 control sprites 0–7 respectively.

Register No. 29 Address 53277 $D01D
     Function: Sprite X – Expand

Each bit in this register determines whether a sprite is expanded in the horizontal direction or not. When a bit is set the sprite is expanded, when cleared the sprite is normal size. Bits 0–7 control sprites 0–7 respectively.

Register No. 30 Address 53278 $D01E
     Function: Sprite/Sprite Collision

Each bit in this register determines whether a sprite has collided with another. When a sprite collides with another sprite the corresponding bit is set in this register. Thus when a collision occurs there will be at least two bits set, from which we may deduce which sprites have collided. Bits 0–7 describe sprites 0–7 respectively.

Having been checked a bit can be cleared (set to zero) in this register by writing a '1' to it.

Register No. 31 Address 53279 $D01F
Function: Sprite/Data Collision

Each bit in this register determines whether a sprite has collided with screen data the corresponding bit is set in this register. Thus when a collision occurs the contents of this register indicate which sprite or sprites have collided with data. Having been checked a bit can be cleared (set to zero) by writing a '1' to it. Bits 0–7 describe sprites 0–7 respectively.

Register No. 32 Address 53280 $D020
Function: Border color

Bits 0–3 – These four bits form a value which represents the color of the screen border.

Bits 4–7 no connect.

Register No. 33 Address 53281 $D021
Function: Background Color No. 1

Bits 0–3 – These four bits form a value which represents the screen background color.

Bits 4–7 – no connect.

Register No. 34 Address 53282 $D022
Function: Background Color No. 2

Bits 0–3 – These four bits form a value which represents Extended color #1 or Multicolor #1.

Bits 4–7 – no connect.

Register No. 35 Address 53283; $D023
Function: Background Color No. 3

Bits 0–3 – These four bits form a value which represents Extended color #2 or Multicolor #2.

Bits 4–7 – no connect.

Register No. 36 Address 53284; $D024
Function: Background Color No. 4

Bits 0–3 – These four bits form a value which represents Extended color #3.

Bits 4–7 – no connect.

Register No. 37 Address 53285; $D025
Function: Sprite Multicolor #1

Bits 0–3 – These four bits form a value which represents the color of Sprite Multicolor #1.

Bits 4–7 – no connect.

Register No. 38 Address 53286; $D026
    Function: Sprite Multicolor #2

Bits 0–3 – These four bits form a value which represents the color of Sprite Multicolor No. 2.

Bits 4–7 – no connect.

Register No. 39 Address 53287; $D027
    Function: Sprite 0 Color

Bits 0–3 – These four bits form a value which represents the color of Sprite No. 0.

Bits 4–7 – no connect.

Register No. 40 Address 53288; $D028
    Function: Sprite 1 Color

Bits 0–3 – These four bits form a value which represents the color of Sprite No. 1.

Bits 4–7 – no connect.

Register No. 41 Address 53289; $D029
    Function: Sprite 2 Color

Bits 0–3 – These four bits form a value which represents the color of Sprite No. 2.

Bits 4–7 – no connect.

Register No. 42 Address 53290; $D02A
    Function: Sprite 3 Color

Bits 0–3 – These four bits form a value which represents the color of Sprite No. 3.

Bits 4–7 – no connect.

Register No. 43 Address 53291; $D02B
    Function: Sprite 4 Color

Bits 0–3 – These four bits form a value which represents the color of Sprite No. 4.

Bits 4–7 – no connect.

Register No. 44 Address 53292; $D02C
    Function: Sprite 5 Color

Bits 0–3 – These four bits form a value which represents the color of Sprite No. 5.

Bits 4–7 – no connect.

Register No. 45 Address 53293; $D02D
    Function: Sprite 6 Color.

Bits 0–3 — These four bits form a value which represents the color of Sprite No. 6.

Bits 4–7 — no connect.

Register No. 46 Address 53294; $D02E
        Function: Sprite 7 Color

Bits 0–3 — These four bits form a value which represents the color of Sprite No. 7.

Bits 4–7 — no connect.

6

Animation and sprites

INTRODUCTION

An attractive feature of the Commodore 64 is the capability of the VIC-II chip to simultaneously display up to eight independent high resolution 'mini-screens'. Originally termed Mobile Object Blocks (MOBs), these 'mini-screens' were eventually renamed Sprites.

Sprites measure 21 pixels vertically by 24 horizontally. This the data for one sprite occupies $21*3=63$ bytes. Pointers for each sprite are located at the end of the screen memory. These pointers tell the VIC-II chip where in its current 16K window it can find the 63 bytes of sprite data for each sprite.

Each sprite can be moved around the display screen very easily; although it must be said that this movement is rather slow from BASIC. We can also expand or contract sprites by a factor of 2 and detect collisions between sprites or between sprites and objects displayed on the screen. Thus the provision of sprites make the CBM 64 a highly versatile games machine.

Needless to say all this screen activity cannot take place without considerable programming effort. In this chapter we shall describe the step-by-step process of first getting a correctly drawn sprite displayed on the screen and then making it do what you want.

To help you on the way there is the 'SPRITE EDITOR' program. A 'Sprite Editor' is a program which takes the hassle out of designing sprites. A normal low resolution display is used to create an enlarged image of the sprite within which each character cell represents a single pixel dot in the sprite. The cursor moves about the enlarged image using the normal cursor controls, bits in the sprite memory can be set or cleared accordingly. When the sprite is designed to our satisfaction the bytes of the sprite data are printed up for our inspection. This program allows you to design up to 8 sprites at one time. The program 'DATASTATE' can then be used to create a program consisting of data statements for the sprite data.

Animation is achieved either by moving sprites around the screen or by switching data pointers to 'instantaneously' replace one set of sprite data by another. This second technique is illustrated by the program 'HELLO HOUSE' (courtesy of Steve Colwill and the 'Groove Monitors'). Here a picture of a house is made to mouth the word 'Hello' using rapid substitution of sprites.

GETTING STARTED ON SPRITES

To create a sprite we have to POKE sixty-three bytes into the current VIC-II window and set a one-byte pointer to direct VIC-II to the sprite data. The sprite will then be nearly ready to display.

Example:

```
1000  REM****SPRITE DEMO*****
1010  PRINTCHR$(147):REM CLEAR SCREEN
1020  POKE56,48:CLR:REM LOWER MRMTOP
1030  VIC=53248:REM VIC BASE ADDRESS
1040  SB=12288:REM SPRITE DATA BASE
1050  POKE2040,INT(SB/64):REM DATA POINTER SPR 0
1060  REM***READ SPRITE DATA***
1070  FORI=SBTOSB+62:READA:POKE,A:NEXT
1080  REM***COLOR SPRITE BLACK***
1090  POKEVIC+39,0
1100  REM***POSITION SPRITE******
1110  POKEVIC,100:REM X COORD LO
1120  POKEVIC+1,100:REM Y COORD
1130  REM***TURN ON SPRITE*******
1140  POKEVICI+21,1:REM ENABLE SPRITE
1150  REM***WAIT FOR KEYPRESS****
1160  GETA$:IFA$=" " THEN 1160
1170  REM***TERMINATE************
1180  POKEVIC+21,0:REM DISABLE SPRITE
1190  POKE56,160:CLR:REM RESET MEMTOP
1200  END
1210  REM***SPRITE DATA**********
1220  DATA255,0,255,0,254,0,127,252,0,63
1230  DATA240,0,15,232,0,23,228,0,39
1240  DATA194,0,67,129,24,129,0,189,0
1250  DATA0,102,0
1260  DATA0,102,0
1270  DATA0,102,0
1280  DATA0,189,0,129,24,129,194,0,67
1290  DATA228,0,39,232,0,23,240,0,15
1300  DATA252,0,63,254,0,127,255,0,255
```

As you can see the data pointer is set in multiples of 64 from the base of the VIC-II window. This example is using sprite 0 whose data pointer lives at 2040 plus the VIC-II window base address (which here takes its default value of zero). Another way to look at 2040 is that it is SC+1016, where SC is the base address of the currently displayed screen; if you are moving the screen about the sprite data pointers should go with it, so this second formula is really more appropriate. The sprite data base address is SB so that to set the pointer we POKE2040,INT(SB/64) in line 1050. Having READ in the sprite data it only remains to set its color and position before turning it on.

A SPRITE READY-RECKONER

In order to manipulate several sprites easily we need to systemize the information on sprites given in the description of the VIC-II registers at the end of the previous chapter. All the information is there, but in that form it is not really very useful. In the guide which follows:

VIC=53248
DB is base address for sprite data
PIC is any data block (0<=PIC<=Number of data blocks)
SPR is a sprite number, in the range 0 to 7.
POW=2↑SPR, i.e. 2 to the power of the sprite number.
CC, C1, C2 are color codes, in the range 0 to 15.

Quick reference guide to Sprites

Function	BASIC code
Data pointer for SPR to block PIC	POKE2040+SPR,INT(DB/64)+PIC
Enable SPR	POKEVIC+21,PEEK(VIC+21)ORPOW
Disable SPR	POKEVIC+21,PEEK(VIC+21)AND(255−POW)
Set X coord lo-byte	POKEVIC+2*SPR,X
Set X coord Hi-byte (1)	POKEVIC+16,PEEK(VIC+16)ORPOW
Set Y coord	POKEVIC+1+2*SPR,Y
Expand X-wise	POKEVIC+29,PEEK(VIC+29)ORPOW
Contract X-wise	POKEVIC+29,PEEK(VIC+29)AND(255−POW)
Expand Y-wise	POKEVIC+23,PEEK(VIC+23)ORPOW
Contract Y-wise	POKEVIC+23,PEEK(VIC+23)AND(255−POW)
Sprite SPR under text/graphics	POKEVIC+27,PEEK(VIC+27)ORPOW
Sprite SPR over text/graphics	POKEVIC+27,PEEK(VIC+27)AND(255−POW)
Define SPR color	POKEVIC+39+SPR,CC
Multicolor mode ON for SPR	POKEVIC+28,PEEK(VIC+28)ORPOW
Multicolor mode OFF for SPR	POKEVIC+28,PEEK(VIC+28)AND(255−POW)
Define Multicolor #1	POKEVIC+37,C1
Define Multicolor #2	POKEVIC+38,C2

Although it is only possible to have a maximum of eight sprites on the screen at any one time (Remark: at least this is true from BASIC; one could go to an awful lot of trouble to get round the restriction in machine code by using raster scan interrupts, but this would probably produce a lot of screen flicker anyway), we can have up to 64 sprites in total and display any of them we wish by switching sprite data pointers.

In the next section we put the 'ready-reckoner' to use and create a useful tool for sprite making.

THE SPRITE EDITOR PROGRAM

Obviously drawing out each sprite on a 21 (vertical) by 24 (horizontal) grid and converting all those zeros and ones into 63 bytes of data could develop into a pretty tiresome chore. However, this is exactly the sort of thing that computers are good at. So why not get the CBM 64 to do it for us? This is the philosophy behind the 'SPRITE EDITOR' program; it allows you to design up to eight sprites at a time using the cursor controls to move about within an enlarged picture of the current sprite. In this way pixels are set or unset in the sprite, which is also displayed on the screen. At the touch of key the program will print out all 63 bytes which describe the sprite. An even better way to get the sprite data is: having RUN 'SPRITE EDITOR' use the program 'DATA-STATE' to 'save' the block of sprite data memory as a program of DATA statements. The entire process is then automated.

```
1000 REM***CBM 64 SPRITE GENERATOR***
859 POKE55,255:POKE56,47:CLR:REM LOWER MEMTOP
1010 PRINTCHR$(147)
1020 POKE53280,5:REM GREEN BORDER
1030 POKE53281,0:REM BLACK SCREEN
1040 SC=1024+81:CO=55296+81:REM SCR/COL
1050 VIC=53248:REM VIC CHIP BASE ADDR
1060 DB=12288:REM SPRITES BASE ADDR
1070 I=0:X=0:Y=0:KEY=0:ZC=0:ZN=0
1080 CC=6:REM SPRITE/DIS COLOR
1090 TM=0:REM MULTCOL/NORM TOGGLE
1100 M1C=2:REM MULTICOL1 RED
1110 M2C=1:REM MULTICOL2 BLUE
1120 KP$="█▐▌▟▟▐DOTS▚▚▚01234567":REM 21 CTRLS
1130 DW$="▚▟▟▟▟▟▟▟▟▟▟▟▟▟▟▟▟▟▟▟▟▟▟▟▟":REM HOME+25
CURSOR DOWN
1140 R$="▐▐▐▐▐▐▐▐▐▐▐▐▐▐▐▐▐▐▐▐▐▐▐▐▐▐▐▐▐":REM 29 CUR
SOR RIGHT
1150 SP$="                            ":REM 28 SPA
CES
1160 FORI=0TO7:C%(I)=2↑(7-I):NEXT
1170 KEY=14:REM SPRITE ZERO
1180 GOSUB1810:REM SETUP SPRITE ZERO
1190 GOSUB2420:REM SCREEN DISPLAY
1200 GOSUB2020:REM COPY SPRITE TO DISPL
```

ERRATA 2
Pages 187-188

```
1610 GOSUB2420:REM SCREEN DISPLAY
1620 RETURN
1630 REM**SET INSERT PIXEL MODE**
1640 F=0:REM INSERT FLAG
1650 POKE53280,5:REM GREEN BORDER
1660 RETURN
1670 REM**SET DELETE PIXEL MODE**
1680 F=1:REM DELETE FLAG
1690 POKE53280,2:REM RED BORDER
1700 RETURN
1710 REM**NEW SPRITE NUMBER**
1720 IFKEY<140RKEY>22THENRETURN
1730 GOSUB1810:REM SETUP NEW SPRITE
```

```
1210 REM********* MAIN LOOP *********
1220 ZC=40*Y+X:REM CURRENT CURSOR PSN
1230 POKESC+ZC,219:POKECO+ZC,CC
1240 GETA$:IFA$=""THEN1240
1250 KEY=0
1260 FORI=1TOLEN(KP$)
1270 IFA$<>MID$(KP$,I,1)THENNEXT:GOTO1240:REM NOT
FOUND
1280 KEY=I:I=LEN(KP$):NEXT:REM FOUND SO END LOOP A
ND CONTINUE
1290 ON KEY GOSUB 1470,1500,1530,1560,1590,1630,16
70,2990,1950,2140,2360,2390
1300 IFKEY=13THENGOTO3220:REM END
1310 GOSUB1710:REM SELECT NEW SPRITE?
1320 IFF=0THENPOKESC+ZC,160:GOSUB1370
1330 IFF=1THENPOKESC+ZC,32:GOSUB1420
1340 ZN=40*Y+X:ZC=ZN:REM NEW CURSOR POS
1350 GOTO1210:REM BACK ROUND MAIN LOOP
1360 REM***************GOSUBS***************
1370 REM****INSERT PIXEL IN SPRITE***
1380 TH=INT(X/8):BI=X-8*TH
1390 BY=SB+3*Y+TH
1400 POKEBY,PEEK(BY)ORC%(BI)
1410 RETURN
1420 REM****DELETE PIXEL IN SPRITE***
1430 TH=INT(X/8):BI=X-8*TH
1440 BY=SB+3*Y+TH
1450 POKEBY,PEEK(BY)AND(255-C%(BI))
1460 RETURN
1470 REM**CURSOR RIGHT**
1480 X=X+1:IFX>23THENX=0
1490 RETURN
1500 REM**CURSOR LEFT**
1510 X=X-1:IFX<0THENX=23
1520 RETURN
1530 REM**CURSOR UP**
1540 Y=Y-1:IFY<0THENY=20
1550 RETURN
1560 REM**CURSOR DOWN**
1570 Y=Y+1:IFY>20THENY=0
1580 RETURN
1590 REM**CLEAR SPRITE/RESET SCREEN**
1600 GOSUB1770:REM CLEAR SPRITE
1610 GOSUB2420:REM SCREEN DISPLAY
```

Listing continued next page

```
1730 GOSUB1810:REM SETUP NEW SPRITE
1740 GOSUB2420:REM SCREEN DISPLAY
1750 GOSUB2020:REM COPY SPRITE TO DISPL
1760 RETURN
1770 REM***CLEAR SPRITE DATA***
1780 FORI=0TO63:POKESB+I,0:NEXT
1790 X=0:Y=0:RETURN
1800 RETURN
1810 REM****SETUP SELECTED SPRITE***
1820 POKEVIC+21,PEEK(VIC+21)AND(255-POW):REM DISAB
LE OLD SPRITE
1830 SPR=KEY-14:REM SPRITE NUMBER
1840 SB=DB+64*SPR:REM SPRITE DATA BASE
1850 POW=2↑SPR:REM SPRITE NUM AS POWER2
1860 POKEVIC+21,PEEK(VIC+21)ORPOW:REM ENBLE NEW SP
RITE
1870 POKE2040+SPR,INT(DB/64)+SPR:REM SPR PTR
1880 POKEVIC+2*SPR,5:REM X COORD LO
1890 POKEVIC+16,PEEK(VIC+16)ORPOW:REM X COORD HI(S
ET)
1900 POKEVIC+1+2*SPR,95:REM Y COORD
1910 POKEVIC+39+SPR,CC:REM COLOR
1920 POKEVIC+29,PEEK(VIC+29)ORPOW:REM EXPAND XWISE
1930 POKEVIC+23,PEEK(VIC+23)ORPOW:REM EXPAND YWISE
1940 RETURN
1950 REM****TOGGLE MULTICOL/NORM****
1960 POKEVIC+37,M1C:REM COL REG 1
1970 POKEVIC+38,M2C:REM COL REG 2
1980 TM=1-TM:REM TOGGLE FLAG
1990 IFTM=1THENPOKEVIC+28,PEEK(VIC+28)ORPOW
2000 IFTM=0THENPOKEVIC+28,PEEK(VIC+28)AND(255-POW)
2010 RETURN
2020 REM**COPY SPRITE BACK TO DISPLAY**
2030 M$="-OPYING !ACK":GOSUB2860
2040 FORX=0TO23
2050 TH=INT(X/8):BI=X-8*TH
2060 FORY=0TO20
2070 BY=SB+3*Y+TH
2080 ZC=40*Y+X
2090 IF(PEEK(BY)ANDC%(BI))=C%(BI)THENPOKECO+ZC,CC:
POKESC+ZC,160
2100 NEXT:NEXT
2110 X=0:Y=0:REM REST COORDS
2120 GOSUB2910:REM CLEAR WAIT MESS
```

```
2130 RETURN
2140 REM**SYMMETRISE ABOUT VERT AXIS**
2150 M$="*YMMETRISING":GOSUB2860
2160 FORX=0TO11
2170 T1H=INT(X/8):B1I=X-8*T1H
2180 T2H=INT((23-X)/8):B2I=23-X-8*T2H
2190 FORY=0TO20
2200 SET=0
2210 AB=SB+3*Y+T1H
2220 BB=SB+3*Y+T2H
2230 IF(PEEK(AB)ANDC%(B1I))=C%(B1I)THENSET=1
2240 IF(PEEK(BB)ANDC%(B2I))=C%(B2I)THENSET=1
2250 IFSET=0THEN2320:REM SKIP
2260 ZC=40*Y+X
2270 POKECO+ZC,CC:POKESC+ZC,160
2280 POKEAB,PEEK(AB)ORC%(B1I)
2290 ZC=40*Y+23-X
2300 POKECO+ZC,CC:POKESC+ZC,160
2310 POKEBB,PEEK(BB)ORC%(B2I)
2320 NEXT:NEXT
2330 X=0:Y=0:REM RESET COORDS
2340 GOSUB2910:REM CLEAR WAIT MESS
2350 RETURN
2360 REM**ROTATE SCREEN COLOR**
2370 POKE53281,(PEEK(53281)+1)AND15
2380 RETURN
2390 REM**ROTATE BORDER COLOR**
2400 POKE53280,(PEEK(53280)+1)AND15
2410 RETURN
2420 REM ********* MAIN DISPLAY *********
2430 PRINTCHR$(14);:REM LOWER/UPPER
2440 REM**HEADER/CURRENT SPRITE NUMBER
2450 PRINTCHR$(156);:REM PURPLE
2460 PRINTCHR$(147)CHR$(18)" *** ~!\ 64 - *7_\!~ #
";RIGHT$(STR$(SPR),1);
2470 PRINTCHR$(18)" !ENERATOR ***   ";
2480 REM**DISPLAY FRAME**
2490 PRINTCHR$(154);:REM LIGHT BLUE
2500 PRINTCHR$(146)" ▬▬▬▬▬▬▬▬▬▬▬▬▬▬▬"CHR$(30)"▬▬"CHR$(
154)"▬▬▬▬▬▬▬▬▬▬▬▬▬ "
2510 FORT=0TO20
2520 IFT=10THENPRINTCHR$(30);
2530 PRINTCHR$(18)"▌ "CHR$(146)SPC(24)"▌"
2540 IFT=10THENPRINTCHR$(154);
```

Listing continued next page

```
2550 NEXT
2560 PRINTCHR$(146)" ""CHR$(18)"▬▬▬▬▬▬▬▬▬▬▬"CHR$(30
     )"▬▬";
2570 PRINTCHR$(154)"▬▬▬▬▬▬▬▬▬▬"CHR$(146)"* "
2580 REM**LEGENDS**
2590 PRINTCHR$(5);:REM WHITE
2600 R=2:C=26:GOSUB2960:PRINT"◆PR IASE"SB
2610 PRINTCHR$(158);:REM YELLOW
2620 R=12:C=26:GOSUB2960:PRINT"╲ =╲NSERT MODE"
2630 PRINTCHR$(30);:REM GREEN
2640 R=13:C=26:GOSUB2960:PRINT"(IRN BORDER)"
2650 PRINTCHR$(158);:REM YELLOW
2660 R=14:C=26:GOSUB2960:PRINT"─ =─ELETE MODE"
2670 PRINTCHR$(28);:REM RED
2680 R=15:C=26:GOSUB2960:PRINT"(╲ED BORDER)"
2690 PRINTCHR$(158);:REM YELLOW
2700 R=16:C=26:GOSUB2960:PRINT"I =╲ULTICOL";
2710 PRINTCHR$(154);:REM LIGHT BLUE
2720 R=17:C=26:GOSUB2960:PRINT"(IOGGLE)"
2730 PRINTCHR$(158);:REM YELLOW
2740 R=18:C=26:GOSUB2960:PRINT"◆ = ╲ERT ◆YMT"
2750 R=19:C=26:GOSUB2960:PRINT"┌ = ╨RT ─ATA"
2760 R=20:C=26:GOSUB2960:PRINT"0/7 ◆PRITE"
2770 R=21:C=26:GOSUB2960:PRINT"─╨─ ─LEAR ◆PR"
2780 R=22:C=26:GOSUB2960:PRINT"─1  ╨ND ╨ROG"
2790 REM**SPRITE FRAME**
2800 PRINTCHR$(5);:REM WHITE
2810 R=4:C=27:GOSUB2960:PRINT"* ◆╚╲I╨. *"
2820 PRINTCHR$(156);:REM PURPLE
2830 R=5:C=29:GOSUB2960:PRINT" ┌──────┐"
2840 R=11:C=29:GOSUB2960:PRINT" └──────┘"CHR$(30)
2850 RETURN
2860 REM**M$+WAIT MESSAGE**
2870 R=24:C=8:GOSUB2960
2880 PRINTCHR$(156);:REM PURPLE
2890 PRINTCHR$(18)M$+" ╨LEASE ╨AIT";
2900 RETURN
2910 REM**CLEAR WAIT MESSAGE**
2920 R=24:C=8:GOSUB2960
2930 PRINTCHR$(144);:REM BLACK
2940 PRINTSP$;
2950 RETURN
2960 REM**POSITION CURSOR**
2970 PRINTLEFT$(DW$,R+1)LEFT$(R$,C);
```

```
2980 RETURN
2990 REM******OUTPUT SPRITE DATA*******
3000 PRINTCHR$(147)CHR$(142)
3010 PRINTCHR$(5);:REM WHITE
3020 R=8:C=10:GOSUB2960
3030 PRINT"_____SPRITE. _____"CHR$(18)"▼"CHR$(146)
3040 R=9:C=10:GOSUB2960
3050 PRINT"_____▼"
3060 R=12:C=0:GOSUB2960
3070 PRINT"SPRITE BASE ADDRESS "SB
3080 PRINT
3090 PRINT"SPRITE DATA:-"
3100 PRINT:CH=44
3110 FORI=0TO63
3120 IFI=63THENCH=32
3130 PRINTRIGHT$(" "+STR$(PEEK(SB+I)),3);CHR$(CH);
3140 NEXT
3150 R=24:C=8:GOSUB2960
3160 PRINTCHR$(156);:REM PURPLE
3170 PRINTCHR$(18)"PRESS ANY KEY TO CONTINUE";
3180 GETC$:IFC$=""THEN3180
3190 GOSUB2420:REM SCREEN DISPLAY
3200 GOSUB2020:REM COPY SPRITE TO DISPL
3210 RETURN
3220 REM**TERMINATE**
3230 POKEVIC+21,PEEK(VIC+21)AND(255-POW):REM DISAB
LE CURRENT SPRITE
3240 POKE53280,254:REM NORMALISE BORDER
3250 POKE53281,246:REM NORMALISE SCREEN
3260 PRINTCHR$(147)CHR$(154)CHR$(142)
3270 POKE55,0:POKE56,160:CLR
3280 END
```

PRIORITIES AND COLLISIONS

When the sprites are moving about the screen some will pass in front of others. This is determined by the sprite priority rule, which is very simple. Sprite 0 passes over (in front of) every other sprite, Sprite 1 passes over every sprite except Sprite 0 and so on.

As was described in Chapter 5, the VIC-II chip has the capability to flag the occurrence of certain events. Among these are:

(1) Sprite to sprite collisions.
(2) Sprite to screen character collisions.

Sprite to sprite collisions are latched (stored until cleared) in register VIC+30 (53278 $D01E). A bit is set if the corresponding sprite was involved in a collision. Thus if bits 2 and 3 are set we know that Sprite 2 collided with Sprite 3. However, if bits 1, 2 and 3 are set, we can only conclude that all three sprites were involved in a collision, but just who collided with who must remain a mystery (unless we check another way). There is one point to watch when using this register to detect collisions: namely, *the register does not clear when it is read*. To clear the register and so be able to detect further collisions we must write a '1' to every bit we have checked. Thus a subroutine to detect if Sprite number SPR was involved in a sprite to sprite collision might go like this:

Example:

```
1000  REM**DID SPRITE SPR COLLIDE WITH ANOTHER SPRITE**
1010  FLAG$="NO":VIC=53248:POW=2↑SPR
1020  IFPEEK(VIC+30)ANDPOW=POWTHENFLAG$="YES"
1030  POKEVIC+30,PEEK(VIC+30)ORPOW:REM CLEAR POW BIT
1040  RETURN
```

Sprite to screen character collision detection works in very much the same way except that the register involved is VIC+31 (53279 $D01F). Again there is no quick way to detect which screen character the sprite collided with.

Example:

```
1000  REM**DID SPRITE SPR COLLIDE WITH SCREEN CHAR**
1010  FLAG$="NO":VIC=53248:POW=2↑SPR
1020  IFPEEK(VIC+31)ANDPOW=POWTHENFLAG$="YES"
1030  POKEVIC+31,PEEK(VIC+31)ORPOW:REM CLEAR POW BIT
1040  RETURN
```

ANIMATION WITH SPRITES

There are two ways in which we can create moving pictures using sprites. To begin with we can simply move a single sprite around the screen.

Example:
A subroutine to move Sprite SPR from left to right across the screen would look like this. (Note it assumes the Y co-ordinate is set before the subroutine is called.)

```
1000  REM**MOVE SPRITE SPR ACROSS SCREEN**
1010  VIC=53248:POW=2↑SPR
1020  FORX=0TO319
1030  XH=INT(X/256):XL=X-256*XH
1040  POKEVIC+2*SPR,XL:REM LO BYTE
1050  IFXH=0THENPOKEVIC+16,PEEK(VIC+16)AND(255-POW)
1060  IFXH=1THENPOKEVIC+16,PEEK(VIC+16)ORPOW
1070  NEXTX
1080  RETURN
```

Notice that the hi-byte of the X coordinate needs special treatment and that it can only be 0 or 1. With the Y coordinate this does not occur since the maximum possible value (199) is less than 255.

A subroutine to move Sprite SPR from the top to the bottom of the screen might look like this. (Note it assumes the X coordinate is set before the subroutine is called.)

```
1000  REM**MOVE SPRITE SPR DOWN THE SCREEN**
1010  VIC=53248:POW=2↑SPR
1020  FORY=0TO199
1030  POKEVIC+1+2*SPR,Y:REM Y COORD
1040  NEXTY
1050  RETURN
```

Writers of transatlantic software should note that there is a slight PAL/NTSC difference here. The NTSC screen has 262 raster lines per screen with a frame rate of 60 per second, and PAL has 312 lines per screen at a frame rate of 50 per second. The vertical positioning of sprites is the same on both systems but the upper and lower limits on the X coordinate between which the sprite is visible are different. If it is necessary to take account of this difference there is a flag set on power-up in address 678 ($02A6): it is '0' on NTSC and '1' on PAL.

Another approach to animation is to instantaneously change the appearance of a sprite by changing its data pointer. By changing successive sprites by small amounts very convincing moving images can be obtained. Of course there is nothing to stop us (except possibly the amount of work involved) from defining large numbers of sprites to use as successive 'frames' in this way.

To give you some idea of how this works Steve Colwill composed the following program in which a house says 'Hello'. Unfortunately we were not up to getting 'Hello' out of the SID chip so you will have to lip-read!

```
1000 REM** HELLO HOUSE!!! **
1010 REM**BY STEVE COLWILL**
1020 POKE56,48:CLR:REM LOWER MEMTOP
1030 PRINTCHR$(147):POKE53280,6:REM BLUE BORDER
1040 VIC=53248
1050 SC=1024:CO=55296:REM SCREEN/COL
1060 DB=12288:REM SPRITE DATA BASE ADDR
1070 REM***READ IN SPRITE DATA********
1080 FORK=0TO5:REM 6 DATA BLOCKS
1090 SB=DB+64*K:REM SPR BASE
1100 FORI=SBTOSB+62:READA:POKEI,A:NEXT
1110 NEXTK
1120 REM***SET MULTICOL FOR SPRITES 0-4
1130 POKEVIC+28,31:REM MULTICOL ON 0-4
1140 POKEVIC+37,1:REM MULTICOL #1
1150 POKEVIC+38,0:REM MULTICOL #2
1160 REM***SET SPRITE COLORS**********
1170 POKEVIC+39,2:REM SPR 0 RED
```
Listing continued next page

```
1180 FORSPR=1TO4:REM SPRITES 1 TO4
1190 POKEVIC+39+SPR,4:REM PURPLE
1200 NEXT
1210 REM***SET SPRITE DATA POINTERS***
1220 POKE2040,INT(DB/64):REM SPR 0/DOOR DATA
1230 FORSPR=1TO4:REM 4 CURTAIN/WINDOWS
1240 POKE2040+SPR,INT(DB/64)+4:REM ALL CLOSED
1250 NEXT
1260 REM***POSITION DOOR*************
1270 POKEVIC,164:POKEVIC+1,192:REM 0
1280 REM***POSITION HOUSE WINDOWS*****
1290 POKEVIC+2,116:POKEVIC+3,158:REM 1
1300 POKEVIC+4,214:POKEVIC+5,158:REM 2
1310 POKEVIC+6,116:POKEVIC+7,200:REM 3
1320 POKEVIC+8,214:POKEVIC+9,200:REM 4
1330 REM***EXPAND SPRITE 0***********
1340 POKEVIC+23,1:REM XWISE
1350 POKEVIC+29,31:REM YWISE
1360 REM***BUILD HOUSE***************
1370 PRINT:PRINT:PRINT
1380 PRINTTAB(24)"        "
1390 PRINTTAB(23) "          "
1400 PRINTTAB(24)"        "
1410 PRINTTAB(7)"                    "
1420 PRINTTAB(7)"                    "
1430 PRINTTAB(7)"                    "
1440 PRINTTAB(7)"                    "
1450 PRINTTAB(7)"                    "
1460 PRINTTAB(7)"                    "
1470 FORI=1TO8
1480 PRINTTAB(10)"                    "
1490 NEXT
1500 PRINT"                                  
        "
1510 FORI=1TO3
1520 PRINT"                                  
        "
1530 NEXT
1540 PRINT"";
1550 FORI=920TO959:POKESC+I,160:POKECO+I,5:NEXT
1560 FORI=960TO977:POKESC+I,214:POKECO+I,5:NEXT
1570 FORI=978TO982:POKESC+I,160:POKECO+I,5:NEXT
1580 FORI=983TO999:POKESC+I,214:POKECO+I,5:NEXT
1590 REM***TURN ON SPRITES 0TO4********
```

```
1600 POKEVIC+21,31:REM ENABLE SPRITES
1610 REM***MAIN LOOP********************
1620 GETA$:GOSUB1800:IFA$=""THEN1620
1630 IFA$=CHR$(13)THEN2630:REM TERMINATE
1640 POKE2041,INT(DB/64)+5:REM CURTAINS
1650 POKE2042,INT(DB/64)+5:REM OPEN
1660 FORL=1TO9:GOSUB1800:NEXT
1670 REM***TALKING ROUTINE************
1680 POKEVIC,163:REM 0 POSN
1690 POKE2040,INT(DB/64)+1:REM HELL
1700 FORI=1TO230:NEXT:REM DELAY
1710 POKE2040,INT(DB/64)+2:REM ELL
1720 FORI=1TO70:NEXT:REM DELAY
1730 POKE2040,INT(DB/64)+3:REM OH !
1740 FORI=1TO800:NEXT:REM DELAY
1750 POKE2040,INT(DB/64):REM DOOR AGAIN
1760 FORI=1TO500:NEXT:REM DELAY
1770 POKE2041,INT(DB/64)+4:REM CURTAINS
1780 POKE2042,INT(DB/64)+4:REM CLOSED
1790 GOTO1620:REM BACK ROUND LOOP
1800 REM***SMOKE SUBROUTINE*****
1810 F=1-F:S=102-128*(F=0)
1820 POKESC+104,S:POKECO+104,1
1830 POKESC+105,S:POKECO+105,1
1840 POKESC+65,S:POKECO+65,1
1850 POKESC+66,S:POKECO+66,1
1860 FORI=0TO2
1870 POKESC+26+I,S:POKECO+26+I,1
1880 NEXT
1890 IFF=0THEN1950
1900 POKESC+30,S:POKECO+30,1
1910 POKESC+31,32
1920 POKESC+32,S:POKECO+32,1
1930 POKESC+33,S:POKECO+33,1
1940 IFF=1THEN1990
1950 POKESC+30,S:POKECO+30,1
1960 POKESC+31,S:POKECO+31,1
1970 POKESC+32,32
1980 POKESC+33,S:POKECO+33,1
1990 RETURN
2000 REM***SPRITE DATA STARTS HERE****
2010 REM****DOOR DATA*******
2020 DATA0,0,0
2030 DATA2,170,128,2,170,128
```

Listing continued next page

```
2040 DATA2,255,128,2,255,128
2050 DATA2,255,128,2,255,128
2060 DATA2,255,128,2,255,128
2070 DATA2,63,128,2,63,128
2080 DATA2,255,128,2,255,128
2090 DATA2,195,128,2,255,128,2,255,128
2100 DATA2,255,128,2,255,128
2110 DATA2,255,128,2,255,128
2120 DATA2,255,128
2130 REM****HELL DATA*******
2140 DATA0,195,0,0,195,0,0,0,0,0,0,0
2150 DATA0,0,0,0,0,0
2160 DATA10,130,160,43,235,232,191,255
2170 DATA254,191,255,254,191,255,254
2180 DATA191,255,254,43,255,232,10
2190 DATA190,160,0,40,0
2200 DATA0,0,0,0,0,0,0,0,0
2210 DATA0,0,0,0,0,0,0,0,0
2220 REM****ELL DATA********
2230 DATA0,195,0,0,195,0,0,0,0,0,0,0
2240 DATA0,0,0,0,0,0
2250 DATA10,130,160,43,235,232,191,255
2260 DATA254,191,239,254,191,171,254
2270 DATA190,170,254,43,239,232,10
2280 DATA190,160,0,40,0
2290 DATA0,0,0,0,0,0,0,0,0
2300 DATA0,0,0,0,0,0,0,0,0
2310 REM****OH DATA*********
2320 DATA0,195,0,0,195,0,0
2330 DATA0,0,0,0,0,0,0,0
2340 DATA0,40,0,0,170,0,2,190,128
2350 DATA2,255,128,2,255,128,11,255,224
2360 DATA11,255,224,2,255,128,2,255,128
2370 DATA2,190,128,0,170,0,0,170,0
2380 DATA0,0,0,0,0,0,0,0,0,0,0,0
2390 REM***CURTAINS CLOSED DATA****
2400 DATA170,154,168,170,154,168
2410 DATA170,154,168,170,154,168
2420 DATA170,154,168,170,154,168
2430 DATA170,154,168,170,154,168
2440 DATA85,85,84,85,85,84
2450 DATA170,154,168,170,154,168
2460 DATA170,154,168,170,154,168
2470 DATA170,154,168,170,154,168
```

```
2480 DATA170,154,168,170,154,168
2490 DATA170,154,168,170,154,168
2500 DATA0,0,0
2510 REM***CURTAINS OPEN DATA******
2520 DATA170,222,168,170,222,168
2530 DATA171,223,168,171,223,168
2540 DATA175,223,232,175,223,232
2550 DATA191,223,248,191,223,248
2560 DATA85,85,84,85,85,84
2570 DATA191,223,248,191,223,248
2580 DATA191,223,248,191,223,248
2590 DATA191,223,248,191,223,248
2600 DATA191,223,248,191,223,248
2610 DATA191,223,248,191,223,248
2620 DATA0,0,0
2630 REM***TERMINATE****************
2640 POKEVIC+21,0:REM DISABLE SPRITES
2650 POKE56,160:CLR:REM RAISE MEMTOP
2660 PRINTCHR$(154)CHR$(147):POKE53280,254:END
```

7

Peripheral devices

INTRODUCTION

To get the best from any microcomputer it must have some support from external devices. At the very least a tape cassette unit is required to store program and data files. In this chapter we consider the Commodore 64 as it interacts with various peripheral devices, as they are usually called. Among these are: Cassette unit, Printer, Disk drive and Joysticks. The microcomputer really starts to be amazingly useful when it sits at the heart of a well-organized system.

There are three different types of peripheral device: those that input data to the CBM 64 ('talk'), those that receive data ('listen') and those that do both. For example a Cassette unit can do both, whereas most Printers can only listen and Joysticks can only talk. To prevent confusion each device (including the screen and keyboard but excluding Joysticks or Paddles) is given a unique device number, which serves to identify it. A table of standard device numbers can be found in that part of Section I which deals with the OPEN statement.

The first fact to consider about a peripheral is where to plug it into the computer so that the two can communicate. Apart from audio/video connections, the Cassette port and the Joyports there are three other possible places, or 'ports' where external devices may be connected. We begin with a brief description of each of these ports before going on to discuss specific peripherals in detail.

The Serial Port

This is the 6-pin DIN socket between the Cassette port and the audio/video socket. The Serial port is the place to plug in Commodore serial printers or the 1541 disk drive. Devices connected to the Serial port can be daisy-chained so that it is perfectly possible to have several devices connected simultaneously. None but the very brave or knowledgeable would attempt to use the Serial port except to Commodore equipment through BASIC or the Kernal routines. (The problem is in part due to significant differences in timing between one machine and another, probably due to DMA's). The only non-standard device we have come across which uses this port is Interpod by Oxford Computer Systems. Interpod permits the CBM 64 to communicate with standard PET peripherals on a Parallel IEEE bus, the Serial bus (since it provides another Serial port socket) and also to send to an RS232 device at the correct 12-volt levels. With Interpod it is possible to use the Serial port to address a mixture of several parallel and serial devices on all three busses. As far as we are aware Interpod is the only serial/parallel interface whose operation makes no demands on the CBM 64 whatsoever, a point worth bearing in mind if you are developing machine code software.

The User Port
This is a flat 24-way, .15-pitch male edge connector next to the Cassette port. The User port can be used to connect the CBM 64 to non-Commodore printers treated as RS232 devices, to a modem, to a robot arm, or to a host of other devices already on the market. Unlike the Serial port the User port is relatively easy to program for I/O. From BASIC a logical file OPENed to device number 2 will address this port (OPEN1,2:PRINT#2,"IS THERE ANYONE THERE?"). When attempting to connect an RS232 device don't forget that standard RS232 uses 12-volt levels whereas the CBM 64 uses 5-volt levels (VS64–0904 will accomplish this conversion in the UK). At the low baud rate suitable for an RS232 device, timing is unlikely to be a problem; machine code programs at higher baud rates may experience difficulty. Finally the user port can also be used for 8-bit parallel communication: if you want to transfer 8 bits of parallel data to a non-standard device with your own routines then this is the port to use.

The Expansion Port
When you write code destined for a plug-in cartridge for the Expansion port you are going for the jugular. The Expansion bus is a 44-pin female edge connector which gives access to all the main control lines, address and data lines of the CBM 64. This gives you total control of the machine (awsome isn't it!). Needless to say that this port needs treating with special respect. *Turn off the machine before plugging or unplugging a cartridge or connector to the Expansion port.* This port is used for games cartridges, Parallel IEEE cartridges (again to enable CBM 64's to talk to PET peripherals), the promised CP/M† Z–80 card and (hopefully) software that is so good people want it on an EPROM or ROM.

All I/O not through the Expansion port is dealt with either by the 6510 itself (the 6510 has its own I/O capability) or by two special chips on the CBM 64 board, known as Complex Interface Adapters (CIAs). These 6526 chips will be discussed in some detail in the last chapter, for the present it is enough to know that the CIA's handle I/O and timing functions.

THE KEYBOARD
From the first appearance of the flashing cursor after the CBM 64 is switched on, the operating system scans the matrix of keyboard switches every 1/60 second. This is part of the periodic service routine triggered by an IRQ interrupt generated by one of the CIA 6526s. When a key is pressed, a number derived from the key's position in the keyboard matrix is stored in address 197 ($00C5). The contents of 197 are used as a pointer to the address in a keyboard character table

†CP/M is a registered trademark of Digital Research, Inc.

where the ASCII code corresponding to the key pressed is stored. The final ASCII code is then transferred to a 10-byte keyboard buffer at addresses 631–640 ($0277–$0280). For a key pressed in conjunction with SHIFT, CTRL, CBM, SHIFT+CBM, alternative tables are consulted for the ASCII codes. Distinct from all other keys are RUN/STOP and RESTORE. If RUN/STOP is pressed the number 254 ($FE) is placed in address 145 ($0091). When RUN/STOP is pressed in conjunction with RESTORE an NMI interrupt is generated which results in a system reset or warm start, any BASIC program present should remain intact. When a new character code is stored in the keyboard buffer, the buffer counter, contained in address 198 ($00C6), is incremented by 1. This directs the next keyboard input to the next available buffer location

Character codes are extracted from the keyboard buffer one at a time, in the order in which they were stored In direct mode this is done by the screen-handling routines which allow you to edit a program and issue direct mode commands As each character is removed, the keyboard buffer counter is decremented by 1 and the buffer closed up. In practice, character codes are removed from the keyboard buffer as they are stored unless a program is RUNning. If a program is RUNning character codes are queued in the keyboard buffer until the program performs a GET from the keyboard. (INPUT differs from GET in that during an INPUT characters are transferred to the screen, where a limited amount of editing may occur, and when the 'RETURN' key is pressed INPUT reads a character string from the screen.) If no GET statements are executed any characters input during program execution will be displayed on the screen upon a return to direct mode. If the keyboard buffer is full, further keypresses are lost. The contents of address 649 ($0289), normally 10, are used to determine the maximum number of characters permitted in the keyboard buffer If this number is changed to a value greater than 10 the keyboard and screen handling routines tend to get confused but it is sometimes useful to use a smaller value

Address 650 ($028A) holds the keyboard repeat flag, which is normally 0 for cursor controls only. The following commands are sometimes useful

POKE650.64	Disables all repeats
POKE650 128	Enables all keys to repeat

The following program PRINTs the keyboard matrix number and the ASCII code of the last key pressed.

```
1000 PRINTCHR$(147):REM CLEAR SCREEN
1010 GETA$:IFA$=" "THEN1010
1020 PRINT"MATRIX NO="PEEK(197)
1030 PRINT"SHIFT FLAG="PEEK(653)
1040 PRINT"RVS FLAG="PEEK(199)
1050 PRINT"ASCII CODE="ASC(A$)
1060 PRINT"CHAR="A$
1070 PRINT:GOTO1010
```

When RUNning this program, note how the Shift flag varies as either 'SHIFT' or the 'CBM' key is pressed in conjunction with another. In some programs we may wish to disable the shifted keys. This can be accomplished with

POKE657,0	or PRINTCHR$(8)	Disables shifted keys
POKE657,128	or PRINTCHR$(9)	Enables shifted keys.

In normal use it is unnecessary to specify a device number for keyboard and screen as the contents of 153 ($0099), default input device, and 154 ($009A), default output device, are automatically set to 0 (keyboard) and 3 (screen) respectively. However, it is possible, if you are cunning, to manipulate the choice of input and output device directly. Jim Butterfield, patron saint of all PET, VIC-20 and CBM 64 users, has published several ingenious procedures which make use of this idea.

THE C2N CASSETTE OR DATASETTE UNITS

The CBM 64 communicates with the cassette unit via four lines: Motor, Read, Write and Sense. A separate power supply of 5 volts D.C. and Ground are also used. Three of these lines (Write, Sense and Motor) are connected direct to the 6510's own I/O port. The remaining line (Read) is connected to CIA #1. Fig. 7.1 gives the CBM 64 edge connections for the cassette unit. The separate power lines through pins A and B are not used by the cassette motor, but are instead used to supply signal amplification and pulse-shaping circuitry within the cassette. The Motor line supplies +9 volts at 500 mA to the cassette motor. The Sense line is used to detect that 'PLAY' has been pressed, often in response to the screen prompt "PRESS PLAY ON TAPE" or "PRESS RECORD AND PLAY ON TAPE". It is worth remarking that the pressing of 'FAST FORWARD' or 'REWIND' are also sensed as depression of 'PLAY'. Similarly, if when attempting to SAVE to tape, 'PLAY' is pressed but not 'RECORD', the operating system cannot sense that 'RECORD' has not been pressed and will continue a fruitless effort to write to tape until 'RUN/STOP' is pressed.

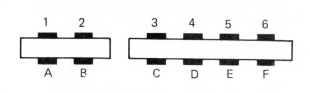

Viewed looking into port.

Pins	Function	Direction	
A/1	Ground	—	
B/2	+5 volts	From	CBM 64
C/3	Motor (power)	From	CBM 64
D/4	Record	To	CBM 64
E/5	Write	From	CBM 64
F/6	Sense	To	CBM 64

Fig. 7.1 – Cassette port connections.

The cassette unit is allocated a 192-byte buffer at addresses 828 ($033C) to 1019 ($03FB), through which all data to be read from or written to tape normally passes. When writing to tape the operating system waits until the buffer is full, or the file is CLOSEd, before blanking the screen and turning on the cassette motor: thus tape data files (SEQ) are written to tape in 192-byte blocks. When the buffer is empty the motor is turned off and the screen unblanked.

There are two good reasons why it makes sense to use a dedicated, manufacturer-supplied, tape unit. Firstly, if the microcomputer has some degrees of sensing and control over the tape deck then it becomes far easier to write data files. Secondly, if the manufacturer dictates the specification of the tape deck it becomes feasible to implement error correction procedures in read operations. As far as we are aware Commodore is unusual in this last respect. The result is a very low failure rate when reading from tape. The actual read rate is around 1100–1200 bits per second (baud) but all data is actually written twice so that when error detection and correction are taken into account an effective rate of data transfer is about 300 baud, or roughly 30 characters per second.

The whole tape operation is software controlled; '1's and '0's are written to tape as different length pulses.

$$1 = MMSS \quad \text{where} \quad \left\{ \begin{array}{l} \text{M is a medium pulse of duration 256 } \mu s \\ \text{S is a short pulse of duration 176 } \mu s \end{array} \right.$$
$$0 = SSMM$$

Further pulse widths are used as synchronizing markers.

Word marker $=$ LLMM   where L is a long pulse of duration 336 μs
File leader $=$ Fifty short pulses
File end $=$ L + Leader

You can hear all this when a computer tape is played back through an audio cassette.

It is possible to write two kinds of file to the cassette: program files (PRG) and data files (SEQ). This terminology can be confusing since data may be stored as a PRG file (the 'SCREEN EDITOR' program does this), and programs can be stored as an SEQ file, although they rarely are.

Program files (PRG)

Program files are normally SAVEd as a RAM image from the bottom of the user BASIC program area to the end of the BASIC program in RAM. A PRG file is therefore normally a copy of the bytes which describe the compressed text of a BASIC program. The format of a PRG file on tape is broadly as follows.

Format of a program file on tape

Header block	Id byte(1)+191 bytes
Repeated header	Id byte(1)+191 bytes
Program	One long block
Repeated program	One long block
End header	Id byte(5)+191 bytes
Repeated End header	Id byte(5)+191 bytes

Note that the first byte of the header block identifies the file type (1 for a PRG file and 4 for a SEQ file). The second two bytes are the start address of the RAM save and the next two bytes the end address. This means the correct LOAD address for a PRG file is easy to determine by OPENning a PRG file and using GET# to find the second and third bytes.

The command

SAVE"PROGNAME"

writes the current program to tape. The SAVE routine places a pointer to the start address of the RAM to be SAVEd in addresses 172 ($00AC) and 173 ($00AD). If the start of user BASIC is in the normal place the numbers 1 and 8 would be placed in 172 and 173 respectively, since as we saw earlier these are the Lo- and Hi-bytes of the start address of BASIC. Similarly SAVE places the Lo- and Hi-bytes of the address at which the program ends in 174 ($00AE) and 175 ($00AF) respectively. Upon pressing 'RECORD' and then 'PLAY' the operating system takes about 7 seconds to run the motor up to speed and avoid any leader tape. It then writes a synchronizing File leader followed by a PRG file in the above format. From machine code the Kernal subroutine 'Save' performs much the same function (except that it requires more care to set up). This is to be expected since, of course, the BASIC SAVE includes a call to the Kernal subroutine.

The command

LOAD"PROGNAME"

searches the cassette tape for a file header containing the specified file name, and upon locating it attempts to perform the LOAD. A 'LOAD ERROR' is generated if the file is of the wrong type. LOAD will then proceed to load the PRG file into RAM from the bottom of user BASIC and, assuming LOAD"PROGNAME",1,1 was not used, will rebuild link addresses as it goes.

The command

VERIFY"PROGNAME"

operates in a similar manner to LOAD except that when a file is found its contents are compared with the current program in memory. This provides a positive check on the accuracy of SAVE; except of course if the program was SAVEd from a different bottom of memory, in which case a 'VERIFY ERROR' will be generated because the link addresses will be different.

In the same way that SAVE uses addresses 172–173 ($$00AC–$00AD) and 174–175 ($00AE–$00AF) to mark the start and end addresses of the RAM in question so does LOAD. This fact can be useful if you need to know where a LOAD ended, for it is only necessary to PEEK the address from 174 and 175.

From within a BASIC program a LOAD or a LOAD"NAME",1,1 will cause the resulting program in memory to be RUN. This may be either a new program if LOAD was used or the original program if LOAD"NAME",1,1 was used to load to outside the BASIC program area. In either case when performing a LOAD from a BASIC program the variable pointers of the original program are left intact. This may or may not be a good thing depending on what you are doing. It is a good thing if you are LOADing a new BASIC program which is shorter than the original program and you wish the second program to share the variables and dynamic strings of the first. It is a bad thing if the second BASIC program is longer than the first. Because then the variable pointers will be too low and horrible things will happen to the second program as it attempts to write variables all over itself. However, this problem can be overcome by having the second program immediately reset its variable pointers upon being RUN (see, for example, the program 'DATASTATE' where the pointers are reset for a different reason).

When LOAD"NAME",1,1 is used from within a program to write to a block of RAM outside the user BASIC area of memory we probably want the original program to keep running. Of course after the LOAD"NAME",1,1 the original program will be reRUN from the start. If we want to avoid an infinite loop of LOADing and reRUNning, the program must leave a memo for itself. This technique is illustrated by the following example.

Example:
LOADing from within a program, A LOAD from BASIC will not reset ST so we can check that
each LOAD performs correctly at the start of the program.

```
1000  REM**ON TAPE– FILE ORDER MATTERS**
1010  IFST<>0THENPRINT"ERROR ST IS"ST:STOP
1020  REM IFPEEK(56)<>WANTED THEN LOWER MEMTOP
1030  IFA=0THENA=1:LOAD"LOAF BREAD",1,1
1040  IFA=1THENA=2:LOAD"FLASK WINE",1,1
1050  IFA=2THENA=3:LOAD"THOU",1,1
1060  REM**ALL PRG FILES NOW LOADED**
```

By the time line 1060 is finally reached the program has been RUN four times; once for the
original RUN and once after each LOAD. It can keep a record of its progress using the variable
A since the variable pointers remain intact. By replacing the multiple IF statements by ON A
GOTO... a program can do a LOAD"NAME",1,1 and continue at the right point (even though
it will reRUN).

Data Files (SEQ)
In order to create a data file (SEQ) on tape the command

OPEN1,1,1or2,"FILENAME"

can be used. This OPENs logical file 1 to device 1 (Cassette) with secondary address 1 (write with
end of file marker 64) or 2 (write with end of tape marker −128) as discussed in Section I. The
file is then written using the commands PRINT# or CMD, which take a logical file number as a
parameter. The format of a data file is broadly as follows.

Format of a data file on tape

Header block	Id byte(4)+191 bytes
Repeated header	Id byte(4)+191 bytes
Data block	Id byte(2)+191 bytes of data
Repeated Data block	Id byte(2)+191 bytes of data
. . .	
Continued to end of last Data block padded with spaces	
. . .	
End header	Id byte(5)+191 bytes
Repeated End header	Id byte(5)+191 bytes

At the end of the write operation a data file *must* be CLOSEd (else the last Data block and
the End header will not be written to tape). Failure to CLOSE a write file will result in loss of data
and problems when attempting to read the file.
Data files are read back by OPENing a file for read

OPEN1,1,0,"FILENAME"

and using either GET# or INPUT# as described in Section I.

Error checking and ST

Regardless of which type of file is to be stored the method of storing an individual byte is the same. Each character is stored on tape using 10 'bits': 8 bits for the data byte, a parity bit used in error checking, and the Word marker pulse. The parity bit of each byte is computed prior to writing the data byte and indicates whether the number of '1's is odd or even. In additon, for every 8 bytes of data a ninth checksum byte is recorded; computed as the least significant byte of the sum of the preceding eight.

When the tape is read back the parity bit of each byte, and the checksum for each 8 bytes, are recomputed. If a byte is bad and cannot be recovered an error count is incremented and the location where the error occurred is stored. The operating system then picks the best data from each pass. In the event of there being more errors than the system can handle either an unrecoverable read error (ST=16) or a checksum error (ST=32) is generated.

ST=4 (short block) or ST=8 (long) block are apt to occur if a PRG file is read as an SEQ file.

In addition to these checks the operating system measures the time taken to read each bit and compensates for speed variations of the motor. In this way a variation of up to ±20% can be accommodated. Unfortunately VIC-II DMAs put the system right on the edge of its limit and so the screen is blanked.

DISK DRIVES

The addition of a disk drive dramatically increases the power and flexibility of the CBM 64. Program and data files can be accessed directly, without the necessity of winding the tape to the right place, and files can be written to or read from disk far faster than with a cassette unit.

Unlike many microcomputer systems all Commodore disk drives are intelligent peripherals and make no demands on the memory of the computer. The standard disk drive for use with the CBM 64 is the Commodore 1541 which plugs into the Serial port. In this section we shall mostly discuss the 1541 but it is worth noting that, using a Serial to Parallel Interface, any Commodore disk drive can be used with the CBM 64. A factor to consider here is the relative read/write compatability of the differing disk drives, a topic which we shall return to later.

A disk drive can also be used to create Random Access files, in which a specified part of a file can be accessed without having to needlessly process all the preceding data. Such files are not possible in cassette since tape data access is necessarily sequential.

The 1541 disk drive is an intelligent peripheral controlled by its own 6502 microprocessor, two 6522 chips, 2K of RAM and 8K of ROM. The ROM (located at $C000 in terms of the internal addressing of the disk drive) contains the Disk Operating System (DOS) which performs all disk management routines. This enables many powerful new commands to be issued directly from BASIC. Error messages from the disk drive can also be easily read from BASIC. Part of the 2K of RAM is used for three 256 byte buffers (located at internal addresses $0300, $0400 and $0500), through which all communication between the CBM 64 and the disk drive must pass. In practice this last fact limits the number of separate channels (logical files) which may be OPEN to the unit at any one time; a 'NO CHANNELS' error will result when this limit is exceeded. The disk drive comes with a preset device number of 8, but this is easily changed from software so that several disk drives can be used 'simultaneously'. Up to five devices may be daisy-chained in this way. In what follows it is assumed that the reader is familiar with the file handling procedures outlined in Section I.

Any 5¼-inch single-sided, soft-sectored, floppy disk can be used in the 1541 (double-sided disks can be used but it is pointless). Floppy disks should always be handled with *great care*: the disk surface should *never* be touched and the disk should always be replaced in its sleeve after removal from the disk drive. The read/write head moves over the disk in contact with the surface, therefore any small particle on the disk surface creates the possibility of a read/write error. The disk drive should not be turned on or off with a disk already in place (there is a possibility that data on the disk might be corrupted). Compared to the other components of the CBM 64 system the disk drive is delicate and should be treated accordingly. It represents an example of precision engineering comparable to a traditional Swiss watch and will not take kindly to rough treatment. Do not move the disk drive without placing the cardboard insert supplied with the unit into the drive, this restrains the read/write head. The early 1540/1s were subject to a number of design faults which resulted in an urgent need for servicing more often than was acceptable, but later models seem to have overcome these problems.

WARNING If you suspect the disk drive is faulty do NOT write to important disks, this is likely to corrupt the data on the disk.

Storage of data on a diskette is in *blocks* of 254 bytes, an additional 2 bytes are used to point to the next linked block (if any). A data (SEQ) or program (PRG) file therefore consists of a sequence of linked blocks. Physically the blocks are distributed within *tracks* and *sectors*. On a 1541 disk there are 35 tracks each consisting of an area of diskette between two concentric circles (an annulus). Other disk drives may arrange this differently. A sector is an arc of a track which, in addition to one data block with its 2-byte pointer, also contains information relating to timing, self-identification and checksums.

To determine which block is where, in terms of track and sector, is the job of the DOS. To perform this task the DOS creates a Block Availability Map (BAM) and a disk *Directory*. The BAM consists of 144 bytes, contained in track 18 sector 0, recording which blocks are in use and which are free to accept data. The Directory, which begins on track 18 sector 1, is a list of up to 144 data or program files which have already been stored on the disk. Both the BAM and the directory are continually updated as disk write operations are performed. When a data or program file is specified for reading back into the CBM 64, the DOS looks up the track and sector of the first block and begins sending linked blocks.

A useful feature of Commodore DOS is that the disk directory may be LOADed into the microcomputer as a BASIC program. Of course as a program the directory is meaningless and will not RUN, but as a list of all files on the disk the directory is invaluable. The directory is loaded by entering the command

LOAD"$0",8

and then LISTed in the normal way. The '0' after the '$' sign refers to drive zero. Although the 1541 is a single disk drive it is an excellent idea to include the drive number in all interactions with the disk drive, especially in programs. This ensures that your habits and software are compatible with all Commodore disk drives.

A BASIC program file listed in the directory can be loaded by first entering NEW, to delete the directory as a program in RAM, and then entering the command

LOAD"0:PROGNAME", 8

A PRG file can be loaded back into the memory locations from which it was originally SAVEd by

LOAD"0:FILENAME", 8.1

The first step in preparing a new disk is to *format* it. Until it is formatted a disk has no BAM, no directory and no timing markers. Formatting is accomplished by the commands

OPEN15,8,15"N0:DISKTITLE,DI":CLOSE15

WARNING. If a previously used disk is reformatted all data on the disk is lost.

Here 'N0' (New disk on drive 0) is the disk maintenance command and DI is a two-character disk identifier assigned by the user. It is good practice to arrange that no two of your disks have the same identifier; otherwise a change of disk may go unnoticed by DOS, which will probably cause a mess and loss of data. Formatting takes about 85 seconds.

On the front panel of the 1541 disk drive there are two LEDs. The green LED merely indicates whether the unit is on or off. The red LED is more useful:

Red on   : reading or writing to disk
Red off   : awaiting command
Red flashing   : DOS has detected an error

If the red LED is flashing at the end of formatting it is possible that the disk is faulty. Suspect disks are best discarded but can be tested using the 'CHECK DISK' program on the 'TEST/DEMO' disk supplied with the unit. However, be warned that 'CHECK DISK' takes about 3 hours to RUN!

The DOS error channel may be read with the following BASIC program.

```
1000  REM**DISK ERROR CHECK**
1010  OPEN15,8,15
1020  INPUT#15,EN,EM$,ET,ES
1030  PRINT"ERROR NUMBER"EN
1040  PRINTEM$
1050  PRINT"TRACK"ET:PRINT"SECTOR"ES
1060  CLOSE15:END
```

A list of error codes and their meanings is contained in the VIC-1541 User's Manual. Upon execution of this program the flashing red LED should go out since the error status is returned to normal following a read out of the error channel.

In this program, and in the previously given command sequence, the secondary address of 15 in the OPEN statement has special significance for the disk drive. Here '15' refers to the command channel on which information supplied by DOS may be read after every I/O operation, and through which the user transmits disk maintenance commands such as 'N0'.

It is good programming practice to include the error-checking routine after every BASIC read or write to disk. As noted in Section I there is one slight problem in that CLOSEing the command channel will also CLOSE all other logical files OPENED to the disk drive! Hence

IMPORTANT NOTE. The command channel should be OPENed early in a disk-handling program and CLOSEd only after the last read or write.

The maximum length of a disk maintenance command string is 40 characters. Assuming OPEN15,8,15 the syntax of the disk-handling commands is.

New   PRINT#15,"N0:DISKITTLE,DI"
Initialize PRINT#15,"I0"
Validate   PRINT#15,"V0"
Rename   PRINT#15,"R0:NEWNAME=0:OLDNAME"
Scratch   PRINT#15,"S0:FIRSTFILE,SECONDFILE, . . ."
Copy (i) To make multiple copies of the same file on the same disk

PRINT#15,"C0:COPYNAME=0:FILENAME"

(ii) To concatenate SEQ files on the same disk into a single file also on the same disk.

PRINT#15,"C0:BIGFILE=0:ONENAME,TWONAME, . . ."

Ideally every disk should be initialized when inserted into a disk drive, this is certainly the case if it is intended to write to the disk. Initialization ensures that the BAM held in the disk drive RAM corresponds to the BAM recorded on the disk. Failure to initialize can result in a 'DISK ID MISMATCH ERROR' and/or loss of data. However, it is not necessary for the user to initialize disks if every disk used has a distinct two-character identifier.

Validate is a powerful disk maintenance command which in common with Scratch should be used with extreme care. If a write file was not properly CLOSEd it will appear on the directory with an asterisk against the file type. *At this point you must proceed with care.* If you don't want the data in the unCLOSEd file then perform Validate immediately. *Do* NOT *Scratch* the *file, this will sow the seed for data corruption on the disk at some later time (a 'time bomb' disk scenario). If you do need the data on the disk then see the appropriate paragraph below. Execution of Validate causes the DOS to trace through each block contained in all the files on the disk. Any blocks which have been allocated by more advanced disk-handling command, such as Block-Allocate, and which are not associated with an explicit directory entry will be freed for use.

WARNING. Don't Validate disks containing Random Access files created by advanced disk-handling commands. Reserve separate disks for such data files.

In addition to constructing a new BAM, Validate also deletes *files. If the block trace is unsuccessful a Validate error will be generated and the disk left in its original state. If this happens *immediately Initialize the disk,* since the BAM in the disk drive is the uncompleted version produced by the aborted Validate. If you get a Validate error start copying files from the disk onto another one. Do NOT write to the disk until you have got all the data you need or can get off it, then New it. To continue using it is to court disaster. Regular validation is the best protection against a 'time bomb' disk error.

Rename changes the directory listing of the specified file, without changing its contents, and *Scratch* removes the specified files from the disk.

Copy is more useful on a dual disk drive, where it is commonly used to copy files from a disk in one drive to a disk in the other. When used on the 1541 disk drive Copy can make multiple copies of the same file or concatenate SEQ files.

In addition to the disk maintenance commands the familiar BASIC commands LOAD, SAVE, and VERIFY are used with device number 8 to handle BASIC programs on disk, as in

VERIFY"0:PROGNAME",8

The logical file handling commands OPEN, CLOSE, PRINT#, GET#, and INPUT# are used, as with the cassette unit, to read and write data for an SEQ file. There are slight variations in the format of the OPEN command for disk, in that the file type and whether the operation is read or write should be specified in the command string.

Examples:

OPEN1,8,2,"0:FILENAME,S,W"	Open SEQ file for write.
OPEN1,8,2,"0:FILENAME,S,R"	Open SEQ file for read.
OPEN1,8,2,"0:FILENAME,P,W"	Open PRG file for write.
OPEN1,8,2,"0:FILENAME,P,R"	Open PRG file for read.
OPEN1,8,1,"$0"	Open directory for write (care!).
OPEN1,8,0,"$0"	Open directory for read.

EXTRACTING DATA FROM A *FILE

We owe to Mike Todd[†] the following procedure for recovering data on a *file. The obvious way to try to read the data back is to OPEN the *file for a read. Unfortunately this won't work; you'll get a 'WRITE FILE OPEN ERROR'. Apart from its interest to collectors of arcane error messages this is not very helpful! Now it happens that Commodore very kindly provided a command to cover this situation, but they neglected to tell anyone about it. Fortunately for desperate souls Mike discovered the 'M' command (sort of midway between Read and Write?). All that is necessary is to OPEN the *file like this

OPEN1,8,2,"0:FILENAME,S,M"

and read the data back in the normal way. Even so, some care is needed since ST will not be set to 64 at the end of the file. Also, you must remember that the last block of data would never have been written to disk, so there is no hope of getting that back.

PATTERN MATCHING AND '@'

A nice feature of all Commodore DOS is the special use of '*' and '?' in filenames. You can't use these symbols in the filename when creating the file for reasons which will become clear. The power of these commands becomes apparent at the point where we wish to LOAD a file or OPEN it for reading. The following examples illustrate this

LOAD"0:FILE*",8	This will load the first file on the disk directory whose file name matches 'FILE' in the first four characters.
LOAD"0:*",8	This loads the first file on the directory.

[†]ICPUG Newsletter, 5, 4, July 1983.

LOAD"0:FI?EN*"   This loads the first file which meets the following requirements. (1) The first two characters of the file name must be 'FI'. (2) Any third character is acceptable. (3) The fourth and fifth characters must be 'EN'. After 'EN' any character or no character is acceptable in the filename.

Similarly

        OPEN2,8,2,"0:FILE*,S,R"
        OPEN2,8,2,"0:FI?EN*,S,R"

You can also use the 'wild card' (?) and the 'don't care what happens after this' (*) in disk maintenance commands. For example,

        OPEN15,8,15"S0:*"

will Scratch every file on the disk (so be careful using wild cards and 'don't cares' with Scratch).

This facility makes it very easy to be systematic when developing programs on disk. As the process of development proceeds successive versions of the program can be SAVEd with prefixes, for example

        (1)MEGAPROG
        (2)MEGAPROG
        (3)MEGAPROG
        etc.

When the final version is written you SAVE and VERIFY it as MEGAPROG and then just

        OPEN15,8,15,"S0:(?)MEGAPROG":CLOSE15

thereby getting rid of all earlier versions of MEGAPROG.

The last special symbol in disk file manipulation is '@', which can be used to SAVE and replace or OPEN and replace. Unlike 'M' this is an official Commodore command, so it should be bug-free. Nevertheless '@' fell into disfavor since earlier versions of Commodore disk drives were reputed to have a bug related to SAVE and replace. However, we have it on no less an authority than Harry Broomhall that "there is no such thing as a SAVE and replace bug", which is good enough for us (although we don't use it, on the grounds that it is good to keep earlier versions until you are absolutely sure the program is fully developed and tested)[†]. Thus

        SAVE"@0:MEGAPROG",8

will SAVE the current program in memory under the name of 'MEGAPROG', replacing any earlier version of MEGAPROG.

RELATIVE ACCESS FILES

The idea of a Relative file (REL) is that it is made up of a large number of records each of which can be accessed directly for read/write operations without having to process any other part of the file. The price to be paid for this flexibility is that each record must be of fixed length less than 255 bytes. This makes Relative files ideal where the number of records is large (the practical limit on the 1541 is around 650) but each record is fairly small, for example a mailing list. Indi-

†However, not all experts agree on this.

vidual records do not appear on the disk directory (a good thing since the directory can only hold 144 entries) but the main file name appears as a REL file. The internal structure of a relative file on the disk is quite complicated (an interesting account can be found in Raeto West's book *Programming the PET/CBM*) so we shall confine our comments to practical uses.

To create a Relative file you first decide how many bytes an individual record is going to have. A simple way to do this is to break each record up into a series of subfields, not forgetting to allow extra characters, say R$=CHR$(13), to use as field separators within each record.

Example:

Field name	Length	
First name	12+1 separator	FN$(RN)+R$
Last name	15+1	LN$(RN)+R$
Phone	10+1	PH$(RN)+R$
Address line 1	20+1	A1$(RN)+R$
Address line 2	20+1	A2$(RN)+R$
City	12+1	CT$(RN)+R$
Zip/Postal code	9+1	ZP$(RN)+R$
Comments	40+1	CM$(RN)+R$
Total	146	

To OPEN a Relative file with room for 500 records each of length 146 we first OPEN a file to the disk drive command channel

        OPEN15,8,15

and then use the command

        OPEN1,8,3,"MAILING LIST,L,"+CHR$(146)

Finally we define the expected number of records by writing a dummy last record using

        HI=INT(500/256):LO=500−256*HI
        PRINT#15,"P"+CHR$(3)CHR$(LO)CHR$(HI)
        CLOSE1:CLOSE15

Here 'P' signifies a reference to the record pointer, CHR$(3) is the channel number and corresponds to the secondary address used in the OPEN statement, and the next two characters represent the Lo-and Hi-bytes, respectively, of the number of records expected. You are not stuck forever with this number of records, the file can be extended if necessary, but data access is speeded up if the right number of records are created initially.

Once the file has been created there is no need to use the full syntax of the OPEN statement every time the file is used, although nothing bad will happen if you do since DOS first checks to see if the file already exists. It suffices to use

        OPEN15,8,15
        OPEN1,8,3,"MAILING LIST"

DOS will know when it checks that 'MAILING LIST' is a REL file.

To read or write to an OPENed REL file we must first position the record pointer to the record number we wish to access. It is even possible to position the pointer to any desired byte within an individual record. This is done with

PRINT#15,"P"+CHR$(3)+CHR$(RL)+CHR$(RH)+CHR$(PN)

Here RL is the Lo-byte of the record number, RH is the Hi-byte and PN (optional) is the position of the first byte within the record which we wish to read or write from.

Finally we read or write a string from the indicated position with

INPUT#1,A$ or   PRINT#1,A$;CHR$(13);

respectively.

When writing software using Relative files it is important to check that each field string is the right length before writing it to the record. Short strings should be padded with spaces and the program should not accept input strings for a field which are too long. Secondly the strings should be separated by a valid separator, a good choice here is a carriage return CHR$(13). Thus to write a single full record for the 'MAILING LIST' file we could use

F1$=FN$(RN)+R$+LN$(RN)+R$+PH$(RN)+R$+A1$(RN)+R$
F2$=A2$(RN)+R$+CT$(RN)+R$+ZP$(RN)+R$+CM$(RN)+R$
RC$(RN)=F1$+F2$
PRINT#1,RC$(RN);

Here RN is the record number and R$=CHR$(13).

Notice that records are accessed by their number. This is nice for the computer but not so good for us when we want to know Bill Smith's telephone number in a hurry. The answer is to use another file: of record numbers against one of the fields (for example, last name) in the Relative file. The field chosen is called the *key field*. This second file can be a sequential file which is loaded in when the whole program is first RUN, updated if new records are created or old records altered in the key field, and rewritten to disk when the program is terminated. For example 'INDEX PREP' would provide the essentials of such a key file. Given a key file in the machine, 'Smith' can be entered by the user, his record number located by a binary search and finally his record read from the Relative access file.

We have covered the basics of relative file construction. There are a number of useful examples in the manual which comes with the disk drive. An interesting project would be to put this all together and write your own record system. For those who have not got the time or inclination there are a number of excellent software packages on the market.

ADVANCED DISK-HANDLING COMMANDS

Using advanced disk-handling, or 'Direct Access' commands as they are often called, it becomes possible to do a variety of clever things with the disk drive. For example, you can place a short machine code program within the disk drive RAM and then get its 6502 to execute your own code. To do this kind of thing it is obviously necessary to have some knowledge about the internal structure of the disk drive. This poses problems since very little detailed information on the 1540/1 disk drives has been officially released. However, a modest amount of information is in general circulation and no doubt this will be added to by the Independent User groups as time goes on. Moreover, there are many useful things which can be done using direct access commands without knowing anything at all about the internal structure of the drive itself.

At this stage it is helpful to know the number of sectors on each track. For 4040 and 1541 disk drives, see Table 7.1. Direct access commands are transmitted through the disk drive command channel and the data being handled is held in one of the disk drive's internal buffers. To prepare to issue direct access commands which handle data we must first OPEN the disk drive command channel and then a channel to a buffer. This is done as follows.

OPEN 15,8,15

OPEN1,8,5,"#"   (Channel 5, any buffer)

or

OPEN1,8,5,"#2"   (Channel 5, Buffer 2)

Note the channel number is identical to the secondary address used in the OPEN statement.

Table 7.1 — Track/sectors for the 1541/40 and 4040

Track number	Sector range	Total sectors
1–17	0–20	21
18–24	0–18	19
25–30	0–17	18
31–35	0–16	17

The following is a list of direct access commands.

Block–Allocate

Given a valid track T and sector S this command flags the defined block as allocated in the BAM. This action prevents the block from being overwritten when further data is SAVEd or written to disk. It may be that the requested block is already in use. In this case the next available T and S will be returned with error number number 65 in the command channel. Assuming the block is successfully allocated it will remain so until either the disk is Validated or the block is de-allocated using Block-Free.

Example:

```
1000  OPEN15,8,15,"I0":GOSUB5000
1010  T=10:S=10
1020  PRINT#15,"B–A";0;T;S:REM DRIVE 0,TRACK T,SECTOR S
1030  GOSUB5000:IFEN=65THENT=ET:S=ES:GOTO1020
1040  CLOSE1:CLOSE15
1050  END
5000  REM**DISK ERROR CHECK**
5010  INPUT#15,EN,EM$,ET,ES
5020  IFEN=0THENRETURN
```

```
5030  PRINTEN:PRINTEM$
5040  IFEN=65THENPRINT"ALLOCATING"
5050  PRINT"TRACK"ET:PRINT"SECTOR"ES
5060  RETURN
```

Here no data is being moved about so there is no need to OPEN a channel and reserve a buffer. You can check that a block has been allocated by looking at the disk directory. The number of blocks free should be decreased by 1.

Block-Execute
Given a valid track T and sector S this command will load the specified block into the reserved buffer and the disk drive 6502 will begin execution of the machine code program which (if you put it there!) the block contained. To use Block-Execute a detailed knowledge of the disk drive is required. The syntax is

PRINT#15,"B−E";CH;0;T;S;

where CH is the channel number to a previously reserved buffer.

Block-Free
This command is the reverse of Block-Allocate since it de-allocates a block, specified by its track and sector, in the BAM. The data will still be on the block but can be overwritten at any time. The syntax is

PRINT#15,"B−F";0;T;S

Block Read
This is the command which enables the programmer to read any specified block, or part of a block, from the disk into a reserved buffer (from where it can be recovered by GET# or INPUT#). Amongst other things it can be useful for recovering data from corrupted disks. The syntax is

PRINT#15,"U1:"CH;0;T;S

where CH is the channel number to a previously reserved buffer. The companion command is:

Block Write
This writes the contents of a buffer onto the specified block. The syntax is

PRINT#15,"U2:"CH;0;T;S

Example: Block Read/Write:
```
1000  REM**BLOCK READ/WRITE**
1010  OPEN15,8,15"I0":GOSUB 5000
1020  OPEN1,8,5,"#":GOSUB5000
1030  INPUT"TRACK,SECTOR";T,S
1060  INPUT"MESSAGE";M$
```

```
1070  PRINT"WRITING TO BLOCK"T,S
1080  PRINT#15,"B–P";5;1:REM B–P TO FIRST BYTE IN BUFFER
1090  PRINT#1,M$;CHR$(13);:REM WRITE M$ TO BUFFER
1100  PRINT#15,"U2:"5;0;T;S:REM WRITE BUFFER TO DISK
1110  GOSUB5000:IFEN=0THENPRINT"SEEMS OK"
1120  PRINT"NOW READING BACK"
1130  PRINT#15,"U1:"5;0;T;S: REM READ BLOCK INTO BUFFER
1140  PRINT#15,"B–P";5;1:REM BLOCK POINTER TO FIRST BYTE
1150  INPUT#1,B$:REM GET STRING FROM BUFFER
1160  PRINT"MESSAGE IS "B$
1170  CLOSE1:CLOSE15:END
5000  REM**DISK ERROR CHECK**
5010  INPUT#15,EN,EM$,ET,ES
5020  IFEN=0THENRETURN
5030  PRINTEN:PRINTEM$
5050  PRINT"TRACK"ET:PRINT"SECTOR"ES
5060  RETURN
```

Buffer Pointer

This positions the buffer pointer to the position in the buffer (1–255) to which data is to be written, or from which it is to be read. The above example uses this command. The syntax is

> PRINT#15,"B–P";CH;P

where CH is the channel number to a previously reserved buffer, and P is the required position within the buffer.

Memory Execute

This takes an address inside the disk drive as a parameter, specified by a Lo-and Hi-byte. Upon receiving the Memory-Execute command the disk drive 6502 begins execution of the machine code program which (hopefully) starts at the given address. If you know enough about the disk drive this is the way to use its own routines for your purposes. Alternatively you can write code into a buffer using the Memory Write and then jump to it using Memory-Execute. The syntax is

> PRINT#15,"M–E"CHR$(LO)CHR$(HI)

where LO is the address Lo-byte and HI the Hi-byte.

Memory Read

This enables you to read any part of the 6502 disk controller's memory. Added to a disassembler one could use this command to obtain a disassembled version of the disk drive ROM, although this is of limited use since of course it will be without comments. The requested byte is placed in the disk drive error channel, where it can be retrieved using GET#15,A$. If A$=" " we must replace it by CHR$(0). The error channel remains in this non-standard state until it receives its next command; in the meantime avoid interrogating the error channel with INPUT#. The syntax is

```
PRINT#15,"M-R"CHR$(LO)CHR$(HI)
```

where LO and HI specify the address as before.

Example:

```
1000  REM**READ DISK DRIVE MEMORY**
1010  OPEN15,8,15,"I0"
1020  INPUT"START ADDRESS";A$:A=VAL(A$)
1030  AH=INT(A/256):AL=A-256*AH
1040  PRINT#15,"M-R"CHR$(AL)CHR$(AH)
1050  GET#15,BY$:IFBY$=" "THENBY$=CHR$(0)
1060  PRINTASC(BY$),A
1070  GETCC$:IDCC$=" "THEN1070
1080  IFCC$=CHR$(13)THEN1100
1090  A=A+1:GOTO1030:REM GET NEXT BYTE
1100  REM**TERMINATE**
1110  CLOSE15:END
```

Memory Write

This command enables the programmer to deposit up to 34 bytes into the disk drive RAM. The first two bytes define the Lo- and Hi-bytes respectively of the desired start address of the byte string, the following bytes represent the byte string itself. Thus the general syntax is

```
PRINT#15,"M-W"CHR$(LO)CHR$(HI)CHR$(B1)CHR$(B2) . . . CHR$(BN)
```

Example:

The following is based on a Commodore public domain release which in essence is due to Jim Butterfield. The function of the program is to alter the device number of a disk drive from software. This is an essential step to take if more than one disk drive is to be used on the Serial bus at the same time. The procedure is to connect only the unit whose device number is to be changed (for example, from 8 to 9), RUN this program and then connect the next unit, and so on. Of course, this program produces a 'soft' change, so if the unit is turned off its device number will revert to 8. A permanent 'hard' change of the device number is a straightforward alteration but probably best avoided since then the drive will not function with most software.

```
1000  REM**CHANGE DEVICE NUMBER CBM DISK DRIVE*
1010  REM**WORKS WITH 1541/0 2040 4040 8050        *
1020  REM*********************************************
1030  DATA 12,50,119,0
1040  INPUT "OLD DEVICE NUMBER";DO
1050  IFDO<8ORDO>15THEN1040
1060  INPUT"NEW DEVICE NUMBER";DN
1070  IFDN<8ORDN>15THEN1060
1080  OPEN15,8,15:REM COMMAND CHANNEL
1090  AS=CHR$(DO+32):B$=CHR$(DO+64)
1100  REM**MAIN LOOP TO ID DEVICE TYPE**
1110  READA:IFA=0THENPRINT"UNIT NOT RECOGNISED!":GOTO1160
1120  PRINT#15,"M-R"CHR$(A)CHR$(0):GET#15,X$:IFX$<>A$THEN1100
```

```
1130 PRINT#15,"M–R"CHR$(A+1)CHR$(0):GET#15,X$:IFX$<>B$THEN1100
1140 REM**NOW CHANGE DEVICE NUMBER***
1150 PRINT#15,"M–W"CHR$(A)CHR$(0)CHR$(2)CHR$(DN+32)CHR$(DN+64)
1160 REM**TERMINATE**
1170 CLOSE15:END
```

The above is only a brief summary of the advanced disk handling commands. There are a number of variations and subtleties which we shall not go into. The principal use of these commands is to make it possible for the programmer to create file structures like Relative files but without the restriction that maximum length of an individual record is 254; such files are called *Random Access files*. In a Random Access file there is still a maximum length for each record, but this number is under the programmer's control and can therefore be chosen appropriately for the specific application. If you can get hold of a TEST/DEMO disk for a 4040 disk drive (which is read compatible with the 1541) try the program 'RANDOM 1.00' which illustrates the entire process very nicely.

1541/0 AND 4040 COMPATIBILITY

For those with a CBM 64 and a Parallel IEEE Interface there is a strong temptation to move up the disk drive range and get a dual disk drive. The obvious choice was a 4040 since 1541/0 and 4040 drives are certainly read compatible. Unfortunately the thoroughly reliable and much-loved 4040 is now defunct and it remains to be seen what the new range of Commodore disk drives will look like. If you don't care about compatibility with 1541/0 and can afford it then a good bet is the new 8250 with a healthy 2.12 Mb capacity on two double-sided $5\frac{1}{4}$-inch disks. With a little care 8250s can also read 8050 disks.

Still, a number of commercial software packages for the CBM 64 are being produced on 4040 disks, so the question of write compatibility between 1541/0 and 4040 disks is of current interest.

According to Commodore, 1541/0 and 4040 disks are fully compatible. We have to say that our experience suggests otherwise. The situation seems to be that any disk, whether formatted on a 1541/0 or 4040, which has been written to using a 1541/0 must NOT subsequently be written to using a 4040. If this happens there will be persistent read errors.

The best explanation which we have come across of this problem was given by Mike Todd (in *IPUG,* **5**, 4, July 1983) and goes something like this.

Each sector on the disk consists of a sector header, giving details of the disk ID, the track and the sector number. This is followed by a short gap and the data block itself. The header block is preceded by 40 '1's used as a SYNC pulse, the 6 'bytes' (actually 60 bits) of the header, the first being an identifier to tell the drive that it is reading a header and not a data block. This process is exactly identical on the 1541/0 and 4040.

There then follows a gap, known as the 'header gap', another sequence of '1's as the SYNC for the data block, then the data block itself followed by yet another gap, known as the 'tail gap', before the start of the next sector. On the 4040 the header gap is about 90 bits long, followed by 40 SYNC bits. On the 1541/0 there are only about 80 bits of gap and 48 SYNC bits. The header block is only ever written during the formatting operation, but the data block, including the SYNC bits, are written as required.

Now, imagine a 4040 about to write to a block which has already been written on by a 1541/0. It waits until it has found the correct header, waits the time required for 90 bits to be read and then writes its 40 SYNC bits followed by the data itself. Unfortunately the last 10 bits of the gap already contain the start of the SYNC bits which the 1541/0 had written.

When the 4040 reads this back, it will see the redundant SYNC bits and treat them as true SYNC bits, waiting for the first '0' as a signal to start reading the data block. However, the start of the proper (i.e. 4040 written) SYNC pulses will usually be a little 'ragged' and contain a '0' or two. The result is that the 4040 will see these as the start of the data and proceed to read the start of the SYNC bits as data. The first character that it expects to see is the data block identifier, which it doesn't see. So it assumes the data block does not exist.

Mike Todd also suggests a couple of 'fixes'. The first is for those using a 4040 (with DOS 2.1 or 2.2) to write to a disk which has already been written on by a 1541/0 (a 'prevention is better than cure' fix), namely, having performed OPEN15,8,15 and before writing to the disk do

PRINT#15,"M−W"CHR$(157)CHR$(16)CHR$(1)CHR$(8)

This makes the 4040 write as if it were a 1541/0 (so the new block is 4040 'write incompatible').

The second is for those who have already got a disk which is producing read errors (error 22, DATA BLOCK NOT PRESENT). This will not guarantee a successful read, but should improve the probability significantly.

PRINT#15,"M−W"CHR$(92)CHR$(52)CHR$(1)CHR$(31)

If a disk read operation fails it is normally attempted automatically up to about 10 times. The above line forces the drive to make up to 31 attempts, the maximum possible, thereby giving a better chance of a successful read. The 'raggedness' at the start of the SYNC pulses is often variable, and occasionally a '0' will not be found. When this happens the end of the sequence of SYNC pulses is identified correctly.

PRINTERS AND PLOTTER/PRINTER

There are a number of Commodore printers which can be connected directly to the CBM 64 through the Serial port. These include the VIC-1515 Printer, the 1525/6 and the MPS 801, all normally taking device number 4. In addition there is a small four-color Plotter/Printer, the 1520, which takes device number 6 (ours does anyway !). The Plotter/Printer is relatively inexpensive and great for plotting Multicolor graphs or pictures; as a printer it is very slow and unsuitable for listing a program of any length. Several non-Commodore printers are in common use with the CBM 64, many can be supplied with the necessary interfacing, and popular amongst these are Epsom printers. However, it should be noted that non-Commodore printers will not usually be supplied with a character ROM containing Commodore graphics and control codes. Hence special software is required to produce intelligible program LISTings.

The brief printer routines and comments in this section apply to the 1515 and the MPS 801.

In normal operation characters are printed by a print hammer as a 7×5 matrix of dots, corresponding to the appropriate CBM ASCII code as illustrated in Fig. 7.2. A sixth column is addressed by the printer in normal mode but is always empty to provide a space between characters. To enable high resolution printing in 'graphic' mode each column of 7 dots is bit-addressable in a maximum 480-column print line. The printer also has a capability to print double-width characters giving a bold 7×10 dot matrix character.

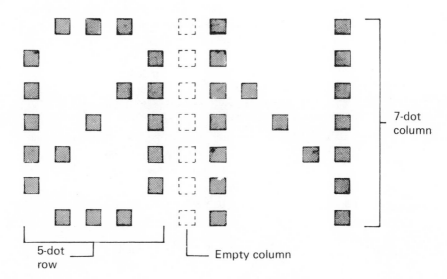

Fig. 7.2 – Character construction.

Data is input by the printer and stored in a small buffer until the buffer is full. In normal operation characters are transferred by the printer's own microprocessor to the print head sequentially, one character at a time, in the order stored. In graphic mode the contents of the buffer are printed as a block followed by the return of the print head to the start position to await the next buffer block.

The VIC-1515 printer is fitted with a switch at the rear of its case that enables the user to change the printer device number from 4 to 5. In the case of the MPS 810 the device number is switch selectable as 7, 5 or 4. These facilities allow the use of more than one printer on the Serial bus at the same time.

As a Serial bus device the printer is subject to the OPEN, CLOSE, CMD, PRINT# commands in the usual way. In addition, the printer can be commanded by the use of special CBM ASCII codes as in Table 7.2.

To address the printer we first have to OPEN a logical file. We can do this in one of several ways:

OPEN4,4	Just OPENs a channel to the printer.
OPEN4,4,0	OPENs channel with Cursor-down mode.
OPEN4,4,7	OPENs channel with Cursor-up mode.

Cursor-up mode selects the character set containing upper-case characters and CBM Graphics characters. Cursor-down mode selects lower-case/upper-case characters. It is usually unnecessary to specify a secondary address as control codes CHR$(145) and CHR$(17) perform the same function within a program or command sequence.

Table 7.2 – CBM ASCII printer codes (1515/MPS 801)

Control code	Function
CHR$(8)	Set Graphic (Hi-res) mode
CHR$(10)	Line Feed (do not use)
CHR$(13)	Carriage return
CHR$(14)	Set double-width character mode
CHR$(15)	Set standard width characters
CHR$(16)	Next two bytes define print position
CHR$(26)	Set graphics data repeat
CHR$(27)	Set dot address start position in graphic mode
CHR$(145)	Cursor-up mode (upper-case/graphics)
CHR$(17)	Cursor-down mode (lower-case/upper-case)
CHR$(18)	Reverse field on
CHR$(146)	Reverse field off

The normal sequence to LIST a program from direct mode is

    OPEN4,4:CMD4:LIST

At the end of the LIST operation 'READY' is sent to the printer and the output device reverts to the screen. At which point the command

    PRINT#4:CLOSE4

should be used to 'un-listen' the printer.

When writing a program to send normal character output to the printer we can define the character in four ways:

    (i)   Cursor-up or Cursor-down character set.
    (ii) Reverse field on or off.
    (iii) Normal or double width.
    (iv) The CBM ASCII code for the character.

For example, to print the normal width, lower-case character 'a' in reverse field we select the lower-case/upper-case character set (cursor down), reverse field on and the CBM ASCII code for 'a'. Thus referring to Table 7.2 and the Appendices the program would be

    1000 OPEN4,4
    1010 PRINT#4,CHR$(17)CHR$(18)CHR$(65)
    1020 PRINT#4:CLOSE4

Alternatively

    1000 OPEN4,4
    1010 PRINT#4,CHR$(17)CHR$(18)"A"
    1020 PRINT#4:CLOSE4

On initialization the printer is set to output normal-width characters. If we change the above to

```
1000  OPEN4,4
1010  PRINT#4,CHR$(17)CHR$(18)CHR$(14)CHR$(65)
1020  PRINT#4,CHR$(15)
1030  PRINT#4:CLOSE4
```

the double-width, reverse field character 'a' is printed. Note the addition of CHR$(15). This returns the printer to normal width character output. The CLOSE command has no effect on printer modes.

The following program 'LO-DUMP' uses control codes to print an exact copy of the current screen display. The use of the graphics mode control code CHR$(8) in line 1150 is explained in the paragraph on direct dot addressing.

```
1000  REM**LO-RES SCREEN DUMP**
1010  SC=1024:REM SET TO SCREEN BASE ADDRESS
1020  A(0)=2:FORI=1TO3:A(I)=I-1:NEXT
1030  IFPEEK(53272)AND2=0THENP=145:REM SET 1
1040  IFPEEK(53272)AND2=2THENP=17:REM SET 2
1050  OPEN4,4
1060  FORR=0TO24
1070  FORC=0TO39
1080  SK=PEEK(SC+40*R+C):REM SCREEN CODE
1090  I=(SKAND96)/32
1100  CH=A(I)*32+(SKAND127):REM CHR$ CODE
1110  RF=146:IF(SKAND128)=128THENRF=18:REM REVERSE FIELD OFF/ON
1120  C$=CHR$(15)+CHR$(P)+CHR$(RF)+CHR$(CH)
1130  PRINT#4,C$;
1140  NEXTC
1150  PRINT#4,CHR$(8)CHR$(13);:REM NO VERT SPACE BETWEEN ROWS
1160  NEXTR
1170  PRINT#4,CHR$(15)CHR$(145)
1180  PRINT#4:CLOSE4:END
```

If character cells are numbered across a line from 0 to 79, the Nth character cell can be selected by use of the control code CHR$(16). Thus

```
1000  OPEN4,4
1010  PRINT#4,CHR$(16)CHR$(51)CHR$(48)"CBM 64"
1020  PRINT#4:CLOSE4
```

will result in "CBM 64" being printed in character cell 30, since 51 is the ASCII code for 3 and 48 and ASCII code for 0. The use of CHR$(16) on the printer is therefore analogous to the ordinary BASIC command SPC(.

To address an individual pixel dot on a printer line, the printer is first set to graphic mode with CHR$(8). The control code CHR$(27) is then used in conjunction with CHR$(16). Following CHR$(8)CHR$(27)CHR$(16) the printer expects to receive two numbers, which together describe the column (0 to 479) in which the dot is to be printed. We may call these numbers HP (Hi-printer byte) and LP (Lo-printer byte). Thus if the dot is to be printed in column 258 we have HP=1, LP=2. Plainly HP is either 0 (columns 0 to 255) or 1 (columns 256 to 479).

Having selected the correct column, the required dot or dots are printed by assembling a vertical single column character. The process is illustrated in Fig. 7.3.

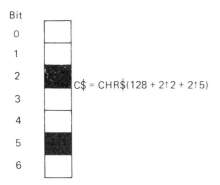

Fig. 7.3 – A vertical byte for the printer.

Example:

In this program individual dot addressing is illustrated by drawing a sawtooth wave, one character cell high across the whole of one line. The required column is specified by the variable X and the vertical dot co-ordinate by Y ($0<=Y<=6$) measured downwards. As Y is computed the program displays the current value on the screen.

```
1000  REM***PRINTER DOT ADDRESSING***
1010  OPEN4,4
1020  FORX=0TO479
1020  HP=INT(X/256):LP=X-256*LP
1030  A=INT(X/13):B=X-13*A:Y=INT(B/2):PRINTY
1040  C$=CHR$(128+2↑Y)
1050  IFB=12THENC$=CHR$(255):REM VERT LINE
1060  PRINT#4,CHR$(8)CHR$(27)CHR$(16)CHR$(HP)CHR$(LP)C$;
1070  NEXT
1080  PRINT#4,CHR$(15)
1090  PRINT#4:CLOSE4
```

It should be noted that there were occasional Serial bus problems with early 1515 printers when run with a VIC-20. This caused the 1515 printer to sometimes hang in the middle of a LISTing, particularly at the end of a long line. We have had no such problems running the MPS 801 with a CBM 64.

Finally we should mention the VIC-1520 Plotter/Printer. This is basically a four-color X–Y plotter that uses ball-point pens as its writing instruments. It uses 114 mm wide plain rolled paper with up to 80 characters per line when used as a printer. This is a fun, low-cost plotter with rather limited print capability. Although suitable for continuous plotting (pen down) with occasional changes of color, the 1520 would not be suitable for a Hi-resolution screen dump for example. For a Hi-res screen dump we need to plot a large number of unconnected pixel dots for which a dot matrix printer is ideal.

THE JOYSTICKS

The CBM 64 has two 9-pin ports which allow the use of joysticks, paddles, or a light pen. Joysticks can be plugged into both ports but a light pen can only connect to port A. Both sets of joystick lines are connected to CIA #1 (base address 56320 or $DC00). This 6526 chip also performs the scan of keyboard switches every 1/60 second. One consequence of this fact is that port A cannot be used to read the keyboard if a joystick is connected and being used. The 6526 cannot tell the difference between a keypress and a joystick switch being closed on this port. In practice the effect manifests itself by GET obtaining spurious characters. Thus the rule should be:

(i)   If using one joystick only, then program for port B; this will enable the keyboard to be read as well if required.

(ii) If using both joyports then don't plan on being able to read the keyboard.

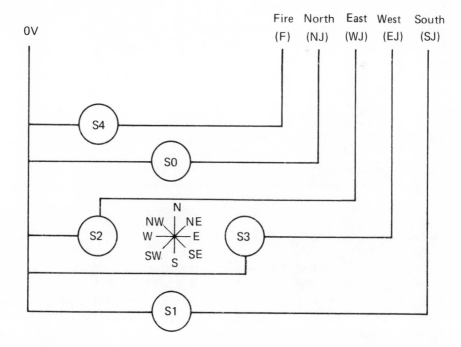

Fig. 7.4 – Switch joystick operation.

The input from a joystick is derived from the operation of 5 switches contained within the joystick. Normally the joystick provides a means of control during a graphics-based game. Four switches indicate a direction of movement and a fifth switch can be used for any additional purpose required by the program, usually as a 'FIRE' button. Fig. 7.4. shows the switch configurations with their outputs. All five switches are normally open circuit. S0 to S3 are closed when the stick control is pushed in their respective directions. In between, 45-degree angles are detected by adjacent switches both being closed. Switch closures connect 0 volts to their respective I/O lines, the level of which can be read by PEEKing addresses 56320 ($DC00) for the port A joystick and 56321 ($DC01) for port B. The bit/switch relationship is as follows:

				Bit					
Address	7	6	5	4	3	2	1	0	
56320	–	–	–	F1	E1J	W1J	S1J	N1J	Port A/Joy 1
56321	–	–	–	F2	E2J	W2J	S2J	N2J	Port B/Joy 2

where E, W, S, N refer to East, West, South and North, F refers to the fire button, and the numbers 1 or 2 refer to Joy 1 or Joy 2 respectively.

These bits are normally 1 and will go to zero when the corresponding switch is closed. The following program demonstrates both joysticks.

```
1000 REM**JOYSTICK DEMO**
1010 REM*********************
1020 SC=1024:CO=55296:REM SCR/COL BASE
1030 PRINTCHR$(147)
1040 REM**MAIN LOOP STARTS HERE**
1050 J1=PEEK(56320):REM JOY #1
1060 J2=PEEK(56321):REM JOY #2
1070 REM**JOY #1 BITS**
1080 N1J=J1AND1:S1J=(J1AND2)/2
1090 W1J=(J1AND4)/4:E1J=(J1AND8)/8
1100 F1=(J1AND16)/16
1110 REM**JOY #2 BITS**
1120 N2J=J2AND1:S2J=(J2AND2)/2
1130 W2J=(J2AND4)/4:E2J=(J2AND8)/8
1140 F2=(J2AND16)/16
1150 REM**COMPUTE #1 COORDS**
1160 IFN1J=0THENY1=Y1-1:IFY1<0THENY1=0
1170 IFS1J=0THENY1=Y1+1:IFY1>24THENY1=24
1180 IFW1J=0THENX1=X1-1:IFX1<0THENX1=0
1190 IFE1J=0THENX1=X1+1:IFX1>39THENX1=39
1200 REM**PLOT #1 ON SCREEN**
1210 S1L=40*Y1+X1
1220 POKESC+S1L,42:POKECO+S1L,1
```

```
1230 IFF1=0THENPRINTCHR$(147)
1240 REM**COMPUTE #2 COORDS**
1250 IFN2J=0THENY2=Y2-1:IFY2<0THENY2=0
1260 IFS2J=0THENY2=Y2+1:IFY2>24THENY2=24
1270 IFW2J=0THENX2=X2-1:IFX2<0THENX2=0
1280 IFE2J=0THENX2=X2+1:IFX2>39THENX2=39
1290 REM**PLOT #2 ON SCREEN**
1300 S2L=40*Y2+X2
1310 POKESC+S2L,42:POKECO+S2L,2
1320 IFF2=0THENPRINTCHR$(147)
1330 GOTO1040
```

If a fast response to the joystick is required then the program must sample the Joyport at regular intervals. This does not leave a BASIC program time to do very much else. Also for moving sprites horizontally we need 9 bits which further slows things up. In order to leave BASIC time to do its thing and still be able to keep up-to-date on the joystick we have written '2BYTJOY' as a utility which is easily RUN from BASIC but is in fact a machine code wedge. This program scans both Joyports every 1/60 second and updates two-byte wide counters for each direction of travel. The whole thing is easily LOADed from BASIC and can be found in the introductory chapter on machine code.

8

System architecture

INTRODUCTION

In this chapter we will take a closer look at what really goes on inside your CBM 64. We will start off by looking at the layout and 'hardware' of the 64 and will then go on to consider the 6510 chip, the heart of the CBM 64.

CBM 64 System Architecture

Fig. 8.1 is a block diagram of the CBM 64 system showing the interaction of the principal components, which are:

> The 6510A microprocessor
>
> The 6566/6569 video interface chip II
>
> The 6581 sound interface device
>
> The two 6526 complex interface adaptors
>
> The associated RAM and ROM chips

The 6510 chip is an 8-bit microprocessor. This means that each operation of the 6510 processes or transfers 8 bits of data at a time. Each instruction cycle can be broken down into three distinct stages. Firstly the instruction is fetched from memory in the form of a single 8-bit byte, then it is decoded by the processor, which is simply a switching process within the processor, and finally the instruction is executed. In reality the system uses a method called pipelining to speed things up, this involves fetching the next instruction whilst executing the current one, which is rather like reaching for the next slice of cake while you're still chewing the piece in your mouth. The 6566/9 VIC-II chip (6566 in the USA and 6569 in Europe), the 6581 SID chip and the two 6526 CIAs provide the means for the CBM 64 to communicate with the outside world. The

6566/9 controls the output of the picture to your TV including control of sprites on the 64 and light pen data. This chip is discussed in detail in Chapter 5. The 6581 controls the very versatile range of sounds that the CBM 64 can produce, and also handles the potentiometer joysticks and paddles. The chip was discussed in detail in Chapter 4. Finally the two 6526 CIAs handle all remaining input/output functions, including the keyboard, user port, cassette port, switch joysticks and serial bus which is used to communicate with the disk drive and printer.

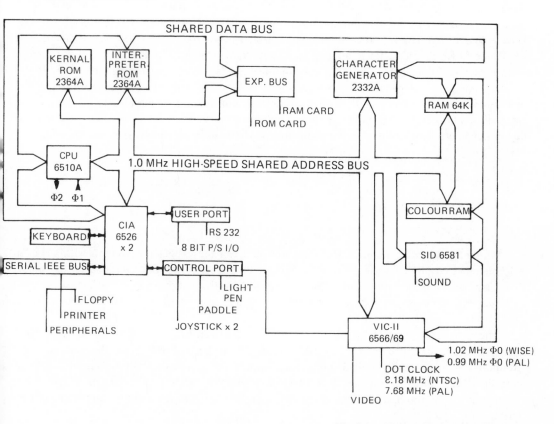

Fig. 8.1 – Block diagram of the CBM 64.

The other main component of the CBM 64 is the RAM and ROM which form the system's memory.

RAM stands for Random Access Memory and was originally used to describe memory where the access time is the same irrespective of the address, i.e. whatever the address required the memory will always be accessed in the same, known, time. However, this has now become the standard form of memory and the phrase Random Access Memory has come to mean memory which is alterable, i.e. can be written to as well as read from.

The Commodore 64 has 64K of RAM consisting of 8 8264 memory chips, each of which is organized as 65536 1-bit units. All 64K of RAM can be accessed by the 6510 at any time, and any one of four 16K blocks can be accessed by the VIC-II chip.

The ROM, or Read Only Memory, is not alterable, that is it can be read but any attempt to write to it will have no effect. There are several different types of ROM. The first type is used to hold information which is determined by the manufacturer, such as the BASIC Interpreter, the KERNAL, and the CHARACTER SET. The information is put onto the chip at manufacture and cannot be changed or erased, so although the chip is physically the same as others of its type it may be unique in the information it holds. The second type of ROM chip is called a Programmable Read Only Memory or PROM, this type of chip is popular amongst the games cartridge manufacturers, who buy in blank chips and 'burn' the program onto the chip with a special machine. Once the data is burned onto the chip it cannot be changed or erased. The final type is the Erasable PROM or EPROM. This chip is programmed in the same manner as a PROM, but if exposed to intense ultraviolet light for about 20–30 minutes can be erased and reprogrammed. EPROMs are very popular with people who are developing a program, but do not want to lose it if the power is turned off. All of the ROM chips are called 'non-volatile' which means that they retain their information even when power is turned off, unlike most RAM which is volatile. In order to do anything useful with all these components the 6510 has to be able to achieve the following:

> Select the right component
> Select the right part of the component
> Control the direction of data flow
> Read or write data

In order to keep the number of connections between the various components within reasonable bounds everything in the CBM 64 is connected to three *buses*. Each bus is a set of parallel lines along which information passes. Since everything in the computer works in binary we only need the values 0 and 1 to appear on the lines, and these are represented by 0 volts and +5 volts respectively.

The first of the three buses is the *address bus*. This consists of sixteen parallel lines, which means any one of $2\uparrow16$ (65536) possible addresses can be accessed. Since the data is moved around in bytes or blocks of eight bits the second bus, the *data bus* comprises eight bi-directional data lines. The third bus on the 64 is the *control bus* which consists of a series of signal lines which control the timing and direction of data transfers between the various components on the buses.

The major control lines are:

Read/Write (R/$\overline{W}$)

This line controls the direction of data transfer. When the R/$\overline{W}$ line is low (0 V) the transfer of data is from the processor to the memory, this is a *write* operation. When high, the data is transferred from memory to the processor, a *read* operation. It is customary to indicate that a function occurs when the line goes low by putting a bar over its symbol, thus R/$\overline{W}$ indicates that a write occurs when the line is low.

Reset ($\overline{RES}$)

When this line goes low, all of the components in the 64 including the 6510 are reset. It is this line which starts the processor and other components when the CBM 64 is switched on.

Non-maskable interrupt ($\overline{\text{NMI}}$)

When this line goes low the 6510 finishes the instruction it is executing and then jumps off to a predetermined program. As the name implies it is not possible to prevent the occurrence of an NMI from software. The only thing which takes precedence over an NMI is a RES.

Interrupt request ($\overline{\text{IRQ}}$)

The function of this line is very similar to the NMI, the chip is again interrupted and a (different) predetermined routine is executed. The effect of the IRQ line can, however, be disabled from software using the SEI and CLI instructions, thus allowing the processor to ignore IRQs when required. The NMI line takes precedence over the IRQ line.

Direct Memory Access (DMA)

Apart from the 6510's requirements for the bus there is another chip which also needs to access memory, this is the 6566/9 video chip. So the buses have to be shared between the two chips using a system called *Direct Memory Access* (DMA). To understand how this works we must look at the function of the *system clock*. On the CBM 64 circuit board is a tiny crystal which, when a voltage is applied to it, vibrates at a frequency of 8.181840 MHz for NTSC and 7.882000 MHz for PAL, this is called the dot clock and is just like the quartz crystal in your quartz watch. This high frequency signal is fed into the VIC-II chip and all operations in the VIC-II chip occur at this speed. This is necessary because there is so much information for the video chip to send to the screen of your TV. One of the functions of the VIC-II chip is to divide this frequency by eight and output it. This produces the system clock for the CBM 64, at 1·022730 MHz for NTSC and 0.985250 MHz for PAL, which means that it changes from high to low and back again very rapidly. The period of time the clock is low is called the *phase 1* portion of the cycle and when it is high it is the *phase 2* portion of the cycle. Now because the 6510 doesn't want the buses all of the time as it has to do internal processing as well, the 6510 only accesses the buses during phase 2 of the clock cycle, and the video chip uses the buses during phase 1. Thus neither chip need ever know that the other is using the buses. Obviously maintaining this timing is quite complex and this is where two more of the control bus lines feature. The first of these is the *Address Enable Control* (AEC) line. The state of this line is controlled by the video chip. When this line goes low the 6510's address bus drivers are disabled, which means that the 6510 cannot put an address on the address bus, this allows the 6566/9 to use the address bus. This line is only activated during phase 1 of the clock so that the normal function of the 6510 is not affected. Because of this 'bus sharing' all memory accesses must be completed in 1/2 cycle, which is approximately 500 nanoseconds (1 nanosecond = 1 thousand-millionth of a second). Some operations on the video chip require data more quickly than is possible using phase 1 accesses only, in particular the access of character pointers from the video matrix and the accessing of sprite data. As a result of this every so often the VIC-II chip must steal some time from the 6510 by disabling it and using phase 2 for video accesses. This is achieved using the *Bus Available* (BA) line. When this line is pulled low by the VIC-II chip during phase 1 it indicates that the video chip will require a phase 2 data access. The 6510 then has three more phase 2 accesses which allow it to complete its current instruction, and on the fourth phase 2 after the BA line goes low, the AEC line will remain low during phase 2 while the video chip does a data access.

The amount of time stolen from the 6510 by the VIC-II chip is quite significant. For example, the character pointer fetches are required every eighth raster line displayed on the screen and require 40 consecutive phase 2 accesses to fetch the video matrix pointers. When you consider that in the UK the video chip refreshes every other line of the 625 raster lines on your TV roughly 25 times a second, and in the US 524 lines 30 times per second, this is quite a lot of time. Additional time is also required to display sprites. Because of the large amounts of time taken from the 6510 by the video chip, the 6510 does not execute instructions at a constant speed, and when dealing with non-intelligent peripherals, such as the C2N cassette which transmit or receive data at a steady rate, the screen must be blanked.

THE OPERATING SYSTEM

When you switch your CBM 64 on, you find yourself in the world of BASIC which is a nice easy programming language for us to use. However, it has no meaning to the 6510 chip, which only understands 6510 machine code. So, somewhere along the line between entering a BASIC program and actually having it run, something must translate from BASIC into 6510 machine code. This is one of the functions of what we have so far called the 'operating system'. The operating system is a large machine code program which is about 16K in total, and comprises two major components, the *Interpreter* and the *Kernal*.

The Interpreter

The main function of the Interpreter is to translate BASIC into machine code, and to help it in this task it has a library of useful subroutines which it can call on. This library is called the Kernal, and we shall discuss it in detail in the next section.

In its way the BASIC Interpreter is one of the great achievements of our generation; certainly without the Interpreter, or something conceptually equivalent, microcomputers as we know them could not exist. Representing, as it does, thousands of man-hours of work, we can do little more than briefly describe the main functions of the Interpreter, which in the CBM 64 can be found in ROM at addresses 40960–49151 ($A000–$BFFF).

When computing was in its infancy all programs had to be written as a sequence of 0s and 1s. Plainly this is a very tedious, time-consuming and error-prone process. Even writing programs using 64-MON is open to the same objections. To meet this problem various high level languages were developed. A *high level* language, such as FORTRAN, PASCAL or BASIC, is a programming language which is more closely related to English than to Assembler or the 0s and 1s of pure machine code. When, for example, a FORTRAN program has been written for a mainframe computer the entire program must then be translated into machine code, a process known as *compilation*. Compilation is carried out by a large program (which itself can be written in any convenient language) which has to be developed in accordance with the high level language. Most compilers perform a syntax check before beginning any serious translating and it is at this stage that the error messages usually start to appear. From the user's point of view this arrangement is less than satisfactory, mainly because if you make a syntax error in your program there is no way to find out about it until the program is compiled: there is a lack of interactive editing at the time of entering the program. From the computer's viewpoint too there are problems, mainly relating to how much RAM is needed. Not only has the computer to store and run the compiler, it also has to hold the high level source program whilst creating the machine code equivalent, or *object code* as it is called. Typically a mainframe compiler can use several hundred kilobytes of RAM.

The program language BASIC (Beginner's All-purpose Symbolic Instruction Code) was developed at Dartmouth College, New York, in the 1960s as an easy-to-learn and easy-to-use high level language. BASIC was designed to need no initial declaration (such as is required by every PASCAL program) and so, once a line of BASIC has been written, it can be immediately executed using the RUN time Interpreter.

The essential difference between an interpreter and a compiler is that an interpreter does not try to translate the entire program in one fell swoop. Instead, when RUN time comes, the Interpreter translates the first program statement, executes the corresponding machine code and then goes back to fetch the next program statement and so on. The advantage of this technique is that two copies of the program, one in the high level language and one in machine code, never have to co-exist in RAM. A disadvantage is that translating each program statement, essentially via a jump table of keyword tokens, is time-consuming and often inefficient, since the same line may be translated many times during a complete RUN of the program. Thus RUNning a program with an Interpreter may be 100 times slower than RUNning the compiled equivalent. Still, the fact remains that it was the concept of an Interpreter which made microcomputers like the CBM 64 possible and, as we know, the idea works very well.

The other principal function of the Interpreter is to provide the Screen Editor. When a program is being entered from the keyboard the Editor, an associate of the Interpreter, takes control, allowing you to edit any line until the 'RETURN' key is pressed. When this is done the line is translated, not into machine code, but into compressed text, changing all BASIC keywords into one-byte tokens as explained in Chapter 3. Next the Interpreter searches memory, in the user BASIC program area, for a program line with the same line number. If such a line is found it is replaced by the new one; if not, the line is inserted in the appropriate place in memory in relation to the other existing lines. The reasons for this intermediate phase of storing the program as compressed text are that it takes up less RAM in this form and secondly, at RUN time, it makes the process of translation into machine code faster.

One of the advantages of the CBM 64 is that because we can 'switch out' the Interpreter from software, we can LOAD a completely different Interpreter for another high level language. Already an Interpreter for LOGO is available from Commodore, and it can be expected that more will follow.

Apart from the BASIC Interpreter and possibly a true BASIC-to-machine/code compiler there is a third way to turn BASIC into machine code: the so called pseudo-code, or *p-code compiler*. The idea of a p-code is as follows. The BASIC is first compiled into a language very near to machine code called *pseudo-code*. Pseudo-code is a kind of archetypal machine language which is close to most microprocessor instruction sets without being identical to any. At RUN time the p-code is translated into the machine language of the particular microprocessor being used, in this case the 6510, by a RUN time p-code interpreter which must be saved as part of the complete program.

There are several p-code compilers for the CBM 64 currently on the market. These include the very popular PETSPEED (Oxford Systems) and DTL (Drive Technology Ltd) compilers. Typically these carry around an 8K overhead for the p-code interpreter. By using a p-code compiler on a BASIC program the execution time can often be decreased by more than a factor of 10. The other main advantage of p-code compilers is software security. Whilst a skilled programmer can often understand an uncommented disassembled machine code program, it is virtually impossible to make any sense of p-code (unless you happen to be the person who wrote the RUN time interpreter). The DTL compiler also has an optional facility to include a test for a key or 'dongle' as they are called. This is a device which is plugged into the joyport or cassette port, without which the compiled program will not RUN. You might consider this an advantage if you were writing software sufficiently valuable to justify the expense of a dongle.

Each of these p-code compilers has its own advantages and disadvantages. The DTL compiler will allow the program to include arrays dimensioned by a variable, and will permit SYS to call machine code subroutines, whereas PETSPEED will allow neither of these. However, in fairness it must also be said that PETSPEED compiles everything and does not rely on the normal BASIC Interpreter, whereas DTL hands all PRINT statements over to the Interpreter.

The only aspect of the standard BASIC Interpreter which we shall discuss in some detail is the numeric floating point routines. These routines all operate on the floating point accumulators located in the zero page at addresses 97–102 ($61–$66) and 105–110 ($69–$6E). The format of data within these accumulators is that discussed in Chapter 3 (the last byte of each is used as a convenient temporary store for the sign bit).

Here is a list of the most useful functions and their call addresses in ROM. Detailed comments for each of these routines can be found at the end of this chapter. It should be noted that, unlike the Kernal routines which can (and should) be routed through the jump table, the Interpreter routines must be called directly. Consequently any programs which use these routines will not be portable across different machines. In this list the following abbreviations are used:

FAC   Floating Point Accumulator (#1)
ARG   Argument (FAC #2)
MFPTN   Memory Floating Point Number

NAME	HEX	DECIMAL	FUNCTION
ABS	$BC58	48216	Perform ABS(FAC)
ANDOP	$AFE9	45033	Perform FAC AND ARG
ATN	$E30E	58126	Perform ATN(FAC)
AYINT	$B1BF	45503	Convert FAC to INT in FAC+3
CONUPK	$BA8C	47756	Load ARG from MFPTN
COS	$E264	57956	Perform COS(FAC)
DIV10	$BAFE	47870	Divide FAC/10 (Result always positive)
EXP	$BFED	49133	Perform EXP(FAC)
FACINX	$B1AA	45482	Convert FAC to INT in A,Y
FADD	$B867	47207	Add MFPTN+FAC
FADDH	$B849	47177	Add 0.5 to FAC
FADDT	$B86A	47210	Add ARG+FAC
FCOMP	$BC5B	48219	Compare FAC with MFPTN
FDIV	$BB0F	47887	Divide MFPTN/FAC
FDIVF	$BB07	47879	Divide ARG/MFPTN
FDIVT	$BB12	47890	Divide ARG/FAC
FMULT	$BA28	47656	Multiply MFPTN*FAC
FMULTT	$BA2B	47659	Multiply FAC*ARG
FPWRT	$BF7B	49019	Perform ARG↑FAC
FSUB	$B850	47184	Subtract MFPTN−FAC

NAME	HEX	DECIMAL	FUNCTION
FSUBT	$B853	47187	Subtract ARG—FAC
GIVAYF	$B391	45969	Convert INT in A,Y to FAC
INT	$BCCC	48332	Perform INT(FAC)
LOG	$B9EA	47594	Perform LOG(FAC)
MOVAF	$BC0C	48140	Load ARG from FAC
MOVFA	$BBFC	48124	Load FAC from ARG
MOVFM	$BBA2	48034	Load FAC from MFPTN
MOVMF	$BBD4	48084	Store FAC into MFPTN
MUL10	$BAE2	47842	Multiply FAC*10
NEGOP	$BFB4	49076	Negate FAC
NUMREL	$B01B	45083	Perform numeric comparison
OROP	$AFE6	45030	Perform FAC OR ARG
QINT	$BC9B	48283	Convert FAC to 4-byte INT in FAC+1 to 4
RND	$E097	57495	Put random number in FAC
ROUND	$BC1B	48155	Round FAC
SGN	$BC39	48185	Perform SGN(FAC)
SIGN	$BC2B	48171	Get sign of FAC
SIN	$E26B	57963	Perform SIN(FAC)
SNGFT	$B3A2	45986	Convert 1-byte INT in Y to FAC
SQR	$BF71	49009	Perform SQR(FAC)
TAN	$E2B4	58036	Perform TAN(FAC)

Further details of these routines may be found at the end of this chapter.

THE KERNAL

The KERNAL is a library of useful subroutines which are called by the Interpreter, and can be called from your own machine code. The KERNAL can be found between addresses 53248 and 65536 ($E000 to $FFFF). The advantage of having this type of set-up is that a user program can call the routines that the operating system uses for input/output, memory management and general housekeeping. The other advantage of having a kernal is that all major routines in it can be called from a 'jump table'. This is a table of pointers to the locations of the routines, which means that even if the physical location of the routine changes between Commodore machines the jump address to call is the same. Many of these routines will not function with interrupts turned off.

Here is a list of the user-callable kernal routines:

NAME	HEX	DECIMAL	FUNCTION
ACPTR	$FFA5	65445	Input a byte from serial port
CHKIN	$FFC6	65478	Open a channel for input
CHKOUT	$FFC9	65481	Open a channel for output
CHRIN	$FFCF	65487	Input a character from channel

NAME	HEX	DECIMAL	FUNCTION
CHROUT	$FFD2	65490	Output a character to channel
CIOUT	$FFA8	65448	Output a byte to serial port
CINT	$FF81	65409	Initialize the screen editor
CLALL	$FFE7	65511	Close all channels and logical files
CLOSE	$FFC3	65475	Close a logical file
CLRCHN	$FFCC	65484	Close all channels
GETIN	$FFE4	65508	Get a character from the keyboard buffer
IOBASE	$FFF3	65523	Get base address of I/O devices
IOINIT	$FF84	65412	Initialize input/output
LISTEN	$FFB1	65457	Command serial device to LISTEN
LOAD	$FFD5	65493	Load RAM from a device
MEMBOT	$FF9C	65436	Read/Set bottom of memory
MEMTOP	$FF99	65433	Read/Set top of memory
OPEN	$FFC0	65472	Open a logical file
PLOT	$FFF0	65520	Read/set Cursor Co-ordinates
RAMTAS	$FF87	65415	Initialize RAM, reset screen to $0400, allocate tape buffer
RDTIM	$FFDE	65502	Read real time clock
READST	$FFB7	65463	Read I/O status
RESTOR	$FF8A	65418	Restore default I/O vectors
SAVE	$FFD8	65496	Save RAM to device
SCNKEY	$FF9F	65439	Scan keyboard
SCREEN	$FFED	65517	Return number of screen rows and columns
SECOND	$FF93	65427	Send secondary address after LISTEN
SETLFS	$FFBA	65466	Set logical, first and second addresses
SETMSG	$FF90	65424	Control KERNAL messages
SETNAM	$FFBD	65469	Set filename
SETTIM	$FFDB	65499	Set real time clock
SETTMO	$FFA2	65442	Set timeout on serial bus
STOP	$FFE1	65505	Scan STOP key
TALK	$FFB4	65460	Command serial device to TALK
TKSA	$FF96	65430	Send secondary address after TALK
UDTIM	$FFEA	65514	Increment real time clock
UNLSN	$FFAE	65454	Command serial device to UNLISTEN
UNTLK	$FFAB	65451	Command serial device to UNTALK
VECTOR	$FF8D	65421	Read/Set vectored I/O

Here are some example routines which use the KERNAL routines to perform a LOAD and a SAVE.

```
LINE# LOC    CODE        LINE

00001 0000               ;********************************
00002 0000               ;*                              *
00003 0000               ;*           LOAD 64            *
00004 0000               ;*                              *
00005 0000               ;* 49984 = DEVICE NUMBER        *
00006 0000               ;*                              *
00007 0000               ;* TO USE   - POKE VALS ABOVE   *
00008 0000               ;*                              *
00009 0000               ;* CALL FILENAME STRING THEN    *
00010 0000               ;*                              *
00011 0000               ;*           SYS 49988          *
00012 0000               ;*                              *
00013 0000               ;*                              *
00014 0000               ;* E.G.                         *
00015 0000               ;* 10 FN$="FILENAME"            *
00016 0000               ;* 20 POKE 49984,DEVICE         *
00017 0000               ;* 30 FN$=FN$                   *
00018 0000               ;* 40 SYS49988                  *
00019 0000               ;*                              *
00020 0000               ;* NOTE: THIS ROUTINE WILL FIND *
00021 0000               ;* THE ADDRESS IN MEMORY OF THE *
00022 0000               ;* FILENAME. A FULL DISCUSSION  *
00023 0000               ;* OF VARIABLE STORAGE CAN BE   *
00024 0000               ;* FOUND IN CHAPTER 2.          *
00025 0000               ;*                              *
00026 0000               ;********************************

00028 0000               VARNAM = $45           ;CURRENT BASIC VAR NAME
00029 0000               VARPTR= $47            ;POINTER CURRENT VARIABLE
00030 0000               SETLFS = $FFBA         ;KERNAL SETLFS
00031 0000               SETNAM = $FFBD         ;KERNAL SETNAM
00032 0000               LOAD   = $FFD5         ;KERNAL LOAD
00033 0000               *      = $C340
00034 C340               DEVNUM *=*+1           ;DEVICE NUMBER
00035 C341               FNLEN  *=*+1           ;FILENAME LENGTH
00036 C342               FNADDR *=*+2;FILENAME ADDRESS

00038 C344  A0 02            LDY #$02
00039 C346  B1 47            LDA (VARPTR),Y
00040 C348  8D 41 C3         STA FNLEN
00041 C34B  C8               INY
00042 C34C  B1 47            LDA (VARPTR),Y
00043 C34E  8D 42 C3         STA FNADDR
00044 C351  C8               INY
00045 C352  B1 47            LDA (VARPTR),Y
00046 C354  8D 43 C3         STA FNADDR+1

00048 C357             ;
00049 C357             ;
00050 C357  A9 01          LDA #$01
00051 C359  AE 40 C3       LDX DEVNUM        ;SETLFS (1,DEVNUM,1)
00052 C35C  A0 01          LDY #$01
00053 C35E  20 BA FF       JSR SETLFS
00054 C361             ;
00055 C361             ;
00056 C361  AD 41 C3       LDA FNLEN
00057 C364  AE 42 C3       LDX FNADDR
```

Listing continued next page

```
00058  C367  AC 43 C3          LDY FNADDR+1        ;SETNAM
00059  C36A  20 BD FF          JSR SETNAM
00060  C36D               ;
00061  C36D               ;
00062  C36D  A9 00             LDA #$00
00063  C36F  A2 FF             LDX #$FF            ;LOAD TO ADDRESS SPECIFIED
00064  C371  A0 FF             LDY #$FF            ;IN FILE HEADER
00065  C373  20 D5 FF          JSR LOAD            ;LOAD
00066  C376               ;
00067  C376          EXIT
00068  C376  60             RTS
00069  C377          .END
```

ERRORS = 00000

SYMBOL TABLE

SYMBOL VALUE
```
  DEVNUM   C340     EXIT     C376     FNADDR   C342     FNLEN    C341
  LOAD     FFD5     SETLFS   FFBA     SETNAM   FFBD     VARNAM   0045
  VARPTR   0047
```

END OF ASSEMBLY

```
LINE# LOC    CODE          LINE


00001  0000                ;****************************************
00002  0000                ;*                                    *
00003  0000                ;*              SAVE 64                *
00004  0000                ;*                                    *
00005  0000                ;*                                    *
00006  0000                ;* 50048 = START ADDR LO-BYTE         *
00007  0000                ;*                                    *
00008  0000                ;* 50049 = START ADDR HI-BYTE         *
00009  0000                ;*                                    *
00010  0000                ;* 50050 = END ADDR LO-BYTE           *
00011  0000                ;*                                    *
00012  0000                ;* 50051 = END ADDR HI-BYTE           *
00013  0000                ;*                                    *
00014  0000                ;* 50052 = DEVICE NUMBER              *
00015  0000                ;*                                    *
00016  0000                ;*                                    *
00017  0000                ;*                                    *
00018  0000                ;* TO USE   - POKE VALS ABOVE         *
00019  0000                ;*                                    *
00020  0000                ;* CALL FILENAME STRING THEN          *
00021  0000                ;*                                    *
00022  0000                ;*           SYS 50056                *
00023  0000                ;*                                    *
00024  0000                ;*                                    *
00025  0000                ;* E.G.                               *
00026  0000                ;* 10 FN$="FILENAME"                  *
00027  0000                ;* 20 POKE50048,SL:POKE50049,SH *
00028  0000                ;* 30 POKE50050,EL:POKE50051,EH *
00029  0000                ;* 40 POKE 50052,DEVICE               *
00030  0000                ;* 50 FN$=FN$                         *
00031  0000                ;* 60 SYS50056                        *
00032  0000                ;*                                    *
00033  0000                ;* NOTE: THIS ROUTINE WILL FIND *
00034  0000                ;* THE ADDRESS IN MEMORY OF THE *
00035  0000                ;* FILENAME. A FULL DISCUSSION  *
00036  0000                ;* OF VARIABLE STORAGE CAN BE   *
00037  0000                ;* FOUND IN CHAPTER 2.          *
00038  0000                ;*                                    *
00039  0000                ;****************************************

00041  0000                VARNAM = $45              ;CURRENT BASIC VAR NAME
00042  0000                VARPTR= $47              ;POINTER CURRENT VARIABLE
00043  0000                SADDR  = $FB              ;ZP SAVE ADDRESSS
00044  0000                SETLFS = $FFBA            ;KERNAL SETLFS
00045  0000                SETNAM = $FFBD            ;KERNAL SETNAM
00046  0000                SAVE   = $FFD8            ;KERNAL SAVE
00047  0000                *      = $C380
00048  C380                START  *=*+2              ;SAVE START ADDRESS
00049  C382                END    *=*+2              ;SAVE END ADDRESS
00050  C384                DEVNUM *=*+1              ;DEVICE NUMBER
00051  C385                FNLEN  *=*+1             ;FILENAME LENGTH
00052  C386                FNADDR *=*+2;FILENAME ADDRESS

00054  C388  A0 02         LDY #$02
00055  C38A  B1 47         LDA (VARPTR),Y
00056  C38C  8D 85 C3      STA FNLEN
```

Listing continued next page

```
00057   C38F   C8                      INY
00058   C390   B1 47                   LDA (VARPTR),Y
00059   C392   8D 86 C3                STA FNADDR
00060   C395   C8                      INY
00061   C396   B1 47                   LDA (VARPTR),Y
00062   C398   8D 87 C3                STA FNADDR+1

00064   C39B   AD 80 C3                LDA START            ;
00065   C39E   85 FB                   STA SADDR            ;PUT START ADDRESS IN
00066   C3A0   AD 81 C3                LDA START+1          ;ZERO PAGE
00067   C3A3   85 FC                   STA SADDR+1          ;
00068   C3A5                   ;
00069   C3A5                   ;
00070   C3A5   A9 01                   LDA #$01
00071   C3A7   AE 84 C3                LDX DEVNUM           ;SETLFS (1,DEVNUM,1)
00072   C3AA   A0 01                   LDY #$01
00073   C3AC   20 BA FF                JSR SETLFS
00074   C3AF                   ;
00075   C3AF                   ;
00076   C3AF   AD 85 C3                LDA FNLEN
00077   C3B2   AE 86 C3                LDX FNADDR
00078   C3B5   AC 87 C3                LDY FNADDR+1         ;SETNAM
00079   C3B8   20 BD FF                JSR SETNAM
00080   C3BB                   ;
00081   C3BB                   ;
00082   C3BB   A9 FB                   LDA #SADDR           ;ZP POINTER TO START ADDR
00083   C3BD   AE 82 C3                LDX END
00084   C3C0   AC 83 C3                LDY END+1            ;END ADDRESS
00085   C3C3   20 D8 FF                JSR SAVE             ;SAVE
00086   C3C6                   ;
00087   C3C6                  EXIT
00088   C3C6   60                      RTS
00089   C3C7                  .END

ERRORS = 00000


SYMBOL TABLE

SYMBOL VALUE
  DEVNUM    C384      END      C382      EXIT     C3C6      FNADDR   C386
  FNLEN     C385      SADDR    00FB      SAVE     FFD8      SETLFS   FFBA
  SETNAM    FFBD      START    C380      VARNAM   0045      VARPTR   0047


END OF ASSEMBLY
```

When the concept of the KERNAL routines was devised it was decided that upon returning from any routine, carry clear would indicate no error, and carry set would indicate an error. However, our own experience has proved this not to be reliable.

Let us take a look at each routine and how to use it.

Routine: ACPTR
Function: Get a byte from the serial bus.
Address: $FFA5   65445
Registers used: A,X
Prior to this Execute: TALK,TKSA
Possible errors: See READST

This routine is used to get a byte of data from the serial bus. No data needs to be passed to this routine, and the byte is returned in the accumulator. Prior to calling this routine the device must be instructed to TALK on the serial bus using the TALK routine, and if the device requires a secondary address the TKSA routine must also be used.

How to use: Call this routine.

Routine: CHKIN
Function: Open a channel for input
Address: $FFC6   65478
Registers used: X
Prior to this Execute: OPEN
Possible errors: See below

This routine will define any logical file already opened using the OPEN routine as an input channel. The device on the channel must, of course, be an input device, otherwise an error will occur and the routine will abort. When used with devices on the serial bus the TALK and if required TKSA commands are automatically sent.

How to use: Load the logical file number into X
             Call this routine
Possible Errors: 3 − File not open
                 5 − Device not present
                 6 − File not an input file.

Routine: CHKOUT
Function: Open a channel for output
Address: $FFC9   65481
Registers used: X
Prior to this Execute: OPEN
Possible errors: See below

This routine will define any logical file already opened using the OPEN routine as an output channel. The device on the channel must, of course, be an output device, otherwise an error will occur and the routine will abort. When used with devices on the serial bus the LISTEN and if required SECOND commands are automatically sent.

How to use: Load the logical file number into X
             Call this routine
Possible errors: 3 — File not open
                  5 — Device not present
                  7 — File not an output file.

Routine: CHKIN
Function: Get a byte from the input channel
Address: $FFCF   65487
Registers used: A
Prior to this Execute: OPEN,CHRIN
Possible errors: See READST

This routine is used to get a byte of data from the input channel. No data needs to be passed to this routine, and the byte is returned in the accumulator. Prior to calling this routine the input channel must be defined using the CHKIN routine, unless input is required from the keyboard.

How to use: Call this routine.

Routine: CHROUT
Function: Send a byte to the output channel
Address: $FFD2   65490
Registers used: A
Prior to this Execute: OPEN,CHKOUT
Possible errors: See READST

This routine is used to send a byte of data to the output channel. The byte to be transmitted should be in the accumulator before calling this routine. Prior to calling this routine the output channel must be defined using the CHKOUT routine, unless output is required to the screen.

How to use: Load byte into A
             Call this routine.

Routine: CIOUT
Function: Send a byte to the serial bus
Address: $FFA8   65448
Registers used: A
Prior to this Execute: LISTEN,SECOND
Possible errors: See READST

This routine is used to send a byte of data to the serial bus. The byte to be sent should be loaded into the accumulator before calling this routine. Prior to calling this routine the device must be instructed to LISTEN on the serial bus using the LISTEN routine, and if the device requires a secondary address the SECOND routine must also be used.

How to use: Load byte into A
             Call this routine

Routine: CINT
Function: Initialize screen editor
Address: $FF81   65409
Registers used: A,X,Y
Prior to this Execute: None
Possible errors: None.

This routine is used to reinitialize the screen editor, and the VIC-II video chip.

How to use: Call this routine

Routine: CLALL
Function: Close all logical files and channels
Address: $FFE7   65511
Registers used: A,X
Prior to this Execute: None
Possible errors: None

This routine is used to close all logical files and channels which are open.

How to use: Call this routine.

Routine: CLOSE
Function: Close a specified logical file
Address: $FFC3   65475
Registers used: A,X,Y
Prior to this Execute: None
Possible errors: See READST

This routine is used to close a specified logical file. The logical file number should be loaded into the accumulator before calling this routine.

How to use: Load logical file number into A
             Call this routine

Routine: CLRCHN
Function: Clear the current input/output channels
Address: $FFCC   65484
Registers used: A,X
Prior to this Execute: None
Possible errors: See READST

This routine is used to clear the current input/output channels.

How to use: Call this routine.

Routine: GETIN
Function: Get a byte from the keyboard buffer
Address: $FFE4   65508

Registers used: A,X,Y
Prior to this Execute: None
Possible errors: See READST

This routine is used to get a byte of data from the keyboard buffer. The data is returned in the accumulator.

How to use: Call this routine

Routine: IOBASE
Function: Get the base address of the I/O devices
Address: $FFF3   65523
Registers used: X,Y
Prior to this Execute: None
Possible errors: None

This routine returns with the base address of the I/O devices, i.e. CIA#1, in the X and Y registers, the X register holding the Lo-byte. If all calls to the I/O devices are made as an offset from this then programs should be compatible with future versions of the CBM 64.

How to use: Call this routine

Routine IOINIT
Function: Initialize I/O devices.
Address: $FF84   65412
Registers used: A,X,Y
Prior to this Execute: None
Possible errors: None

This routine initializes all I/O devices and routines.

How to use: Call this routine

Routine: LISTEN
Function: Command serial device to listen
Address: $FFB1   65457
Registers used: A
Prior to this Execute: None
Possible errors: None

This routine will command a device on the serial bus to LISTEN. The accumulator must be loaded with the device number before calling the routine.

How to use: Load device number into A
              Call this routine

Routine: LOAD
Function: Load/Verify RAM from a device
Address: $FFD5   65493
Registers used: A,X,Y

Prior to this Execute: SETLFS,SETNAM
Possible errors: See READST

This routine can be used to either load or verify RAM from a device. The accumulator must be set to a 0 for a load and a 1 for a verify. If a secondary address of zero has been specified then the header information from the device is ignored, and the start address for the load is taken from the X and Y registers, with the Hi-byte in the Y register. If the secondary address is a one then the load will start from the address specified in the header information.

Before using this routine the SETLFS and SETNAM routines must be called.

How to use: Call SETLFS and SETNAM
             Load 1 for load or 0 for verify into A
             Load start address if required into X and Y
             Call this routine

Routine: MEMBOT
Function: Read/Set the bottom of memory
Address: $FF9C   65436
Registers used: X,Y
Prior to this Execute: None
Possible errors: None

If the carry bit of the 6510 status register is set when this routine is called the X and Y registers will return with the pointer to the bottom of memory. If the carry bit is cleared then the values in the X and Y registers will be put into the bottom of memory pointers.

How to use: Load pointer values, if required, into X and Y
             Clear carry to set pointers, set carry to read pointers
             Call this routine

Routine: MEMTOP
Function: Read/Set the top of memory
Address: $FF99   65433
Registers used: X,Y
Prior to this Execute: None
Possible errors: None

If the carry bit of the 6510 status register is set when this routine is called the X and Y registers will return with the pointer to the top of memory. If the carry bit is cleared then the values in the X and Y registers will be put into the top of memory pointers.

How to use: Load pointer values, if required, into X and Y
             Clear carry to set pointers, set carry to read pointers
             Call this routine

Routine: OPEN
Function: Open a logical file
Address: $FFC0   65472

Registers used: A,X,Y
Prior to this Execute: SETLFS,SETNAM
Possible errors: See READST

This routine is used to open a logical file. Once opened a logical file may then be used by the various I/O kernal routines. No parameters need be passed to this routine, but before using this routine the SETLFS and SETNAM routines must be called.

How to use: Call SETLFS and SETNAM
                Call this routine

Routine: PLOT
Function: Read/Set cursor position
Address: $FFF0   65520
Registers used: A,X,Y
Prior to this Execute: None
Possible errors: None

If the carry bit of the 6510 status register is set when this routine is called the X and Y registers will return with the co-ordinates of the cursor position on the current *logical* screen line (vertical and horizontal respectively!). If the carry bit is cleared then the values in the X and Y registers will be used to set the cursor position.

How to use: Load pointer values, if required, into X and Y
                Clear carry to set position, set carry to read position
                Call this routine

Routine: RAMTAS
Function: Perform RAM test, and initialize RAM
Address: $FF87   65415
Registers used: A,X,Y
Prior to this Execute: None
Possible errors: None

This routine will test RAM and set the top and bottom of memory pointers according to how much RAM it finds. It will also clear the zero page and page 2.

How to use: Call this routine

Routine: RDTIM
Function: Read the real time system clock
Address: $FFDE   65502
Registers used: A,X,Y
Prior to this Execute: None
Possible errors: None

This routine will read the system real time (jiffy) clock. The MSB is returned in the accumulator, the next significant byte is in the X register, and the LSB in the Y register.

How to use: Call this routine.

Routine: READST
Function: Read the I/O status byte
Address: $FFB7   65463
Registers used: A
Prior to this Execute: None
Possible errors: None

This routine returns the I/O status byte in the accumulator. The information contained within this byte is tabulated in the description of ST in Section I. (See also Chapter 7.)

How to use: Call this routine.

Routine: RESTOR
Function: Restore default system and interrupt vectors
Address: $FF8A   65418
Registers used: A,X,Y
Prior to this Execute: None
Possible errors: None

This routine restores the default values to the system and interrupt vectors in page 2.

How to use: Call this routine

Routine: SAVE
Function: Save RAM to a device
Address: $FFD8   65496
Registers used: A,X,Y
Prior to this Execute: SETLFS,SETNAM
Possible errors: See READST

This routine is used to either save RAM to a device. The accumulator holds a single byte pointer to a pair of zero page locations which contain the start address of the save, and the X and Y registers should hold the end address of the save, with the Hi-byte in the Y register.
    Before using this routine the SETLFS and SETNAM routines must be called.

How to use: Call STLFS and SETNAM
              Load zero page pointer to start address into A
              Load end address into X and Y
              Call this routine

Routine: SCNKEY
Function: Scan the keyboard
Address: $FF9F   65439
Registers used: A,X,Y
Prior to this Execute: IOINIT
Possible errors: None

This routine will scan the keyboard, and if a key is being pressed it will place the ASCII value of the character in the keyboard buffer.

How to use: Call IOINIT (if you have been using the I/O chips)
                Call this routine

Routine: SCREEN
Function: Return the screen format
Address: $FFED   65517
Registers used: X,Y
Prior to this Execute: None
Possible errors: None

This routine returns the number of rows and columns displayed on the screen. The number of rows is returned in the Y register and the number of columns in the X register.

How to use: Call this routine

Routine: SECOND
Function: Send secondary address for LISTEN
Address: $FF93   65427
Register used: A
Prior to this Execute: LISTEN
Possible errors: See READST

This routine is used to send a secondary address to a device which has been commanded to LISTEN. The secondary address should be loaded into the accumulator before calling this routine.

How to use: Call LISTEN
                Load secondary address into A
                Call this routine

Routine SETLFS
Function: Set logical file number, first and second addresses
Address: $FFBA   65466
Registers used: A,X,Y
Prior to this Execute: None
Possible errors: None

This routine sets the logical file number, first and second addresses, which are required by the OPEN, LOAD and SAVE routines. The logical file number should be put into the accumulator, the device number into the X register, and the secondary address into the Y register before calling this routine.

How to use: Load the logical file number into A
                Load the device number into X
                Load the secondary address into Y
                Call this routine

Routine: SETMSG
Function: Control KERNAL messages
Address $FF90   65424
Registers used: A
Prior to this Execute: None
Possible errors: None

This routine controls the output of KERNAL control and error messages. Control messages are of the type 'SEARCHING FOR . . .' and error messages are of the type 'DEVICE NOT PRESENT'. The control byte should be loaded into the accumulator before calling this routine. The important parts of the control byte are bits 6 and 7. When bit 6 is set Control messages will output, when cleared they are inhibited. Bit 7 has the same effect on Error messages.

How to use: Load control byte into A
             Call this routine

Routine: SETNAM
Function: Set filename
Address: $FFBD   65469
Registers used: A,X,Y
Prior to this Execute: None
Possible errors: None

This routine is used to set the filename which is required for the OPEN, LOAD and SAVE routines. The length of the filename must be loaded into the accumulator, and the address of the filename string in memory must be loaded into the X and Y registers with the Hi-byte in the Y register, before calling the routine. If no filename is desired (with a tape save for example) the accumulator should be set to zero.

How to use: Load the filename length into A
             Load the address of the filename string into X and Y
             Call this routine

Routine: SETTIM
Function: Set real time (jiffy) clock
Address: $FFDB   65499
Registers used: A,X,Y
Prior to this Execute: None
Possible errors: None

This routine is used to set the value of the jiffy clock. Before calling the routine the MSB of the value should be loaded into the accumulator, the next significant byte in the X register and the LSB in the Y register.

How to use: Load MSB into A
             Load NSB into X
             Load LSB into Y
             Call this routine

Routine: SETTMO
Function: Set serial port timeout
Address: $FFA2 65442
Registers used: A
Prior to this Execute: None
Possible errors: None

This routine is used to enable and disable serial bus timeouts. The command byte should be loaded into the accumulator before calling the routine. If bit 7 of the command byte is set to a one timeouts will be disabled, if cleared they will be enabled.

How to use: Load command byte into A
            Call this routine

Routine: STOP
Function: Check if STOP key is pressed
Address: $FFE1 65505
Registers used: A,X
Prior to this Execute: None
Possible errors: None

If the stop key was pressed during the last call of the UDTIM routine, a call of this routine will return with the Z flag of the processor status byte set.

How to use: Call UDTIM
            Call this routine

Routine: TALK
Function: Command serial device to TALK
Address: $FFB4 65460
Registers used: A
Prior to this Execute: None
Possible errors: See READST

To use this routine the accumulator must first be loaded with the device number before calling the routine.

How to use: Load device number into A
            Call this routine

Routine: TKSA
Function: Send secondary address for TALK
Address: $FF96 65430
Registers used: A
Prior to this Execute: TALK
Possible errors: See READST

This routine is used to send a secondary address to a device which has been commanded to TALK. The secondary address should be loaded into the accumulator before calling this routine.

How to use: Call TALK
                     Load secondary address into A
                     Call this routine

Routine: UDTIM
Function: Update the system (jiffy) clock
Address: $FFEA   65514
Registers used: A,X
Prior to this Execute: None
Possible errors: None

This routine increments the value of the jiffy clock by one. It is normally called by the operating system every 60th of a second on an interrupt. If you are handling interrupts yourself you must call this routine to update the clock. In addition this routine must be called in conjunction with STOP in order to keep the stop key functioning.

How to use: Call this routine

Routine: UNLSN
Function: Command serial device to UNLISTEN
Address: $FFAE   65454
Registers used: A
Prior to this Execute: None
Possible errors: None

This routine will command all devices on the serial bus which are LISTENing to UNLISTEN. No parameters are required.

How to use: Call this routine

Routine: UNTLK
Function: Command serial device to UNTALK
Address: $FFAB   65451
Registers used: A
Prior to this Execute: None
Possible errors: See READST

This routine will command all devices on the serial bus which are TALKing to UNTALK. No parameters are required.

How to use: Call this routine

Routine: VECTOR
Function: Read/Set RAM vectors
Address: $FF8D   65421
Registers used: A,X,Y
Prior to this Execute: None
Possible errors: None

Before calling this routine the X and Y registers should contain a pointer to memory. If the routine is then called with the carry bit set the contents of the RAM vectors at locations $0314 to $0333 (788 to 819) are copied into the block of memory pointed to by the X and Y registers. If the carry is clear, the values pointed to by the X and Y registers are copied into the RAM vectors.

How to use: Set up pointers in X and Y registers
Set carry to read vectors, clear carry to set vectors
Call this routine

INTERPRETER FLOATING POINT ROUTINES

Here is a more detailed description of the interpreter floating point routines, which were mentioned earlier in this chapter.

Routine: ABS
Function: Perform ABS(FAC)
Address: $BC58   48216

FAC = ABS(FAC)

Routine: ANDOP
Function: Perform FAC AND ARG
Address: $AFE9   45033

FAC = (FAC) AND (ARG)

Routine: ATN
Function: Perform ATN(FAC)
Address: $E30E   58126

FAC = ATN(FAC)

Routine: AYINT
Function: Convert FAC to INT
Address: $B1BF   45503

Convert FAC to integer in the range 0 to 32767, result in FAC+3.

Routine: CONUPK
Function: Load ARG from MFPTN
Address: $BA8C   47756

Load ARG from a MFPTN whose address is stored in A and Y registers (Lo, Hi) upon entry.

Routine: COS
Function: Perform COS(FAC)
Address: $E264   57956

FAC = COS(FAC).

Routine: DIV10
Function: Divide FAC/10
Address: $BAFE   47870

FAC = ABS(FAC/10). Divides FAC by 10, but result always positive.

Routine: EXP
Function: Perform EXP(FAC)
Address: $BFED   49133

FAC = EXP(FAC)

Routine: FACINX
Function: Convert DAC to INT
Address: $B1AA   45482

Convert FAC to an integer in the range −32768 to +32767. Result in A and Y registers upon exit.

Routine: FADD
Function: Add FAC + MFPTN
Address: $B867   47207

FAC = FAC + MPRTN. Address of MRPTN in A and Y (Lo, Hi) upon entry.

Routine: FADDH
Function: Add FAC + 0.5
Address: $B849   47177

FAC = FAC + 0.5.

Routine: FADDT
Function: Add FAC + ARG
Address: $B86A   47210

FAC = FAC + ARG.

Routine: FCOMP
Function: Compare FAC with MFPTN
Address: $BC5B   48219

Upon entry address of MFPTN is in A and Y (Lo, Hi). Upon exit A contains:

        00 if FAC = MFPTN
        01 if FAC > MFPTN
        FF if FAC < MFPTN.

Routine: FDIV
Function: Divide MFPTN/FAC
Address: $BB0F   47887

FAC = MFPTN/FAC. Address MFPTN in A and Y (Lo, Hi) upon entry.

Routine: FDIVF
Function: Divide ARG/MFPTN
Address: $BB07   47879

FAC = ARG/MFPTN. Address of MFPTN in A and Y (Lo, Hi), sign of result in X upon entry.

Routine: FDIVT
Function: Divide ARG/FAC
Address: $BB12   47890

FAC = ARG/FAC.

Routine: FMULT
Function: Multiply FAC*MFPTN
Address: $BA28   47656

FAC = FAC*MFPTN. Address of MFPTN in A and Y (Lo, Hi) upon entry.

Routine: FMULTT
Function: Multiply FAC*ARG
Address: $BA2B   47659

FAC = FAC*ARG.

Routine: FPWRT
Function: Perform ARG↑FAC
Address $BF7B   49019

FAC = ARG↑FAC. Set A = FAC exponent on entry.

Routine: FSUB
Function: Subtract MFPTN–FAC
Address: $B850   47184

FAC = MFPTN − FAC. Address of MFPTN in A and Y (Lo, Hi) upon entry.

Routine: FSUBT
Function: Subtract ARG–FAC
Address: $B853   47187

FAC = ARG − FAC.

Routine: GIVAYF
Function: Convert INT in A/Y to FPT
Address: $B391   45969

Takes an integer, in the range 0 to 32767, held in A and Y (Lo, Hi) and converts it to a floating point value in FAC.

Routine: INT
Function: Perform INT(FAC)
Address: $BCCC   48332

FAC = INT(FAC)

Routine: LOG
Function: Perform LOG(FAC)
Address: $B9EA   47594

FAC = LOG(FAC)

Routine: MOVAF
Function: Load ARG from FAC
Address: $BC0C   48140

ARG = FAC.

Routine: MOVFA
Function: Load FAC from ARG
Address: $BBFC   48124

FAC = ARG.

Routine: MOVFM
Function: Load FAC from MFPTN
Address: $BBA2   48034

FAC = MFPTN. Address of MFPTN in A and Y (Lo, Hi) upon entry. Note this converts from 5 byte format to 7 byte.

Routine: MOVMF
Function: Store FAC in MFPTN
Address: $BBD4   48084

MFPTN = FAC. Address of MFPTN in X and Y (Lo, Hi) upon entry.

Routine: MUL10
Function: Multiply FAC*10
Address: $BAE2   47842

FAC = FAC*10.

Routine: NEGOP
Function: Negate FAC
Address: $BFB4   49076

FAC = −FAC.

Routine: NUMREL
Function: Perform numeric comparison
Address: $B01B   45083

Compare FAC and ARG. Results as described under FCOMP.

Routine: OROP
Function: Perform (FAC) OR (ARG)
Address: $AFE6   45030

FAC = (FAC) OR (ARG).

Routine: QINT
Function: Convert FAC into 4-byte INT
Address: $BC9B   48283

Convert FAC into 4-byte integer in FAC+1 to FAC+4.

Routine: RND
Function: Put random number into FAC
Address: $E097   57495

FAC = RND(FAC), where:
    seed is 'random' register of 6526 if FAC = 0;
    seed is last random number (in RNDX) if FAC > 0;
    seed is ABS(FAC) if FAC < 0.

Routine: ROUND
Function: Round FAC
Address: $BC1B   48155

FAC = INT(FAC+0.5).

Routine: SGN
Function: Perform SGN(FAC)
Address: $BC39   48185

FAC = SGN(FAC).

Routine: SIGN
Function: Check sign of FAC
Address: $BC2B   48171

Upon exit A contains:
        01 if FAC +ve
        00 if FAC 0
        FF if FAC −ve

Routine: SIN
Function: Perform SIN(FAC)
Address: $E26B   57963

FAC = SIN(FAC)

Routine: SNGFT
Function: Convert Y to FPT
Address: $B3A2   45986

FAC = Y, where Y is in the range 0 to 255. Note this converts from 1-byte integer to floating point.

Routine: SQR
Function: Perform SQR(FAC)
Address: $BF71   49009

FAC = SQR(FAC).

Routine: TAN
Function: Perform TAN(FAC)
Address: $E2B4   58036

FAC = TAN(FAC).

An introduction to machine-code programming

INTRODUCTION

We will now take a brief look at 6510 machine code programming on the CBM 64. A machine code program is a sequence of bytes which represent instructions and data. Because a series of bytes is simply a collection of numbers in the range 0 to 255 it is rather difficult to follow, especially since each instruction may have a different number of bytes of data following it. Instead of trying to follow this by hand it is easier to get the machine to do it for us. We can use a set of three character *mnemonics* to represent the various instructions, or op-codes, and then run a program called an ASSEMBLER to turn these mnemonics into true machine code. Similarly, if we wish to look at a machine code program we use a DISASSEMBLER, which translates bytes into mnemonics for us. This form of writing programs using mnemonics is called ASSEMBLER, and it is just as much a language as BASIC. For writing virtually any machine language program an assembler and a disassembler is essential. Most disassemblers or m/c monitors will allow you to write programs which they will assemble byte by byte, while the Assembler will assemble a whole program in one go. This is rather like the comparison of an interpreter and a compiler given in the previous chapter. Although a disassembler is not as convenient as a separate assembler it is perfectly adequate for writing short routines.

64-MON[†] is just such a disassembler (often called a 'debugger' on other systems). It is widely available, and really is a must for anyone attempting to learn about machine code programming. It has a variety of commands, a few of which we will discuss briefly here.

D ADDR1,ADDR2

Disassemble code from memory address ADDR1 to address ADDR2. This command will read bytes from memory and display them on the screen as mnemonics. Here is a short piece of code from the KERNAL disassembled by 64-MON.

†64-MON is a registered trade-mark of CBM.

```
,,   FCE2   A2 FF      LDX  #$FF
,,   FCE4   78         SEI
,,   FCE5   9A         TXS
,,   FCE6   D8         CLD
,,   FCE7   20 02 FD   JSR  $FD02
,,   FCEA   D0 03      BNE  $FCEF
,,   FCEC   6C 00 80   JMP  ($8000)
,,   FCEF   8E 16 D0   STX  $D016
,,   FCF2   20 A3 FD   JSR  $FDA3
,,   FCF5   20 50 FD   JSR  $FD50
,,   FCF8   20 15 FD   JSR  $FD15
,,   FCFB   20 5B FF   JSR  $FF5B
,,   FCFE   58         CLI
,,   FCFF   6C 00 A0   JMP  ($A000)
,,   FD02   A2 05      LDX  #$05
,,   FD04   BD 0F FD   LDA  $FD0F,X
,,   FD07   DD 03 80   CMP  $8003,X
,,   FD0A   D0 03      BNE  $FD0F
,,   FD0C   CA         DEX
,,   FD0D   D0 F5      BNE  $FD04
,,   FD0F   60         RTS
```

M ADDR1,ADDR2

Memory dump for ADDR1 to ADDR2. This displays the actual byte values between ADDR1 and ADDR2. Here is the same block of memory dumped.

```
, :FCE2 A2 FF 78 9A D8 20 02 FD
, :FCEA D0 03 6C 00 80 8E 16 D0
, :FCF2 20 A3 FD 20 50 FD 20 15
, :FCFA FD 20 5B FF 58 6C 00 A0
, :FD02 A2 05 BD 0F FD DD 03 80
, :FD0A D0 03 CA D0 F5 60 C3 C2
```

R

Displays the contents of the Accumulator, X and Y registers, Status Register, Stack Pointer and Program Counter.

```
    PC   SR AC XR YR SP
, ;803E 32 00 83 00 F6
```

The instructions given above will produce a listing on the screen. To list to the printer you should direct output to the printer using the BASIC commands OPEN,4,4:CMD4 before entering 64-MON.

Code may be written using 64-MON by simply Disassembling the block of memory you wish to put your code into, positioning the cursor on the right line and entering your program.

You may then test your programs using the BP, set breakpoint, and G, go (or execute) code, and they may then be saved to tape or disk using the L, load, and S, save, commands. However, because moving blocks of programs about to insert and delete code is quite a complex task, a disassembler is not recommended for writing lengthy routines.

Each machine code instruction performs a very simple task, changing one internal register on the chip or moving one byte of data, but because no interpreting is required the instructions can be executed at such an incredible speed (about 250,000 per second!) that a great deal can be achieved. The great advantage of machine code programming is that it gives you total control of the computer — you could write a completely new operating system if you wanted to — but the big disadvantage is that if you get it wrong there's no operating system to say 'SYNTAX ERROR' and let you try again; the machine just crashes on you! Learning about Assembly language programming can be very rewarding, but it can also be very frustrating. It's worth it in the end, so hang in there!

The first bit of good news is that the 6510 instruction set is identical to the 6502. So if you've done any Assembler on a VIC-20 or a PET you have a head start.

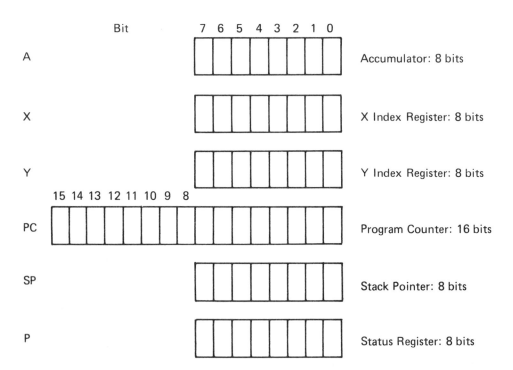

Fig. 9.1 – The 6510 Internal Registers.

THE INTERNAL REGISTERS OF THE 6510

The 6510 microprocessor has five 8-bit registers and one 16-bit register available to the programmer. These are shown in Fig. 9.1. Let's take a look at each of these registers in turn.

The Accumulator

This is the register which is most used by the programmer. All arithmetic and logical operations (with the exception of increment and decrement by 1) are performed on the contents of this register, and no other. This register can also be used to transfer bytes from one memory location to another. This latter function can also be performed by the X and Y Index registers.

Examples:
Throughout this chapter we will use the mnemonic form of the instruction set, a complete list of which can be found at the end of this chapter.

        LDA $1000   Load accumulator with contents of address $1000
        STA $2000   Store accumulator contents in address $2000

Similarly

        LDX $1000 or LDY $1000
        STX $2000 or STY $2000

The X and Y index registers

Like the accumulator data can be moved in and out of these registers, but their main function is to hold offset values which can be used as pointers to blocks of memory, or counters. The contents of each index register can be incremented by one or decremented by one, using the following instructions:

        INX and INY
        DEX and DEY

There are some differences in the way these registers can be used but we will discuss these differences when we look at addressing modes later in this chapter.

The program counter

This is the only 16-bit register and it always contains the address in memory of the next instruction to be executed. The first step of executing each instruction is to set the R/$\overline{W}$ line high for a read, and to place the contents of the program counter onto the address bus. The microprocessor then reads the instruction into its internal *instruction register*, which is not accessible to the programmer, where it is held whilst it is decoded. At this point the program counter is automatically incremented by one to point to the next byte, which may be data or another instruction. The next step is the actual execution of the instruction, during this period more data may be read in, and each read increments the program counter to the next byte, so that by the end of the instruction the program counter will be pointing to the next instruction.

We can see that the program counter allows the microprocessor to step through a program sequentially; but of course sometimes we will want jump from one part of a program to another. There are two types of instruction which allow us to alter the contents of the program counter.

The JSR and JMP instructions cause the two bytes which follow them to be put into the program counter, and the branch on condition instruction causes the byte following it to be added to the program counter. This gives us the equivalent of GOSUB and GOTO in BASIC.

The stack pointer

Before we consider the function of the stack pointer we should consider the stack itself. The stack is the block of memory between $100 and $1FF, and comprises what is technically called a LIFO of last-in-first-out structure. To visualize it think of one of those plate dispensers that you find in cafeterias. You take a plate off the top and another pops up, if you push one back on top it has to be removed again before you can get to the one beneath. Now, in the plate stacker the plates physically move up and down: to achieve the same effect in memory we would be continually shuffling bytes, so instead we employ a *stack pointer* to tell us where the top of the stack is. Just to be a little perverse we build our stack from the top down (who need gravity anyway?) so when the stack is empty the stack pointer is at $1FF and when the stack is full it's at $100 Since the stack pointer is only an 8-bit register, it is assumed that the stack is on page one, and so when the stack is empty the stack pointer contains $FF and when full it contains $00. Now that we know where the stack is and how the stack pointer works, we had better find something to put on the stack.

Consider the instruction JSR, this instruction is like a BASIC GOSUB command. It 'pushes' the contents of the program counter onto the stack, and increments the stack pointer to allow for the two extra bytes on the stack. The 16-bit address which follows the JSR instruction is then loaded into the program counter which causes execution to transfer to the desired subroutine. The return-from-subroutine instruction RTS uses the stack pointer to retrieve the original address from the stack and decrements the stack pointer as it takes the bytes back off, returning them to the program counter, and incrementing the program counter to point to the next instruction following the JSR. It is also possible for the programmer to 'push' and 'pull' the contents of the accumulator of the status register onto and from the stack, for temporary storage using the following commands:

> PHA Push accumulator onto stack and decrement stack pointer
> PLA Pull accumulator from stack and increment stack pointer
> PHP Push status register onto stack and decrement stack pointer
> PLP Pull status register from stack and increment stack pointer

In certain situations the programmer may wish to change or set the contents of the stack pointer directly. This can be achieved by using the instructions:

> TSX Transfer stack pointer to X index register
> TXS Transfer X index register to stack pointer

By loading the X index register with some value and using the TXS instruction, the stack pointer may be set, and by using the TSX command the stack pointer may be manipulated and returned using TXS. Some care should be taken in using these instructions since a foul-up of the stack is one of the more spectacular means of causing a crash.

The status register

The 8-bit status register provides the means for decision making. Each bit of this register has its own individual meaning as shown below:

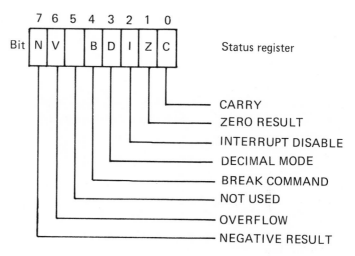

Fig. 9.2 – The 6510 Status Register.

Carry

The carry bit is used to show that the result of an arithmetic operation has generated a carry. In many respects the carry bit is like a ninth bit of the accumulator. The carry bit is set to a one if a carry has occurred, and cleared to a zero if not. However, the meaning of this is inverted when subtraction operations are performed. Thus, after execution of an SBC (Subtract with Borrow) instruction, the carry bit is cleared if a borrow was required, and set if no borrow was needed. The programmer may also set and clear the carry using the instructions:

        SEC Set Carry
        CLC Clear Carry

Apart from the arithmetic operations, the carry bit is also affected by the ASL, BIT, CMP, LSR, ROL and ROR instructions.

Zero result

This flag is automatically set by the processor whenever the contents of the accumulator is zero. This bit cannot be changed by the programmer directly, but any instruction which changes the contents of the accumulator, including arithmetic, logical and data movement, can affect the zero result flag.

Interrupt disable

There are only two instructions which affect the state of this bit, they are

        SEI Set Interrupt Bit
        CLI Clear Interrupt Bit

When the interrupt bit is set all IRQ interrupts to the microprocessor are ignored, and when clear the processor will respond to IRQs. The interrupt bit is automatically set when an interrupt occurs, to prevent further interrupts occurring whilst the current one is dealt with.

Decimal mode
The state of this bit determines whether arithmetic functions performed on the accumulator are done in binary or *binary-coded decimal*, when this bit is set BCD is used, when cleared normal binary is used. In BCD each nybble (4 bits) is used to represent a decimal digit. Thus any value for a nybble of greater than nine is illegal. The largest BCD value that can be represented in 8 bits is therefore 99. BCD is normally only used, for example, when doing things like digital clock displays. Here is an example to show the difference between binary and BCD arithmetic.

	BINARY		BCD	
	0000 1000	(8)	0000 1000	
+	0000 0101	(5)	0000 0101	
	0000 1101	(13)	0001 0011	

The Decimal Mode flag is set and cleared using the instructions

SED Set Decimal Mode
CLD Clear Decimal Mode

Break flag
The break flag is automatically set by the processor, and is used by the interrupt handling routines to determine whether the interrupt was caused by the IRQ line or by a BRK instruction. When an interrupt occurs a copy of the status register is pushed onto the stack, with the break bit set for a BRK and clear for a normal interrupt, from whence it can be examined.

Overflow flag
The overflow flag is used in signed binary arithmetic to determine the validity of the sign bit (bit 7). In signed binary arithmetic a single byte is used to represent values in the range −128 to +127, the lowest seven bits (0–6) representing the value, and bit 7 representing the sign. If bit 7 is set the number is negative, if clear the number is positive. If during an arithmetic operation there is a carry from bit 6 to bit 7, there will be an error in the state of the sign, and then the overflow bit is set.

The other use of the overflow flag is in conjunction with the BIT instruction. The instruction BIT $2000 will perform an AND operation between the contents of the accumulator and memory address $2000, without actually changing either. If the result of this operation is zero then the zero result flag will be set, but more usefully the resultant state of bit 7 is stored in the negative flag, and of bit 6 in the overflow flag. This provides a simple means of testing the state of bit 6. The programmer can directly clear the overflow flag using the CLV instruction.

Negative flag
This bit is set according to the sign of the result of an operation. It will contain the same value as bit 7 after any arithmetic or logical operation. That is 1 if the result is negative and 0 if positive.

All arithmetic, logical and data transfer commands will affect this flag. The programmer cannot directly set or clear this flag.

As we have seen the 6510 microprocessor has one 8-bit status register which contains all of the flags discussed above. The contents of this register provide the means for making decisions about the flow of program control. There are a set of eight branch instructions which test the status register for various conditions. These instructions are:

BCC	Branch on Carry Clear	Test Carry Flag
BCS	Branch on Carry Set	Test Carry Flag
BEQ	Branch on result zero	Test Zero Flag
BNE	Branch on result Not Zero	Test Zero Flag
BVC	Branch on Overflow Clear	Test Overflow Flag
BVS	Branch on Overflow Set	Test Overflow Flag
BMI	Branch on result Negative	Test Negative Flow
BPL	Branch on result Not Negative	Test Negative Flag

ADDRESSING MODES

Each complete instruction to the 6510 comprises a single byte op-code followed by 0.1 or 2 bytes of data, as required. Since an op-code is represented by a single byte, there are 256 possible op-codes. However, on the 6510 microprocessor only 151 of them are implemented. There are actually 56 different mnemonics, but because the same mnemonic may be used in several different *addressing modes* we end up with 151 distinct op-codes. The addressing mode is used to describe which part of memory or which internal register the instruction applies to.

Immediate addressing – 2 bytes – op-code,operand
In immediate mode the instruction operates on the byte following the opcode. For example:

      LDA #$80   appears in memory as A9 80

This instruction loads the value $80 into the accumulator. The #sign signifies immediate addressing.

Absolute addressing – 3 bytes – op-code, two-byte address
In this mode the two bytes following the op-code represent the Lo-byte and the Hi-byte of an address in memory.

      LDA $8056   (AD 56 80)

This instruction will load the contents of address $8056 into the accumulator.

Zero page addressing – 2 bytes – op-code, single-byte address
In this mode the byte following the op-code is the Lo-byte of an address, and can be used when the memory location is in the zero page. Because the Hi-byte is assumed to be zero, less time is spent on producing the address, and thus this instruction is quicker than the previous one.

      LDA $80   (A5 80)

This instruction will load the contents of address $80 into the accumulator.

Implied addressing – 1 byte – op-code
In this mode no memory accesses are required, and the operations on the internal registers of the 6510 are implied by the instructions. Examples of this TSX,TXS,CLC,SEC and so on.

Relative Addressing – 2 bytes – op-code, offset
This type of addressing is used by the Branch instructions. The offset is treated as a signed binary number in the range −128 to +127, and is added to the current value of the program counter. Therefore the instruction BEQ $10 means 'if the zero flag is set add $10 to the program counter and continue execution'. In reality, however, it is tedious to have to work out the required offset, so we normally specify the target address we want,

e.g.   BEQ $1234   (F0 offset)

and the assembler or disassembler will convert this into the required offset. If the offset is out of range, i.e. greater than 127 or less than −128, then the assembler will report an error. In the case of most disassemblers available they will print ? against the line of code.

Indirect addressing – 3 bytes – op-code, 2-byte address
The only instruction which can take advantage of this form of addressing is the unconditional jump instruction JMP. The actual result of the instruction:

JMP ($1000)   (6C 00 10)

is jump to the address which is held in $1000 and $1001. Thus if we compute the address we want to end up at, store it in Lo-byte, Hi-byte form in $1000 and $1001 the JMP instruction above will get us to the right place. This instruction has two major uses. Firstly where we need to compute a jump address and then 'GOTO' it, and secondly in the form of VECTORS, which we will discuss in detail later on in the section on Interrupts. The only point to bear in mind is not to make the indirect address a page boundary, e.g. JMP ($10FF), because instead of picking up the final address from $10FF and $1100 the processor will pick up from $10FF and $1000. Therefore both bytes of the final address must be on the same page.

We now turn to the various forms of indexed addressing. This is where the X and Y registers really come into their own. This type of addressing is particularly useful when dealing with arrays and tables.

Absolute indexed addressing – 3 bytes – op code, two-byte address
This mode implies that the contents of one of the Index Registers is to be added to the address supplied in the two following bytes. Thus if the Y register contains $3C and the following instruction is encountered:

LDA $1000,Y   (B9 00 10)

then the contents of address $103C will be loaded into the accumulator. It should be noted that whilst some instructions allow indexing by either register, others don't. The instructions which may use either are ADC,AND,CMP,EOR,LDA,ORA,SBC and STA. Instructions which only use the X register are ASL,DEC,INC,LDY,LSR and ROL, and the only instruction that permits Y indexing only with this addressing mode is LDX.

Zero page indexed addressing − 2 bytes − op-code, single-byte address
This mode is a short form of Absolute Indexed which is used when the address is on the zero page.
The Hi-byte of the address is assumed to be zero. Thus if the X register contains the value $20, the
instruction:

LDA $35,X   (B5 35)

will cause the contents of address $55 to be loaded into the accumulator. It should be noted that
if the sum of the address and the Index Register is more than $FF the address wraps around onto
the zero page, i.e. LDA $F0,X produces an address of $110, but the data will be read from $10.

Zero page indexed addressing is only available with the X Index Register, with the exception
of the LDX and STX instructions, which are indexed by Y.

Example:

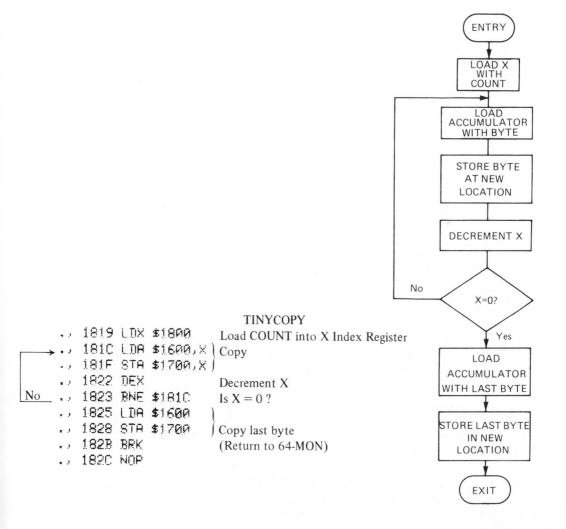

TINYCOPY

```
  .,  1819  LDX  $1800    Load COUNT into X Index Register
→ .,  181C  LDA  $1600,X ⎱ Copy
  .,  181F  STA  $1700,X ⎰
  .,  1822  DEX           Decrement X
  .,  1823  BNE  $181C    Is X = 0 ?
  .,  1825  LDA  $1600   ⎫
  .,  1828  STA  $1700   ⎬ Copy last byte
  .,  182B  BRK          ⎭ (Return to 64-MON)
  .,  182C  NOP
```

Pre-indexed indirect addressing – 2 bytes – op-code, single-byte address
Pre-indexed indirect addressing can only be used with the X register. This mode is a combination of two previous modes, zero page indexed and zero page indirect. If the X register contains the value $20 then the instruction:

LDA ($16,X)   (A1 16)

will load the accumulator with the contents of the address which is stored in addresses $36 and $37. Let's look at a simple example to try and clarify that.

Suppose we put the value $FF into address $1234, and the value $34 into address $36 and the value $12 into address $37. Since the X index register contains $20, the instruction LDA ($16,X) will load the value $FF into the accumulator from address $1234.

This may seem a rather tortuous route for getting data but is in fact a very useful means of picking up data from tables and lists. As with zero page indexed addressing, if the sum of the single-byte address and the index register exceed $FF then the value will wrap around onto the beginning of the zero page.

Post-indexed indirect addressing
This mode employs a slightly different combination of zero page indirect and zero page indexed addressing, and is considered by many to be the most powerful of the addressing modes. It allows you to set up a pointer to anywhere in memory with reasonable ease. This form of addressing is only available using the Y Index Register. Suppose the Y Index Register contains the value $20. The instruction:

LDA ($01),Y   (A1 01)

will load the accumulator with the contents of the address which is contained in $01 and $04 added to the contents of the Y register. Thus if address $01 contains $04 and address $02 contains $1A giving an address of $1A04 plus the contents of the Y register we get an effective address of $1A14. Here is the same thing in more graphical form:

Fig. 9.3 – Post-Indexed Indirect Addressing.

Example:
In this example we will use post-indexed indirect addressing to copy any specified block of memory to a new block, also specified.

```
LINE#  LOC   CODE        LINE

00001  0000                        ;********************************
00002  0000                        ;*                              *
00003  0000                        ;*              COPY 64          *
00004  0000                        ;*                              *
00005  0000                        ;*                              *
00006  0000                        ;* KEY VALUES (DECIMAL):         *
00007  0000                        ;*                              *
00008  0000                        ;* 49872 = START ADDR LO-BYTE    *
00009  0000                        ;*                              *
00010  0000                        ;* 49873 = START ADDR HI-BYTE    *
00011  0000                        ;*                              *
00012  0000                        ;* 49874 = END ADDR LO-BYTE      *
00013  0000                        ;*                              *
00014  0000                        ;* 49875 = END ADDR HI-BYTE      *
00015  0000                        ;*                              *
00016  0000                        ;* 49876 = TO ADDR LO-BYTE       *
00017  0000                        ;*                              *
00018  0000                        ;* 49877 = TO ADDR HI-BYTE       *
00019  0000                        ;*                              *
00020  0000                        ;* 49878 = SWAP=1/COPY=0         *
00021  0000                        ;*                              *
00022  0000                        ;*                              *
00023  0000                        ;*                              *
00024  0000                        ;*                              *
00025  0000                        ;* TO USE   - POKE VALS ABOVE    *
00026  0000                        ;*                              *
00027  0000                        ;*              THEN SYS 49879   *
00028  0000                        ;*                              *
00029  0000                        ;* NOTE: THIS ROUTINE WORKS      *
00030  0000                        ;* FROM THE BOTTOM UP. THUS IF   *
00031  0000                        ;* YOU ATTEMPT TO COPY A BLOCK   *
00032  0000                        ;* 100 BYTES LONG TO A DESTINA-  *
00033  0000                        ;* TION OF 'FROM + 50', THE LAST *
00034  0000                        ;* 50 BYTES OF THE COPY WILL BE  *
00035  0000                        ;* CORRUPTED.                    *
00036  0000                        ;*                              *
00037  0000                        ;********************************


00039  0000               PNTR1  = $FB              ;ZP POINTER FOR INDIRECTS
00040  0000               PNTR2  = $FD              ;ZP POINTER FOR INDIRECTS
00041  0000               ZTEMP1 = $F7              ;
00042  0000               ZTEMP2 = $F9              ;ZP TEMPORARY STORAGE
00043  0000               ZTEMP3 = $FA              ;
00044  0000               *      = $C2D0
00045  C2D0               STRT   *=*+2              ;START ADDRESS
00046  C2D2               END    *=*+2              ;END ADDRESS
00047  C2D4               TO     *=*+2              ;DESTINATION ADDRESS
00048  C2D6               SWAP   *=*+1              ;COPY/SWAP FLAG

00050  C2D7  AD D2 C2            LDA END
00051  C2DA  CD D0 C2            CMP STRT           ;IS STRT < END?
00052  C2DD  AD D3 C2            LDA END+1
00053  C2E0  ED D1 C2            SBC STRT+1
00054  C2E3  90 4E               BCC EXIT           ;NO...BRANCH
```

Listing continued next page

```
00056   C2E5   AD D0 C2            LDA STRT
00057   C2E8   85 FB               STA PNTR1
00058   C2EA   AD D1 C2            LDA STRT+1
00059   C2ED   85 FC               STA PNTR1+1
00060   C2EF   AD D4 C2            LDA TO
00061   C2F2   85 FD               STA PNTR2        ;COPY POINTERS DOWN
00062   C2F4   AD D5 C2            LDA TO+1         ;TO ZERO PAGE
00063   C2F7   85 FE               STA PNTR2+1
00064   C2F9   AD D2 C2            LDA END
00065   C2FC   85 F7               STA ZTEMP1
00066   C2FE   AD D3 C2            LDA END+1
00067   C301   85 F8               STA ZTEMP1+1
00068   C303   AD D6 C2            LDA SWAP
00069   C306   85 F9               STA ZTEMP2

00071   C308   A0 00               LDY #$00
00072   C30A              NEXT
00073   C30A   A5 F7               LDA ZTEMP1
00074   C30C   C5 FB               CMP PNTR1        ;FINISHED?
00075   C30E   A5 F8               LDA ZTEMP1+1
00076   C310   E5 FC               SBC PNTR1+1
00077   C312   90 1F               BCC EXIT         ;YES.. END
00078   C314   B1 FB               LDA (PNTR1),Y
00079   C316   A6 F9               LDX ZTEMP2       ;COPY OR SWAP
00080   C318   F0 08               BEQ NOSWAP       ;COPY...BRANCH
00081   C31A   85 FA               STA ZTEMP3
00082   C31C   B1 FD               LDA (PNTR2),Y
00083   C31E   91 FB               STA (PNTR1),Y
00084   C320   A5 FA               LDA ZTEMP3
00085   C322              NOSWAP
00086   C322   91 FD               STA (PNTR2),Y

00088   C324   E6 FB               INC PNTR1
00089   C326   D0 02               BNE NOFLO1       ;INCREMENT POINTERS
00090   C328   E6 FC               INC PNTR1+1
00091   C32A              NOFLO1
00092   C32A   E6 FD               INC PNTR2
00093   C32C   D0 02               BNE NOFLO2
00094   C32E   E6 FE               INC PNTR2+1
00095   C330              NOFLO2
00096   C330   4C 0A C3            JMP NEXT

00098   C333              EXIT
00099   C333   60                  RTS              ;FINISHED
00100   C334              .END


ERRORS = 00000


SYMBOL TABLE

SYMBOL VALUE
  END       C2D2       EXIT      C333      NEXT      C30A      NOFLO1    C32A
  NOFLO2    C330       NOSWAP    C322      PNTR1     00FB      PNTR2     00FD
  STRT      C2D0       SWAP      C2D6      TO        C2D4      ZTEMP1    00F7
  ZTEMP2    00F9       ZTEMP3    00FA

END OF ASSEMBLY
```

```
, ,  C2D7    AD D2 C2   LDA $C2D2
, ,  C2DA    CD D0 C2   CMP $C2D0
, ,  C2DD    AD D3 C2   LDA $C2D3
, ,  C2E0    ED D1 C2   SBC $C2D1
, ,  C2E3    90 4E      BCC $C333
, ,  C2E5    AD D0 C2   LDA $C2D0
, ,  C2E8    85 FB      STA $FB
, ,  C2EA    AD D1 C2   LDA $C2D1
, ,  C2ED    85 FC      STA $FC
, ,  C2EF    AD D4 C2   LDA $C2D4
, ,  C2F2    85 FD      STA $FD
, ,  C2F4    AD D5 C2   LDA $C2D5
, ,  C2F7    85 FE      STA $FE
, ,  C2F9    AD D2 C2   LDA $C2D2
, ,  C2FC    85 F7      STA $F7
, ,  C2FE    AD D3 C2   LDA $C2D3
, ,  C301    85 F8      STA $F8
, ,  C303    AD D6 C2   LDA $C2D6
, ,  C306    85 F9      STA $F9
, ,  C308    A0 00      LDY #$00
, ,  C30A    A5 F7      LDA $F7
, ,  C30C    C5 FB      CMP $FB
, ,  C30E    A5 F8      LDA $F8
, ,  C310    E5 FC      SBC $FC
, ,  C312    90 1F      BCC $C333
, ,  C314    B1 FB      LDA ($FB),Y
, ,  C316    A6 F9      LDX $F9
, ,  C318    F0 08      BEQ $C322
, ,  C31A    85 FA      STA $FA
, ,  C31C    B1 FD      LDA ($FD),Y
, ,  C31E    91 FB      STA ($FB),Y
, ,  C320    A5 FA      LDA $FA
, ,  C322    91 FD      STA ($FD),Y
, ,  C324    E6 FB      INC $FB
, ,  C326    D0 02      BNE $C32A
, ,  C328    E6 FC      INC $FC
, ,  C32A    E6 FD      INC $FD
, ,  C32C    D0 02      BNE $C330
, ,  C32E    E6 FE      INC $FE
, ,  C330    4C 0A C3   JMP $C30A
, ,  C333    60         RTS
,
,
```

INTERRUPTS AND THEIR USES

The two main uses of interrupts within the BASIC operating system are dealing with unpredictable events, such as peripherals wanting to send or receive data, the user pressing the RUN/STOP and RESTORE keys, and for the periodic housekeeping functions such as scanning the keyboard and updating the jiffy clock, all of which are done every 1/60th of a second.

At the end of executing each instruction the 6510 checks the interrupt system to see if an interrupt has occurred, and in the case of an IRQ interrupt whether the interrupt disable bit in the status register is clear. If a valid interrupt has been received then the first thing the 6510 will do is push the Program Counter Hi (PCH), followed by the Program Counter Lo (PCL) and the status register onto the stack. Next it sets the interrupt disable bit to prevent further IRQ interrupts. Finally it reads two bytes of data from high memory and puts them into the program counter. These bytes are of course the start of the 'Interrupt Service Routines'. Apart from the NMI and IRQ interrupts we have mentioned earlier there is a third source of interrupt which occurs when the microprocessor performs a BRK instruction. The locations at which these addresses are found, and the actual addresses are:

Interrupt	Address location	Address
NMI	$FFFA/$FFFB	$FE43
BRK & IRQ	$FFFE/$FFFF	$FF48

The next stage of the interrupt routine is very important to the programmer. Let's take a look at the NMI routine at $FE43 first. If we were to disassemble the first few bytes of this routine we would see:

```
SEI
JMP ($0318)
PHA
TXA
```

The instruction that we are really interested in is the Indirect Jump to the address which is stored in $0318 and $0319. Normally this would send us on to the PHA instruction at $FE47 that follows the JMP — this seems rather silly until you realize that the programmer can change the contents of $0318 and $0318 to point to his own routine. These locations at $0318 and $0319 are called the NMI *RAM vector*, because they point to the next instruction to be executed. Rather predictably the NMI routine is not the only interrupt routine with a RAM vector. Both the IRQ and the BRK routines have their own vectors, as do many other KERNAL routines. Here is a list of these vectors:

ROUTINE	VECTOR LOCATION	NORMAL CONTENTS
IRQ	$0314/$0315	$EA31
BRK	$0316/$0317	$FE66
NMI	$0318/$0319	$FE47
OPEN	$031A/$031B	$F34A
CLOSE	$031C/$031D	$F291
CHKIN	$031E/$031F	$F20E
CHKOUT	$0320/$0321	$F250
CLRCHN	$0322/$0323	$F333

CHRIN	$0324/$0325	$F157
CHROUT	$0326/$0327	$F1CA
STOP	$0328/$0329	$F6ED
GETIN	$032A/$032B	$F13E
CLALL	$032C/$032D	$F32F
User vector	$032E/$032F	$FE66
LOAD	$0330/$0331	$F4A5
SAVE	$0332/$0333	$F5ED

If an IRQ or BRK occur the program first jumps to $FF48 where it pushes the accumulator, and X and Y registers onto the stack so that they are preserved for use when the interrupt is completed. The routine then determines whether an IRQ or a BRK has occurred and jumps to the appropriate vector.

All of this jumping about may seem a bit unnecessary. The NMI routine could go straight onto $FE47 without the indirect jump. However, if the whole of the interrupt routine were in ROM the user would have no control over it at all. As it is, the provision of vectors in RAM allows the user to either substitute his own routine or to insert some of his own code before executing the normal interrupt routine. This is a very powerful tool, but one which is also very dangerous. Have you ever tried stopping a computer that doesn't bother to scan the keyboard!

A *system wedge* is the name for a piece of code which is inserted into the normal routine, and there are two types of system wedge which can be easily implemented — an *interrupt wedge* and a *charget wedge.* An interrupt wedge works by changing the appropriate RAM vector to point to the user's wedge code. The other type of wedge is inserted into the routine in RAM which reads the next keyword from the BASIC input buffer prior to interpreting it. When the CBM 64 is switched on charget is copied down from ROM to locations $73 to $8A (115–138) in the zero page. Using a charget wedge it is possible to create new commands in BASIC, and this is the principle used in some of the programmer's aid and extended BASIC packages available.

Any wedge comprises three distinct parts:

(1) A routine to initialize the wedge. This is the routine which stores the present RAM vector somewhere in memory and then changes the RAM vector to point to the code which is to be executed.
(2) The wedge code itself. This performs the new or additional functions required, and should always end with an indirect jump through the original RAM vector values you have stored away. Note that the method of indirect jumping is better than a simple jump to $EA31 in the case of the IRQ. This means that if the RAM vector has already been modified by another wedge there will be no conflict, and both wedges will be executed, whereas a jump absolute will prevent the other wedge from executing. Using this technique it is possible to 'daisy chain' several wedges together.
(3) A routine to disable the wedge when it is not required, by restoring the values of the RAM vector to those that were there previously.

Example:
The following is an example of an IRQ driven wedge which reads and displays the 24-hour clock on board the 6526 chip.

```
LINE# LOC    CODE        LINE

00001  0000              ;*********************************
00002  0000              ;*                               *
00003  0000              ;*         CLOCK IRQ WEDGE        *
00004  0000              ;*                               *
00005  0000              ;*                               *
00006  0000              ;* 50128 = AM=0 / PM=128         *
00007  0000              ;*                               *
00008  0000              ;* 50129 = HOURS                 *
00009  0000              ;*                               *
00010  0000              ;* 50130 = MINUTES               *
00011  0000              ;*                               *
00012  0000              ;* 50131 = SECONDS               *
00013  0000              ;*                               *
00014  0000              ;* 50132 = CLOCK COLOUR          *
00015  0000              ;*                               *
00016  0000              ;* 50133 = DISPLAY ON=1/OFF=0    *
00017  0000              ;*                               *
00018  0000              ;*                               *
00019  0000              ;*                               *
00020  0000              ;* WEDGE INSERT   SYS 50138      *
00021  0000              ;*                               *
00022  0000              ;* WEDGE REMOVE   SYS 50237      *
00023  0000              ;*                               *
00024  0000              ;*********************************

00026  0000              IRQVEC = $0314           ; IRQ RAM VECTOR
00027  0000              CLOCK  = $DD08           ; TOD REGISTER
00028  0000              D2CRA  = $DD0E           ;VIA#2 CRA
00029  0000              D2CRB  = $DD0F           ;VIA#2 CRB
00030  0000              PALNTS = $02A6           ;PAL/NTSC FLAG
00031  0000              RATE   = $06             ;DISPLAY EVERY 6 IRQS
00032  0000              DIGIT  = $30             ;SCREEN CODE FOR '0'
00033  0000              POINT  = $2E             ;SCREEN CODE FOR '.'
00034  0000              SLASH  = $2F             ;SCREEN CODE FOR '/'
00035  0000              COLON  = $3A             ;SCREEN CODE FOR ':'
00036  0000              HZ50   = $80             ; 50 HZ MASK FOR TODIN
00037  0000              HZ60   = $7F             ; 60 HZ MASK FOR TODIN
00038  0000              AY     = $01             ;SCREEN CODE FOR 'A'
00039  0000              PEE    = $10             ;SCREEN CODE FOR 'P'
00040  0000              EM     = $0D             ;SCREEN CODE FOR 'M'
00041  0000              WRITE  = 127             ;MASK TO SET CLOCK IN CRB
00042  0000              SCNLOC = $041C           ;CLOCK ADDR ON SCREEN
00043  0000              COLLOC = $D81C           ;ADDR ON VIDEO MATRIX
00044  0000              TRNCLO = $0F             ;MASK FOR LOW NYBBLE
00045  0000              *      = $C3D0
00046  C3D0              AMPM   *=*+1             ;AM/PM FLAG
00047  C3D1              HOURS  *=*+1             ;HOURS VAL (FOR INITIALISE)
00048  C3D2              MINS   *=*+1             ;MINUTES VALUE
00049  C3D3              SECS   *=*+1             ;SECONDS VALUE
00050  C3D4              COLOR  *=*+1             ;CLOCK COLOUR
00051  C3D5              DISPLY *=*+1             ; DISPLAY/HIDE FLAG
00052  C3D6              VECTOR *=*+2             ;STORAGE FOR OLD IRQ VEC
00053  C3D8              COUNT  *=*+1             ;IRQ COUNTER
00054  C3D9              TEMP1  *=*+1
00056  C3DA              ;
00057  C3DA              ;INSERT WEDGE
00058  C3DA              ;
```

```
00059   C3DA   AD A6 02           LDA PALNTS        ;PAL OR NTSC
00060   C3DD   F0 0A              BEQ NTSC          ;BRANCH FOR NTSC
00061   C3DF   A9 80              LDA #HZ50         ;MUST BE PAL
00062   C3E1   0D 0E DD           ORA D2CRA
00063   C3E4   8D 0E DD           STA D2CRA         ;SET TODIN FOR 50 HZ
00064   C3E7   30 08              BMI PALDUN
00065   C3E9             NTSC
00066   C3E9   A9 7F              LDA #HZ60         ;NTSC
00067   C3EB   2D 0E DD           AND D2CRA
00068   C3EE   8D 0E DD           STA D2CRA         ;SET TODIN FOR 60 HZ
00069   C3F1             PALDUN
00070   C3F1   A9 7F              LDA #WRITE
00071   C3F3   2D 0F DD           AND D2CRB         ;SET CLOCK NOT ALARM
00072   C3F6   8D 0F DD           STA D2CRB
00073   C3F9   AD D0 C3           LDA AMPM
00074   C3FC   29 80              AND #128          ;MAKE AMPM VALUE VALID
00075   C3FE   8D D0 C3           STA AMPM
00076   C401   AD D1 C3           LDA HOURS         ;GET HOURS
00077   C404   20 1C C5           JSR BINBCD        ;CONVERT TO BCD
00078   C407   0D D0 C3           ORA AMPM          ;OR WITH AM/PM FLAG
00079   C40A   8D 0B DD           STA CLOCK+3       ;STORE IN CLOCK
00080   C40D   AD D2 C3           LDA MINS          ;GET MINUTES
00081   C410   20 1C C5           JSR BINBCD        ;CONVERT TO BCD
00082   C413   8D 0A DD           STA CLOCK+2       ;STORE IN CLOCK
00083   C416   AD D3 C3           LDA SECS          ;GET SECONDS
00084   C419   20 1C C5           JSR BINBCD        ;CONVERT TO BCD
00085   C41C   8D 09 DD           STA CLOCK+1       ;STORE IN CLOCK
00086   C41F   A9 00              LDA #00           ;ALWAYS SET 10THS TO 0
00087   C421   8D 08 DD           STA CLOCK         ;START CLOCK
00088   C424             ;
00089   C424   78                 SEI               ;DISABLE INTERRUPTS
00090   C425   AD 14 03           LDA IRQVEC
00091   C428   8D D6 C3           STA VECTOR        ;SAVE OLD IRQ VECTOR
00092   C42B   AD 15 03           LDA IRQVEC+1
00093   C42E   8D D7 C3           STA VECTOR+1
00094   C431             ;
00095   C431   A9 4C              LDA #<WEDGE
00096   C433   8D 14 03           STA IRQVEC
00097   C436   A9 C4              LDA #>WEDGE       ;INSERT WEDGE
00098   C438   8D 15 03           STA IRQVEC+1
00099   C43B   58                 CLI               ;ENABLE INTERRUPTS
00100   C43C   60                 RTS

00102   C43D             ;
00103   C43D             ; REMOVE WEDGE
00104   C43D             ;
00105   C43D   78                 SEI               ;DISABLE INTERRUPTS
00106   C43E   AD D6 C3           LDA VECTOR
00107   C441   8D 14 03           STA IRQVEC        ;RESTORE RAM VECTOR
00108   C444   AD D7 C3           LDA VECTOR+1
00109   C447   8D 15 03           STA IRQVEC+1
00110   C44A   58                 CLI               ;ENABLE INTERRUPTS
00111   C44B   60                 RTS

00113   C44C             ;
00114   C44C             ;WEDGE STARTS HERE
00115   C44C             ;
00116   C44C             WEDGE
00117   C44C   AD D8 C3           LDA COUNT         ;
00118   C44F   C9 06              CMP #RATE         ;DO CLOCK THIS IRQ?
```

Listing continued next page

```
00119   C451   F0 03                  BEQ CONT              ;
00120   C453                   OUT
00121   C453   4C 08 C5               JMP EXIT              ; NO
00122   C456                   CONT
00123   C456   A9 FF                  LDA #$FF              ;RESET IRQ COUNTER
00124   C458   8D D8 C3               STA COUNT
00125   C45B   AD D5 C3               LDA DISPLAY           ;DISPLAY?
00126   C45E   F0 F3                  BEQ OUT               ;NO...BRANCH

00128   C460   AD 0B DD               LDA CLOCK+3           ;GET HOURS/AM/PM
00129   C463   AA                     TAX                   ;PUT A COPY IN X REG
00130   C464   29 80                  AND #$80              ;GET AM/PM
00131   C466   D0 05                  BNE PM                ;BRANCH IF PM
00132   C468   A9 01                  LDA #AY               ;DISPLAY 'A'
00133   C46A   4C 6F C4               JMP MERIDP
00134   C46D                   PM
00135   C46D   A9 10                  LDA #PEE              ;DISPLAY 'P'
00136   C46F                   MERIDP
00137   C46F   8D 26 04               STA SCNLOC+10
00138   C472   AD D4 C3               LDA COLOR             ;GET COLOUR
00139   C475   8D 26 D8               STA COLLOC+10         ;SET COLOUR
00140   C478   A9 0D                  LDA #EM               ;DISPLAY 'M'
00141   C47A   8D 27 04               STA SCNLOC+11
00142   C47D   AD D4 C3               LDA COLOR             ;SET COLOUR
00143   C480   8D 27 D8               STA COLLOC+11
00144   C483                   ;
00145   C483                   ;DO HOURS
00146   C483                   ;
00147   C483   8A                     TXA                   ;GET HOURS
00148   C484   29 10                  AND #$10              ;JUST WANT HIGH DIGIT
00149   C486   20 0E C5               JSR HIDIGT            ;GET SCREEN CODE
00150   C489   8D 1C 04               STA SCNLOC            ;DISPLAY IT
00151   C48C   AD D4 C3               LDA COLOR
00152   C48F   8D 1C D8               STA COLLOC            ;SET COLOUR
00153   C492   8A                     TXA                   ;GET BYTE AGAIN
00154   C493   20 16 C5               JSR LODIGT            ;GET LOW DIGIT
00155   C496   8D 1D 04               STA SCNLOC+1          ;DISPLAY IT
00156   C499   AD D4 C3               LDA COLOR
00157   C49C   8D 1D D8               STA COLLOC+1          ;SET COLOUR
00158   C49F                   ;
00159   C49F   A9 3A                  LDA #COLON            ; HRS/MINS SEPARATOR
00160   C4A1   8D 1E 04               STA SCNLOC+2
00161   C4A4   AD D4 C3               LDA COLOR
00162   C4A7   8D 1E D8               STA COLLOC+2
00163   C4AA                   ;
00164   C4AA                   ;NOW DO MINUTES
00165   C4AA                   ;
00166   C4AA   AD 0A DD               LDA CLOCK+2           ;GET MINUTES
00167   C4AD   AA                     TAX
00168   C4AE   20 0E C5               JSR HIDIGT            ;DO HIGH DIGIT
00169   C4B1   8D 1F 04               STA SCNLOC+3          ;DISPLAY IT
00170   C4B4   AD D4 C3               LDA COLOR
00171   C4B7   8D 1F D8               STA COLLOC+3          ;AND COLOUR
00172   C4BA   8A                     TXA                   ;GET BYTE AGAIN
00173   C4BB   20 16 C5               JSR LODIGT            ;DO LOW DIGIT
00174   C4BE   8D 20 04               STA SCNLOC+4          ;DISPLAY IT
00175   C4C1   AD D4 C3               LDA COLOR
00176   C4C4   8D 20 D8               STA COLLOC+4          ;SET COLOUR
00177   C4C7                   ;
```

```
00178   C4C7   A9 2F              LDA #SLASH        ; MIN/SEC SEPARATOR
00179   C4C9   8D 21 04           STA SCNLOC+5
00180   C4CC   AD D4 C3           LDA COLOR
00181   C4CF   8D 21 D8           STA COLLOC+5
00182   C4D2                   ;
00183   C4D2               ;NOW DO SECONDS
00184   C4D2                   ;
00185   C4D2   AD 09 DD           LDA CLOCK+1       ;GET SECONDS
00186   C4D5   AA                 TAX
00187   C4D6   20 0E C5           JSR HIDIGT        ;DO HIGH DIGIT
00188   C4D9   8D 22 04           STA SCNLOC+6      ;DISPLAY IT
00189   C4DC   AD D4 C3           LDA COLOR
00190   C4DF   8D 22 D8           STA COLLOC+6      ;AND COLOUR
00191   C4E2   8A                 TXA               ;GET BYTE AGAIN
00192   C4E3   20 16 C5           JSR LODIGT        ;DO LOW DIGIT
00193   C4E6   8D 23 04           STA SCNLOC+7      ;DISPLAY IT
00194   C4E9   AD D4 C3           LDA COLOR
00195   C4EC   8D 23 D8           STA COLLOC+7 AND COLOUR
00196   C4EF                   ;
00197   C4EF   A9 2E              LDA #POINT        ; SECS/TENTHS SEPARATOR
00198   C4F1   8D 24 04           STA SCNLOC+8
00199   C4F4   AD D4 C3           LDA COLOR
00200   C4F7   8D 24 D8           STA COLLOC+8
00201   C4FA                   ;
00202   C4FA               ;NOW DO TENTHS
00203   C4FA                   ;
00204   C4FA   AD 08 DD           LDA CLOCK         ;GET TENTHS VALUE
00205   C4FD   69 30              ADC #DIGIT        ;ADD $30 FOR SCREEN CODE
00206   C4FF   8D 25 04           STA SCNLOC+9      ;DISPLAY IT
00207   C502   AD D4 C3           LDA COLOR
00208   C505   8D 25 D8           STA COLLOC+9      ;AND COLOUR
00209   C508                   ;
00210   C508                   ;
00211   C508               EXIT
00212   C508   EE D8 C3           INC COUNT         ;INCREMENT IRQ COUNTER
00213   C50B   6C D6 C3           JMP (VECTOR)      ;GO TO REST OF IRQ

00215   C50E                   ;
00216   C50E               ;SUBROUTINES
00217   C50E                   ;
00218   C50E               HIDIGT
00219   C50E   4A                 LSR A
00220   C50F   4A                 LSR A             ;MOVE HIGH NYBBLE INTO LOW
00221   C510   4A                 LSR A
00222   C511   4A                 LSR A
00223   C512   18                 CLC
00224   C513   69 30              ADC #DIGIT        ;ADD $30 FOR SCREEN CODE
00225   C515   60                 RTS

00227   C516               LODIGT
00228   C516   29 0F              AND #TRNCLO       ;MASK OFF HIGH NYBBLE
00229   C518   18                 CLC
00230   C519   69 30              ADC #DIGIT        ;ADD $30 FOR SCREEN CODE
00231   C51B   60                 RTS

00233   C51C                   ;
00234   C51C               ;CONVERT BINARY TO BCD
00235   C51C                   ;
00236   C51C               BINBCD
```

Listing continued next page

```
00237   C51C   A0 FF                    LDY  #$FF
00238   C51E   38                       SEC
00239   C51F   C8              D10      INY
00240   C520   E9 0A                    SBC  #10          ;SUBTRACT 10 UNTIL -VE
00241   C522   B0 FB                    BCS  D10
00242   C524   69 0A                    ADC  #10          ;ADD 10 BACK ON
00243   C526   8D D9 C3                 STA  TEMP1        ;STORE REMAINDER
00244   C529   98                       TYA              ;GET NUMBER PF 10S SUBTRACTED
00245   C52A   0A                       ASL  A
00246   C52B   0A                       ASL  A
00247   C52C   0A                       ASL  A            ;SHIFT INTO HIGH NYBBLE
00248   C52D   0A                       ASL  A
00249   C52E   0D D9 C3                 ORA  TEMP1        ;PUT REMAINDER IN LOW NYBBLE
00250   C531   60                       RTS
00251   C532                   .END
```

ERRORS = 00000

SYMBOL TABLE

SYMBOL	VALUE								
AMPM	C3D0	AY	0001	BINBCD	C51C	CLOCK	DD08		
COLLOC	D81C	COLON	003A	COLOR	C3D4	CONT	C456		
COUNT	C3D8	D10	C51F	D2CRA	DD0E	D2CRB	DD0F		
DIGIT	0030	DISPLY	C3D5	EM	000D	EXIT	C508		
HIDIGT	C50E	HOURS	C3D1	HZ50	0080	HZ60	007F		
IRQVEC	0314	LODIGT	C516	MERIDP	C46F	MINS	C3D2		
NTSC	C3E9	OUT	C453	PALDUN	C3F1	PALNTS	02A6		
PEE	0010	PM	C46D	POINT	002E	RATE	0006		
SCNLOC	041C	SECS	C3D3	SLASH	002F	TEMP1	C3D9		
TRNCLO	000F	VECTOR	C3D6	WEDGE	C44C	WRITE	007F		

END OF ASSEMBLY

CHARGET

We have mentioned previously the CHARGET routine. When a BASIC program is being RUN the tokenized BASIC of each program line is copied from the BASIC program area into the BASIC input buffer, addresses $200 to $258 (512 to 600). The function of CHARGET is to scan through the text in the input buffer, ignoring spaces, until a byte of BASIC is found, whether it be a keyword token or a character. Having found such a byte CHARGET then passes it back to the Interpreter where it is dealt with. Thus the CHARGET routine is the fundamental link between the Interpreter and your BASIC program. The CHARGET routine can be found in the zero page at addresses $73 to $8A. By changing CHARGET we can add new functions and commands. CHARGET itself is a seemingly simple little routine only 23 bytes long, and is listed below.

```
B*
       PC   SR AC XR YR SP
.;C03E 32 00 C3 00 F6
   "
```

```
 ,  0073  E6 7A     INC $7A
 ,  0075  D0 02     BNE $0079
 ,  0077  E6 7B     INC $7B
 ,  0079  AD 08 02  LDA $0208
 ,  007C  C9 3A     CMP #$3A
 ,  007E  B0 0A     BCS $008A
 ,  0080  C9 20     CMP #$20
 ,  0082  F0 EF     BEQ $0073
 ,  0084  38        SEC
 ,  0085  E9 30     SBC #$30
 ,  0087  38        SEC
 ,  0088  E9 D0     SBC #$D0
 ,  008A  60        RTS
 "
 "
```

However, there is a sting in the tail of CHARGET which makes it very devious. CHARGET modifies itself as it is executed. What it does is to change the absolute address stored in locations $7A and $7B, thus changing the character which it accesses within the BASIC input buffer. This peculiar behaviour necessitates the routine being in RAM. The state of the carry bit on exit from this routine is significant, and is determined in the following manner.

If the character has an ASCII code greater than $39 (the character '9'), the carry bit will be set.

If the ASCII code of the character is between $30 and $39 (it is a numerical character), the carry bit will be clear.

If the character has an ASCII code of less than $30 (the character '0'), the carry bit will be set.

· Examples of CHARGET wedges are the DOS support program supplied by Commodore with their disk drives, and the programmer's aid program POWER.

To give a simple modification to CHARGET which can be tried from BASIC, enter the following line:

POKE128,234:POKE129,234:POKE130,234:POKE131,234

The effect of this is to remove the check which looks for spaces, by replacing it with NOP instructions. Any BASIC the 64 now encounters with spaces in will produce a syntax error.

If we wish to add new commands to BASIC, using a CHARGET wedge, the normal method is to place a JMP command at the beginning of CHARGET to our wedge routine. The routine must perform the task of CHARGET, get a valid byte and check to see if it is one of the newly defined functions. If so the wedge deals with it and goes on until it finds a character which is not special, it must then pass this on to the Interpreter through CHARGET in the normal way. Here is an example of a CHARGET wedge.

```
LINE# LOC   CODE           LINE

00001 0000                 ;***********************************
00002 0000                 ;*                                 *
00003 0000                 ;*           CHARGET WEDGE          *
00004 0000                 ;*                                 *
00005 0000                 ;*                                 *
00006 0000                 ;* WHEN WEDGE IS RUNNING LEFT      *
00007 0000                 ;* ARROW KEY WILL GIVE THE SIZE    *
00008 0000                 ;* OF THE CURRENT BASIC PROGRAM    *
00009 0000                 ;*                                 *
00010 0000                 ;*                                 *
00011 0000                 ;* WEDGE  INSERT   SYS 50496       *
00012 0000                 ;*                                 *
00013 0000                 ;* WEDGE  REMOVE   SYS 50513       *
00014 0000                 ;*                                 *
00015 0000                 ;***********************************

00017 0000                 CHRGET = $73
00018 0000                 CHRGOT = $79
00019 0000                 CHDGOT = $E3A8
00020 0000                 MAIN   = $A48C
00021 0000                 TEMP   = $FB
00022 0000                 STROUT = $AB1E
00023 0000                 LINPRT = $BDCD
00024 0000                 TXTTAB = $2B
00025 0000                 VARTAB = $2D
00026 0000                 CMD    = 95

00028 0000                 *      = $C540
00029 C540  4C 46 C5              JMP START
00030 C543                 ;
00031 C543                 ;BYTES TO BE INSERTED INTO CHARGET
00032 C543                 ;
00033 C543                 JUMP
00034 C543  4C 5C C5              JMP WEDGE
00035 C546                 ;
00036 C546                 ;INSERT WEDGE
00037 C546                 ;
00038 C546                 START
00039 C546  A2 02                 LDX #$02
00040 C548                 INSERT
00041 C548  BD 43 C5              LDA JUMP,X
00042 C54B  95 7C                 STA CHRGOT+3,X  ;INSERT 'JMP WEDGE'
00043 C54D  CA                    DEX             ;INTO $7C TO $7E
00044 C54E  10 F8                 BPL INSERT
00045 C550  60                    RTS
00046 C551                 ;
00047 C551                 ;REMOVE CHARGET WEDGE
00048 C551                 ;
00049 C551                 REMOVE
00050 C551  A2 02                 LDX #$02
00051 C553                 REST                   ;RESTORE 'CHRGET'
00052 C553  BD AB E3              LDA CHDGOT+3,X  ;GET FROM ROM COPY
00053 C556  95 7C                 STA CHRGOT+3,X  :STORE IN RAM COPY
00054 C558  CA                    DEX
00055 C559  10 F8                 BPL REST
00056 C55B  60                    RTS
00057 C55C                 ;
```

```
00059  C55C                          ;
00060  C55C                          ;WEDGE CODE STARTS HERE
00061  C55C                          ;
00062  C55C                          WEDGE
00063  C55C   85 FB                      STA TEMP          ;SAVE .A, .X
00064  C55E   86 FC                      STX TEMP+1
00065  C560   BA                         TSX               ;FIND WHERE CHARGET
                                                                 CALLED FROM
00066  C561   BD 01 01                   LDA $0101,X       ;GET PREV PCL FROM STACK
00067  C564   C9 8C                      CMP #<MAIN        ;FROM DIRECT MODE??
00068  C566   D0 0D                      BNE NOTCMD
00069  C568   BD 02 01                   LDA $0102,X       ;GET PREV PCH FROM STACK
00070  C56B   C9 A4                      CMP #>MAIN        ;DIRECT?
00071  C56D   D0 06                      BNE NOTCMD        ;BRANCH IF NOT DIRECT MODE
00072  C56F   A5 FB                      LDA TEMP          ;GET THE COMMAND BACK
00073  C571   C9 5F                      CMP #CMD          ;CHECK IF NEW COMMAND
00074  C573   F0 0E                      BEQ FOUND
00075  C575                          ;
00076  C575                          NOTCMD
00077  C575   A5 FB                      LDA TEMP          ;RESTORE REGS
00078  C577   A6 FC                      LDX TEMP+1
00079  C579   C9 3A                      CMP #$3A          ;COMPLETE CHRGOT
00080  C57B   B0 03                      BCS STRTS
00081  C57D   4C 80 00                   JMP CHRGOT+7
00082  C580                          STRTS
00083  C580   4C 8A 00                   JMP CHRGOT+17     ;TO THE END OF CHRGOT
00084  C583                          ;
00085  C583                          ;GOT COMMAND
00086  C583                          ;
00087  C583                          FOUND
00088  C583   A5 2D                      LDA VARTAB        ;GET POINTER TO END OF BASIC
00089  C585   A6 2E                      LDX VARTAB+1
00090  C587   38                         SEC
00091  C588   E5 2B                      SBC TXTTAB
00092  C58A   B0 01                      BCS NOBORW
00093  C58C   CA                         DEX               ;SUBTRACT BOTTOM OF BASIC
00094  C58D                          NOBORW
00095  C58D   85 FB                      STA TEMP
00096  C58F   8A                         TXA
00097  C590   38                         SEC
00098  C591   E5 2C                      SBC TXTTAB+1
00099  C593   A6 FB                      LDX TEMP
00100  C595   20 CD BD                   JSR LINPRT        ;OUTPUT RESULT TO SCREEN
00101  C598   A9 A7                      LDA #<STRING
00102  C59A   A0 C5                      LDY #>STRING      ;OUTPUT CR & READY
00103  C59C   20 1E AB                   JSR STROUT        ;OUTPUT A STRING UNTIL A
00104  C59F                                                ;ZERO IS FOUND
00105  C59F                          CLEAR
00106  C59F   20 73 00                   JSR CHRGET        ;CALL CHARGET UNTIL
00107  C5A2   D0 FB                      BNE CLEAR         ;LINE CLEARED
00108  C5A4   4C 79 00                   JMP CHRGOT        ;EXIT TO CHARGOT
00109  C5A7                          ;
00110  C5A7                          ;STRING TO FOLLOW NUMBER OUTPUT
00111  C5A7                          STRING
00112  C5A7   20 42                      .BYT ' BYTES',$0D,$0D,'READY.',$0D,$00
00112  C5AD   0D
00112  C5AE   0D
00112  C5AF   52 45
00112  C5B5   0D
00112  C5B6   00
```

Listing continued next page

```
00113   C5B7                    .END
ERRORS = 00000


SYMBOL TABLE

SYMBOL VALUE
  CHDGOT   E3A8     CHRGET   0073     CHRGOT   0079     CLEAR    C59F
  CMD      005F     FOUND    C583     INSERT   C548     JUMP     C543
  LINPRT   BDCD     MAIN     A48C     NOBORW   C58D     NOTCMD   C575
  REMOVE   C551     REST     C553     START    C546     STRING   C5A7
  STROUT   AB1E     STRTS    C580     TEMP     00FB     TXTTAB   002B
  VARTAB   002D     WEDGE    C55C

END OF ASSEMBLY
```

USING AN ASSEMBLER

Now that we have had a chance to look at code produced by a disassembler, such as 64-MON, you begin to realize that assembly language is pretty powerful stuff, but does have its disadvantages in that it is quite time-consuming and difficult to write.

One of the most annoying problems with a disassembler or machine code monitor is having to calculate branch addresses. For example if you want to branch forward to a routine, but you don't yet know what address it will be at. An assembler is one of the ways to solve this type of problem.

One of the things that an assembler does is to allow you to use labels in your assembler program. We can illustrate how labels help us by looking at a piece of code.

```
0400          LDA      $03FF
0403          CMP      #$80
0405          BEQ      $0420
0407          Code 1  .......
041E          JMP      $0433
0420          Code 2  ........
0433          Common Code ..
```

If this code were entered into a disassembler you would have to calculate the branch and jump addresses. Now let's take a look at the same piece of code written using labels.

```
0400              LDA      $03FF
0403              CMP      #$80
0405              BEQ      LABEL1
0407              Code1 .........
041E              JMP      LABEL2
0420     LABEL1 Code2 .........
0433     LABEL 2 Common Code..
```

As you can see no calculation is required when you write the code. The assembler will take your piece of code and substitute the correct numbers in place of the labels for you. If you later change the contents and therefore the length of Code1 or Code2 you don't have to worry about recalculating the addresses.

We have shown above that we can use a label in place of any number, and so we can also use one in place of the operand for any machine instruction. In the above example we could have defined a label called, for example, ADDR1 as follows:

        ADDR1 = $03FF

we can then use the instruction

        LDA   ADDR1

and this will load the accumulator with the contents of $03FF in exactly the same way as:

        LDA $03FF

Obviously from the above example the method of using labels instead of numbers makes the program longer. We now need two lines instead of one. One to define the label and at least one to call the value. However, there are still great advantages to be had.

Imagine we were writing a long program, and we may want to perform the instruction LDA $03FF several times. If we use the label form of the instruction, LDA ADDR1, and then later decide that we don't really want $03FF, but we want $13FF instead, by simply changing the statement ADDR1 = $03FF to ADDR1 = $13FF and re-assembling the program the change is done, and we don't have to search through the code looking for every occurrence of the incorrect address. This facility can be useful in a variety of ways. Firstly, as we have seen above, if we get an address wrong it is an easy matter to correct it; secondly we may perhaps have a program written for the CBM 64 which we would like to run on a VIC-20, it's easy to change the values assigned to the labels to suit the change of machine, and if we define as many of our labels as possible at the beginning of the program it becomes an even easier task.

Immediately it can be seen that an assembler is a useful, time-saving tool, but it will do much more for you than that! Let's look at some of its other features.

Firstly most assemblers will do some simple arithmetic for you. Imagine we want to read an address from one place in memory (two consecutive bytes) and store it somewhere else. For example let's take two bytes from $0314 and $0315 and store them in $FB and $FC. First we define two labels:

        FROM   = $0314
        TO   = $FB

then to perform our task we write a piece of code like this:

        LDA   FROM
        STA   TO
        LDA   FROM+1
        STA   TO+1

The assembler will evaluate FROM+1 for you, as it will for any value in the range −32768 to +32767.

Another facility of the assembler is the evaluation of the Lo-byte or the Hi-byte of a two-byte number, e.g. an address. This is particularly useful when writing things like the wedges discussed earlier.

When we write a wedge we have to put the address of our piece of code into the RAM vector of the CBM 64. Here's an example of a routine to insert a wedge:

```
IRQVEC  =      $0314
WEDGE   =      $400D
        SEI
        LDA    #<WEDGE
        STA    IRQVEC
        LDA    #>WEDGE
        STA    IRQVEC+1
        CLI
        RTS
```

In this example the < sign means 'Lo-byte of' and the > sign means 'Hi-byte of'. Thus the routine puts the value $0D into $0314 and the value $40 into $0315, which inserts the wedge as required. As you can see, writing programs like this invites careful structuring. In fact it's getting much nearer to the higher level languages (like good old BASIC), and so it's about time we started putting comments in our programs. The equivalent to the REM statement in assembly language is the semicolon ';' – the assembler will treat anything on a line after a ';' as comments and ignore it when it assembles the program into machine code.

THE PROGRAM COUNTER VARIABLE

The star symbol '*' is one of the most important symbols and probably the most powerful available to the assembly language programmer. When we discussed machine code we looked at the program counter of the 6510, this is a counter which tells the processor where in memory the next instruction to be processed is. In order to execute a BRANCH or JUMP instruction the value of the program counter is changed.

Similarly, the assembler has a variable '*' which tells it where in memory the byte it is processing will go. Star, as with any other variable takes an initial value of zero, and if it is not changed the assembler will think your code is to live from address $0000 upwards, which will have a spectacular and definitely disastrous effect on your CBM 64 when you load it. So perhaps we had better find somewhere else for our program. Let's start it from address $4000, all we have to do to achieve this is to enter at the beginning of our code the line:

```
* = $4000
```

The 'program counter' is now set at $4000, and so our program is now located at $4000.

We can also assign a label to the value of the 'program counter' at any point in our program by simply entering:

```
LABEL = *
```

Suppose you have a subroutine in your program called SBRTN1. The first line of your subroutine might look like:

    SBRTN1 LDA #$00

but what happens if you want to insert some more code at the beginning of the subroutine? You have to knock out the label, insert the extra code, and then replace the label. If you forget the label then you'll have trouble later.

However, we could write the following:

    SBRTN1   =   *
             LDA   #$00

This will do exactly the same as the previous code, but to insert more code we just slot it in between the two lines.

As can be seen, using an assembler does allow us to produce far more 'readable' programs. which, due to the simplicity of having only one instruction to a line, are often better annotated than many BASIC programs.

There is a large variety of assemblers available for every microprocessor on the market, but the two most popular ones for the CBM 64 are the Commodore assembler, and the PAL (Pro-Line Software) assembler. Each have their advantages and disadvantages. PAL will allow you to include BASIC in your program, to handle the difficult bits, and will assemble a routine in memory without needing any peripherals; but its listings cannot be formatted so you may get a line of code on the fold of your paper. The Commodore assembler does not allow BASIC to be mixed in, and requires a disk drive to assemble files, but does have well-formatted output. Writing files for these assemblers usually requires you to write a file like a BASIC program with line numbers, and whilst there are some good program writing aids around this can be a nuisance. The Commodore assembler does have an advantage here since it stores its files as sequential (SEQ) rather than program (PRG) files. This means that a file can be written using many of the commonly available word processor packages such as Paperclip 64 (Batteries Included) or Easyscript (Commodore), with all their text editing facilities, and without the restriction of line numbers to create source files for the assembler.

Each of these attributes of an assembler can be called upon by the programmer, along with many others. The way this is done is by putting 'assembler directives' into your code. These directives tell the assembler to do something. Because each assembler has its own set of directives it is not possible to give a definitive list. However, there are some assembler functions which are common to virtually all assemblers, although the actual syntax of the directives may differ. Here are some of the more common ones using the directives required for the Commodore assembler.

.BYTE — This directive tells the assembler to reserve a byte of memory, and put a specified value into it. For example:

    .BYTE $FF,175,$20,'HELLO'

will put the values $FF,175,$20 and the ASCII codes of the string 'HELLO' into eight consecutive locations in memory, as determined by the program counter. This directive is commonly used to create look-up tables, such as a table of powers of two.

.WORD is used to store a two-byte value in memory, in the common Hi-byte, Hi-byte form used in indirect addressing. For example:

.WORD $0314

would store the values $14 and $03 in consecutive bytes. As with the .BYTE directive, several numbers may be specified in either hexadecimal or decimal, but strings may not be used.

.DBYTE stores double bytes in the opposite order to that of .WORD, and as with .WORD will take hexadecimal or decimal values, but not strings.

The equals sign which we saw earlier is also an assembler directive, which tells the assembler to identify a label with value.

The .END directive is used to signify the end of the file to be assembled, and prompts the assembler to produce a symbol table, which is an alphabetically ordered list of labels and their equivalent values, and in certain assemblers a cross-reference table which lists each label, along with all the numbers of lines in which the label is used.

Here is a sample routine along with its symbol table and cross reference.

```
LINE# LOC    CODE          LINE


00001  0000                ;******************************
00002  0000                ;*                            *
00003  0000                ;*         LOAD 64            *
00004  0000                ;*                            *
00005  0000                ;* 49984 = DEVICE NUMBER      *
00006  0000                ;*                            *
00007  0000                ;* TO USE   - POKE VALS ABOVE *
00008  0000                ;*                            *
00009  0000                ;* CALL FILENAME STRING THEN  *
00010  0000                ;*                            *
00011  0000                ;*         SYS 49988          *
00012  0000                ;*                            *
00013  0000                ;*                            *
00014  0000                ;* E.G.                       *
00015  0000                ;* 10 FN$="FILENAME"          *
00016  0000                ;* 20 POKE 49984,DEVICE       *
00017  0000                ;* 30 FN$=FN$                 *
00018  0000                ;* 40 SYS49988                *
00019  0000                ;*                            *
00020  0000                ;* NOTE: THIS ROUTINE WILL FIND*
00021  0000                ;* THE ADDRESS IN MEMORY OF THE*
00022  0000                ;* FILENAME. A FULL DISCUSSION *
00023  0000                ;* OF VARIABLE STORAGE CAN BE  *
00024  0000                ;* FOUND IN CHAPTER 2.         *
00025  0000                ;*                            *
00026  0000                ;******************************

00028  0000                VARNAM = $45        ;CURRENT BASIC VAR NAME
00029  0000                VARPTR= $47         ;POINTER CURRENT VARIABLE
00030  0000                SETLFS = $FFBA      ;KERNAL SETLFS
00031  0000                SETNAM = $FFBD      ;KERNAL SETNAM
00032  0000                LOAD   = $FFD5      ;KERNAL LOAD
00033  0000                *      = $C340
00034  C340                DEVNUM *=*+1        ;DEVICE NUMBER
00035  C341                FNLEN  *=*+1        ;FILENAME LENGTH
```

```
00036   C342                    FNADDR *=*+2;FILENAME ADDRESS

00038   C344   A0 02            LDY #$02
00039   C346   B1 47            LDA (VARPTR),Y
00040   C348   8D 41 C3         STA FNLEN
00041   C34B   C8               INY
00042   C34C   B1 47            LDA (VARPTR),Y
00043   C34E   8D 42 C3         STA FNADDR
00044   C351   C8               INY
00045   C352   B1 47            LDA (VARPTR),Y
00046   C354   8D 43 C3         STA FNADDR+1

00048   C357                  ;
00049   C357                  ;
00050   C357   A9 01            LDA #$01
00051   C359   AE 40 C3         LDX DEVNUM        ;SETLFS (1,DEVNUM,1)
00052   C35C   A0 01            LDY #$01
00053   C35E   20 BA FF         JSR SETLFS
00054   C361                  ;
00055   C361                  ;
00056   C361   AD 41 C3         LDA FNLEN
00057   C364   AE 42 C3         LDX FNADDR
00058   C367   AC 43 C3         LDY FNADDR+1      ;SETNAM
00059   C36A   20 BD FF         JSR SETNAM
00060   C36D                  ;
00061   C36D                  ;
00062   C36D   A9 00            LDA #$00
00063   C36F   A2 FF            LDX #$FF          ;LOAD TO ADDRESS SPECIFIED
00064   C371   A0 FF            LDY #$FF          ;IN FILE HEADER
00065   C373   20 D5 FF         JSR LOAD          ;LOAD
00066   C376                  ;
00067   C376            EXIT
00068   C376   60               RTS
00069   C377            .END


ERRORS = 00000


SYMBOL TABLE

SYMBOL VALUE
  DEVNUM   C340     EXIT     C376     FNADDR   C342     FNLEN    C341
  LOAD     FFD5     SETLFS   FFBA     SETNAM   FFBD     VARNAM   0045
  VARPTR   0047

END OF ASSEMBLY


   DEVNUM $C340     34   51
*  EXIT   $C376     67
   FNADDR $C342     36   43   46   57   58
   FNLEN  $C341     35   40   56
   LOAD   $FFD5     32   65
   SETLFS $FFBA     30   53
   SETNAM $FFBD     31   59
*  VARNAM $0045     28
   VARPTR $0047     29   39   42   45
```

There are many directives used for things such as formatting printouts and so on, but since these are far less universal we will not discuss them here.

SOME EXAMPLE PROGRAMS

In this section we give two sample machine code programs PLOTSUB and 2BYTJOY. The first of these is a high resolution PLOTSUB which reproduces the corresponding BASIC subroutine in HIRES DEMO. The second 2BYTJOY is a routine designed to sample both joyports and return X and Y co-ordinates 2 bytes wide. In this way the routine can be used to drive either high or low resolution graphics.

In the Appendices you will find a BASIC loader for each of the programs (prepared using DATASTATE) which POKEs the machine code into memory. Each loader is followed by a short TEST program.

```
LINE# LOC    CODE        LINE


00001  0000              ;*******************************
00002  0000              ;*                             *
00003  0000              ;*         PLOTSUB 64           *
00004  0000              ;*                             *
00005  0000              ;*                             *
00006  0000              ;* KEY VALUES (DECIMAL):        *
00007  0000              ;*                             *
00008  0000              ;* 49496 = X VALUE LO-BYTE      *
00009  0000              ;*                             *
00010  0000              ;* 49497 = X VALUE HI-BYTE      *
00011  0000              ;*                             *
00012  0000              ;* 49498 = Y VALUE              *
00013  0000              ;*                             *
00014  0000              ;* 49499 = ERASE=1/PLOT=0       *
00015  0000              ;*                             *
00016  0000              ;* 49500 = COLOUR BYTE          *
00017  0000              ;*                             *
00018  0000              ;*                             *
00019  0000              ;* TO SETUP - SYS 49509         *
00020  0000              ;*                             *
00021  0000              ;* TO RESET - SYS 49594         *
00022  0000              ;*                             *
00023  0000              ;* TO PLOT  - POKE VALS ABOVE   *
00024  0000              ;*                             *
00025  0000              ;*            THEN SYS 49634    *
00026  0000              ;*                             *
00027  0000              ;*******************************

00029  0000              POINTR = $FB        ;0 PAGE LOC FOR INDIRECTS
00030  0000              VICREG = $D000      ;BASE ADDR OF VIC-II
00031  0000              DDR2A  = $DD02      ;ADDR OF VIA#2 PORT A
00032  0000              PORT2A = $DD00      ;ADDR OF VIA#2 DDR A
00033  0000              CMBASE = $6000      ;BASE OF CHAR MATRIX
00034  0000              VMBASE = $5C00      ;BASE OF VIDEO MATRIX
00035  0000              MASK0  = $03        ;
00036  0000              MASK1  = $FC        ;
00037  0000              BANK1  = $02        ;MASKS FOR BANK SELECT
00038  0000              BANK0  = $03        ;
```

```
00039   0000                        NEWPTR  = $78           ;HIRES VM & CM POINTER
00040   0000                        OLDPTR  = $14           ;NORMAL VM & CM POINTER
00041   0000                        BMMODE  = $20           ;MASK FOR BIT-MAP MODE
00042   0000                        TXMODE  = 223           ;MASK FOR NORMAL MODE
00043   0000                        SEVEN   = $07
00044   0000                        FORTY   = 40
00045   0000                        YMAX    = 200           ;BORDER Y VAL
00046   0000                        XMAXL   = 64            ;BORDER X LO VAL
00047   0000                        XMAXH   = 2             ;BORDER X HI VAL
00048   0000                        *       = $C150
00049   C150                        POWERS                  ; POWERS OF TWO TABLE
00050   C150   80                   .BYT    128,64,32,16,8,4,2,1
00050   C151   40
00050   C152   20
00050   C153   10
00050   C154   08
00050   C155   04
00050   C156   02
00050   C157   01
00051   C158                        XLO     *=*+1           ; LO-BYTE OF X VAL
00052   C159                        XHI     *=*+1           ;HI-BYTE OF X VAL
00053   C15A                        YVAL    *=*+1           ;Y VAL
00054   C15B                        ERFLAG  *=*+1           ;ERASE/DRAW FLAG
00055   C15C                        COLOUR  *=*+1           ;COLOUR BYTE
00056   C15D                        RVAL    *=*+1           ; R VALUE
00057   C15E                        CVAL    *=*+1           ; C VALUE
00058   C15F                        UVAL    *=*+1           ; U VALUE
00059   C160                        VVAL    *=*+1           ; V VALUE
00060   C161                        TEMP1   *=*+1
00061   C162                        TEMP2   *=*+1
00062   C163                        TEMP3   *=*+1           ;TEMPORARY STORAGE
00063   C164                        TEMP4   *=*+1

00065   C165                        ;
00066   C165                        ;ROUTINE TO SET UP HIRES SCREEN
00067   C165                        ;FOR PLOTSUB
00068   C165                        ;
00069   C165   48                           PHA
00070   C166   8A                           TXA
00071   C167   48                           PHA             ;SAVE REGISTERS
00072   C168   98                           TYA
00073   C169   48                           PHA

00075   C16A   A9 00                        LDA #<VMBASE    ;SET ZP POINTER TO VM
00076   C16C   85 FB                        STA POINTR
00077   C16E   A9 5C                        LDA #>VMBASE
00078   C170   85 FC                        STA POINTR+1
00079   C172   A0 00                        LDY #$00        ;ZERO OFFSET
00080   C174   AD 5C C1                     LDA COLOUR      ;GET SCREEN COLOUR
00081   C177                        BLKCOL
00082   C177   91 FB                        STA (POINTR),Y  ;STORE IN VM
00083   C179   E6 FB                        INC POINTR      ;INC LO-BYTE POINTER
00084   C17B   D0 FA                        BNE BLKCOL      ;NO CARRY.. BRANCH
00085   C17D   E6 FC                        INC POINTR+1    ;CARRY.. INC HI-BYTE
00086   C17F   A6 FC                        LDX POINTR+1
00087   C181   E0 60                        CPX #>CMBASE    ;HI-BYTE= CMBASE?
00088   C183   D0 F2                        BNE BLKCOL      ;NO.. BRANCH BACK

00090   C185                        ;POINTER NOW AT CHAR MATRIX
00091   C185   A9 00                        LDA #$00        ;GET BLANK VALUE
```

Listing continued next page

```
00092   C187                    BLKSCN
00093   C187   91 FB                    STA (POINTR),Y   ;STORE IN CM
00094   C189   E6 FB                    INC POINTR       ;INC LO-BYTE POINTER
00095   C18B   D0 FA                    BNE BLKSCN       ;NO CARRY.. BRANCH
00096   C18D   E6 FC                    INC POINTR+1     ;CARRY.. INC HI-BYTE
00097   C18F   A6 FC                    LDX POINTR+1
00098   C191   E0 80                    CPX #>CMBASE+32  ;HI-BYTE = END OF CM?
00099   C193   D0 F2                    BNE BLKSCN       ;NO.. BRANCH BACK

00101   C195   AD 11 D0                 LDA VICREG+17
00102   C198   09 20                    ORA #BMMODE      ;SET BIT-MAP MODE
00103   C19A   8D 11 D0                 STA VICREG+17
00104   C19D   AD 02 DD                 LDA DDR2A
00105   C1A0   09 03                    ORA #MASK0       ;SET DDR FOR BANK
00106   C1A2   8D 02 DD                 STA DDR2A        ;SELECT
00107   C1A5   AD 00 DD                 LDA PORT2A
00108   C1A8   29 FC                    AND #MASK1
00109   C1AA   09 02                    ORA #BANK1       ;SELECT BANK 1
00110   C1AC   8D 00 DD                 STA PORT2A
00111   C1AF   A9 78                    LDA #NEWPTR      ;SET CM & VM
00112   C1B1   8D 18 D0                 STA VICREG+24    ;POINTERS

00114   C1B4   68                       PLA
00115   C1B5   A8                       TAY
00116   C1B6   68                       PLA              ;RESTORE REGISTERS
00117   C1B7   AA                       TAX
00118   C1B8   68                       PLA
00119   C1B9   60                       RTS              ;RETURN

00121   C1BA                    ;
00122   C1BA                    ;ROUTINE TO RESTORE NORMAL TEXT
00123   C1BA                    ;SCREEN AFTER PLOTSUB
00124   C1BA                    ;
00125   C1BA   48                       PHA
00126   C1BB   8A                       TXA
00127   C1BC   48                       PHA              ;SAVE REGISTERS
00128   C1BD   98                       TYA
00129   C1BE   48                       PHA

00131   C1BF   AD 11 D0                 LDA VICREG+17
00132   C1C2   29 DF                    AND #TXMODE      ;SET TEXT MODE
00133   C1C4   8D 11 D0                 STA VICREG+17
00134   C1C7   AD 02 DD                 LDA DDR2A
00135   C1CA   09 03                    ORA #MASK0       ;SET DDR FOR BANK
00136   C1CC   8D 02 DD                 STA DDR2A        ;SELECT
00137   C1CF   AD 00 DD                 LDA PORT2A
00138   C1D2   09 03                    ORA #BANK0       ;SELECT BANK 0
00139   C1D4   8D 00 DD                 STA PORT2A
00140   C1D7   A9 14                    LDA #OLDPTR      ;RESET CM & VM
00141   C1D9   8D 18 D0                 STA VICREG+24    ;POINTER

00143   C1DC                    EXIT
00144   C1DC   68                       PLA
00145   C1DD   A8                       TAY
00146   C1DE   68                       PLA
00147   C1DF   AA                       TAX              ;RESTORE REGISTERS
00148   C1E0   68                       PLA
00149   C1E1   60                       RTS              ;RETURN FROM ROUTINE

00151   C1E2                    ;
```

```
00152   C1E2                        ;PLOTSUB HIRES PLOTTING ROUTINE
00153   C1E2                        ;
00154   C1E2                        ;
00155   C1E2    48              PHA
00156   C1E3    8A              TXA
00157   C1E4    48              PHA                 ;SAVE REGISTERS
00158   C1E5    98              TYA
00159   C1E6    48              PHA
00161   C1E7    AD 5A C1        LDA YVAL
00162   C1EA    10 04           BPL NOWX
00163   C1EC    C9 C8           CMP #YMAX
00164   C1EE    10 EC           BPL EXIT
00165   C1F0                NOWX
00166   C1F0    AD 59 C1        LDA XHI         ;CHECK VALUES IN
00167   C1F3    F0 0B           BEQ OK          ;RANGE
00168   C1F5    C9 02           CMP #XMAXH      ;IF NOT - EXIT
00169   C1F7    10 E3           BPL EXIT        ;PLOTSUB
00170   C1F9    AD 58 C1        LDA XLO
00171   C1FC    C9 40           CMP #XMAXL
00172   C1FE    10 DC           BPL EXIT

00174   C200                OK
00175   C200    AD 5A C1        LDA YVAL
00176   C203    4A              LSR A
00177   C204    4A              LSR A               ;U = INT(Y/8)
00178   C205    4A              LSR A
00179   C206    8D 5F C1        STA UVAL

00181   C209    AD 59 C1        LDA XHI
00182   C20C    8D 61 C1        STA TEMP1
00183   C20F    AD 58 C1        LDA XLO
00184   C212    6E 61 C1        ROR TEMP1           ;V = INT(X/8)
00185   C215    6A              ROR A
00186   C216    4A              LSR A
00187   C217    4A              LSR A
00188   C218    8D 60 C1        STA VVAL

00190   C21B                    ;
00191   C21B                    ;COMPUTE 40*U
00192   C21B                    ;
00193   C21B                    ;FAST 8 BIT MULTIPLICATION ROUTINE
00194   C21B                    ;MULTIPLICAND IN TEMP1
00195   C21B                    ;MULITPLIER IN TEMP2
00196   C21B                    ;RESULT (16 BIT) IN TEMP3 (LO) AND
00197   C21B                    ;ACCUMULATOR (HI)
00198   C21B                    ;
00199   C21B
00200   C21B    AD 5F C1        LDA UVAL
00201   C21E    8D 61 C1        STA TEMP1           ;MULTIPLICAND
00202   C221    A9 28           LDA #FORTY
00203   C223    8D 62 C1        STA TEMP2           ;MULTIPLIER
00204   C226    A9 00           LDA #$00
00205   C228    8D 63 C1        STA TEMP3           ;CLEAR RESULT LO
00206   C22B    A2 08           LDX #$08            ;LOOP COUNTER (8 BIT MULT)
00207   C22D                LOOP
00208   C22D    4E 62 C1        LSR TEMP2           ;SHIFT LSB INTO CARRY
00209   C230    90 04           BCC NOADD           ;IF A 0 BRANCH
00210   C232    18              CLC                 ;ELSE CLEAR CARRY
00211   C233    6D 61 C1        ADC TEMP1           ;AND ADD MPAND TO RESULT
```

Listing continued next page

```
00212   C236                        NOADD
00213   C236   6A                        ROR  A              ;SHIFT RES 1 BIT TO RIGHT
00214   C237   6E 63 C1                   ROR  TEMP3          ;DROP LSB INTO MSB OF TEMP3
00215   C23A   CA                         DEX                 ;DONE 8 TIMES?
00216   C23B   D0 F0                      BNE  LOOP           ;NO.. BRANCH BACK
00217   C23D   8D 64 C1                   STA  TEMP4          ;YES.. PUT RES HI IN TEMP4

00219   C240   AD 60 C1                   LDA  VVAL           ;GET V
00220   C243   18                         CLC
00221   C244   6D 63 C1                   ADC  TEMP3          ;ADD TO RESULT LO
00222   C247   8D 63 C1                   STA  TEMP3
00223   C24A   90 03                      BCC  NOFLO1         ;BRANCH IF NO CARRY
00224   C24C   EE 64 C1                   INC  TEMP4          ;ELSE INC RESULT HI

00226   C24F                        NOFLO1
00227   C24F   AD 63 C1                   LDA  TEMP3
00228   C252   0A                         ASL  A
00229   C253   2E 64 C1                   ROL  TEMP4
00230   C256   0A                         ASL  A
00231   C257   2E 64 C1                   ROL  TEMP4
00232   C25A   0A                         ASL  A              ;MULTIPLY 16 BIT VALUE
00233   C25B   2E 64 C1                   ROL  TEMP4          ;BY 8 (3 SHIFT RIGHTS)
00234   C25E   8D 63 C1                   STA  TEMP3

00236   C261   AD 5A C1                   LDA  YVAL
00237   C264   29 07                      AND  #SEVEN         ;R = YAND7
00238   C266   8D 5D C1                   STA  RVAL
00239   C269   AD 58 C1                   LDA  XLO
00240   C26C   29 07                      AND  #SEVEN         ;C = XAND7
00241   C26E   8D 5E C1                   STA  CVAL

00243   C271   A9 00                      LDA  #<CMBASE
00244   C273   18                         CLC
00245   C274   6D 63 C1                   ADC  TEMP3          ;ADD CM BASE VALUE
00246   C277   8D 63 C1                   STA  TEMP3
00247   C27A   90 03                      BCC  NOFLO2
00248   C27C   EE 64 C1                   INC  TEMP4
00249   C27F                        NOFLO2
00250   C27F   A9 60                      LDA  #>CMBASE
00251   C281   18                         CLC
00252   C282   6D 64 C1                   ADC  TEMP4
00253   C285   8D 64 C1                   STA  TEMP4

00255   C288   AD 5D C1                   LDA  RVAL
00256   C28B   18                         CLC
00257   C28C   6D 63 C1                   ADC  TEMP3          ;ADD R
00258   C28F   8D 63 C1                   STA  TEMP3
00259   C292   90 03                      BCC  NOFLO3
00260   C294   EE 64 C1                   INC  TEMP4

00262   C297                        NOFLO3
00263   C297   AD 63 C1                   LDA  TEMP3
00264   C29A   85 FB                      STA  POINTR         ;PUT FINAL ADDR IN
00265   C29C   AD 64 C1                   LDA  TEMP4          ;ZERO PAGE
00266   C29F   85 FC                      STA  POINTR+1

00268   C2A1   AC 5E C1                   LDY  CVAL
00269   C2A4   B9 50 C1                   LDA  POWERS,Y       ;GET 2↑C
00270   C2A7   A0 00                      LDY  #$00
```

```
00271  C2A9  AE 5B C1          LDX ERFLAG       ;PRINT OR ERASE?
00272  C2AC  D0 07             BNE ERASE        ;NON ZERO.. ERASE
00273  C2AE  11 FB             ORA (POINTR),Y   ;PRINT PIXEL
00274  C2B0  91 FB             STA (POINTR),Y
00275  C2B2  4C BB C2          JMP END          ;FINISHED
00276  C2B5          ERASE
00277  C2B5  49 FF             EOR #$FF         ;INVERT BIT PATTERN
00278  C2B7  31 FB             AND (POINTR),Y   ;ERASE PIXEL
00279  C2B9  91 FB             STA (POINTR),Y

00281  C2BB          END
00282  C2BB  68                PLA
00283  C2BC  A8                TAY
00284  C2BD  68                PLA
00285  C2BE  AA                TAX              ;RESTORE REGISTERS
00286  C2BF  68                PLA
00287  C2C0  60                RTS
00288  C2C1                    .END
```

```
ERRORS = 00000

SYMBOL TABLE

SYMBOL VALUE
  BANK0     0003    BANK1     0002    BLKCOL    C177    BLKSCN    C187
  BMMODE    0020    CMBASE    6000    COLOUR    C15C    CVAL      C15E
  DDR2A     DD02    END       C2BB    ERASE     C2B5    ERFLAG    C15B
  EXIT      C1DC    FORTY     0028    LOOP      C22D    MASK0     0003
  MASK1     00FC    NEWPTR    0078    NOADD     C236    NOFLO1    C24F
  NOFLO2    C27F    NOFLO3    C297    NOWX      C1F0    OK        C200
  OLDPTR    0014    POINTR    00FB    PORT2A    DD00    POWERS    C150
  RVAL      C15D    SEVEN     0007    TEMP1     C161    TEMP2     C162
  TEMP3     C163    TEMP4     C164    TXMODE    00DF    UVAL      C15F
  VICREG    D000    VMBASE    5C00    VVAL      C160    XHI       C159
  XLO       C158    XMAXH     0002    XMAXL     0040    YMAX      00C8
  YVAL      C15A

END OF ASSEMBLY
```

```
LINE# LOC    CODE           LINE

00001  0000                 ;*********************************
00002  0000                 ;*                               *
00003  0000                 ;*                               *
00004  0000                 ;*    JOYSTICK READ ROUTINE       *
00005  0000                 ;*                               *
00006  0000                 ;*                               *
00007  0000                 ;* KEY VALUES (DECIMAL) :         *
00008  0000                 ;* 49152=XMIN2 LO :49153=XMIN2 HI *
00009  0000                 ;* 49154=XMIN1 LO :49155=XMIN1 HI *
00010  0000                 ;* 49156=XMAX2 LO :49157=XMAX2 HI *
00011  0000                 ;* 49158=XMAX1 LO :49159=XMAX1 HI *
00012  0000                 ;* 49160=YMIN2 LO :49161=YMIN2 HI *
00013  0000                 ;* 49162=YMIN1 LO :49163=YMIN1 HI *
00014  0000                 ;* 49164=YMAX2 LO :49165=YMAX2 HI *
00015  0000                 ;* 49166=YMAX1 LO :49167=YMAX1 HI *
00016  0000                 ;*                               *
00017  0000      /          ;* 49168=READ RATE               *
00018  0000                 ;* (0= 1/60 SEC:255= 4.3 SECS)    *
00019  0000                 ;*                               *
00020  0000                 ;* ABOVE VALUES (0 TO 255) MUST   *
00021  0000                 ;* BE POKED BEFORE CALLING        *
00022  0000                 ;* ROUTINE.                       *
00023  0000                 ;*                               *
00024  0000                 ;* 49169=DX2 - LO :49170=DX2 - HI *
00025  0000                 ;* 49171=DX1 - LO :49172=DX1 - HI *
00026  0000                 ;* 49173=DY2 - LO :49174=DY2 - HI *
00027  0000                 ;* 49175=DY1 - LO :49176=DY1 - HI *
00028  0000                 ;* THESE ARE JOYSTICK X & Y VALS. *
00029  0000                 ;* 49177=FIRE-JOY2:49178=FIRE-JOY1*
00030  0000                 ;*                               *
00031  0000                 ;* TO TURN WEDGE ON SYS 49183     *
00032  0000                 ;* TO TURN WEDGE OFF SYS 49208    *
00033  0000                 ;*                               *
00034  0000                 ;*********************************

00036  0000                                    ;DEFINE VARIABLES
00037  0000                                    ;
00038  0000                 PORT1A = $DC00      ;VIA#1 PORT A
00039  0000                 DDR1A  = $DC02      ;VIA#1 DDR A
00040  0000                 IRQVEC = $0314      ;IRQ RAM VECTOR
00041  0000                 INPUT  = $E0        ;MASK FOR DDR
00042  0000                 *      = $C000
00043  C000                 XMIN2  *=*+2        ;MIN LEGAL X-VAL JOY2
00044  C002                 XMIN1  *=*+2        ;MIN LEGAL X-VAL JOY1
00045  C004                 XMAX2  *=*+2        ;MAX LEGAL X-VAL JOY2
00046  C006                 XMAX1  *=*+2        ;MAX LEGAL X-VAL JOY1
00047  C008                 YMIN2  *=*+2        ;MIN LEGAL Y-VAL JOY2
00048  C00A                 YMIN1  *=*+2        ;MIN LEGAL Y-VAL JOY1
00049  C00C                 YMAX2  *=*+2        ;MAX LEGAL Y-VAL JOY2
00050  C00E                 YMAX1  *=*+2        ;MAX LEGAL Y-VAL JOY1
00051  C010                 DELAY  *=*+1        ;READ RATE
00052  C011                 DX2    *=*+2        ;X-VAL JOY2
00053  C013                 DX1    *=*+2        ;X-VAL JOY1
00054  C015                 DY2    *=*+2        ;Y-VAL JOY2
00055  C017                 DY1    *=*+2        ;Y-VAL JOY1
00056  C019                 FIRE   *=*+2        ;FIRE BUTTONS 1 & 2
00057  C01B                 COUNT  *=*+1        ;#IRQ'S SINCE LAST READ
```

```
00058   C01C                          OLDDDR  *=*+1              ;PREVIOUS DDR VALUE
00059   C01D                          VECTOR  *=*+2              ;PREVIOUS RAM VECTOR

00061   C01F                  ;
00062   C01F                  ;INSERT WEDGE
00063   C01F                  ;
00064   C01F    78                    SEI
00065   C020    AD 14 03              LDA IRQVEC
00066   C023    8D 1D C0              STA VECTOR               ;SAVE OLD IRQ
00067   C026    AD 15 03              LDA IRQVEC+1             ;RAM VECTOR
00068   C029    8D 1E C0              STA VECTOR+1
00069   C02C    A9 47                 LDA #<WEDGE
00070   C02E    8D 14 03              STA IRQVEC               ;INSERT WEDGE ADDRESS
00071   C031    A9 C0                 LDA #>WEDGE              ;INTO RAM VECTOR
00072   C033    8D 15 03              STA IRQVEC+1
00073   C036    58                    CLI
00074   C037    60                    RTS

00076   C038                  ;
00077   C038                  ; REMOVE WEDGE
00078   C038                  ;
00079   C038    78                    SEI
00080   C039    AD 1D C0              LDA VECTOR
00081   C03C    8D 14 03              STA IRQVEC
00082   C03F    AD 1E C0              LDA VECTOR+1             ;RESTORE OLD RAM VECTOR
00083   C042    8D 15 03              STA IRQVEC+1
00084   C045    58                    CLI
00085   C046    60                    RTS

00087   C047                  ;
00088   C047                  ;WEDGE STARTS HERE
00089   C047                  ;
00090   C047                  WEDGE
00091   C047    AD 1B C0              LDA COUNT                ;CHECK IF READ REQUIRED
00092   C04A    CD 10 C0              CMP DELAY                ;THIS IRQ
00093   C04D    F0 03                 BEQ CONTRD               ;BRANCH IF REQUIRED
00094   C04F    4C 41 C1              JMP EXIT                 ;ELSE EXIT
00095   C052                  CONTRD
00096   C052    A9 FF                 LDA #$FF                 ;RESET COUNT
00097   C054    8D 1B C0              STA COUNT
00098   C057    A2 00                 LDX #00
00099   C059    A0 00                 LDY #00                  ;CLEAR INDEX REGS
00100   C05B                  READ
00101   C05B    B9 02 DC              LDA DDR1A,Y              ;GET OLD DDR VALUE
00102   C05E    8D 1C C0              STA OLDDDR               ;SAVE IT
00103   C061    A9 E0                 LDA #INPUT               ;SET DDR FOR JOYSTICK READ
00104   C063    99 02 DC              STA DDR1A,Y
00105   C066    B9 00 DC              LDA PORT1A,Y             ;READ JOYSTICK
00106   C069    48                    PHA                      ;TEMP STORE ON STACK
00107   C06A    AD 1C C0              LDA OLDDDR               ;RESTORE DDR FOR KEYBOARD
00108   C06D    99 02 DC              STA DDR1A,Y              ;READ BY OP-SYSTEM

00110   C070                  ;
00111   C070                  ;UPDATE DY
00112   C070                  ;
00113   C070                  ;DOWN BIT FIRST
00114   C070                  ;
00115   C070    BD 08 C0              LDA YMIN2,X
00116   C073    DD 15 C0              CMP DY2,X
```

Listing continued next page

```
00117   C076   BD 09 C0            LDA YMIN2+1,X   ;CHECK VALUES STILL IN
00118   C079   FD 16 C0            SBC DY2+1,X     ;USER DEFINED RANGE
00119   C07C   90 12              BCC INRNG1      ;BRANCH IF IN RANGE
00120   C07E   BD 08 C0            LDA YMIN2,X
00121   C081   9D 15 C0            STA DY2,X
00122   C084   BD 09 C0            LDA YMIN2+1,X   ;IF NOT, PUT LIMIT
00123   C087   9D 16 C0            STA DY2+1,X     ;INTO DY
00124   C08A   68                 PLA             ;GET JOYSTICK BYTE FROM STAC
00125   C08B   4A                 LSR A           ;SHIFT LSB INTO CARRY
00126   C08C   48                 PHA             ;PUSH BYTE BACK
00127   C08D   4C A2 C0            JMP NEXT1       ;JUMP TO NEXT DIRECTION
00128   C090              ;
00129   C090              ;IN RANGE
00130   C090              ;
00131   C090              INRNG1
00132   C090   68                 PLA             ;GET JOYSTICK BYTE FROM STAC
00133   C091   4A                 LSR A           ;SHIFT LSB INTO CARRY
00134   C092   48                 PHA             ;PUSH BYTE BACK
00135   C093   B0 0D              BCS NEXT1       ;CARRY SET.. NEXT DIRECTION
00136   C095   DE 15 C0            DEC DY2,X       ;DECREMENT LO-BYTE
00137   C098   BD 15 C0            LDA DY2,X
00138   C09B   C9 FF              CMP #$FF        ;BORROW REQUIRED
00139   C09D   D0 03              BNE NEXT1       ;NO.. BRANCH
00140   C09F   DE 16 C0            DEC DY2+1,X     ;YES.. DEC HI-BYTE

00142   C0A2              ;
00143   C0A2              ;NOW DO UP BIT
00144   C0A2              ;
00145   C0A2              NEXT1
00146   C0A2   BD 15 C0            LDA DY2,X
00147   C0A5   DD 0C C0            CMP YMAX2,X
00148   C0A8   BD 16 C0            LDA DY2+1,X     ;CHECK VALUES STILL IN
00149   C0AB   FD 0D C0            SBC YMAX2+1,X   ;USER DEFINED RANGE
00150   C0AE   90 12              BCC INRNG2      ;BRANCH IF IN RANGE
00151   C0B0   BD 0C C0            LDA YMAX2,X
00152   C0B3   9D 15 C0            STA DY2,X
00153   C0B6   BD 0D C0            LDA YMAX2+1,X   ;IF NOT PUT LIMIT
00154   C0B9   9D 16 C0            STA DY2+1,X     ;INTO DY
00155   C0BC   68                 PLA             ;GET JOYSTICK BYTE FROM STAC
00156   C0BD   4A                 LSR A           ;SHIFT LSB INTO CARRY
00157   C0BE   48                 PHA             ;PUSH BYTE BACK
00158   C0BF   4C CF C0            JMP NEXT2       ;JUMP TO NEXT DIRECTION
00159   C0C2              ;
00160   C0C2              ;IN RANGE
00161   C0C2              ;
00162   C0C2              INRNG2
00163   C0C2   68                 PLA             ;GET JOYSTICK BYTE FROM STAM
00164   C0C3   4A                 LSR A           ;SHIFT LSB INTO CARRY
00165   C0C4   48                 PHA             ;PUSH BYTE BACK
00166   C0C5   B0 08              BCS NEXT2       ;CARRY SET NEXT DIRECTION
00167   C0C7   FE 15 C0            INC DY2,X       ;INCREMENT LO-BYTE
00168   C0CA   D0 03              BNE NEXT2       ;CARRY?
00169   C0CC   FE 16 C0            INC DY2+1,X     ;YES.. INC HI-BYTE
00170   C0CF              ;
00171   C0CF              ; UPDATE DX
00172   C0CF              ;
00173   C0CF              ; LEFT BIT
00174   C0CF              ;
00175   C0CF              NEXT2
```

```
00176   C0CF   BD 00 C0              LDA XMIN2,X
00177   C0D2   DD 11 C0              CMP DX2,X
00178   C0D5   BD 01 C0              LDA XMIN2+1,X      ;CHECK VALUES STILL IN
00179   C0D8   FD 12 C0              SBC DX2+1,X        ;USER DEFINED RANGE
00180   C0DB   90 12                 BCC INRNG3         ;BRANCH IF IN RANGE
00181   C0DD   BD 00 C0              LDA XMIN2,X
00182   C0E0   9D 11 C0              STA DX2,X
00183   C0E3   BD 01 C0              LDA XMIN2+1,X      ;IF NOT PUT LIMIT
00184   C0E6   9D 12 C0              STA DX2+1,X        ;INTO DX
00185   C0E9   68                    PLA                ;GET JOYSTICK BYTE FROM STACK
00186   C0EA   4A                    LSR A              ;SHIFT LSB INTO CARRY
00187   C0EB   48                    PHA                ;PUSH BYTE BACK
00188   C0EC   4C 01 C1              JMP NEXT3          ;JUMP TO NEXT DIRECTION
00189   C0EF                   ;
00190   C0EF                   ;IN RANGE
00191   C0EF                   ;
00192   C0EF                   INRNG3
00193   C0EF   68                    PLA                ;GET JOYSTICK BYTE FROM STACK
00194   C0F0   4A                    LSR A              ;SHIFT LSB INTO CARRY
00195   C0F1   48                    PHA                ;PUSH BYTE BACK
00196   C0F2   B0 0D                 BCS NEXT3          ;CARRY SET.. NEXT DIRECTION
00197   C0F4   DE 11 C0              DEC DX2,X          ;DECREMENT LO-BYTE
00198   C0F7   BD 11 C0              LDA DX2,X
00199   C0FA   C9 FF                 CMP #$FF           ;BORROW REQUIRED?
00200   C0FC   D0 03                 BNE NEXT3          ;NO BRANCH
00201   C0FE   DE 12 C0              DEC DX2+1,X        ;YES.. DEC HI-BYTE

00203   C101                   ;
00204   C101                   ;NOW DO RIGHT BIT
00205   C101                   ;
00206   C101                   NEXT3
00207   C101   BD 11 C0              LDA DX2,X
00208   C104   DD 04 C0              CMP XMAX2,X
00209   C107   BD 12 C0              LDA DX2+1,X        ;CHECK VALUES STILL IN
00210   C10A   FD 05 C0              SBC XMAX2+1,X      ;USER DEFINED RANGE
00211   C10D   90 12                 BCC INRNG4         ;BRANCH IF IN RANGE
00212   C10F   BD 04 C0              LDA XMAX2,X
00213   C112   9D 11 C0              STA DX2,X
00214   C115   BD 05 C0              LDA XMAX2+1,X      ;IF NOT PUT LIMIT
00215   C118   9D 12 C0              STA DX2+1,X        ;INTO DX
00216   C11B   68                    PLA                ;GET JOYSTICK BYTE FROM STACK
00217   C11C   4A                    LSR A              ;SHIFT LSB INTO CARRY
00218   C11D   48                    PHA                ;PUSH BYTE BACK
00219   C11E   4C 2E C1              JMP NEXT4          ;JUMP TO CHECK FIRE
00220   C121                   ;
00221   C121                   ;IN RANGE
00222   C121                   ;
00223   C121                   INRNG4
00224   C121   68                    PLA                ;GET JOYSTICK BYTE FROM STACK
00225   C122   4A                    LSR A              ;SHIFT LSB INTO CARRY
00226   C123   48                    PHA                ;PUSH BYTE BACK
00227   C124   B0 08                 BCS NEXT4          ;CARRY SET.. CHECK FIRE
00228   C126   FE 11 C0              INC DX2,X          ;INCREMENT LO-BYTE
00229   C129   D0 03                 BNE NEXT4          ;CARRY?
00230   C12B   FE 12 C0              INC DX2+1,X        ;YES.. INC HI-BYTE
00231   C12E                   ;
00232   C12E                   ;NOW CHECK FIRE BUTTON
00233   C12E                   ;
00234   C12E                   NEXT4
```

Listing continued next page

```
00235   C12E    68                      PLA                 ;GET JOYSTICK BYTE FROM STAC
00236   C12F    4A                      LSR A               ;SHIFT LSB INTO CARRY
00237   C130    B0 05                   BCS NEXT5           ;CARRY SET.. NO FIRE
00238   C132    A9 01                   LDA #01
00239   C134    99 19 C0                STA FIRE,Y          ;SET FIRE FLAG
00240   C137            NEXT5
00241   C137    C8                      INY                 ;NEXT JOYSTICK
00242   C138    E8                      INX
00243   C139    E8                      INX
00244   C13A    E0 04                   CPX #04 ARE WE FINISHED?
00245   C13C    F0 03                   BEQ EXIT            ;YES.. BRANCH
00246   C13E    4C 5B C0                JMP READ            ;NO.. GO BACK
00247   C141            EXIT
00248   C141    EE 1B C0                INC COUNT           ;INC IRQ COUNTER
00249   C144    6C 1D C0                JMP (VECTOR)        ;GO TO REST OF IRQ
00250   C147                            .END
```

ERRORS = 00000

SYMBOL TABLE

SYMBOL VALUE
```
 CONTRD    C052      COUNT     C01B      DDR1A     DC02      DELAY     C010
 DX1       C013      DX2       C011      DY1       C017      DY2       C015
 EXIT      C141      FIRE      C019      INPUT     00E0      INRNG1    C090
 INRNG2    C0C2      INRNG3    C0EF      INRNG4    C121      IRQVEC    0314
 NEXT1     C0A2      NEXT2     C0CF      NEXT3     C101      NEXT4     C12E
 NEXT5     C137      OLDDDR    C01C      PORT1A    DC00      READ      C05B
 VECTOR    C01D      WEDGE     C047      XMAX1     C006      XMAX2     C004
 XMIN1     C002      XMIN2     C000      YMAX1     C00E      YMAX2     C00C
 YMIN1     C00A      YMIN2     C008
```

END OF ASSEMBLY

THE 6510/6502 MICROPROCESSOR INSTRUCTION SET

ADC	Add Memory to Accumulator with Carry		**JSR**	Jump to New Location Saving Return Address
AND	"AND" Memory with Accumulator			
ASL	Shift Left One Bit (Memory or Accumulator)		**LDA**	Load Accumulator with Memory
			LDX	Load Index X with Memory
			LDY	Load Index Y with Memory
BCC	Branch on Carry Clear		**LSR**	Shift Right One Bit (Memory or Accumulator)
BCS	Branch on Carry Set			
BEQ	Branch on Result Zero			
BIT	Test Bits in Memory with Accumulator		**NOP**	No Operation
BMI	Branch on Result Minus		**ORA**	"OR" Memory with Accumulator
BNE	Branch on Result not Zero		**PHA**	Push Accumulator on Stack
BPL	Branch on Result Plus		**PHP**	Push Processor Status on Stack
BRK	Force Break		**PLA**	Pull Accumulator from Stack
BVC	Branch on Overflow Clear		**PLP**	Pull Processor Status from Stack
BVS	Branch on Overflow Set			
			ROL	Rotate One Bit Left (Memory or Accumulator)
CLC	Clear Carry Flag			
CLD	Clear Decimal Mode		**ROR**	Rotate One Bit Right (Memory or Accumulator)
CLI	Clear Interrupt Disable Bit			
CLV	Clear Overflow Flag		**RTI**	Return from Interrupt
CMP	Compare Memory and Accumulator		**RTS**	Return from Subroutine
CPX	Compare Memory and Index X			
CPY	Compare Memory and Index Y		**SBC**	Subtract Memory from Accumulator with Borrow
DEC	Decrement Memory by One		**SEC**	Set Carry Flag
DEX	Decrement Index X by One		**SED**	Set Decimal Mode
DEY	Decrement Index Y by One		**SEI**	Set Interrupt Disable Status
			STA	Store Accumulator in Memory
EOR	"Exclusive-Or" Memory with Accumulator		**STX**	Store Index X in Memory
			STY	Store Index Y in Memory
INC	Increment Memory by One		**TAX**	Transfer Accumulator to Index X
INX	Increment Index X by One		**TAY**	Transfer Accumulator to Index Y
INY	Increment Index Y by One		**TSX**	Transfer Stack Pointer to Index X
			TXA	Transfer Index X to Accumulator
JMP	Jump to New Location		**TXS**	Transfer Index X to Stack Pointer
			TYA	Transfer Index Y to Accumulator

The following notation applies to this summary:

A	Accumulator	$+$	Add	$\leftarrow$	Transfer to
X, Y	Index Registers	$\wedge$	Logical AND	V	Logical OR
M	Memory	$-$	Subtract	PC	Program Counter
P	Processor Status Register	$\forall$	Logical Exclusive Or	PCH	Program Counter High
S	Stack Pointer	$\uparrow$	Transfer from Stack	PCL	Program Counter Low
$\sqrt{}$	Change	$\downarrow$	Transfer to Stack	OPER	Operand
$-$	No Change	$\rightarrow$	Transfer to	#	Immediate addressing mode

Note. At the top of each table is located in parentheses a reference number (Ref: XX) which directs the user to that section in the *MCS6500 Microcomputer Family Programming Manual* in which the instruction is defined and discussed.

ADC — Add Memory to Accumulator with Carry — ADC

Operation: A + M + C → A, C

N Z C I D V
✓ ✓ ✓ − − ✓

(Ref: 2.2.1)

Addressing Mode	Assembly Language Form		OP CODE	No. Bytes	No. Cycles
Immediate	ADC	# Oper	69	2	2
Zero Page	ADC	Oper	65	2	3
Zero Page, X	ADC	Oper, X	75	2	4
Absolute	ADC	Oper	6D	3	4
Absolute, X	ADC	Oper, X	7D	3	4*
Absolute, Y	ADC	Oper, Y	79	3	4*
(Indirect, X)	ADC	(Oper, X)	61	2	6
(Indirect), Y	ADC	(Oper), Y	71	2	5*

* Add 1 if page boundary is crossed.

AND — "AND" Memory with Accumulator — AND

Logical AND to the accumulator

Operation: A ∧ M → A

N Z C I D V
✓ ✓ − − − −

(Ref: 2.2.3.0)

Addressing Mode	Assembly Language Form		OP CODE	No. Bytes	No. Cycles
Immediate	AND	# Oper	29	2	2
Zero Page	AND	Oper	25	2	3
Zero Page, X	AND	Oper, X	35	2	4
Absolute	AND	Oper	2D	3	4
Absolute, X	AND	Oper, X	3D	3	4*
Absolute, Y	AND	Oper, Y	39	3	4*
(Indirect, X)	AND	(Oper, X)	21	2	6
(Indirect), Y	AND	(Oper), Y	31	2	5

* Add 1 if page boundary is crossed.

ASL — ASL Shift Left One Bit (Memory or Accumulator) — ASL

Operation: C ← |7|6|5|4|3|2|1|0| ← 0

N Z C I D V
✓ ✓ ✓ − − −

(Ref: 10.2)

Addressing Mode	Assembly Language Form	OP CODE	No. Bytes	No. Cycles
Accumulator	ASL A	0A	1	2
Zero Page	ASL Oper	06	2	5
Zero Page, X	ASL Oper, X	16	2	6
Absolute	ASL Oper	0E	3	6
Absolute, X	ASL Oper, X	1E	3	7

BCC — BCC Branch on Carry Clear — BCC

Operation: Branch on C = 0

N Z C I D V
− − − − − −

(Ref: 4.1.1.3)

Addressing Mode	Assembly Language Form	OP CODE	No. Bytes	No. Cycles
Relative	BCC Oper	90	2	2*

* Add 1 if branch occurs to same page.
* Add 2 if branch occurs to different page.

BCS — BCS Branch on Carry Set — BCS

Operation: Branch on C = 1

N Z C I D V
− − − − − −

(Ref: 4.1.1.4)

Addressing Mode	Assembly Language Form	OP CODE	No. Bytes	No. Cycles
Relative	BCS Oper	B0	2	2*

* Add 1 if branch occurs to same page.
* Add 2 if branch occurs to next page.

BEQ — BEQ Branch on Result Zero — BEQ

Operation: Branch on Z = 1

(Ref: 4.1.1.5)

N Z C I D V
− − − − − −

Addressing Mode	Assembly Language Form	OP CODE	No. Bytes	No. Cycles
Relative	BEQ Oper	F0	2	2*

* Add 1 if branch occurs to same page.
* Add 2 if branch occurs to next page.

BIT — BIT Test Bits in Memory with Accumulator — BIT

Operation: A ∧ M, M_7 → N, M_6 → V

Bit 6 and 7 are transferred to the status register. N Z C I D V
If the result of A ∧ M is zero then Z = 1, otherwise M_7 ✓ − − − M_6
Z = 0

(Ref: 4.2.1.1)

Addressing Mode	Assembly Language Form	OP CODE	No. Bytes	No. Cycles
Zero Page	BIT Oper	24	2	3
Absolute	BIT Oper	2C	3	4

BMI — BMI Branch on Result Minus — BMI

Operation: Branch on N = 1

N Z C I D V
− − − − − −

(Ref: 4.1.1.1)

Addressing Mode	Assembly Language Form	OP CODE	No. Bytes	No. Cycles
Relative	BMI Oper	30	2	2*

* Add 1 if branch occurs to same page.
* Add 2 if branch occurs to different page.

BNE — BNE Branch on Result not Zero — BNE

Operation: Branch on Z = 0

N Z C I D V
− − − − − −

(Ref: 4.1.1.6)

Addressing Mode	Assembly Language Form	OP CODE	No. Bytes	No. Cycles
Relative	BNE Oper	D0	2	2*

* Add 1 if branch occurs to same page.
* Add 2 if branch occurs to different page.

BPL   BPL *Branch on Result Plus*   BPL

Operation: Branch on N = 0

N Z C I D V
− − − − − −

(Ref: 4.1.1.2)

Addressing Mode	Assembly Language Form	OP CODE	No. Bytes	No. Cycles
Relative	BPL Oper	10	2	2*

* Add 1 if branch occurs to same page.
* Add 2 if branch occurs to different page.

BRK   BRK *Force Break*   BRK

Operation: Forced Interrupt PC + 2 ↓ P ↓

N Z C I D V
− − − 1 − −

(Ref: 9.11)

Addressing Mode	Assembly Language Form	OP CODE	No. Bytes	No. Cycles
Implied	BRK	00	1	7

1. A BRK command cannot be masked by setting I.

BVC   BVC *Branch on Overflow Clear*   BVC

Operation: Branch on V = 0

N Z C I D V
− − − − − −

(Ref: 4.1.1.8)

Addressing Mode	Assembly Language Form	OP CODE	No. Bytes	No. Cycles
Relative	BVC Oper	50	2	2*

* Add 1 if branch occurs to same page.
* Add 2 if branch occurs to different page.

BVS   BVS *Branch on Overflow Set*   BVS

Operation: Branch on V = 1

N Z C I D V
− − − − − −

(Ref: 4.1.1.7)

Addressing Mode	Assembly Language Form	OP CODE	No. Bytes	No. Cycles
Relative	BVS Oper	70	2	2*

* Add 1 if branch occurs to same page.
* Add 2 if branch occurs to different page.

CLC   CLC *Clear Carry Flag*   CLC

Operation: 0 → C

N Z C I D V
− − 0 − − −

(Ref: 3.0.2)

Addressing Mode	Assembly Language Form	OP CODE	No. Bytes	No. Cycles
Implied	CLC	18	1	2

CLD   CLD *Clear Decimal Mode*   CLD

Operation: 0 → D

N Z C I D V
− − − − 0 −

(Ref: 3.3.2)

Addressing Mode	Assembly Language Form	OP CODE	No. Bytes	No. Cycles
Implied	CLD	D8	1	2

CLI   CLI *Clear Interrupt Disable Bit*   CLI

Operation: 0 → I

N Z C I D V
− − − 0 − −

(Ref: 3.2.2)

Addressing Mode	Assembly Language Form	OP CODE	No. Bytes	No. Cycles
Implied	CLI	58	1	2

CLV   CLV *Clear Overflow Flag*   CLV

Operation: 0 → V

N Z C I D V
− − − − − 0

(Ref: 3.6.1)

Addressing Mode	Assembly Language Form	OP CODE	No. Bytes	No. Cycles
Implied	CLV	B8	1	2

CMP   CMP *Compare Memory and Accumulator*   CMP

Operation: A - M

N Z C I D V
√ √ √ − − −

(Ref: 4.2.1)

Addressing Mode	Assembly Language Form	OP CODE	No. Bytes	No. Cycles
Immediate	CMP #Oper	C9	2	2
Zero Page	CMP Oper	C5	2	3
Zero Page, X	CMP Oper, X	D5	2	4
Absolute	CMP Oper	CD	3	4
Absolute, X	CMP Oper, X	DD	3	4*
Absolute, Y	CMP Oper, Y	D9	3	4*
(Indirect, X)	CMP (Oper, X)	C1	2	6
(Indirect), Y	CMP (Oper), Y	D1	2	5*

* Add 1 if page boundary is crossed.

CPX   CPX *Compare Memory and Index X*   CPX

Operation X - M

N Z C I D V
√ √ √ − − −

(Ref: 7.8)

Addressing Mode	Assembly Language Form	OP CODE	No. Bytes	No. Cycles
Immediate	CPX #Oper	E0	2	2
Zero Page	CPX Oper	E4	2	3
Absolute	CPX Oper	EC	3	4

CPY   CPY *Compare Memory and Index Y*   **CPY**

Operation: Y - M   N Z C I D V
                            √ √ √ — — —
              (Ref: 7.9)

Addressing Mode	Assembly Language Form	OP CODE	No. Bytes	No. Cycles
Immediate	CPY #Oper	C0	2	2
Zero Page	CPY Oper	C4	2	3
Absolute	CPY Oper	CC	3	4

DEC   DEC *Decrement Memory by One*   **DEC**

Operation: M - 1 → M   N Z C I D V
                            √ √ — — — —
              (Ref: 10.7)

Addressing Mode	Assembly Language Form	OP CODE	No. Bytes	No. Cycles
Zero Page	DEC Oper	C6	2	5
Zero Page, X	DEC Oper, X	D6	2	6
Absolute	DEC Oper	CE	3	6
Absolute, X	DEC Oper, X	DE	3	7

DEX   DEX *Decrement Index X by One*   **DEX**

Operation: X - 1 → X   N Z C I D V
                            √ √ — — — —
              (Ref: 7.6)

Addressing Mode	Assembly Language Form	OP CODE	No. Bytes	No. Cycles
Implied	DEX	CA	1	2

DEY   DEY *Decrement Index Y by One*   **DEY**

Operation: Y - 1 → Y   N Z C I D V
                            √ √ — — — —
              (Ref: 7.7)

Addressing Mode	Assembly Language Form	OP CODE	No. Bytes	No. Cycles
Implied	DEY	88	1	2

EOR   EOR *"Exclusive Or" Memory with Accumulator*   **EOR**

Operation: A ∀ M → A   N Z C I D V
                            √ √ — — — —
              (Ref: 2.2.3.2)

Addressing Mode	Assembly Language Form	OP CODE	No. Bytes	No. Cycles
Immediate	EOR #Oper	49	2	2
Zero Page	EOR Oper	45	2	3
Zero Page, X	EOR Oper, X	55	2	4
Absolute	EOR Oper	4D	3	4
Absolute, X	EOR Oper, X	5D	3	4*
Absolute, Y	EOR Oper, Y	59	3	4*
(Indirect, X)	EOR (Oper, X)	41	2	6
(Indirect),Y	EOR (Oper), Y	51	2	5*

* Add 1 if page boundary is crossed.

INC   INC *Increment Memory by One*   **INC**

Operation: M + 1 → M   N Z C I D V
                            √ √ — — — —
              (Ref: 10.6)

Addressing Mode	Assembly Language Form	OP CODE	No. Bytes	No. Cycles
Zero Page	INC Oper	E6	2	5
Zero Page, X	INC Oper, X	F6	2	6
Absolute	INC Oper	EE	3	6
Absolute, X	INC Oper, X	FE	3	7

INX   INX *Increment Index X by One*   **INX**

Operation: X + 1 → X   N Z C I D V
                            √ √ — — — —
              (Ref: 7.4)

Addressing Mode	Assembly Language Form	OP CODE	No. Bytes	No. Cycles
Implied	INX	E8	1	2

INY   INY *Increment Index Y by One*   **INY**

Operation: Y + 1 → Y   N Z C I D V
                            √ √ — — — —
              (Ref: 7.5)

Addressing Mode	Assembly Language Form	OP CODE	No. Bytes	No. Cycles
Implied	INY	C8	1	2

JMP   JMP *Jump to New Location*   **JMP**

Operation: (PC + 1) → PCL   N Z C I D V
           (PC + 2) → PCH (Ref: 4.0.2)   — — — — — —
                           (Ref: 9.8.1)

Addressing Mode	Assembly Language Form	OP CODE	No. Bytes	No. Cycles
Absolute	JMP Oper	4C	3	3
Indirect	JMP (Oper)	6C	3	5

JSR   JSR *Jump to New Location Saving Return Address*   **JSR**

Operation: PC + 2 ↓, (PC + 1) → PCL   N Z C I D V
           (PC + 2) → PCH   — — — — — —
              (Ref: 8.1)

Addressing Mode	Assembly Language Form	OP CODE	No. Bytes	No. Cycles
Absolute	JSR Oper	20	3	6

LDA — LDA *Load Accumulator with Memory* — LDA

Operation: M → A

(Ref: 2.1.1)

N Z C I D V
√ √ − − − −

Addressing Mode	Assembly Language Form	OP CODE	No. Bytes	No. Cycles
Immediate	LDA # Oper	A9	2	2
Zero Page	LDA Oper	A5	2	3
Zero Page, X	LDA Oper, X	B5	2	4
Absolute	LDA Oper	AD	3	4
Absolute, X	LDA Oper, X	BD	3	4*
Absolute, Y	LDA Oper, Y	B9	3	4*
(Indirect, X)	LDA (Oper, X)	A1	2	6
(Indirect), Y	LDA (Oper), Y	B1	2	5*

* Add 1 if page boundary is crossed.

LDX — LDX *Load Index X with Memory* — LDX

Operation: M → X

(Ref: 7.0)

N Z C I D V
√ √ − − − −

Addressing Mode	Assembly Language Form	OP CODE	No. Bytes	No. Cycles
Immediate	LDX # Oper	A2	2	2
Zero Page	LDX Oper	A6	2	3
Zero Page, Y	LDX Oper, Y	B6	2	4
Absolute	LDX Oper	AE	3	4
Absolute, Y	LDX Oper, Y	BE	3	4*

* Add 1 when page boundary is crossed.

LDY — LDY *Load Index Y with Memory* — LDY

Operation: M → Y

(Ref: 7.1)

N Z C I D V
√ √ − − − −

Addressing Mode	Assembly Language Form	OP CODE	No. Bytes	No. Cycles
Immediate	LDY # Oper	A0	2	2
Zero Page	LDY Oper	A4	2	3
Zero Page, X	LDY Oper, X	B4	2	4
Absolute	LDY Oper	AC	3	4
Absolute, X	LDY Oper, X	BC	3	4*

* Add 1 when page boundary is crossed.

LSR — LSR *Shift Right One Bit (Memory or Accumulator)* — LSR

Operation: 0 → [7 6 5 4 3 2 1 0] → C

(Ref: 10.1)

N Z C I D V
0 √ √ − − −

Addressing Mode	Assembly Language Form	OP CODE	No. Bytes	No. Cycles
Accumulator	LSR A	4A	1	2
Zero Page	LSR Oper	46	2	5
Zero Page, X	LSR Oper, X	56	2	6
Absolute	LSR Oper	4E	3	6
Absolute, X	LSR Oper, X	5E	3	7

NOP — NOP *No Operation* — NOP

Operation: No Operation (2 cycles)

N Z C I D V
− − − − − −

Addressing Mode	Assembly Language Form	OP CODE	No. Bytes	No. Cycles
Implied	NOP	EA	1	2

ORA — ORA *"OR" Memory with Accumulator* — ORA

Operation: A V M → A

(Ref: 2.2.3.1)

N Z C I D V
√ √ − − − −

Addressing Mode	Assembly Language Form	OP CODE	No. Bytes	No. Cycles
Immediate	ORA # Oper	09	2	2
Zero Page	ORA Oper	05	2	3
Zero Page, X	ORA Oper, X	15	2	4
Absolute	ORA Oper	0D	3	4
Absolute, X	ORA Oper, X	1D	3	4*
Absolute, Y	ORA Oper, Y	19	3	4*
(Indirect, X)	ORA (Oper, X)	01	2	6
(Indirect), Y	ORA (Oper), Y	11	2	5

* Add 1 on page crossing

PHA — PHA *Push Accumulator on Stack* — PHA

Operation: A ↓

(Ref: 8.5)

N Z C I D V
− − − − − −

Addressing Mode	Assembly Language Form	OP CODE	No. Bytes	No. Cycles
Implied	PHA	48	1	3

PHP — PHP *Push Processor Status on Stack* — PHP

Operation: P↓

(Ref: 8.11)

N Z C I D V
− − − − − −

Addressing Mode	Assembly Language Form	OP CODE	No. Bytes	No. Cycles
Implied	PHP	08	1	3

PLA — PLA *Pull Accumulator from Stack* — PLA

Operation: A ↑

(Ref: 8.6)

N Z C I D V
√ √ − − − −

Addressing Mode	Assembly Language Form	OP CODE	No. Bytes	No. Cycles
Implied	PLA	68	1	4

PLP   PLP *Pull Processor Status from Stack*   PLP

Operation: P ↑

N Z C I D V
From Stack

(Ref: 8.12)

Addressing Mode	Assembly Language Form	OP CODE	No. Bytes	No. Cycles
Implied	PLP	28	1	4

ROL   ROL *Rotate One Bit Left (Memory or Accumulator)*   ROL

Operation: $\boxed{7\,6\,5\,4\,3\,2\,1\,0} \leftarrow \boxed{C} \leftarrow$

N Z C I D V
√ √ √ − − −

(Ref: 10.3)

Addressing Mode	Assembly Language Form	OP CODE	No. Bytes	No. Cycles
Accumulator	ROL A	2A	1	2
Zero Page	ROL Oper	26	2	5
Zero Page, X	ROL Oper, X	36	2	6
Absolute	ROL Oper	2E	3	6
Absolute, X	ROL Oper, X	3E	3	7

ROR   ROR *Rotate One Bit Right (Memory or Accumulator)*   ROR

Operation: $\rightarrow \boxed{C} \rightarrow \boxed{7\,6\,5\,4\,3\,2\,1\,0}$

N Z C I D V
√ √ √ − − −

(Ref: 10.4)

Addressing Mode	Assembly Language Form	OP CODE	No. Bytes	No. Cycles
Accumulator	ROR A	6A	1	2
Zero Page	ROR Oper	66	2	5
Zero Page, X	ROR Oper, X	76	2	6
Absolute	ROR Oper	6E	3	6
Absolute, X	ROR Oper, X	7E	3	7

Note: ROR instruction will be available on MCS650X microprocessors after June, 1976.

RTI   RTI *Return from Interrupt*   RTI

Operation: P↑ PC↑

N Z C I D V
From Stack

(Ref: 9.6)

Addressing Mode	Assembly Language Form	OP CODE	No. Bytes	No. Cycles
Implied	RTI	40	1	6

RTS   RTS *Return from Subroutine*   RTS

Operation: PC↑, PC + 1 → PC

N Z C I D V
− − − − − −

(Ref: 8.2)

Addressing Mode	Assembly Language Form	OP CODE	No. Bytes	No. Cycles
Implied	RTS	60	1	6

SBC   SBC *Subtract Memory from Accumulator with Borrow*   SBC

Operation: $A - M - \bar{C} \rightarrow A$

N Z C I D V
√ √ √ − − √

Note: $\bar{C}$ = Borrow   (Ref: 2.2.2)

Addressing Mode	Assembly Language Form	OP CODE	No. Bytes	No. Cycles
Immediate	SBC # Oper	E9	2	2
Zero Page	SBC Oper	E5	2	3
Zero Page, X	SBC Oper, X	F5	2	4
Absolute	SBC Oper	ED	3	4
Absolute, X	SBC Oper, X	FD	3	4*
Absolute, Y	SBC Oper, Y	F9	3	4*
(Indirect, X)	SBC (Oper, X)	E1	2	6
(Indirect), Y	SBC (Oper), Y	F1	2	5*

* Add 1 when page boundary is crossed.

SEC   SEC *Set Carry Flag*   SEC

Operation: 1 → C

N Z C I D V
− − 1 − − −

(Ref: 3.0.1)

Addressing Mode	Assembly Language Form	OP CODE	No. Bytes	No. Cycles
Implied	SEC	38	1	2

SED   SED *Set Decimal Mode*   SED

Operation: 1 → D

N Z C I D V
− − − − 1 −

(Ref: 3.3.1)

Addressing Mode	Assembly Language Form	OP CODE	No. Bytes	No. Cycles
Implied	SED	F8	1	2

SEI   SEI *Set Interrupt Disable Status*   SEI

Operation: 1 → I

N Z C I D V
− − − 1 − −

(Ref: 3.2.1)

Addressing Mode	Assembly Language Form	OP CODE	No. Bytes	No. Cycles
Implied	SEI	78	1	2

STA   STA *Store Accumulator in Memory*   STA

Operation: A → M

N Z C I D V
− − − − − −

(Ref: 2.1.2)

Addressing Mode	Assembly Language Form	OP CODE	No. Bytes	No. Cycles
Zero Page	STA Oper	85	2	3
Zero Page, X	STA Oper, X	95	2	4
Absolute	STA Oper	8D	3	4
Absolute, X	STA Oper, X	9D	3	5
Absolute, Y	STA Oper, Y	99	3	5
(Indirect, X)	STA (Oper, X)	81	2	6
(Indirect), Y	STA (Oper), Y	91	2	6

STX   STX *Store Index X in Memory*   **STX**

Operation: X → M

N Z C I D V
− − − − − −

(Ref: 7.2)

Addressing Mode	Assembly Language Form	OP CODE	No. Bytes	No. Cycles
Zero Page	STX Oper	86	2	3
Zero Page, Y	STX Oper, Y	96	2	4
Absolute	STX Oper	8E	3	4

STY   STY *Store Index Y in Memory*   **STY**

Operation: Y → M

N Z C I D V
− − − − − −

(Ref: 7.3)

Addressing Mode	Assembly Language Form	OP CODE	No. Bytes	No. Cycles
Zero Page	STY Oper	84	2	3
Zero Page, X	STY Oper, X	94	2	4
Absolute	STY Oper	8C	3	4

TAX   TAX *Transfer Accumulator to Index X*   **TAX**

Operation: A → X

N Z C I D V
√ √ − − − −

(Ref: 7.11)

Addressing Mode	Assembly Language Form	OP CODE	No. Bytes	No. Cycles
Implied	TAX	AA	1	2

TAY   TAY *Transfer Accumulator to Index Y*   **TAY**

Operation: A → Y

N Z C I D V
√ √ − − − −

(Ref: 7.13)

Addressing Mode	Assembly Language Form	OP CODE	No. Bytes	No. Cycles
Implied	TAY	A8	1	2

TSX   TSX *Transfer Stack Pointer to Index X*   **TSX**

Operation: S → X

N Z C I D V
√ √ − − − −

(Ref: 8.9)

Addressing Mode	Assembly Language Form	OP CODE	No. Bytes	No. Cycles
Implied	TSX	BA	1	2

TXA   TXA *Transfer Index X to Accumulator*   **TXA**

Operation: X → A

N Z C I D V
√ √ − − − −

(Ref: 7.12)

Addressing Mode	Assembly Language Form	OP CODE	No. Bytes	No. Cycles
Implied	TXA	8A	1	2

TXS   TXS *Transfer Index X to Stack Pointer*   **TXS**

Operation: X → S

N Z C I D V
− − − − − −

(Ref: 8.8)

Addressing Mode	Assembly Language Form	OP CODE	No. Bytes	No. Cycles
Implied	TXS	9A	1	2

TYA   TYA *Transfer Index Y to Accumulator*   **TYA**

Operation: Y → A

N Z C I D V
√ √ − − − −

(Ref: 7.14)

Addressing Mode	Assembly Language Form	OP CODE	No. Bytes	No. Cycles
Implied	TYA	98	1	2

10

Input/output
on the Commodore 64

INTRODUCTION

In this chapter we will take a detailed look at the 6526 Complex Interface Adaptor. There are two such devices within the CBM 64, and they are used to handle all communication with the outside world, with the exception of video output.

The 6526 has two 8-bit data ports, each with individually programmable lines. It is capable of 8- or 16-bit communication, and has two linkable 16-bit timers. In addition it has an 8-bit shift register for serial communications, and a 24-hour programmable time of day clock. It has specific handshaking control lines PC and FLAG. PC will go low for one cycle after data is written to PORT B, and can be used to indicate 'data ready'. Handshaking 16-bit data is possible by writing data to PORT A first. The FLAG line may be used as a control input from another device, and will set the FLAG bit in the interrupt register and, if enabled, interrupt the 6510 processor. Thus it may be used to signal 'data ready' from another device.

In the CBM 64 one of the 6526's (CIA#1, address $DC00) is devoted to the keyboard and joysticks, the other to the serial bus and user port. The cassette is handled directly by the 6510 using its own on-board Input/Output register.

Here is a list of the registers of the 6526.

REG	ADDR	HEX	NAME	FUNCTION
0	56576	$DD00	PRA	Peripheral Data Register A
1	56577	$DD01	PRB	Peripheral Data Register B
2	56578	$DD02	DDRA	Data Direction Register A
3	56579	$DD03	DDRB	Data Direction Register B
4	56580	$DD04	TA LO	Timer A Low Register
5	56581	$DD05	TA HI	Timer A High Register
6	56582	$DD06	TB LO	Timer B Low Register

Fig. 10.1 – User port – view looking in.

PIN TOP SIDE	DESCRIPTION	NOTES
1	GROUND	
2	+5V	(100 mA MAX.)
3	RESET	By grounding this pin, the Commodore 64 will do a COLD START, resetting completely. The pointers to a BASIC program will be reset, but memory will not be cleared. This is also a RESET output for the external devices.
4	CNT1	Serial port counter from CIA #1
5	SP1	Serial port from CIA #1
6	CNT2	Serial port counter from CIA #2
7	SP2	Serial port from CIA #1
8	PC2	Handshaking line from CIA #2
9	SERIAL ATN	This pin is connected to the ATN line of the serial bus.
10	9 VAC+phase	Connected directly to the Commodore 64 transformer (50 mA MAX.).
11	9 VAC−phase	
12	GND	
BOTTOM SIDE		
A	GND	The Commodore 64 gives you control over PORT B on CIA chip #1. Eight lines for input or output are available, as well as 2 lines for handshaking with an outside device. The I/O lines for PORT B are controlled by two locations. One is the PORT itself, and is located at 56577 ($DD01 HEX). Naturally you PEEK it to read an INPUT, or POKE it to set an OUTPUT. Each of the eight I/O lines can be set up as either an INPUT or an OUTPUT by setting the DATA DIRECTION REGISTER properly.
B	FLAG2	
C	PB0	
D	PB1	
E	PB2	
F	PB3	
H	PB4	
J	PB5	
K	PB6	
L	PB7	
M	PA2	
N	GND	

Fig. 10.2 – User port pin description.

7	56583	$DD07	TB HI	Timer B High Register
8	56584	$DD08	TOD 10THS	10ths of Seconds Register
9	56585	$DD09	TOD SEC	Seconds Register
10	56586	$DD0A	TOD MIN	Minutes Register
11	56587	$DD0B	TOD HR	Hours — AM/PM Register
12	56588	$DD0C	SDR	Serial Data Register
13	56589	$DD0D	ICR	Interrupt Control Register
14	56590	$DD0E	CRA	Control Register A
15	56591	$DD0F	CRB	Control Register B

A detailed description of these registers is given at the end of this chapter.

As we have mentioned above, one 6526 is completely tied up with the keyboard, and the other one has to deal with the serial bus, as well as providing us with the user port. As a consequence of this we only have one port to use, unless we are prepared to do without the serial bus, this is PORT B on CIA#2.

Figure 10.1 is a diagram of the user port as seen from the back of the CBM 64, and Fig. 10.2 is a table describing the connection between the user port and the 6526.

Let's look at how to make use of the user port to communicate with other devices.

PARALLEL COMMUNICATIONS

Many external devices today have the necessary wiring to handle parallel communications — eight data lines and a minimum of one control line. If parallel communication is possible then it is usually worth using simply because it is much faster than serial communications. After all sending eight bits at a time must be better than sending one at a time!

The main problem we have to deal with in getting two devices to talk to each other is one of timing. Essentially this means getting device A to listen when device B wants to say something, and vice versa. There are two popular ways of dealing with this problem; the first is the use of a ready/busy control line. When a device wants to send a byte of data or receive a byte of data it looks at the ready/busy line and waits around until the other device is ready. This normally requires two of these lines — the first is set or cleared by device A and looked at by device B, and the second is set by device B and watched by A. However, if we know that one device will *always* be faster than the other, and consequently always the one that has to wait then we may dispense with one line. The following piece of code, written in assembler, will communicate using two ready/busy lines. Some of the code may be omitted if only one line is needed.

```
LINE# LOC   CODE         LINE

00001  0000              ;********************************
00002  0000              ;*                              *
00003  0000              ;*           PARCOMS            *
00004  0000              ;*                              *
00005  0000              ;*                              *
00006  0000              ;* 50624 = START ADDR LO-BYTE   *
00007  0000              ;*                              *
00008  0000              ;* 50625 = START ADDR HI-BYTE   *
00009  0000              ;*                              *
00010  0000              ;* 50626 = END ADDR LO-BYTE     *
00011  0000              ;*                              *
00012  0000              ;* 50627 = END ADDR HI-BYTE     *
00013  0000              ;*                              *
00014  0000              ;* 50628 = INPUT/OUTPUT         *
00015  0000              ;*                              *
00016  0000              ;*                              *
00017  0000              ;*                              *
00018  0000              ;* TO USE   - POKE VALS ABOVE   *
00019  0000              ;*                              *
00020  0000              ;*           THEN               *
00021  0000              ;*                              *
00022  0000              ;*           SYS 50629          *
00023  0000              ;*                              *
00024  0000              ;*                              *
00025  0000              ;* THIS ROUTINE WILL PERFORM A  *
00026  0000              ;* DEDICATED PARALLEL DATA I/O   *
00027  0000              ;* FUNCTION. LINES USED ARE     *
00028  0000              ;*                              *
00029  0000              ;*  PB0-PB7 - DATA LINES        *
00030  0000              ;*  FLAG - HANDSHAKE INPUT      *
00031  0000              ;*  PA2 - READY FOR DATA        *
00032  0000              ;*  PC - DATA VALID             *
00033  0000              ;*                              *
00034  0000              ;********************************

00036  0000              CIA2    = $DD00          ;6526 CHIP BASE ADDR
00037  0000              OUTPUT  = $FF
00038  0000              INPUT   = $00
00039  0000              OUTSHK  = $04
00040  0000              INTMSK  = $10
00041  0000              TOGHI   = $04
00042  0000              TOGLO   = $FC
00043  0000              ZPTEMP  = $FB
00044  0000              *       = $C5C0
00045  C5C0              START   *=*+2            ;START ADDRESS
00046  C5C2              END     *=*+2            ;END ADDRESS
00047  C5C4              MODE    *=*+1            ;INPUT/OUTPUT FLAG

00049  C5C5  AD C4 C5            LDA MODE         ;INPUT OR OUTPUT
00050  C5C8  D0 54               BNE OUTDAT       ;BRANCH IF OUTPUT
00051  C5CA  A9 00               LDA #INPUT
00052  C5CC  8D 03 DD            STA CIA2+3       ;SET DDR FOR INPUT
00053  C5CF  A9 10               LDA #INTMSK
00054  C5D1  8D 0D DD            STA CIA2+13      ;FLAG INTS DISABLED
00055  C5D4  AD 02 DD            LDA CIA2+2
00056  C5D7  09 04               ORA #OUTSHK
```

Listing continued next page

```
00057   C5D9   8D 02 DD              STA CIA2+2          ;SET PA2 FOR OUTPUT
00058   C5DC   AD 00 DD              LDA CIA2
00059   C5DF   09 04                 ORA #TOGHI
00060   C5E1   8D 00 DD              STA CIA2            ;SET HANDSHAKE LINE PA2 HIGH
00061   C5E4   AD C0 C5              LDA START
00062   C5E7   85 FB                 STA ZPTEMP
00063   C5E9   AD C1 C5              LDA START+1         ;MOVE POINTERS TO PAGE 0
00064   C5EC   85 FC                 STA ZPTEMP+1
00065   C5EE                  ;
00066   C67E   85 FC                 STA ZPTEMP+1
00067   C680                  ;
00068   C680                  ;INSERT WEDGE
00069   C680                  ;
00070   C680   AD 18 03              LDA NMIVEC
00071   C683   8D 55 C6              STA VECTOR          ;SAVE OLD NMI VECTOR
00072   C686   AD 19 03              LDA NMIVEC+1
00073   C689   8D 56 C6              STA VECTOR+1
00074   C68C   78                    SEI
00075   C68D   A9 BC                 LDA #<NXTIN
00076   C68F   8D 18 03              STA NMIVEC          ;INSERT WEDGE
00077   C692   A9 C6                 LDA #>NXTIN
00078   C694   8D 19 03              STA NMIVEC+1
00079   C697   58                    CLI
00080   C698   60                    RTS
00081   C699                  ;
00082   C699                  ;
00083   C699                  ;DATA OUTPUT
00084   C699                  ;
00085   C699                  ;
00086   C699                  OUTDAT
00087   C699   A9 FF                 LDA #OUTPUT
00088   C69B   8D 03 DD              STA CIA2+3          ;SET DDR FOR OUTPUT
00089   C69E   A9 90                 LDA #INTMSK
00090   C6A0   8D 0D DD              STA CIA2+13         ;FLAG INTS DISABLED
00091   C6A3                  ;
00092   C6A3                  ;INSERT WEDGE
00093   C6A3                  ;
00094   C6A3   AD 18 03              LDA NMIVEC
00095   C6A6   8D 55 C6              STA VECTOR
00096   C6A9   AD 19 03              LDA NMIVEC+1        ;SAVE OLD NMI VECTOR
00097   C6AC   8D 56 C6              STA VECTOR+1
00098   C6AF   78                    SEI
00099   C6B0   A9 EA                 LDA #<NXTOUT
00100   C6B2   8D 18 03              STA NMIVEC
00101   C6B5   A9 C6                 LDA #>NXTOUT        ;INSERT WEDGE
00102   C6B7   8D 19 03              STA NMIVEC+1
00103   C6BA   58                    CLI
00104   C6BB   60                    RTS
00105   C6BC                  ;
00106   C6BC                  ;
00107   C6BC                  ;
00108   C6BC                  ;
00109   C6BC                  ;
00110   C6BC                  ;HERE WE GO
00111   C6BC                  ;
00112   C6BC                  NXTIN
00113   C6BC   A9 90                 LDA #INTMSK         ;CHECK ICR
00114   C6BE   2C 0D DD              BIT CIA2+13         ;INT CAUSED BY FLAG?
00115   C6C1   F0 24                 BEQ NOTCOM          ;NO.. NORMAL NMI
```

```
00116   C6C3                            ;
00117   C6C3                            ;OK BYTE ON PORT
00118   C6C3                            ;
00119   C6C3    AD 01 DD        LDA CIA2+1          ;READ BYTE
00120   C6C6    91 FB           STA (ZPTEMP),Y     ;STORE IN MEMORY
00121   C6C8    E6 FB           INC ZPTEMP
00122   C6CA    D0 02           BNE TEST1          ;INCREMENT POINTER
00123   C6CC    E6 FC           INC ZPTEMP+1
00124   C6CE                TEST1
00125   C6CE    AD 52 C6        LDA END
00126   C6D1    C5 FB           CMP ZPTEMP
00127   C6D3    AD 53 C6        LDA END+1          ;CHECK TO SEE IF ENDED
00128   C6D6    E5 FC           SBC ZPTEMP+1
00129   C6D8    90 31           BCC DONE           ;BRANCH IF FINISHED
00130   C6DA                        ;
00131   C6DA                    ;TELL DEVICE READY FOR NEXT BYTE
00132   C6DA                        ;
00133   C6DA    AD 00 DD        LDA CIA2
00134   C648    4C 28 C6        JMP NXTOUT
00135   C64B                        ;
00136   C64B                    ;FINISHED
00137   C64B                        ;
00138   C64B                DONE
00139   C64B    60              RTS                ;RETURN
00140   C64C                .END
```

```
ERRORS = 00000


SYMBOL TABLE

SYMBOL VALUE
   CIA2     DD00    DONE    C64B    END     C5C2    INPUT   0000
   INTMSK   0010    MODE    C5C4    NXTIN   C5EE    NXTOUT  C628
   OUTDAT   C61E    OUTPUT  00FF    OUTSHK  0004    START   C5C0
   TOGHI    0004    TOGLO   00FC    WAIT1   C60B    WAIT2   C638
   ZPTEMP   00FB

END OF ASSEMBLY
```

If the two devices are only concerned with passing data and storing it then the above method is quite adequate, but what if we have to do some other things, like playing *Alice's Restaurant* in three-part harmony with full orchestration, at the same time? Obviously we can't afford to wait around while some device in the outside world gets things done, so the alternative method for dealing with the problem is to get on with the things we have to do, and leave the external device to do its own thing and then interrupt us when it is ready to send or receive the next byte.

This method is also useful where the device is very slow, for example a keyboard which will send a byte and then do nothing for a long period of time (in terms of what the 6510 can do), before sending the next byte.

To see how we can achieve this we must take another look at register 13 of the 6526. If we write 1 to bits 4 and 7 of this register, each time the FLG line of the 6526 goes low the 6510 will be interrupted and will go off and execute a special routine in ROM called the Interrupt Service

Routine. This routine has a vector (or pointer) at memory addresses $0314 and $0315. It is possible for us to change this pointer so that our own routine to read or send the next byte of data will be executed. (See Wedges, Chapter 9). Using this method we can do other things with the 6510 in between sending bytes.

There is, however, one disadvantage with this method over the previous one; after all you don't get anything for nothing. If the rate at which you wish to transfer data is sufficiently fast then the time available between bytes becomes so small that it is impossible to get anything else done. In the extreme case your Interrupt Service Routine may take longer to execute than you have time for! When this is the situation, although its pretty unlikely you'll find it so, the former method must be used. One other thing to bear in mind is that the machine uses interrupts for some of its internal functions (reading the stop key and cassette functions, for example), and these routines may take longer to run than you can allow. In this case you must either use the dedicated method, or do without the stop key scan etc., which can be a great way of ensuring that all your efforts at bashing the RUN/STOP and RESTORE keys when your code crashes are in vain! These types of routine are not usually very easy to debug because you soon get sick of reloading your program every few minutes.

Here is an example of a piece of wedge code to handle interrupt-driven input/output.

```
LINE# LOC    CODE        LINE

00001  0000              ;*********************************
00002  0000              ;*                               *
00003  0000              ;*          PARAWEDGE             *
00004  0000              ;*                               *
00005  0000              ;*                               *
00006  0000              ;* 50768 = START ADDR LO-BYTE    *
00007  0000              ;*                               *
00008  0000              ;* 50769 = START ADDR HI-BYTE    *
00009  0000              ;*                               *
00010  0000              ;* 50770 = END ADDR LO-BYTE      *
00011  0000              ;*                               *
00012  0000              ;* 50771 = END ADDR HI-BYTE      *
00013  0000              ;*                               *
00014  0000              ;* 50772 = INPUT/OUTPUT          *
00015  0000              ;*                               *
00016  0000              ;*                               *
00017  0000              ;*                               *
00018  0000              ;* TO USE   - POKE VALS ABOVE    *
00019  0000              ;*                               *
00020  0000              ;*             THEN              *
00021  0000              ;*                               *
00022  0000              ;*           SYS 50775           *
00023  0000              ;*                               *
00024  0000              ;*                               *
00025  0000              ;* THIS ROUTINE WILL PERFORM AN  *
00026  0000              ;* INTERRUPT DRIVEN PARALLEL I/O *
00027  0000              ;* FUNCTION. LINES USED ARE      *
00028  0000              ;*                               *
00029  0000              ;*  PB0-PB7 - DATA LINES         *
00030  0000              ;*  FLAG - HANDSHAKE INPUT       *
00031  0000              ;*  PA2 - READY FOR DATA         *
```

```
00032   0000                      ;*   PC - DATA VALID                  *
00033   0000                      ;*                                    *
00034   0000                      ;**********************************

00036   0000                      CIA2   = $DD00        ;6526 CHIP BASE ADDR
00037   0000                      OUTPUT = $FF
00038   0000                      INPUT  = $00
00039   0000                      OUTSHK = $04
00040   0000                      INTMSK = $90
00041   0000                      TOGHI  = $04
00042   0000                      TOGLO  = $FC
00043   0000                      NMIVEC = $0318
00044   0000                      ZPTEMP = $FB
00045   0000                      *      = $C650
00046   C650                      START  *=*+2         ;START ADDRESS
00047   C652                      END    *=*+2         ;END ADDRESS
00048   C654                      MODE   *=*+1         ;INPUT/OUTPUT FLAG
00049   C655                      VECTOR *=*+2         ;STORAGE FOR NMI VECTOR

00051   C657  AD 54 C6                   LDA MODE      ;INPUT OR OUTPUT
00052   C65A  D0 3D                      BNE OUTDAT    ;BRANCH IF OUTPUT
00053   C65C  A9 00                      LDA #INPUT
00054   C65E  8D 03 DD                   STA CIA2+3    ;SET DDR FOR INPUT
00055   C661  A9 90                      LDA #INTMSK
00056   C663  8D 0D DD                   STA CIA2+13   ;FLAG INTS DISABLED
00057   C666  AD 02 DD                   LDA CIA2+2
00058   C669  09 04                      ORA #OUTSHK
00059   C66B  8D 02 DD                   STA CIA2+2    ;SET PA2 FOR OUTPUT
00060   C66E  AD 00 DD                   LDA CIA2
00061   C671  09 04                      ORA #TOGHI
00062   C673  8D 00 DD                   STA CIA2      ;SET HANDSHAKE LINE PA2 HIGH
00063   C676  AD 50 C6                   LDA START
00064   C679  85 FB                      STA ZPTEMP
00065   C67B  AD 51 C6                   LDA START+1   ;MOVE POINTERS TO PAGE 0
00066   C5EE                      ;HERE WE GO
00067   C5EE                      ;
00068   C5EE                      NXTIN
00069   C5EE  AD C2 C5                   LDA END
00070   C5F1  C5 FB                      CMP ZPTEMP
00071   C5F3  AD C3 C5                   LDA END+1     ;CHECK TO SEE IF ENDED
00072   C5F6  E5 FC                      SBC ZPTEMP+1
00073   C5F8  90 51                      BCC DONE      ;BRANCH IF FINISHED
00074   C5FA                      ;
00075   C5FA                      ;TELL DEVICE READY FOR NEXT BYTE
00076   C5FA                      ;
00077   C5FA  AD 00 DD                   LDA CIA2
00078   C5FD  29 FC                      AND #TOGLO
00079   C5FF  8D 00 DD                   STA CIA2      ;TOGGLE PA2 LOW THEN HIGH
00080   C602  09 04                      ORA #TOGHI
00081   C604  8D 00 DD                   STA CIA2
00082   C607                      ;
00083   C607                      ;NOW WAIT FOR DEVICE
00084   C607                      ;
00085   C607  A0 00                      LDY #$00
00086   C609  A9 10                      LDA #INTMSK
00087   C60B                      WAIT1
00088   C60B  2C 0D DD                   BIT CIA2+13
00089   C60E  F0 FB                      BEQ WAIT1
00090   C610                      ;
```

Listing continued next page

```
00091   C610                            ;OK BYTE ON PORT
00092   C610                            ;
00093   C610    AD 01 DD                LDA CIA2+1          ;READ BYTE
00094   C613    91 FB                   STA (ZPTEMP),Y     ;STORE IN MEMORY
00095   C615    E6 FB                   INC ZPTEMP
00096   C617    D0 D5                   BNE NXTIN          ;INCREMENT POINTER
00097   C619    E6 FC                   INC ZPTEMP+1
00098   C61B    4C EE C5                JMP NXTIN
00099   C61E                            ;
00100   C61E                            ;DATA OUTPUT
00101   C61E                            ;
00102   C61E                            ;
00103   C61E                            OUTDAT
00104   C61E    A9 FF                   LDA #OUTPUT
00105   C620    8D 03 DD                STA CIA2+3         ;SET DDR FOR OUTPUT
00106   C623    A9 10                   LDA #INTMSK
00107   C625    8D 0D DD                STA CIA2+13        ;FLAG INTS DISABLED
00108   C628                            ;
00109   C628                            ;HERE WE GO
00110   C628                            ;
00111   C628                            NXTOUT
00112   C628    AD C2 C5                LDA END
00113   C62B    C5 FB                   CMP ZPTEMP
00114   C62D    AD C3 C5                LDA END+1          ;CHECK TO SEE IF ENDED
00115   C630    E5 FC                   SBC ZPTEMP+1
00116   C632    90 17                   BCC DONE           ;BRANCH IF DONE
00117   C634                            ;
00118   C634                            ;NOW WAIT FOR DEVICE
00119   C634                            ;
00120   C634    A0 00                   LDY #$00
00121   C636    A9 10                   LDA #INTMSK
00122   C638                            WAIT2
00123   C638    2C 0D DD                BIT CIA2+13
00124   C63B    F0 FB                   BEQ WAIT2
00125   C63D                            ;
00126   C63D                            ;OK SEND BYTE
00127   C63D                            ;
00128   C63D    B1 FB                   LDA (ZPTEMP),Y     ;GET BYTE FROM MEMORY
00129   C63F    8D 01 DD                STA CIA2+1         ;OUTPUT IT. PC WILL GO
00130   C642                                               ;LOW FOR 1 CYCLE
00131   C642    E6 FB                   INC ZPTEMP
00132   C644    D0 E2                   BNE NXTOUT         ;INCREMENT POINTER
00133   C646    E6 FC                   INC ZPTEMP+1
00134   C6DD    29 FC                   AND #TOGLO
00135   C6DF    8D 00 DD                STA CIA2           ;TOGGLE PA2 LOW THEN HIGH
00136   C6E2    09 04                   ORA #TOGHI
00137   C6E4    8D 00 DD                STA CIA2
00138   C6E7                            ;
00139   C6E7                            ;NOW DO NORMAL NMI ROUTINE
00140   C6E7                            ;
00141   C6E7                            NOTCOM
00142   C6E7    6C 55 C6                JMP (VECTOR)
00143   C6EA

00145   C6EA                            ;
00146   C6EA                            ;
00147   C6EA                            ;HERE WE GO
00148   C6EA                            ;
00149   C6EA                            NXTOUT
```

```
00150   C6EA   A9 90                       LDA #INTMSK      ;CHECK ICR
00151   C6EC   2C 0D DD                     BIT CIA2+13      ;INTERRUPT CAUSED BY FLAG?
00152   C6EF   F0 F6                        BEQ NOTCOM       ;NO.. DO NORMAL NMI
00153   C6F1                      ;
00154   C6F1                      ;OK SEND BYTE
00155   C6F1                      ;
00156   C6F1   B1 FB                        LDA (ZPTEMP),Y   ;GET BYTE FROM MEMORY
00157   C6F3   8D 01 DD                     STA CIA2+1       ;OUTPUT IT. PC WILL GO
00158   C6F6                                                 ;LOW FOR 1 CYCLE
00159   C6F6   E6 FB                        INC ZPTEMP
00160   C6F8   D0 02                        BNE TEST2        ;INCREMENT POINTER
00161   C6FA   E6 FC                        INC ZPTEMP+1
00162   C6FC                      TEST2
00163   C6FC   AD 52 C6                     LDA END
00164   C6FF   C5 FB                        CMP ZPTEMP
00165   C701   AD 53 C6                     LDA END+1        ;CHECK TO SEE IF ENDED
00166   C704   E5 FC                        SBC ZPTEMP+1
00167   C706   90 03                        BCC DONE         ;BRANCH IF DONE
00168   C708                      ;
00169   C708                      ;CONTINUE NORMAL NMI .ROUTINE
00170   C708                      ;
00171   C708   6C 55 C6                     JMP (VECTOR)
00172   C70B                      ;
00173   C70B                      ;
00174   C70B                      ;FINISHED
00175   C70B                      ;
00176   C70B                      DONE
00177   C70B                      ;REMOVE WEDGE
00178   C70B   78                           SEI
00179   C70C   AD 55 C6                     LDA VECTOR
00180   C70F   8D 18 03                     STA NMIVEC       ;RESET NMI VECTOR TO
00181   C712   AD 56 C6                     LDA VECTOR+1     ;ORIGINAL VALUE
00182   C715   8D 19 03                     STA NMIVEC+1
00183   C718   58                           CLI
00184   C719   6C 18 03                     JMP (NMIVEC)
00185   C71C                      .END
```

ERRORS = 00000

SYMBOL TABLE

```
SYMBOL  VALUE
  CIA2    DD00      DONE    C70B      END     C652      INPUT    0000
  INTMSK  0090      MODE    C654      NMIVEC  0318      NOTCOM   C6E7
  NXTIN   C6BC      NXTOUT  C6EA      OUTDAT  C699      OUTPUT   00FF
  OUTSHK  0004      START   C650      TEST1   C6CE      TEST2    C6FC
  TOGHI   0004      TOGLO   00FC      VECTOR  C655      ZPTEMP   00FB
```

END OF ASSEMBLY

SERIAL COMMUNICATIONS

The other method of communication available to us through the 6526 chip is serial communication. This method is much slower than the parallel method, but it does have the advantage of requiring only one data line and one or two control lines depending upon whether communication is required in only one or both directions. The basic principle of serial communications is that we send each of the bits in a byte one after each other. Thus to send a byte takes approximately 8 times as long as it would in parallel.

To use the serial facilities on the 6526 we must first decide how quickly we wish to send the data. It is not always advantageous, or indeed possible, to send the data out as fast as the 6526 can go. For example, if we are sending data to a modem or acoustic coupler which in turn sends a signal down a telephone line then the speed is limited by the quality of the 'phone line. If the signal is very fast then a slight crackle on the line could easily be read as data. Therefore with an acoustic coupler we normally limit the speed to 300 baud (bits per second), which in terms of the capabilities of the 6526 is extremely slow.

The rate at which the data is transmitted is determined by the value we write into Timer A on the 6526. The timer will count from the specified value down to zero, at this point a bit will be sent and the clock will recommence counting down from the value again. So the smaller the value we put into the timer the faster the data is transmitted.

First we must write this value into registers 4 and 5 (Timer A Lo and Hi) on the chip, memory addresses $DD04 and $DD05 (56580 and 56581). Next we must set bit 6 of register 14 of the chip, address $DD0E (56590), which sets the chip up for serial output. We must also set up the timer to run in continuous mode since we don't want it to stop once it has counted down to zero. This is achieved by clearing bit 3 of register 14. We are now set for serial output. As soon as we write a byte into the serial register the 6526 will take care of the rest for us. All we have to do after this is stay one step ahead of the 6526, to ensure that there is always a byte of data in the serial register ready to go. However, if we write data to this register too quickly we may end up overwriting the previous bytes, so how do we know when to put the next byte into the Serial Register? Fortunately for us this is also taken care of. Bit 3 of register 13 (Interrupt register) at address $DD0D (56589) will be set at the end of each byte being transmitted, and if this interrupt is enabled an IRQ will be sent to the 6510, allowing us to do other things in the meantime.

You will have noticed so far that all of the above routines are written in machine code. The reason for this is that BASIC is simply too slow to cope with this type of thing; but if you want to do serial input/output from BASIC, you can, using the 'pseudo' RS232 chip.

RS232 ON THE COMMODORE 64

RS232 is just a reference number for an agreed system (protocol) for getting different devices to communicate. RS232 is not the only protocol used by machines, but it is by far the most common amongst home microcomputers, and has therefore become something of a standard. The first thing about RS232 on the CBM 64 is that it is not RS232! One of the specifications of RS232 is that voltages on the lines which represent ones and noughts should be +12 V and −12 V, but on the CBM 64 they are +5 V and 0 V. However, apart from this difference, everything else about the CBM 64's RS232 conforms to the RS232 protocol.

WARNING: Check the voltages of other devices before connecting them to the CBM 64, as the wrong voltages could cause damage. One way to avoid this is to purchase the Commodore RS232 interface cartridge, which will handle this problem.

First let's take a look at RS232 and see how it differs from the Serial I/O we were discussing above. Then we'll take a look at how to use it.

The first thing to consider is what makes up the transmission of 1 byte in RS232. The various components are:

> START BIT
> DATA BITS
> PARITY BIT
> STOP BIT(S)

For any given baud rate we can calculate the time between each bit of the byte; for example, at 300 baud a bit is sent every 3.3 milliseconds (1/300 secs), and thus we know that when we receive the start bit the first data bit will be along 3.3 milliseconds later. Therefore the start bit gives us a reference point for the rest of the byte. We then receive the appropriate number of data bits. The number of data bits does not necessarily have to be eight; for example, to send characters to an ASCII printer only requires seven data bits, but as long as the transmitter and the receiver both know how many bits are being sent there should be no problem. Next we come to the parity bit. This bit is optional but can be put to very good use. All parity really means is 'odd or even', and in this case it applies to the number of 1 bits in the byte. Lets consider the transmission of one byte, a carriage return. The ASCII code for a carriage return is 13 ($0D), which in binary is:

> 00001101

As we can see there are three 1 bits and three is an odd number. If we had agreed an odd parity then the parity bit would be 0 because we already have an odd number of 1 bits. If we want even parity then the parity bit will be a one to give us an even number of one bits. Here are a few examples of parity:

Byte	Binary	Parity Bit	No. of 1s	Parity
13	00001101	0	3	ODD
13	00001101	1	4	EVEN
12	00001100	0	2	EVEN
12	00001100	1	3	ODD

We have seen how we can calculate what the value of the parity bit should be, but what do we use it for? Let's say we wish to transmit a carriage return with even parity, we would send the following data and parity bits:

> 00001101   1

Suppose now that the receiving device receives the pattern

> 00101101   1

obviously an error has occurred, perhaps some interference on the data line. The receiver now counts the number of one bits and reaches a total of 5, but since it knows that the parity should be even it rejects the value as erroneous. If the receiver is particularly clever it may have read each bit twice as it came in, and seen a value of 1 and 0 for one particular bit, caused let's say by momentary interference. It can now not only conclude that the byte is in error, but, if it has only detected one bad bit, it can also calculate what its value should be and actually correct an erroneous byte. So parity is a very useful thing and the authors would recommend its use wherever possible. However, your receiving device may not allow for parity, and the CBM64 RS232 caters for this by allowing you to specify that either no parity is sent or that the parity bit is always a one or a zero. Finally we come to the stop bit. The purpose of this bit is not actually to tell the receiver that the byte has ended (the receiver should know how many bits to expect), but to put the data line into the opposite condition to the start bit, i.e. if the start bit is a 1 then the stop bit will be a 0 and vice versa. Without the stop bit the receiver would look for the next start bit, and if the last bit of the previous byte had left the data line in the right state, the receiver would think it had the start of the next byte.

As we can see anyone could, with a little time and patience, implement RS232 on their CBM 64, since all these functions are simply software using the ordinary 6526 chip. However, Commodore have very kindly included all of these routines in the KERNAL and they can thus be utilized from BASIC.

First of all, some warnings about the use of RS232 from Commodore BASIC. As mentioned previously, normal RS232 uses voltage levels of +12 V and −12 V whereas the CBM 64 uses +5 V and 0 V. Care must therefore be taken to ensure that equipments of differing voltages are not connected together as this may cause damage. The KERNAL routines use CIA #2, including its timers and interrupts, for RS232 processing. This means that RS232 will be suspended during cassette or serial bus usage. Finally the KERNAL RS232 routines need two 256-byte buffers which it will take from the top of BASIC memory when an RS232 channel is opened; so if you don't allow for this when writing programs you may end up with a spectacular disaster. Because of this, RS232 channels should be opened before defining dynamic strings, since opening an RS232 channel will perform an automatic CLR. A method of dealing with this is given at the end of the section. Opening an RS232 channel is very similar to opening a logical file to any other device. The syntax is as follows:

OPEN lfn,2,0,'<Control reg><command reg><opt baud lo><opt baud hi>'

for example:

OPEN 1,2,0,CHR$(0)CHR$(97)CHR$(56)CHR$(8)

The device number 2 indicates RS232 and what is normally the filename contains various data required to set up the RS232.

lfn − the logical file number can be any number in the range 1 to 255. However, logical file numbers of more than 127 will cause a line feed character to follow every carriage return.

<control register> − This is a single-byte character whose bits have the following meaning:

Bit 7 − STOP BITS. When this bit is set to a one, two stop bits will be transmitted at the end of each word. When cleared to a zero, one stop bit will be sent.

Bits 6 and 5 — WORD LENGTH. These two bits determine the number of data bits to be sent as follows:

Bit 6	Bit 5	Word length
0	0	8 Bits
0	1	7 Bits
1	0	6 Bits
1	1	5 Bits

Bit 4 — NOT USED.

Bits 3–0 — BAUD RATE. The various combinations of these four bits give 16 different possible baud rates. However, because the 6510 executes KERNAL routines relatively slowly, speeds above 2400 baud are not implemented. Since the KERNAL uses a look-up table for the values (located at 58604, $E4EC), values above 2400 will read part of the cassette timing routine of the KERNAL as data which will result in an unpredictable baud rate. The bit patterns required for the implemented baud rates are:

Bits 3–0	Baud rate
0000	User rate
0001	50 Baud
0010	75
0011	110
0100	134.5
0101	150
0110	300
0111	600
1000	1200
1001	1800
1010	2400
1011 to 1111	*not implemented*

When the User Rate is selected the two other values in the filename field <opt baud lo> and <opt baud hi> are used instead of the preset values.

These values may be calculated as follows:

$$\text{opt baud} = \text{system frequency}/\text{baud}/2 - 100$$

where system frequency = 1,022,730 Hz for NTSC (North American TV Standard), or = 985,250 Hz for PAL (UK and most of Europe) then

$$\text{opt baud hi} = \text{INT}(\text{opt baud}/256)$$

and

$$\text{opt baud lo} = \text{opt baud} - 256*\text{opt baud hi}$$

This byte is mandatory when opening an RS232 channel.

<command register> — This is a single-byte optional character which defines further parameters of the RS232.

Bits 7–5 – PARITY OPTION. These three bits determine the parity used as follows:

Bits 7–5	Parity
––0	Parity disabled, None Transmitted/Received
001	Odd Parity Transmitted/Received
011	Even Parity Transmitted/Received
101	Mark Transmitted (opposite to previous bit)/Parity check disabled
111	Space Transmitted (same as previous bit)/Parity check disabled

Bit 4 – DUPLEX. When this bit is cleared the system uses full duplex, i.e. the receiving device echoes the byte back to the transmitting device. When this bit is set the system works in half duplex and the byte is not echoed.

Bits 3–1 – NOT USED.

Bit 0 – HANDSHAKE. When this bit is cleared a 3-line system is used. The three lines are data in, data out, and ground. This does not therefore provide for one device being able to halt the other until ready, and a steady stream of data will occur. When this bit is set an X-line (or CTS) protocol is assumed. This means that the transmitting device will not send a byte until it receives a 'clear-to-send' signal from the receiving device.

Table 10.1 – RS232 pin connections.

(6526 DEVICE #2 Loc. $DD00–$DD0F)						
PIN ID	6526 ID	DESCRIPTION	EIA	ABV	IN/ OUT	MODES
C	PB0	RECEIVED DATA	(BB)	S_{in}	IN	1 2
D	PB1	REQUEST TO SEND	(CA)	RTS	OUT	1*2
E	PB2	DATA TERMINAL READY	(CD)	DTR	OUT	1*2
F	PB3	RING INDICATOR	(CE)	RI	IN	3
H	PB4	RECEIVED LINE SIGNAL	(CF)	DCD	IN	2
J	PB5	UNASSIGNED	( )	XXX	IN	3
K	PB6	CLEAR TO SEND	(CB)	CTS	IN	2
L	PB7	DATA SET READY	(CC)	DSR	IN	2
B	FLAG2	RECEIVED DATA	(BB)	S_{in}	IN	1 2
M	PA2	TRANSMITTED DATA	(BA)	S_{out}	OUT	1 2
A	GND	PROTECTIVE GROUND	(AA)	GND		1 2
N	GND	SIGNAL GROUND	(AB)	GND		1 2 3

MODES:
1) 3-LINE INTERFACE (S_{in}, S_{out}, GND)
2) X-LINE INTERFACE
3) USER AVAILABLE ONLY (Unused/unimplemented in code.)
* These lines are held high during 3-LINE mode.

Now that we have looked at the various parameters at our disposal, let's take a look at the connections to the user port we must make, and what each line does.

Firstly it must be borne in mind that the EIA specification for RS232 (the definitive article) is a very long and complicated document which is about an inch thick, and consequently we don't intend to repeat it all here. However, we will list each line with its EIA description and definition, and we will then discuss the subset of these lines which is required to set up simple RS232.

Let us now consider a simple X-line protocol. We actually require eight of the above lines.

Firstly, every interconnecting cable between pieces of equipment should have a ground, and RS232 is no exception, so our first two cables are the protective ground and signal ground. Both of these lines should appear on the equipment you wish to connect your CBM 64 to (we'll call it the peripheral from here on; although, if you are hooking up to a mainframe, perhaps it should be the other way around!). Next we need some lines for the data. Your peripheral ought to have a data transmit and a data receive line, as does the CBM 64.

IMPORTANT NOTE. You need to connect your peripheral's transmitted data line to the CBM 64's received data line and the CBM 64's transmit to the peripheral's receive.

It's just like making a phone call. The signal from your mouthpiece goes to the other person's earpiece and vice versa. Otherwise you'd both shout yourselves hoarse and neither of you would hear the other. Now that we have the routes for the data, we need a few signals to control the traffic. Let's take a look at two lines to start with: the RTS or 'Request to Send' line and the CTS or 'Clear to Send' line. These two lines pair together; imagine that the computer is the sending device and the peripheral is receiving. The peripheral needs a method of telling the CBM 64 when it wants another byte. To do this it sends a signal out on its RTS line requesting the computer to send a byte. The computer, meanwhile, is wondering whether it can send another byte yet, so it looks at the CTS line to see if it is 'Clear to Send'. Thus if we connect the peripheral's RTS line to the computer's CTS line we have a handshaking system to control the flow of data in one direction. But what if the peripheral also has to send data back to the computer? Well, we take the computer's RTS line and connect that to the peripheral's CTS line. Now we have handshaking in both directions — great stuff!

We have already produced a system which can be used to do some fairly fancy two-way communications, but so far we've only used six out of the eight lines mentioned. One of the biggest problems with communicating between two devices is that if one goes wrong the other device will tend to hang up, especially if it is waiting to send or receive a byte. We therefore have two further lines the DTR Data Terminal Ready and the DSR Data Set Ready lines. The DTR line can be used as an output to tell the other device that the equipment is turned on and all is well, whilst the DSR line is an input used to check that all is well with the other device. Once again as above we connect the DTR line of one device to the DSR line of the other, and vice versa.

The system will now give us good bi-directional communications and detect any problems; after all, any system will communicate but it takes a good one to sort itself out when things go wrong!

Let's now take a look at the connections we require in diagrammatic form (see Fig. 10.3). Of course if we only want to send data in one direction then we won't need all of these lines.

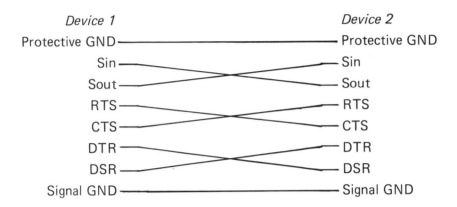

Fig. 10.3 – Wiring connections for RS232.

Now that we have all these fancy facilities set up you might think that we have to write our own machine code routines to handle all this; but not so. The KERNAL CHKOUT and CHKIN routines are designed to work with just this configuration, so you can either call the routines from your own machine code, or simply use the BASIC commands GET# and PRINT#.

Sending Data
When we want to send data from BASIC we first tell the peripheral to listen using the CMD <lfn> command followed by the PRINT#<lfn>,<data list>. From machine code this can be achieved using the CHKOUT and CHROUT KERNAL routines. The data will then be buffered in one of the blocks of memory until it is actually transmitted.

Receiving Data
Data received from a peripheral is stored in one of the 256-byte buffers at the top of memory. It is then up to the user to read data from the buffer before it overflows. If the buffer does overflow then any additional bytes received will be lost. Data is read from the buffer using the GET#<lfn> command. You may use the INPUT#<lfn> command if you wish but there are hazards involved in doing this. If there are no characters in the buffer then GET# will return a null character, but INPUT# will hang until a carriage return is received. The only cure for this is the RESTORE key.

From machine code the KERNAL routines CHKIN and GETIN are recommended whilst CHRIN should be avoided for the same reasons as in the previous paragraph.

Closing the RS232 Channel
The RS232 channel can be closed in the same manner as any other logical file, i.e. CLOSE <lfn> from BASIC, or using the KERNAL routine CLOSE. However, when a CLOSE is executed, any data remaining in the buffers will be lost as both buffers are removed.

Error Checking of RS232
In order to deal with the problems that might arise with RS232, such as buffer overflow or parity errors we can read the status byte ST (from BASIC or using the KERNAL routine READST) and this gives us the following information:

Bit 7 — Break Detected
Bit 6 — DSR Signal Missing
Bit 5 — UNUSED
Bit 4 — CTS Signal Missing
Bit 3 — Receiver Buffer Empty
Bit 2 — Receiver Buffer Overflow
Bit 1 — Framing Error
Bit 0 — Parity Error

Finally if you are using BASIC and you don't like the idea of having 512 bytes taken from the top of memory, here are a few suggestions. Firstly it must be realized that the location of the buffers can be moved by changing the buffer pointers in locations 247/8 ($F7/8) for the input buffer and 249/250 ($F9/A) for the output buffer. Writing a zero into the Hi-byte of the pointer will deallocate the buffer. So if, for example, you are only using the output buffer you can recover 256 bytes by deallocating the input buffer.

If possible OPEN RS232 channels before using dynamic strings. If you do have to OPEN an RS232 channel in the middle of a program the following procedure should be adopted.

Save the pointer to the top of memory
Save the pointer to the bottom of strings
OPEN RS232 channel.
Move or deallocate buffers
Reset pointer to the top of memory
Reset pointer to the bottom of strings.

The following BASIC code performs these actions.

```
1000  POKE828,PEEK(55):POKE829,PEEK(56)
1010  POKE830,PEEK(51):POKE831,PEEK(52)
1020  OPEN1,2,0,CHR$(0)CHR$(97)CHR$(56)CHR$(8):REM AUTO CLR
1030  POKE250,0:REM DEALLOCATE OUTPUT BUFFER
1040  POKE247,0:POKE248,192: REM MOVE INPUT BUFFER TO $C000
1050  POKE55,PEEK(828):POKE56,PEEK(829)
1060  POKE51,PEEK(830):POKE52,PEEK(831)
```

REGISTERS OF THE 6526 CHIP

Here is a detailed description of the functions of the register of the 6526 Complex Interface Adaptor.

Register No. 0   Address 56576 $DD00
Function: Peripheral Data Reg A

This register is the route through which data passes to and from the outside world. If a value is read from this register it reflects the state of the pins on the user port which are connected to it. If a value is written to it then the pins on the user port will reflect this value.

Register No. 1   Address 56577 $DD01
Function: Peripheral Data Reg B

This is the second of the two data registers. Its function is the same as Peripheral Data Register B.

Register No. 2   Address 56578 $DD02
Function: Data Direction Register A

The function of this register allows us to select whether individual pins on the user port (which correspond to individual bits in the register) are used for input or output. If a bit in the Data Direction Register is set to a one then the pin is set for output, if set to a zero the pin will be an input. In order to protect any peripheral device connected to your CBM 64, all of the pins will be set to input (DDR=0) when the CBM 64 is switched on.

Register No. 3   Address 56579 $DD03
Function: Data Direction Register B

This register has the same function as Data Direction Register A, except that it affects the pins connected to PORT B.

Register No. 4,5   Address 56580,56581 $DD04,$DD05
Function: Timer A Low Register, Timer A High Register

These registers give a 16-bit value. If the register is written to them the value written is latched; latching is a hardware function of the chip which involves holding a piece of data irrespective of what then happens until released by a predetermined action, such as the timer reading the data in, and once the Timer A value has counted down to zero it will restart counting down from the value written into the register. When the register is read the value obtained will be the current value of timer A.

Register No. 6,7   Address 56582,56583 $DD06,$DD07
Function: Timer B Low Register, Timer B High Register

These registers perform the same function as Registers 4 and 5, except that they affect Timer B.

Register Number 8   Address 56584 $DD08
Function: 10ths of a Second Register

When written to, this register sets the value of the 10ths of a second of the time of day clock or the alarm depending on the state of the ALARM bit in Control Register B (Register 15). When read, this register gives the value of the 10ths of a second of the time of day clock. Only the lower four bits of this register have any effect, and the value returned or written is in BCD (binary coded decimal).

Register No. 9   Address 56585 $DD09
Function: Seconds Register

When written to, this register sets the seconds value of the time of day clock or the alarm depending on the state of the ALARM bit in Control Register B (Register 15). When read, it returns the current seconds value of the TOD clock. All values are in BCD.

Register No. 10   Address 56586 $DD0A
Function: Minutes Register

When written to, this register sets the minutes value of the time of day clock or the alarm depending on the state of the ALARM bit in Control Register B (Register 15). When read, it returns the current minutes value of the time of day clock. All values are in BCD.

Register No. 11   Address 56587 $DD0B
Function: Hours — AM/PM Register

When written to, this register sets the hours value of the time of day clock or the alarm depending on the state of the ALARM bit in Control Register B (Register 15). When read, it returns the current hours value of the time of day clock.

In this register the lower 5 bits represent the hours value (bit 5 = hours high, bit 0—4 = hours low), whilst bit 7 determines whether the clock reads AM or PM, 1=PM 0=AM. All values are in BCD.

Register No. 12   Address 56588 $DD0C
Function: Serial Data Register

The 6526 chip is capable of sending and receiving serial data (one bit at a time) as well as parallel data. This is accomplished by shifting the data in or out through the shift register. If data is being read in then after every 8 shifts (one byte) the value in the shift register is dumped into the Serial Data Register, and an interrupt occurs. When data is sent out serially an interrupt occurs to indicate that the 6526 is ready to send more data, a value is then written into the Serial Data Register and this is transferred into the shift register and shifted out. If a byte of data is written to this register before the interrupt (i.e. the computer stays one step ahead of the 6526) then a continuous flow of serial data can be achieved.

Register No. 13 Address 56589 $DD0D
Function: Interrupt Control Register

Under certain circumstances the 6526s can cause the 6510 processor in the CBM 64 to stop whatever it is doing and run a short machine code routine called an interrupt service routine (see Chapters 8 and 9). This routine may be part of the Kernal, or a routine the user has written. The Interrupt Control Register decides which events within the 6526 can cause an interrupt to occur. There are five possible causes of an interrupt.

(1) Timer A counting to zero.
(2) Timer B counting to zero.
(3) Alarm on TOD clock.
(4) Eight serial bits sent or received.
(5) Flag line going low.

However, we may not always want an interrupt to occur every time one of these events happens. The Interrupt Control Register allows us to selectively enable or disable these interrupts.

When a value is written into this register each bit has its own function:

Bit 7 — SET/CLR. When a one is written to this bit, all other bits which have a one written to them will be set. When a zero is written to this bit all other bits which have a one written to them will be cleared.

Bits 6 and 5 — Not used.

Bit 4 — FLAG. When this bit is set to a one any negative going transition on the FLG pin of the 6526 will cause an interrupt to occur. When cleared to zero no interrupt will occur.

Bit 3 — SP. When this bit is set and eight bits of serial data have been read in or written out through the serial register an interrupt will occur.

Bit 2 — ALRM. When this bit is set and the value of the TOD clock is equal to the ALARM value set an interrupt will occur.

Bit 1 — TB. When this bit is set and the Timer B counts down to zero an interrupt will occur.

Bit 0 — TA. When this bit is set and Timer A counts down to zero an interrupt will occur.

CIA#1 is connected to the IRQ interrupt line of the 6510, and CIA#2 to the NMI interrupt line.

Register No. 14 Address 56590 $DD0E
Function: Control Register A

This register is used to control various aspects of Timer A. It also has the functions listed below.

Bit 0 — START. When this bit is set to a one Timer A starts counting down. Clearing to zero will stop the Timer.

Bit 1 — PBON. When set to a one the interrupt caused by TIMER A is directed to PB6 on the user port. When cleared PB6 behaves normally.

Bit 2 — OUTMODE. When PBON is set to a one and this bit is set to a one the state of PB6 will change with each interrupt (i.e. if PB6 is high it goes low and vice versa). When OUTMODE is set to a zero PB6 will go high for one cycle and then return to a low state when an interrupt occurs.

Bit 3 — RUNMODE. When this bit is set to a one the timer will count down from the value in the timer latches to zero, generate an interrupt, reload the latched value, clear Bit 0 and stop. When cleared to zero the timer will count down to zero, generate an interrupt, reload the latched value and start counting down again.

Bit 4 — LOAD. When a one is written to this bit the latched value will be forced into the timer whether it is running or not. This bit will not, however, be set to a one, and when read will always be zero. Writing zero to this bit has no effect.

Bit 5 — INMODE. When this bit is cleared the timer is driven by the CBM 64's internal system clock (02 pulses if you are technically minded). When set to a one the timer is driven by positive pulses on the CNT pin of the 6526, and thus may be driven by an external clock, or used as an event counter.

Bit 6 — SPMODE. When this bit is cleared data is output from the serial port. The timing for the output is taken from timer A, and these timing pulses appear in the CNT pin for use by the device that data is being sent to. When this bit is set the serial register reads data in and takes its timing from the signal applied to the CNT pin by the external device.

Bit 7 — TODIN If this bit is set to a one then a 50 Hz signal is required on the TOD pin of the 6526 to keep accurate time. If cleared to a zero a 60 Hz signal will be required. Thus usually TODIN should be set to a one in Europe and cleared to zero in the United States.

Register No. 15 Address 56591 $DD0F
Function: Control Register B

This register is the control register for timer B. Bits 0 to 4 have the same function as the corresponding bits in Control Register A except that bit 1 directs output to PB7 instead of PB6.

Bits 5 and 6 — INMODE. These two bits combine to give four possible sources to drive timer B as follows:

CRB 6	CRB 5	
0	0	Timer B runs on system clock ($\phi2$).
0	1	Timer B counts positive CNT transitions.
1	0	Timer B counts Timer A underflows.
1	1	Timer B counts Timer A underflows while the CNT pin is high.

Bit 7 — ALARM. When this bit is set to a one writing a value to the TOD registers will set the alarm. When this bit is cleared writing to the TOD registers will set the clock.

Appendix 1

Tables

Table A1 — Commodore 64 memory map first 1K block

Label	Hex address	Decimal location	Description
D6510	0000	0	6510 On-Chip Data Direction Register
R6510	0001	1	6510 On-Chip 8-bit Input/Output Register
	0002	2	Unused;
ADRAY1	0003 – 0004	3 – 4	Jump Vector: Convert Floating – Integer
ADRAY2	0005 – 0006	5 – 6	Jump Vector: Convert Integer – Floating
CHARAC	0007	7	Search Character
ENDCHR	0008	8	Flag: Scan for Quote at End of String
TRMPOS	0009	9	Screen Column From Last TAB
VERCKB	000A	10	Flag: 0 = Load, 1 = Verify
COUNT	000B	11	Input Buffer Pointer/ No. of Subscripts
DIMFLG	000C	12	Flag: Default Array DI-Mension
VALTYP	000D	13	Data Type: $FF = String, $00 = Numeric
INTFLG	000E	14	Data Type: $80 = Integer, $00 = Floating
GARBFL	000F	15	Flag: DATA scan/LIST quote/Garbage Coll
SUBFLG	0010	16	Flag: Subscript Ref/User Function Call
INPFLG	0011	17	Flag: $00 = INPUT, $40 = GET, $98 = READ
TANSGN	0012	18	Flag: TAN sign/Comparison Result
	0013	19	Flag: INPUT Prompt
LINNUM	0014 – 0015	20 – 21	Temp: Integer Value
TEMPPT	0016	22	Pointer: Temporary String Stack

Label	Hex address	Decimal location	Description
LASTPT	0017 – 0018	23 – 24	Last Temp String Address
TEMPST	0019 – 0021	25 – 33	Stack for Temporary Strings
INDEX	0022 – 0025	34 – 37	Utility Pointer Area
RESHO	0026 – 002A	38 – 42	Floating-Point Product of Multiply
TXTTAB	002B – 002C	43 – 44	Pointer: Start of BASIC Text
VARTAB	002D – 002E	45 – 46	Pointer: Start of BASIC Variables
ARYTAB	002F – 0030	47 – 48	Pointer: Start of BASIC Arrays
STREND	0031 – 0032	49 – 50	Pointer: End of BASIC Arrays (+1)
FRETOP	0033 – 0034	51 – 52	Pointer: Bottom of String Storage
FRESPC	0035 – 0036	53 – 54	Utility String Pointer
MEMSIZ	0037 – 0038	55 – 56	Pointer: Highest Address Used by BASIC
CURLIN	0039 – 003A	57 – 58	Current BASIC Line Number
OLDLIN	003B – 003C	59 – 60	Previous BASIC Line Number
OLDTXT	003D – 003E	61 – 62	Pointer: BASIC Statement for CONT
DATLIN	003F – 0040	63 – 64	Current DATA Line Number
DATPTR	0041 – 0042	65 – 66	Pointer: Current DATA Item Address
INPPTR	0043 – 0044	67 – 68	Vector: INPUT Routine
VARNAM	0045 – 0046	69 – 70	Current BASIC Variable Name
VARPNT	0047 – 0048	71 – 72	Pointer: Current BASIC Variable Data
FORPNT	0049 – 004A	73 – 74	Pointer: Index Variable for FOR/NEXT
	004B – 0060	75 – 96	Temp Pointer/Data Area
FACEXP	0061	97	Floating-Point Accumulator #1: Exponent
FACHO	0062 – 0065	98 – 101	Floating Accum. #1: Mantissa
FACSGN	0066	102	Floating Accum. #1: Sign
SGNFLG	0067	103	Pointer: Series Evaluation Constant
BITS	0068	104	Floating Accum. #1: Overflow Digit
ARGEXP	0069	105	Floating-Point Accumulator #2: Exponent
ARGHO	006A – 006D	106 – 109	Floating Accum. #2: Mantissa
ARGSGN	006E	110	Floating Accum. #2: Sign
ARISGN	006F	111	Sign Comparison Result: Accum #1 vs #2
FACOV	0070	112	Floating Accum. #1. Low-Order (Rounding)
FBUFPT	0071 – 0072	113 – 114	Pointer: Cassette Buffer
CHRGET	0073 – 008A	115 – 138	Subroutine: Get Next Byte of BASIC Text
CHRGOT	0079	121	Entry to Get Same Byte of Text Again
TXTPTR	007A – 007B	122 – 123	Pointer: Current Byte of BASIC Text
RNDX	008B – 008F	139 – 143	Floating RND Function Seed Value
STATUS	0090	144	Kernal I/O Status Word: ST
STKEY	0091	145	Flag: STOP key/RVS key
SVXT	0092	146	Timing Constant for Tape
VERCK	0093	147	Flag: 0 = Load, 1 = Verify
C3PO	0094	148	Flag: Serial Bus – Output Char. Buffered
BSOUR	0095	149	Buffered Character for Serial Bus
SYNO	0096	150	Cassette Sync No.

Label	Hex address	Decimal location	Description
	0097	151	Temp Data Area
LDTND	0098	152	No. of Open Files/Index to File Table
DFLTN	0099	153	Default Input Device (0)
DFLTO	009A	154	Default Output (CMD) Device (3)
PRTY	009B	155	Tape Character Parity
DPSW	009C	156	Flag: Tape Byte-Received
MSGFLG	009D	157	Flag: $80 = Direct Mode, $00 = Program
PTR1	009E	158	Tape Pass 1 Error Log
PTR2	009F	159	Tape Pass 2 Error Log
TIME	00A0 – 00A2	160 – 162	Real-Time Jiffy Clock (approx) 1/60 Sec
	00A3 – 00A4	163 – 164	Temp Data Area
CNTDN	00A5	165	Cassette Sync Countdown
BUFPNT	00A6	166	Pointer: Tape I/O Buffer
INBIT	00A7	167	RS-232 Input Bits/Cassette Temp
BITCI	00A8	168	RS-232 Input Bit Count/Cassette Temp
RINONE	00A9	169	RS-232 Flag: Check for Start Bit
RIDATA	00AA	170	RS-232 Input Byte Buffer/Cassette Temp
RIPRTY	00AB	171	RS-232 Input Parity/Cassette Short Cnt
SAL	00AC – 00AD	172 – 173	Pointer: Tape Buffer/Screen Scrolling
EAL	00AE – 00AF	174 – 175	Tape End Addresses/End of Program
CMP0	00B0 – 00B1	176 – 177	Tape Timing Constants
TAPE1	00B2 – 00B3	178 – 179	Pointer: Start of Tape Buffer
BITTS	00B4	180	RS-232 Out Bit Count/Cassette Temp
NXTBIT	00B5	181	RS-232 Next Bit to Send/ Tape EOT Flag
RODATA	00B6	182	RS-232 Out Byte Buffer
FNLEN	00B7	183	Length of Current File Name
LA	00B8	184	Current Logical File Number
SA	00B9	185	Current Secondary Address
FA	00BA	186	Current Device Number
FNADR	00BB – 00BC	187 – 188	Pointer: Current File Name
ROPRTY	00BD	189	RS-232 Out Parity/Cassette Temp
FSBLK	00BE	190	Cassette Read/Write Block Count
MYCH	00BF	191	Serial Word Buffer
CAS1	00C0	192	Tape Motor Interlock
STAL	00C1 – 00C2	193 – 194	I/O Start Address
MEMUSS	00C3 – 00C4	195 – 196	Tape Load Temps
LSTX	00C5	197	Current Key Pressed: CHR$(n) 0 = No Key
NDX	00C6	198	No. of Chars. in Keyboard Buffer (Queue)
RVS	00C7	199	Flag: Print Reverse Chars. –1 = Yes, 0 = No Used
INDX	00C8	200	Pointer: End of Logical Line for INPUT
LXSP	00C9 – 00CA	201 – 202	Cursor X-Y Pos. at Start of INPUT

Label	Hex address	Decimal location	Description
SFDX	00CB	203	Flag: Print Shifted Chars.
BLNSW	00CC	204	Cursor Blink enable: 0 = Flash Cursor
BLNCT	00CD	205	Timer: Countdown to Toggle Cursor
GDBLN	00CE	206	Character Under Cursor
BLNON	00CF	207	Flag: Last Cursor Blink On/Off
CRSW	00D0	208	Flag: INPUT or GET from Keyboard
PNT	00D1 – 00D2	209 – 210	Pointer: Current Screen Line Address
PNTR	00D3	211	Curso Column on Current Line
QTSW	00D4	212	Flag: Editor in Quote Mode, $00 = NO
LNMX	00D5	213	Physical Screen Line Length
TBLX	00D6	214	Current Cursor Physical Line Number
	00D7	215	Temp Data Area
INSRT	00D8	216	Flag: Insert Mode, >0 = # INSTs
LDTB1	00D9 – 00F2	217 – 242	Screen Line Link Table/Editor Temps
USER	00F3 – 00F4	243 – 244	Pointer: Current Screen Color RAM loc.
KEYTAB	00F5 – 00F6	245 – 246	Vector: Keyboard Decode Table
RIBUF	00F7 – 00F8	247 – 248	RS-232 Inout Buffer Pointer
ROBUF	00F9 – 00FA	249 – 250	RS-232 Output Buffer Pointer
FREKZP	00FB – 00FE	251 – 254	Free 0-Page Space for User Programs
BASZPT	00FF	255	BASIC Temp Data Area
	0100 – 01FF	256 – 511	Micro-Processor System Stack Area
	0100 – 010A	256 – 266	Floating to String Work Area
BAD	0100 – 013E	256 – 318	Tape Input Error Log
BUF	0200 – 0258	512 – 600	System INPUT Buffer
LAT	0259 – 0262	601 – 610	KERNAL Table: Active Logical File No's.
FAT	0263 – 026C	611 – 620	KERNAL Table: Device No. for Each File
SAT	026D – 0276	621 – 630	KERNAL Table: Second Address Each File
KETD	0277 – 0280	631 – 640	Keyboard Buffer Queue (FIFO)
MEMSTR	0281 – 0282	641 – 642	Pointer: Bottom of Memory for O.S.
MEMSIZ	0283 – 0284	643 – 644	Pointer: Top of Memory for O.S.
TIMOUT	0285	645	Flag: Kernal Variable for IEEE Timeout
COLOR	0286	646	Current Character Color Code
GDCOL	0287	647	Background Color Under Cursor
HIBASE	0288	648	Top of Screen Memory (Page)
XMAX	0289	649	Size of Keyboard Buffer
RPTFLG	028A	650	Flag: REPEAT Key Used, $80 = Repeat
KOUNT	028B	651	Repeat Speed Counter
DELAY	028C	652	Repeat Delay Counter
SHFLAG	028D	653	Flag: Keyboard SHIFT Key/ CTRL Key/ C = Key
LSTSHF	028E	654	Last Keyboard Shift Pattern
KEYLOG	028F – 0290	655 – 656	Vaector: Keyboard Table Setup

Label	Hex address	Decimal location	Description
MODE	0291	657	Flag: $00 = Disable SHIFT Keys, $80 = Enable SHIFT Keys
AUTODN	0292	658	Flag: Auto Scroll Down, 0 = ON
M51CTR	0293	659	RS-232: 6551 Control Register Image
M51CDR	0294	660	RS-232: 6551 Command Register Image
M51AJB	0295–0296	661–662	RS-232 Non-Standard BPS (Time/2-100) USA
RSSTAT	0297	663	RS-232: 6551 Status Register Image
BITNUM	0298	664	RS-232 Number of Bits Left to Send
BAUDOF	0299–029A	665–666	RS-232 Baud Rate: Full Bit Time (μs)
RIDBE	029B	667	RS-232 Index to End of Input Buffer
RIDBS	029C	688	RS-232 Start of Input Buffer (Page)
RODBS	029D	669	RS-232 Start of Output Buffer (Page)
RODBE	029E	670	RS-232 Index to End of Output Buffer
IRQTMP	029F–02A0	671–672	Holds IRQ Vector During Tape I/O
ENABL	02A1	673	RS-232 Enables
	02A2	674	TOD Sense During Cassette I/O
	02A3	675	Temp Storage For Cassette Read
	02A4	676	Temp D1IRQ Indicator For Cassette Read
	02A5	677	Temp For Line Index
	02A6	678	PAL/NTSC Flag, 0 = NTSC, 1 = PAL
	02A7–02FF	679–767	Unused
IERROR	0300–0310	768–769	Vector: Print BASIC Error Message
IMAIN	0302–0303	770–771	Vector: BASIC Warm Start
ICRNCH	0304–0305	772–773	Vector: Tokenize BASIC Text
IQPLOP	0306–0307	774–775	Vector: BASIC Text LIST
IGONE	0308–0309	776–777	Vector: BASIC Char. Dispatch
IEVAL	030A–030B	778–779	Vector: BASIC Token Evaluation
SAREG	030C	780	Storage for 6502 .A Register
SXREG	030D	781	Storage for 6502 .X Register
SYREG	030E	782	Storage for 6502 .Y Register
SPREG	030F	783	Storage for 6502 .SP Register
USRPOK	0310	784	USR Function Jump Instr (4C)
USRADD	0311–0312	785–786	USR Address Low Byte/High Byte
	0313	787	Unused
CINV	0314–0315	788–789	Vector: Hardware IRQ Interrupt
CBINV	0316–0317	790–791	Vector: BRK INstr. Interrupt
NMINV	0318–0319	792–793	Vector: Non-Maskable Interrupt
IOPEN	031A–031B	794–795	KERNAL OPEN Routine Vector
ICLOSE	031C–031D	796–797	KERNAL CLOSE Routine Vector
ICHKIN	031E–031F	798–799	KERNAL CHKIN Routine Vector
ICKOUT	0320–0321	800–801	KERNAL CHKOUT Routine Vector

Label	Hex address	Decimal location	Description
ICLRCH	0322 – 0323	802 – 803	KERNAL CLRCHN Routine Vector
IBASIN	0324 – 0325	804 – 805	KERNAL CHRIN Routine Vector
IBSOUT	0326 – 0327	806 – 807	KERNAL CHROUT Routine Vector
ISTOP	0328 – 0329	808 – 809	KERNAL STOP Routine Vector
IGETIN	032A – 032B	810 – 811	KERNAL GETIN Routine Vector
ICLALL	032C – 032D	812 – 813	KERNAL CLALL Routine Vector
USRCMD	032E – 032F	814 – 815	User-Defined Vector
ILOAD	0330 – 0331	816 – 817	KERNAL LOAD Routine Vector
ISAVE	0332 – 0333	818 – 819	KERNAL SAVE Routine Vector
	0334 – 033B	820 – 827	Unused
TBUFFR	033C – 03FB	828 – 1019	Tape I/O Buffer
	03FC – 03FF	1020 – 1023	Unused
VICSCN	0400 – 07FF	1024 – 2047	1024 Byte Screen Memory Area
	0400 – 07E7	1024 – 2023	Video Matrix: 25 Lines × 40 Columns
	07F8 – 07FF	2040 – 2047	Sprite Data Pointers
	0800 – 9FFF	2048 – 40959	Normal BASIC Program Space
	8000 – 9FFF	32768 – 40959	VSP Cartridge ROM – 8192 Bytes
	A000 – BFFF	40960 – 49151	BASIC ROM – 8192 Bytes (or 8K RAM)
	C000 – CFFF	49152 – 53247	RAM – 4096 Bytes
	D000 – DFFF	53248 – 57343	Input/Output Devices and Color RAM; or Character Generator ROM or RAM – 4096 Bytes
	E000 – FFFF	57344 – 65535	KERNAL ROM – 8192 Bytes (or 8K RAM)

Table A2 – Characters against screen codes and CBM ASCII

	Screen (POKE)	Screen (PRINT)	Printer (PRINT#)
Set 1	POKE53272,(PEEK(53272)AND240)OR4	CHR$(142)	CHR$(145)
Set 2	POKE53272,(PEEK(53272)AND240)OR6	CHR$(14)	CHR$(17)

Set 1 Upper case + miscellaneous/graphics
Set 2 Lower case + miscellaneous/upper case + some graphics

	Screen (PRINT)	Printer (PRINT#)
Reverse field on	CHR$(146)	CHR$(146)
Reverse field off	CHR$(18)	CHR$(18)

ASCII (American Standard Code for Information Interchange) is a widely used code for representing character data. Normally, it is a 7-bit code allowing 128 characters to be represented. CBM computers store characters in an extended 8-bit version of ASCII format, thus allowing 256 characters to be represented. Within compressed BASIC text bit $7 = 1$ signifies a keyword (see Table A4), elsewhere in memory the 8-bit character codes are interpreted as in the following table.

SET 1	SET 2	SCR	ASC	SET 1	SET 2	SCR	ASC
@	@	0	64	Q	q	17	81
A	a	1	65	R	r	18	82
B	b	2	66	S	s	19	83
C	c	3	67	T	t	20	84
D	d	4	68	U	u	21	85
E	e	5	69	V	v	22	86
F	f	6	70	W	w	23	87
G	g	7	71	X	x	24	88
H	h	8	72	Y	y	25	89
I	i	9	73	Z	z	26	90
J	j	10	74	[	[	27	91
K	k	11	75	£	£	28	92
L	l	12	76	]	]	29	93
M	m	13	77	↑	↑	30	94
N	n	14	78	←	←	31	95
O	o	15	79			32	32
P	p	16	80	!	!	33	33

SET 1	SET 2	SCR	ASC	SET 1	SET 2	SCR	ASC
"	"	34	34	⌐	L	76	108
#	#	35	35	╱	M	77	109
$	$	36	36	╲	N	78	110
%	%	37	37	⌐	O	79	111
&	&	38	38	⌐	P	80	112
'	'	39	39	●	Q	81	113
(	(	40	40	─	R	82	114
)	)	41	41	♥	S	83	115
*	*	42	42	│	T	84	116
+	+	43	43	│	U	85	117
,	,	44	44	╳	V	86	118
-	-	45	45	○	W	87	119
.	.	46	46	♠	X	88	120
/	/	47	47	│	Y	89	121
0	0	48	48	♦	Z	90	122
1	1	49	49	+	+	91	123
2	2	50	50	▓	▓	92	124
3	3	51	51	│	│	93	125
4	4	52	52	▟	▨	94	126
5	5	53	53	◣	▨	95	127
6	6	54	54			96	160
7	7	55	55	▌	▌	97	161
8	8	56	56	▄	▄	98	162
9	9	57	57	▔	▔	99	163
:	:	58	58			100	164
;	;	59	59	│	│	101	165
<	<	60	60	▓	▓	102	166
=	=	61	61	│	│	103	167
>	>	62	62	▞	▞	104	168
?	?	63	63	◢	▨	105	169
	@	64	96	│	│	106	170
↑	A	65	97	├	├	107	171
│	B	66	98	▪	▪	108	172
│	C	67	99	└	└	109	173
│	D	68	100	┐	┐	110	174
│	E	69	101	│	│	111	175
─	F	70	102	┌	┌	112	176
│	G	71	103	┴	┴	113	177
│	H	72	104	┬	┬	114	178
│	I	73	105	┤	┤	115	179
╲	J	74	106	│	│	116	180
╱	K	75	107	▌	▌	117	181

SET 1	SET 2	SCR	ASC	SET 1	SET 2	SCR	ASC
		118	182			123	187
		119	183			124	188
		120	184			125	189
		121	185			126	190
		122	186			127	191

Notes.

Screen codes 128 – 255 are the reversed field images of screen codes 0 – 127.

ASC codes 192 – 223 are the same as ASC codes 96 – 127.

ASC codes 224 – 254 are the same as ASC codes 160 – 190.

ASC code   255   is the same as ASC code   126.

The remaining ASC codes 0 – 31 and 128 – 159 are covered in Table A3.

Table A3 – CBM ASCII screen control codes

0 –			128 –		
1 –			129 –		
2 –			130 –		
3 –			131 –		
4 –			132 –		
5	PRINT WHITE	"◼"	133	FUNCTION KEY F1	
6 –			134	FUNCTION KEY F3	
7 –			135	FUNCTION KEY F5	
8	DISABLES SHIFT+CBM		136	FUNCTION KEY F7	
9	ENABLES SHIFT+CBM		137	FUNCTION KEY F2	
10 –			138	FUNCTION KEY F4	
11 –			139	FUNCTION KEY F6	
12 –			140	FUNCTION KEY F8	
13	CARRIAGE RETURN		141	SHIFT CARR RETURN	
14	SWITCH TO LOWER CASE		143 –		
15 –			144	PRINT BLACK	"◼"
16 –			145	CURSOR UP	"⌐"
17	CURSOR DOWN	"◼"	146	REVERSE FIELD OFF	"◼"
18	REVERSE FIELD ON		147	CLEAR HOME	"⌐"
19	HOME		148	INSERT/DEL	"◼"
20	DELETE		149	PRINT BROWN	"◼"
21 –			150	PRINT LIGHT RED	"◼"
22 –			151	PRINT GRAY #1	"◼"
23 –			152	PRINT GRAY #2	"◼"
24 –			153	PRINT LT GREEN	"◼"
25 –			154	PRINT LT BLUE	"⌐"
26 –			155	PRINT GRAY #3	"◼"
27 –			156	PRINT PURPLE	"◼"
28	PRINT RED	"◼"	157	CURSOR LEFT	"◼"
29	CURSOR RIGHT	"◼"	158	PRINT YELLOW	"◼"
30	PRINT GREEN	"◼"	159	PRINT CYAN	"◼"
31	PRINT BLUE	"◼"			

Table A4 — Commodore 64 BASIC keyword codes

Code (decimal)	Character/ Keyword	Code (decimal	Character/ Keyword	Code (decimal)	Character/ Keyword	Code (decimal)	Character/ Keyword
0	End of line	66	B	133	INPUT	169	STEP
1–31	Unused	67	C	134	DIM	170	+
32	space	68	D	135	READ	171	−
33	!	69	E	136	LET	172	·
34	"	70	F	137	GOTO	173	/
35	#	71	G	138	RUN	174	↑
36	$	72	H	139	IF	175	AND
37	%	73	I	140	RESTORE	176	OR
38	&	74	J	141	GOSUB	177	>
39	'	75	K	142	RETURN	178	=
40	(	76	L	143	REM	179	<
41	)	77	M	144	STOP	180	SGN
42	*	78	N	145	ON	181	INT
43	+	79	O	146	WAIT	182	ABS
44	,	80	P	147	LOAD	183	USR
45	−	81	Q	148	SAVE	184	FRE
46	·	82	R	149	VERIFY	185	POS
47	/	83	S	150	DEF	186	SQR
48	0	84	T	151	POKE	187	RND
49	1	85	U	152	PRINT#	188	LOG
50	2	86	V	153	PRINT	189	EXP
51	3	87	W	154	CONT	190	COS
52	4	88	X	155	LIST	191	SIN
53	5	89	Y	156	CLR	192	TAN
54	6	90	Z	157	CMD	193	ATN
55	7	91	[	158	SYS	194	PEEK
56	8	92	\	159	OPEN	195	LEN
57	9	93	]	160	CLOSE	196	STR$
58	:	94	↑	161	GET	197	VAL
59	;	95	←.	162	NEW	198	ASC
60	<	96–127	Unused	163	TAB(	199	CHR$
61	=	128	END	164	TO	200	LEFT$
62	>	129	FOR	165	FN	201	RIGHT$
63	?	130	NEXT	166	SPC(	202	MID$
64	@	131	DATA	167	THEN	203–254	Unused
65	A	132	INPUT#	168	NOT	255	π

```
1000 REM**GIN RUMMY**
1005 GOSUB6970:REM START PAGE
1010 DIMVV$(13),LAY%(3,2),MD(1,4,10)
1015 VV$(1)=" A"
1020 FORI=2TO10:VV$(I)=STR$(I):NEXT
1025 VV$(11)=" J":VV$(12)=" Q":VV$(13)=" K"
1030 SS$(0)="■♠▓":SS$(1)="▓♦▓":SS$(2)="■♦▓":SS$(3)
="▓♦▓"
1035 DIMDD%(52),P%(12),C%(11),CH%(3):CH%(0)=65:CH%(
1)=83:CH%(2)=88:CH%(3)=90
1040 DIMCA%(4,12),DS%(3,12)
1045 SC=1024:CO=55296
1050 DD$="▓██████████████████████████████████████"
1055 W$="                                        "
1060 R$="▶▶▶▶▶▶▶▶▶▶▶▶▶▶▶▶▶▶▶▶▶▶▶▶▶▶▶▶▶▶▶▶▶▶▶▶▶▶▶▶◀"
:CC$="                                        "
1065 P$=LEFT$(DD$,11):D1=255:D2=255
1070 FORI=0TO9:CA%(4,I)=I+1:NEXT
1075 FORI=10TO12:CA%(4,I)=10:NEXT
1080 CV%(1)=2:CV%(2)=7:CV%(3)=4:REM FRAME COLS
1085 CC%(1)=28:CC%(2)=158:CC%(3)=156:REM BLOCK COL
S
1090 TA$="◤        ▇":BA$="▜        ▇"
1095 REM*JOYSTICK WEDGE*
1100 DATA120,173,20,3,141,29,192,173,21
```

```
1105  DATA3,141,30,192,169,71,141,20,3
1110  DATA169,192,141,21,3,88,96,120,173
1115  DATA29,192,141,20,3,173,30,192,141
1120  DATA21,3,88,96,173,27,192,205,16
1125  DATA192,240,3,76,65,193,169,255
1130  DATA141,27,192,162,0,160,0,185,2
1135  DATA220,141,28,192,169,224,153,2
1140  DATA220,185,0,220,72,173,28,192
1145  DATA153,2,220,189,8,192,221,21,192
1150  DATA189,9,192,253,22,192,144,18
1155  DATA189,8,192,157,21,192,189,9,192
1160  DATA157,22,192,104,74,72,76,162
1165  DATA192,104,74,72,176,13,222,21
1170  DATA192,189,21,192,201,255,208,3
1175  DATA222,22,192,189,21,192,221,12
1180  DATA192,189,22,192,253,13,192,144
1185  DATA18,189,12,192,157,21,192,189
1190  DATA13,192,157,22,192,104,74,72,76
1195  DATA207,192,104,74,72,176,8,254,21
1200  DATA192,208,3,254,22,192,189,0,192
1205  DATA221,17,192,189,1,192,253,18
1210  DATA192,144,18,189,0,192,157,17
1215  DATA192,189,1,192,157,18,192,104
1220  DATA74,72,76,1,193,104,74,72,176
1225  DATA13,222,17,192,189,17,192,201
1230  DATA255,208,3,222,18,192,189,17
1235  DATA192,221,4,192,189,18,192,253,5
1240  DATA192,144,18,189,4,192,157,17
1245  DATA192,189,5,192,157,18,192,104
1250  DATA74,72,76,46,193,104,74,72,176
1255  DATA8,254,17,192,208,3,254,18,192
1260  DATA104,74,176,5,169,1,153,25,192
1265  DATA200,232,232,224,4,240,3,76,91
1270  DATA192,238,27,192,108,29,192
1275  DATA35994:REM*CHECKSUM*
1280  CC=0
1285  FORI=49183TO49478
1290  READX:POKEI,X:CC=CC+X:NEXT
1295  READX:IFX<>CCTHENPRINT"CHECKSUM ERROR(1)":END
1300  REM***SETUP PERM J/S POKES***
1305  POKE49152,24:POKE49153,0
```

Listing continued next page

```
1310 POKE49154,0:POKE49155,0
1315 POKE49156,64:POKE49157,1
1320 POKE49158,0:POKE49159,0
1325 POKE49162,0:POKE49163,0
1330 POKE49166,0:POKE49167,0
1335 POKE49168,0
1340 POKE49169,89:POKE49170,1
1345 POKE49171,0:POKE49172,0
1350 POKE49175,0:POKE49176,0
1355 REM**SPRITE    DATA**
1360 DATA0,0,3,0,0,7,0,0,15,0,0,31,0
1365 DATA128,63,1,128,127,1,192,255,0
1370 DATA225,255,0,243,255,0,63,255,0
1375 DATA63,255,0,123,255,0,246,248,1
1380 DATA237,160,3,187,96,7,54,192,14
1385 DATA29,128,28,27,0,24,14,0,0,0,0,0
1390 DATA0,0,53,32
1395 DATA4723:REM*CHECKSUM*
1400 CC=0
1405 FORI=832TO896
1410 READX:POKEI,X:CC=CC+X:NEXT
1415 READX:IFX<>CCTHENPRINT"CHECKSUM ERROR(2)":END
1420 REM**SET UP SPRITE**
1425 POKE2040,13:POKE53248,89:POKE53264,1:POKE5324
9,200:POKE53287,6
1430 GOSUB7080:REM COMMENTS
1435 REM*SHUFFLE*
1440 DA$=""
1445 FORI=1TO52:DA$=DA$+CHR$(I):NEXT
1450 A=RND(0):REM*RND NUM NEW SEED*
1455 FORI=1TO52:A=I+INT((53-I)*RND(1))
1460 A$=MID$(DA$,A,1)
1465 DA$=A$+LEFT$(DA$,A-1)+RIGHT$(DA$,(52-A))
1470 NEXT
1475 FORI=1TO52:D%(I)=ASC(MID$(DA$,I,1)):NEXT:DP=1
1480 P=1:REM*SCREEN INIT FOR CARDS**
1485 PRINT"⯑"CHR$(142):POKE53281,1:POKE53280,5:PRI
NT"⯑":GOSUB3115:DC=0:OF=442
1490 GOSUB5225:PRINT"⯑        DEALING        ⯑"
1495 REM*DEAL ELEVEN/TEN*
1500 FORDP=1TO19STEP2
1505 P%(P)=D%(DP):CD=P%(P):PI=P:CF=13:GOSUB2830:RE
M PLAYER
1510 FL=7:GOSUB3165:REM PLAYERS FLAG
```

Listing continued next page

```
1515 C%(P)=D%(DP+1):CD=C%(P):REM COMP
1520 FL=0:GOSUB3165:REM COMPS FLAG
1525 P=P+1:NEXTDP
1530 P%(P)=D%(DP):CD=P%(P):PI=P:CF=13:GOSUB2830:DP
=DP+1:P%(12)=255:C%(11)=255
1535 FL=7:GOSUB3165:REM PLAYERS FLAG
1540 PI=1:DC=1:OF=82:CF=13:GOSUB2830:DC=0:OF=442
1545 REM*********************************
1550 REM**SET INITIAL FLAGS IN CA%( )**
1555 REM BIT0 IN CBM'S HAND            *
1560 REM BIT1 -                        *
1565 REM BIT2 ROW MELD                 *
1570 REM BIT3 COLUMN MELD              *
1575 REM BIT4 POTENTIAL MELD           *
1580 REM BIT5 CROSSOVER                *
1585 REM BIT6 DISCARDED                *
1590 REM BIT7 IN PLAYERS HAND          *
1595 REM**********************************
1600 FORS=0TO3:REM     SUIT (COL)
1605 FORV=0TO12:REM    VALUE (ROW)
1610 S1=S:V1=V:GOSUB3425:REM FLAG MELDS
1615 NEXTV:REM NEXT CARD IN ROW
1620 NEXTS:REM NEXT SUIT COL
1625 REM**MAIN LOOP**
1630 GOSUB5225:REM CLEAR DISPLAY BOX
1635 PRINT"  PLEASE SORT HAND "
1640 PRINTLEFT$(R$,10);"USE JOYSTICK TO"
1645 PRINTLEFT$(R$,10);"POINT TO CARD/SPACE"
1650 PRINTLEFT$(R$,10);"TO BE SWAPPED AND"
1655 PRINTLEFT$(R$,10);"PRESS FIRE BUTTON."
1660 PRINT
1665 PRINTLEFT$(R$,10);"PRESS TWICE TO END."
1670 GOSUB4765:REM SORT HAND
1675 GETJU$:IFJU$<>""THEN1675
1680 GOSUB5225:REM CLEAR DISPLAY BOX
1685 PRINT"  PLEASE DECLARE    "
1690 PRINT
1695 PRINTLEFT$(R$,10);"  G = GIN"
1700 PRINTLEFT$(R$,10);"  K = KNOCKING"
1705 PRINT
1710 PRINTLEFT$(R$,10);"ELSE HIT ANY OTHER"
1715 PRINTLEFT$(R$,18);"KEY."
1720 GETA$:IFA$=""THEN1720
1725 IFA$="K"ORA$="G"THEN1915:REM PLAYER DECLARES-
```

```
EXIT MAIN LOOP
1730 GOSUB5225:REM CLEAR DISPLAY BOX
1735 PRINT"◆ PLEASE DISCARD  ▇"
1740 PRINTLEFT$(R$,10);"USE JOYSTICK TO"
1745 PRINTLEFT$(R$,10);"POINT TO CARD TO BE"
1750 PRINTLEFT$(R$,14);" DISCARDED."
1755 PRINTLEFT$(R$,17);"THEN"
1760 PRINTLEFT$(R$,10);"PRESS FIRE BUTTON."
1765 GOSUB5050:REM DISCARD ROUTINE
1770 GOSUB5225:REM CLEAR DISPLAY BOX
1775 PRINT"    THANKYOU     "
1780 FL=6:GOSUB3165:CA%(SF,VF)=CA%(SF,VF)AND64
1785 GOSUB4320:S=SF:V=VF:REM CBM PICKUP
1790 GOSUB5225:REM CLEAR DISPLAY BOX
1795 PRINT" HOLD ON PLEASE    "
1800 PRINTLEFT$(R$,13);"I'M THINKING"
1805 GOSUB3400:REM FLAG NEW MELDS
1810 GOSUB3705:REM REFLAG CROSSED MELDS
1815 GOSUB3730:REM OPTIMISE MELDS
1820 GOSUB4210:REM REM GINFINDER
1825 IFGG=1ORGG=2THEN2240:REM CBM HAS GIN - EXIT M
AIN LOOP
1830 GOSUB5225:REM CLEAR DISPLAY BOX
1835 PRINT"JUST DECIDING WHAT "
1840 PRINTLEFT$(R$,14);"TO DISCARD."
1845 GOSUB4660:REM CBM DECIDE DISCARD
1850 IFCC-CA%(4,NV)<11THENGOSUB5150:REM KNOCK
1855 IFKF=1THEN2240:REM CBM IS KNOCKING-EXIT MAIN
LOOP
1860 GOSUB5225:REM CLEAR DISPLAY BOX
1865 PRINT" OK. HERE WE GO    "
1870 GOSUB4540:REM CBM DISCARD
1875 GOSUB5225:REM CLEAR DISPLAY BOX
1880 PRINT"◆PLEASE TAKE A CARD.▇"
1885 PRINTLEFT$(R$,10);"USE JOYSTICK TO"
1890 PRINTLEFT$(R$,10);"POINT TO CARD TO BE"
1895 PRINTLEFT$(R$,14);"PICKED UP."
1900 GOSUB4905:FL=7:REM PICKUP ROUTINE
1905 GOSUB3165:REM SET FLAG USING CD
1910 GOTO1630:REM BACK ROUND MAIN LOOP
1915 REM** PLAYER HAS DECLARED **
1920 DE$="PLAYER":DO$="COMPUTER":DT$=A$
1925 GOSUB5225:REM CLEAR DISPLAY BOX
1930 PRINT"◆ PLAYER DECLARING ▇"
```

Listing continued next page

```
1935 PRINTLEFT$(R$,10);"USE JOYSTICK TO"
1940 PRINTLEFT$(R$,10);"POINT TO CARD TO BE"
1945 PRINTLEFT$(R$,14);" DISCARDED."
1950 PRINTLEFT$(R$,17);"THEN"
1955 PRINTLEFT$(R$,10);"PRESS FIRE BUTTON."
1960 GOSUB5050:REM DISCARD
1965 REM** MARK MELDS **
1970 MP=1
1975 GOSUB2205:REM DISPLAY MESSAGE
1980 GOSUB5290:MD(0,MP,0)=CN-1:CL=0:REM GET ONE ME
LD
1985 FORHP=1TO12
1990 IF(P%(HP)AND128)=0THENCL=CL+1
1995 NEXT
2000 IFCL<3THEN2025
2005 MP=MP+1:GOSUB5495
2010 IFC$="Y"THEN1980
2015 IFC$="S"THENGOSUB5515:GOTO1970:REM ALL FRAMES
 TO GREEN
2020 REM** PLAYER HAPPY WITH MELDS? **
2025 GETJU$:IFJU$<>""THEN2025
2030 GOSUB5225:REM CLR/POSN
2035 PRINT
2040 PRINTLEFT$(R$,10);"ARE MELDS OK? "
2045 PRINTLEFT$(R$,14);"  Y = YES  "
2050 PRINTLEFT$(R$,14);"  N = NO   "
2055 GETC$:IFC$<>"Y"ANDC$<>"N"THEN2055
2060 IFC$="N"THENGOSUB5515:GOTO1970:REM ALL FRAMES
 TO GREEN/RESTART
2065 IFDT$="G"ANDCL=0THEN2120:REM OK - NO UNMELDED
 CARDS
2070 REM** IS POINT COUNT <= 10? **
2075 CT=0:HH=1
2080 FORHP=1TO12
2085 IF(P%(HP)AND128)=128THEN2100
2090 CD=P%(HP):CV=CD-1-13*INT(CD/13):IFCV>10THENCV
=10
2095 CT=CT+CV:MD(0,4,HH)=CD:HH=HH+1
2100 NEXT
2105 MD(0,4,0)=HH-1
2110 IFDT$="K"ANDCT<11THEN2120
2115 WIN$=DO$:PK=CT:GOSUB2800:GOTO2675:REM WRONG D
ECLARATION
2120 LY=0:GOSUB5550:REM CHECK VALID MELDS
```

```
2125 IFFL$="BAD"ORFO$="BAD"THEN2080
2130 PP=PT
2135 REM** DISPLAY CONDENSED HAND **
2140 GOSUB6095:REM BIG GREY BOX
2145 GOSUB5745:REM DISPLAY PLAYER CARDS
2150 GOSUB3730:REM OPTIMISE
2155 GOSUB5850:REM MARK COMPUTER MELDS
2160 GOSUB5990:REM DISPLAY COMPUTER CARDS
2165 FORI=1TO5000:NEXT:REM DELAY
2170 IFDT$="G"THEN2200
2175 GOSUB6145:REM CBM LAY OFF CARDS
2180 IFMF=0THEN2200
2185 GOSUB6095:REM BIG GREY BOX
2190 GOSUB5745:REM DISPLAY PLAYER CARDS
2195 GOSUB5990:REM DISPLAY COMPUTER CARDS
2200 GOTO2555:REM SCORE
2205 REM**DISPLAY MESSAGE**
2210 GOSUB5225:REM CLR/POSN
2215 IFDT$="G"THENPRINT"🮂 PLAYER GOING GIN    ▦"
2220 IFDT$="K"THENPRINT"🮂  PLAYER KNOCKING    ▦"
2225 PRINTLEFT$(R$,10);"  PLEASE INDICATE"
2230 PRINTLEFT$(R$,10);"    YOUR MELDS.      "
2235 RETURN
2240 REM** COMPUTER HAS DECLARED **
2245 DE$="COMPUTER":DO$="PLAYER"
2250 DT$="G":IFKF=1THENDT$="K"
2255 GOSUB2530:REMPRINT"KNOCKING/GIN"
2260 REM DISCARD FACE DOWN
2265 FORHP=1TO11
2270 IFC%(HP)=CDTHENW1=HP:HP=11
2275 NEXT
2280 OF=82:PI=6:CF=13:DC=1:GOSUB2830:OF=442
2285 D2=D1:D1=CD:C%(W1)=255:CA%(DS,DV)=64
2290 FORI=1TO1000:NEXT:REM DELAY LOOP
2295 GOSUB6420:REM CLEAR TOP HALF OF SCREEN
2300 GOSUB5850:REM MARK COMPUTER MELDS
2305 LY=1:GOSUB5550:REM CHECK VALID MELDS
2310 GOSUB5990:REM DISPLAY COMPUTER MELDS
2315 GETJU$:IFJU$<>""THEN2315
2320 M$="DO YOU HAVE ANY MELDS (Y/N)?":GOSUB3090
2325 GETC$:IFC$<>"Y"ANDC$<>"N"THEN2325
2330 IFC$="N"THEN2445
2335 MP=1
2340 REM DISPLAY MESSAGE
```

Listing continued next page

```
2345 GOSUB5290
2350 IFCN-1<3THENGOSUB5515:GOTO2335
2355 MD(0,MP,0)=CN-1:CL=0:REM GET ONE MELD
2360 FORHP=1TO12
2365 IF(P%(HP)AND128)=0THENCL=CL+1
2370 NEXT
2375 IFCL<3THEN2400
2380 MP=MP+1:GOSUB5495
2385 IFC$="Y"THEN2340
2390 IFC$="S"THENGOSUB5515:GOTO2335:REM ALL FRAMES
 TO GREEN
2395 REM** PLAYER HAPPY WITH MELDS? **
2400 GETJU$:IFJU$<>""THEN2400
2405 M$="IS THIS OK (Y/N)? ":GOSUB3090
2410 GETC$:IFC$<>"Y"ANDC$<>"N"THEN2410
2415 IFC$="N"THENGOSUB5515:GOTO2335:REM ALL FRAMES
 TO GREEN-RESTART
2420 HH=1:FORHP=1TO12
2425 IF(P%(HP)AND128)=128THEN2435
2430 CD=P%(HP):MD(0,4,HH)=CD:HH=HH+1
2435 NEXT
2440 MD(0,4,0)=HH-1
2445 IFDT$="G"THEN2510
2450 GETJU$:IFJU$<>""THEN2450
2455 M$="DO YOU WANT TO LAYOFF CARDS (Y/N)?":GOSUB
3090
2460 GETC$:IFC$<>"Y"ANDC$<>"N"THEN2460
2465 IFC$="N"THEN2510
2470 GOSUB6390:REM POINTER BLOCKS
2475 GOSUB6435:REM PLAYER LAY OFF CARD
2480 GOSUB6420:REM CLEAR TOP HALF OF SCREEN
2485 GOSUB5990:REM DISPLAY COMPUTER MELDS
2490 GETJU$:IFJU$<>""THEN2490
2495 M$="ANOTHER LAYOFF (Y/N)?":GOSUB3090
2500 GETC$:IFC$<>"Y"ANDC$<>"N"THEN2500
2505 IFC$="Y"THEN2470
2510 GOSUB6095:REM BIG GREY BOX
2515 GOSUB5990:REM DISPLAY COMPUTER CARDS
2520 GOSUB5745:REM DISPLAY PLAYER CARDS
2525 GOTO2555
2530 REM**DISPLAY MESSAGE**
2535 GOSUB5225:REM CLR/POSN
2540 IFDT$="G"THENPRINT"  COMPUTER HAS GIN ▓"
2545 IFDT$="K"THENPRINT"▓ COMPUTER KNOCKING ▓"
```

```
2550 RETURN
2555 REM** DO SCORES **
2560 PC=0:PP=0
2565 ML=MD(0,4,0):IFML=0THEN2580
2570 FORCN=1TOML:PX=(MD(0,4,CN)AND127):PY=INT((PX-
1)/13):PX=(PX-1)-13*PY
2575 PP=PP+CA%(4,PX):NEXT
2580 ML=MD(1,4,0):IFML=0THEN2595
2585 FORCN=1TOML:PX=(MD(1,4,CN)AND127):PY=INT((PX-
1)/13):PX=(PX-1)-13*PY
2590 PC=PC+CA%(4,PX):NEXT
2595 GOSUB6700:REM DISPLAY POINTS
2600 GETJU$:IFJU$<>""THEN2600
2605 DD=25:RR=14:GOSUB5250:PRINTCHR$(18)"HIT ANY K
EY.";
2610 GETC$:IFC$=""THEN2610
2615 UK$="N":ERR$=""
2620 IFDE$="COMPUTER"THENPK=PC:PO=PP
2625 IFDE$="PLAYER"THENPK=PP:PO=PC
2630 IF(DT$="G")AND(PK<>0)THENERR$="FALSE GIN":GOS
UB 2800
2635 IF(DT$="K")AND(PK>10)THENERR$="FALSE KNOCK":G
OSUB 2800
2640 IFERR$<>""THENGOSUB2800
2645 IFPK>=POTHENUK$="Y"
2650 IFDT$="G"THENPV=PO+20
2655 IFDT$="K"ANDUK$="N"THENPV=PO-PK
2660 IFDT$="K"ANDUK$="Y"THENPV=PK-PO+10
2665 IFUK$="N"THENWIN$=DE$
2670 IFUK$="Y"THENWIN$=DO$
2675 IFWIN$="COMPUTER"THENGOSUB2750
2680 IFWIN$="PLAYER"THENGOSUB2775
2685 IFCS>=100ORPS>=100THEN2715
2690 GETJU$:IFJU$<>""THEN2690
2695 GOSUB6730:REM DISPLAY END OF HAND
2700 GETC$:IFC$=""THEN2700
2705 GOSUB6935:REM CLEAR ARRAYS
2710 GOTO1435:REM NEXT HAND
2715 AC=AC+CS:AP=AP+PS:HG=HG+PG+CG:CG=0:PG=0
2720 GETJU$:IFJU$<>""THEN2720
2725 GOSUB6845:REM DISPLAY END OF GAME
2730 GETC$:IFC$<>"Y"ANDC$<>"N"THEN2730
2735 IFC$="Y"THENGOSUB6935:CS=0:PS=0:GOTO1435:REM
NEXT GAME
```

Listing continued next page

```
2740 POKE53281,6:POKE53280,14:PRINTCHR$(246)CHR$(1
47)"CBYE"
2745 END
2750 REM**COMPUTER WINS**
2755 CS=CS+PV:CG=CG+1
2760 REM--DISPLAY AND PAUSE
2765 IFCS>=100THENCS=CS+100+20*CG
2770 RETURN
2775 REM**PLAYER WINS**
2780 PS=PS+PV:PG=PG+1
2785 REM--DISPLAY AND PAUSE
2790 IFPS>=100THENPS=PS+100+20*PG
2795 RETURN
2800 REM**FALSE DECLARATION**
2805 UK$="Y":PV=PK+10
2810 M$="FALSE KNOCK- "+DE$+" PENALISED":GOSUB3090
2815 M$="FALSE KNOCK- "+DE$+" PENALISED":NN=11:GOS
UB3050
2820 RETURN
2825 REM**GOSUBS START HERE**
2830 REM**CARD GOSUB**
2835 S%=INT(CD/13):V=CD-13*S%:IFV=0THENV=13:S%=S%-
1:REM SUIT & VALUE
2840 RW%=INT((PI-1)/6):CM%=PI-1-6*RW%:DD%=OF+6*CM%
+280*(RW%AND1):REMFR OFFSET
2845 B=SC+DD%:C=CO+DD%
2850 IFCD=255THENGOSUB5210:GOTO 2865
2855 IFDC=2THENGOSUB2380:GOTO2865
2860 GOSUB2870:IFDC=0THENGOSUB2925
2865 RETURN
2870 REM*CARD FRAME*
2875 GOSUB 5210
2880 POKEB,95:POKEB+1,64:POKEB+2,64:POKEB+3,64:POK
EB+4,73 :REM TOP
2885 POKEC,CF:POKEC+1,CF:POKEC+2,CF:POKEC+3,CF:POK
EC+4,CF:REM COLS
2890 POKEB+40,93:POKEB+80,93:POKEB+120,93:POKEB+16
0,93:POKEB+200,93 :REM LEFT
2895 POKEC+40,CF:POKEC+80,CF:POKEC+120,CF:POKEC+16
0,CF:POKEC+200,CF:REM COLS
2900 POKEB+44,93:POKEB+84,93:POKEB+124,93:POKEB+16
4,93:POKEB+204,93:REM RIGHT
2905 POKEC+44,CF:POKEC+84,CF:POKEC+124,CF:POKEC+16
4,CF:POKEC+204,CF:REM COLS
```

```
2910 POKEB+240,74:POKEB+241,64:POKEB+242,64:POKEB+
243,64:POKEB+244,75:REM BOT
2915 POKEC+240,CF:POKEC+241,CF:POKEC+242,CF:POKEC+
243,CF:POKEC+244,CF:REM COLS
2920 RETURN
2925 REM*PATTERN*
2930 A=CHZ(SZ):CC=2*(SZAND1):REM CHAR&COL
2935 ONVGOTO2940,2945,2950,2955,2960,2965,2970,297
5,2980,2985,2990,2995,3000
2940 GOSUB3010:POKEB+41,1:POKEC+41,0:GOTO3005
2945 GOSUB3015:GOTO3005
2950 GOSUB3015:GOSUB3010:GOTO3005
2955 GOSUB3020:GOTO3005
2960 GOSUB3020:GOSUB3010:GOTO3005
2965 GOSUB3020:GOSUB3030:GOTO3005
2970 GOSUB3020:GOSUB3030:GOSUB3010:GOTO3005
2975 GOSUB3020:GOSUB3030:GOSUB3015:GOTO3005
2980 GOSUB3020:GOSUB3035:GOSUB3010:GOTO3005
2985 GOSUB3020:GOSUB3035:GOSUB3015:GOTO3005
2990 GOSUB3010:POKEB+41,10:POKEC+41,0:GOTO3005
2995 GOSUB3010:POKEB+41,17:POKEC+41,0:GOTO3005
3000 GOSUB3010:POKEB+41,11:POKEC+41,0:GOTO3005
3005 RETURN
3010 POKEB+122,A:POKEC+122,CC:RETURN
3015 POKEB+82,A:POKEB+162,A:POKEC+82,CC:POKEC+162,
CC:RETURN
3020 POKEB+41,A:POKEB+43,A:POKEB+201,A:POKEB+203,A
3025 POKEC+41,CC:POKEC+43,CC:POKEC+201,CC:POKEC+20
3,CC:RETURN
3030 POKEB+121,A:POKEB+123,A:POKEC+121,CC:POKEC+12
3,CC:RETURN
3035 POKEB+81,A:POKEB+83,A:POKEB+161,A:POKEB+163,A
3040 POKEC+81,CC:POKEC+83,CC:POKEC+161,CC:POKEC+16
3,CC:RETURN
3045 FORI=0TO2000:NEXT:RETURN
3050 REM**SCROLL MESSAGE**
3055 Z$=W$+M$+W$
3060 P$=LEFT$(DD$,NN)+""
3065 FORN=1TOLEN(Z$)-38
3070 PRINTP$""MID$(Z$,N,38)"";
3075 FORM=0TO20:NEXT
3080 NEXT:PRINTP$+LEFT$(W$,38);
3085 RETURN
3090 REM**STATIC MESSAGE**
```

Listing continued next page

```
3095 Z$=LEFT$(W$,(38-LEN(M$))/2)
3100 M$=Z$+M$+Z$:DD=11:RR=1:GOSUB5250
3105 PRINTCHR$(18)M$CHR$(146):RETURN
3110 REM** CONSTRUCT GREY BOX **
3115 FORL=0TO39:POKESC+9*40+L,99:POKECO+9*40+L,15:
NEXT
3120 FORL=0TO20:POKESC+9+L,160:POKECO+9+L,15:NEXT
3125 FORM=1TO7
3130 L=0:POKESC+40*M+9+L,160:POKECO+40*M+9+L,15
3135 L=20:POKESC+40*M+9+L,160:POKECO+40*M+9+L,15:N
EXT
3140 FORL=0TO20:POKESC+320+9+L,160:POKECO+320+9+L,
15:NEXT
3145 PRINT"█";"  ▌DECK";SPC(25);"DISCARD█"
3150 RETURN
3155 REM ** SET FLAGS & UPDATE **
3160 REM ** DISCARD ARRAY **
3165 REM*SET FLAG USING CD*
3170 SF=INT((CD-1)/13):VF=CD-1-13*SF
3175 REM*SET FLAG USING SF,VF*
3180 CA%(SF,VF)=CA%(SF,VF)OR(2↑FL)
3185 REM *UPDATE DISCARD ARRAY*
3190 ONFL+1GOSUB3195,3195,3200,3200,3210,3195,3220
,3305
3195 RETURN
3200 DS%(SF,VF)=DS%(SF,VF)+30
3205 RETURN
3210 DS%(SF,VF)=DS%(SF,VF)+12
3215 RETURN
3220 REM*CHECK DISCARDS IN COL.*
3225 L1=0
3230 FORSL=0TO3
3235 IFCA%(SL,VF)=64THENL1=L1+1
3240 NEXT
3245 IFL1=0THEN3270
3250 REM*COL MELD RISK LESS*
3255 FOR SL=0TO3
3260 IFCA%(SL,VF)<>64THENDS%(SL,VF)=DS%(SL,VF)-4
3265 NEXT
3270 REM*ROW MELD RISK LESS*
3275 FORVL=VF-2TOVF+2
3280 IFVL<0ORVL>12THEN3290
3285 DS%(SF,VL)=DS%(SF,VL)-2
3290 NEXT
```

```
3295 RETURN
3300 REM
3305 REM*PLAYER WANTS CARD *
3310 IF CA%(SF,VF)<>192THEN3395
3315 L1=0:REM CHECK COL MELD RISK
3320 FORSL=0TO3
3325 IFCA%(SL,VF)=64THENL1=L1+1
3330 NEXT
3335 IFL1<2THEN3360
3340 FORSL=0TO3
3345 IF(CA%(SL,VF)AND1)=1THENDS%(SL,VF)=DS%(SL,VF)
-8
3350 NEXT
3355 GOTO3370
3360 REM*COL MELD RISK INCREASED*
3365 FORSL=0TO3:DS%(SL,VF)=DS%(SL,VF)+30:NEXT
3370 REM*ROW MELD RISK INCREASED*
3375 FORVL=VF-2TOVF+2
3380 IFVL<00RVL>12THEN3390
3385 DS%(SF,VL)=DS%(SF,VL)+25
3390 NEXT
3395 RETURN
3400 REM** FLAG NEW MELDS **
3405 FORV1=V-2TOV
3410 IFV1<0THENV1=0
3415 S1=S:GOSUB3425:NEXT:REMFLAG MELDS
3420 RETURN
3425 REM* FLAG ALL MELDS USING *
3430 REM* CURRENT CARD (S1,V1) *
3435 REM* LEAVES S1,V1 INTACT  *
3440 K=0:REM CURRENT ROW MELD LENGTH
3445 REM*COUNT CARDS IN ROW MELD*
3450 IF(CA%(S1,V1+K)AND1)=1THENK=K+1:IFV1+K<13THEN
3450
3455 IFK=0THEN3700:REM NOT CBM CARD !
3460 REM*FLAG ANY ROW MELD CARDS FOUND*
3465 IFK<3THEN3505
3470 FORL=0TOK-1
3475 SF=S1:VF=V1+L
3480 IF(CA%(SF,VF)AND4)=4THEN3495
3485 FL=2:GOSUB3175:IF(CA%(SF,VF)AND17)=1THENFL=4:
GOSUB3175
3490 IF(CA%(SF,VF)AND12)=12THENFL=5:GOSUB3175
3495 NEXT
```

Listing continued next page

```
3500 GOTO3595
3505 IFK<>2THEN3535
3510 REM*FLAG ANY POTL ROW MELD TYPE1*
3515 SF=S1:VF=V1
3520 IF(CA%(SF,VF)AND17)<>17THENFL=4:GOSUB3175
3525 VF=V1+1:IF(CA%(SF,VF)AND17)<>17THENFL=4:GOSUB
3175
3530 GOTO3595
3535 REM*IS NEW CARD TOP OF ROW MELD?*
3540 SF=S1:VF=V1:IFV1<2THEN3560
3545 IF(CA%(SF,VF-1)AND4)<>4THEN3560
3550 IF(CA%(SF,VF)AND4)<>4THENFL=2:GOSUB3175
3555 IF(CA%(SF,VF)AND17)=1THENFL=4:GOSUB3175
3560 IF(CA%(SF,VF)AND12)=12THENFL=5:GOSUB3175
3565 REM*FLAG ANY POTL ROW MELD TYPE2*
3570 IFV1>10THEN3595:REM NO POTL MELD TYPE2 POSS
3575 FL=4:SF=S1:VF=V1
3580 IF(CA%(SF,VF+2)AND17)=0THEN3595
3585 IF(CA%(SF,VF)AND17)=1THENGOSUB3175
3590 VF=V1+2:IF(CA%(SF,VF)AND17)=1THENGOSUB3175
3595 REM**CHECK FOR COLUMN MELDS**
3600 IF(CA%(S1,V1)AND8)=8THEN3690:REM DONE THIS CO
L
3605 REM*COUNT COL MELD*
3610 M=0:FORSL=0TO3
3615 IF(CA%(SL,V1)AND1)=1THENM=M+1
3620 NEXT
3625 REM*FLAG CARDS IN COL MELD*
3630 IFM<3THEN3665:REM NO COL MELD
3635 FORS3=0TO3
3640 SF=S3:VF=V1
3645 IF(CA%(SF,VF)AND9)=1THENFL=3:GOSUB3175
3650 IF(CA%(SF,VF)AND12)=12THENFL=5:GOSUB3175
3655 IF(CA%(SF,VF)AND17)=1THENFL=4:GOSUB3175
3660 NEXT
3665 REM*FLAG POTL COL MELD*
3670 IFM<>2THEN3690:REM SKIP IF NOT POTL COL MELD
3675 FORS3=0TO3:SF=S3:VF=V1
3680 IF(CA%(SF,VF)AND17)=1THENFL=4:GOSUB3175
3685 NEXT
3690 REM**COL MELDS ALL DONE**
3695 IF(CA%(S1,V1)AND12)=12THENFL=5:SF=S1:VF=V1:GO
SUB3175:REM FLAG CROSSOVERS
3700 RETURN
```

```
3705 REM*REFLAG CROSSED MELDS *
3710 FORS=0TO3:FORV=0TO12
3715 IF(CA%(S,V)AND33)=33THENSF=S:VF=V:GOSUB3400
3720 NEXT:NEXT
3725 RETURN
3730 REM** OPTIMISE MELDS **
3735 FOR S=0TO3:FORV=0TO12
3740 REM**LOOK FOR CROSSOVER POINTS**
3745 IF(CA%(S,V)AND45)<>45THEN3900
3750 REM*CROSSOVER - START COUNTING*
3755 REM *COUNT ROW MELDS ON COL*
3760 R=0:FORSL=0TO3
3765 IF(CA%(SL,V)AND41)=41THENR=R+1
3770 NEXT
3775 REM*R=NUMBER OF ROW MELDS ON COL*
3780 IFR<2THEN3855
3785 CL=0:FORS1=0TO3:RM(S1)=0
3790 IF(CA%(S1,V)AND37)=37THENS4=S1:V4=V:GOSUB4175
:RU(S1)=RU:RD(S1)=RD
3795 IF(CA%(S1,V)AND8)=8THENCL=CL+1
3900 NEXT
3805 IF(CL-R)<2THENGOSUB4025:GOTO3900:REM COL TOO
SHORT
3810 REM *LONG COL WITH 2 CROSSOVERS*
3815 FORSL=0TO3:IF(CA%(SL,V)AND41)<>41THEN3835
3820 IF(RU(SL)>=4)OR(RD(SL)>=3)THEN3830
3825 CA%(SL,V)=CA%(SL,V)AND247:DS%(SL,V)=DS%(SL,V)
-16:CL=CL-1:GOTO3835
3830 LC=SL:REM THIS ROW IS LONG
3835 NEXT
3840 IFCL<3THENGOSUB4025:GOTO3900:REM NOT ENOUGH L
EFT
3845 REM *COL STILL LONG ENOUGH*
3850 V4=LC:RC=RD(LC)+RU(LC):GOSUB4055:GOTO3900
3855 REM *FIND NO. OF CROSSOVERS ON ROW MELD*
3860 VL=V:J=0
3865 IF(CA%(S,VL)AND5)<>5THEN3885:REM END OF MELD
3870 IF(CA%(S,VL)AND37)=37THENJ=J+1
3875 VL=VL-1:IFVL>=0THEN3865
3880 REM *J IS NO.OF CROSSOVERS IN MELD*
3885 S4=S:V4=V:GOSUB4175
3890 IFJ=1ORRC>3THENGOSUB3920:GOTO3900:REM*COL V R
OW VALUE*
3895 GOSUB4055
```

Listing continued next page

```
3900 NEXT:NEXT
3905 REM *ONLY OPTIMUM MELDS ARE FLAGGED*
3910 REM *POTENTIAL MELD FLAGS ARE STILLSET*
3915 RETURN
3920 REM * CHOICE IS ROW MELD(S) OR   *
3925 REM * COLUMN MELD(S)             *
3930 S4=S:V4=V:GOSUB4115:GOSUB4145
3935 FOR SL=0TO3
3940 IF(CA%(SL,V)AND9)<>9THENSL=3:NEXT:GOTO3960
3945 NEXT
3950 CA%(S,V)=CA%(S,V)AND247:DS%(S,V)=DS%(S,V)-16
3955 GOTO4020:REM3-COL &ROW
3960 IFRM<=CMTHEN4055:REM 3 COL ONLY
3965 IFRU<4ANDRD<3THEN4025
3970 CA%(S,V)=CA%(S,V)AND251:DS%(S,V)=DS%(S,V)-16
3975 IF(RU-1)*RD=0THEN4020
3980 IFRD>2THEN4000
3985 FORVL=V-RDTOV-1
3990 CA%(S,VL)=CA%(S,VL)AND251:DS%(S,VL)=DS%(S,VL)
-16
3995 NEXT
4000 IFRU>3THEN4020
4005 FORVL=V+1TOV+RU-1
4010 CA%(S,VL)=CA%(S,VL)AND251:DS%(S,VL)=DS%(S,VL)
-16
4015 NEXT
4020 RETURN
4025 REM ** DELETE COLUMN **
4030 FORSL=0TO3
4035 CA%(SL,V)=CA%(SL,V)AND247:DS%(SL,V)=DS%(SL,V)
-16
4040 NEXT
4045 RETURN
4050 REM *KEEP COLUMN*
4055 IFRC-V+V5>2THEN4080
4060 VL=V+1:IFVL>12THEN4080
4065 IF(CA%(S,VL)AND5)<>5THEN4090
4070 CA%(S,VL)=CA%(S,VL)AND251:DS%(S,VL)=DS%(S,VL)
-16
4075 VL=VL+1:IFVL<13THEN4065
4080 IFV-V5-1>2THEN4105
4085 VL=V-1:IFVL<0THEN4105
4090 IF(CA%(S,VL)AND5)<>5THEN4105
4095 CA%(S,VL)=CA%(S,VL)AND251:DS%(S,VL)=DS%(S,VL)
```

```
-16
4100 VL=VL-1:IFVL>0THEN4090
4105 CA%(S,V)=CA%(S,V)AND251:DS%(S,V)=DS%(S,V)-16
4110 RETURN
4115 REM ** ADD UP ROW MELDS **
4120 V5=V4:RM=0
4125 IF(CA%(S4,V5)AND5)=5THENRM=RM+CA%(4,V5):V5=V5
+1:IFV5<13THEN4125
4130 V5=V4-1:IFV5<0THEN4140
4135 IF(CA%(S4,V5)AND5)=5THENRM=RM+CA%(4,V5):V5=V5
-1:IFV5>=0THEN4135
4140 RETURN
4145 REM ** ADD UP COLUMN MELDS **
4150 CM=0:FORSL=0TO3
4155 IF(CA%(SL,V4)AND9)=0THEN4165
4160 CM=CM+CA%(4,V4)
4165 NEXT
4170 RETURN
4175 REM ** COUNT ROW MELD LENGTH **
4180 V5=V4:RC=0:RU=0:RD=0
4185 IF(CA%(S4,V5)AND5)=5THENRU=RU+1:V5=V5+1:IFV5<
13THEN4185
4190 V5=V4-1:IFV5<0THEN4205
4195 IF(CA%(S4,V5)AND5)=5THENRD=RD+1:V5=V5-1:IFV5>
=0THEN4195
4200 RC=RU+RD
4205 RETURN
4210 REM *** GINFINDER ***
4215 REM MUST RUN 'OPTIMISE' FIRST
4220 GG=2:REM GIN FLAG- 0 FOR NOT GIN
4225 CC=0:FORS=3TO0STEP-1:FORV=12TO0STEP-1
4230 IF(CA%(S,V)AND1)<>1THEN4255:REM NOT IN HAND
4235 IF(CA%(S,V)AND4)=4THENGOSUB4265:GOTO4255:REM
ROW MELD
4240 IF(CA%(S,V)AND8)=8THENGOSUB4290:GOTO4255:REM
COL MELD
4245 GG=GG-1:CC=CC+CA%(4,V):REM CARD NOT IN MELD
4250 DS=S:DV=V:REM USE IT AS DISCARD
4255 NEXT:NEXT:CD=13*DS+DV+1
4260 RETURN
4265 REM** COUNT CARDS IN ROW MELD **
4270 MM=0
4275 IF(CA%(S,V+MM)AND4)=4THENMM=MM+1:IFV+MM<13THE
N4275
```

Listing continued next page

```
4280 IFMM>4ANDGG=2THENDS=S:DV=V
4285 RETURN
4290 REM ** COUNT CARDS IN COL MELD **
4295 MM=0:FORSL=0TO3
4300 IF(CA%(SL,V)AND8)=8THENMM=MM+1
4305 NEXT
4310 IFMM=4ANDGG=2THENDS=S:DV=V
4315 RETURN
4320 REM* CBM PICKUP CARD *
4325 FORHL=0TO11:IFC%(HL)=255THENW1=HL:HL=11
4330 NEXT
4335 CD=D1:S1=INT((CD-1)/13):V1=CD-13*S1-1
4340 P1=1:S2=S1:V2=V1:GOSUB4470
4345 IF8-NA-NB=0THEN4415
4350 NC=0:ND=0:NE=0
4355 FORSL=0TO3
4360 IF(CA%(SL,V1)AND1)=1THENNC=NC+1
4365 NEXT
4370 FORVL=V1-2TOV1-1:IFVL<0THEN4380
4375 IF(CA%(S1,VL)AND1)=1THENND=ND+1
4380 NEXT
4385 FORVL=V1+1TOV1+2:IFVL>12THEN4395
4390 IF(CA%(S1,VL)AND1)=1THENNE=NE+1
4395 NEXT
4400 IF(NC>1)OR(ND=2)OR(NE=2)THEN4440
4405 IFV1<1ORV1>11THEN4415
4410 IF((CA%(S1,V1-1)AND1)=1)AND((CA%(S1,V1+1)AND1
)=1)THEN 4440
4415 GOSUB5225:REM CLEAR DISPLAY BOX
4420 PRINT"      I'LL TAKE        "
4425 PRINTLEFT$(R$,10);"   FROM THE DECK."
4430 CD=D%(DP):DP=DP+1:C%(W1)=CD:FL=0:GOSUB3165
4435 DC=1:OF=82:PI=1:CF=13:GOSUB2830:OF=442:DC=0:G
OTO4465
4440 GOSUB5225:REM CLEAR DISPLAY BOX
4445 PRINT"     I'LL TAKE         "
4450 PRINTLEFT$(R$,10);"    YOUR DISCARD."
4455 CD=D2:PI=6:OF=82:CF=13:GOSUB2830:OF=442
4460 CD=D1:D1=D2:D2=255:C%(W1)=CD:FL=0:GOSUB3165
4465 RETURN
4470 REM* ADJ CARDS*
4475 NA=0:NB=0:FORSL=0TO3
4480 IF(CA%(SL,V2)ANDP1)=0THENNA=NA+1
4485 NEXT
```

```
4490  IFV2=0THEN4505
4495  IF(V2-1)=0)AND((CA%(S2,V2-1)ANDP1)=0)THENNA=N
A+1
4500  IFV2=12THEN4515
4505  IF(V2+1)=0)AND((CA%(S2,V2+1)ANDP1)=0)THENNA=N
A+1
4510  IFV2<2THEN4525
4515  IF(V2-2)=0)AND((CA%(S2,V2-2)ANDP1)=0)THENNB=N
B+1
4520  IFV2>10THEN4530
4525  IF(V2+2)=0)AND((CA%(S2,V2+2)ANDP1)=0)THENNB=N
B+1
4530  PB=(2*NA+NB)/(((50-DP)*(48-DP))OR((51-DP)*(49
-DP)))
4535  RETURN
4540  REM*DISCARD*
4545  FORHP=1TO11:IFC%(HP)=CDTHENW1=HP:HP=11
4550  NEXT
4555  OF=82:PI=6:CF=13:GOSUB2830:OF=442
4560  D2=D1:D1=CD:C%(W1)=255:S=NS:V=NV
4565  REM*CLEAR POT'L MELD FLAGS IF NEC*
4570  IF(CA%(NS,NV)AND29)<>17THEN4650
4575  CA%(NS,NV)=0:FL=6:SF=NS:VF=NV:GOSUB3175
4580  REM COL FLAGS FIRST
4585  FORS2=0TO3:IF(CA%(S2,NV)AND29)<>17THEN4600
4590  CA%(S2,NV)=CA%(S2,NV)AND239:DS%(S2,NV)=DS%(S2
,NV)-8
4595  S1=S2:V1=NV:GOSUB3400
4600  NEXT
4605  REM **POT. ROW FLAGS**
4610  FORVO=0TO2
4615  S2=NS:V2=NV-VO:IFV2<0THENV2=0
4620  IF(CA%(S2,V2)AND29)<>17THEN4630:REM MELD FLAG
  SET
4625  CA%(S2,V2)=CA%(S2,V2)AND239:DS%(S2,V2)=DS%(S2
,V2)-8:S1=S2:V1=V2:GOSUB3400
4630  V2=NV+VO:IFV2>12THENV2=12
4635  IF(CA%(S2,V2)AND29)<>17THEN4645
4640  CA%(S2,V2)=CA%(S2,V2)AND239:DS%(S2,V2)=DS%(S2
,V2)-8:S1=S2:V1=V2:GOSUB3400
4645  NEXT
4650  CA%(NS,NV)=0:FL=6:SF=NS:VF=NV:GOSUB3165
4655  RETURN
4660  REM* CBM DECIDE DISCARD *
```

```
4665 MI=DS%(0,0):MA=MI:FORS=0TO3:FORV=0TO12
4670 IFDS%(S,V)<MITHENMI=DS%(S,V)
4675 IFDS%(S,V)>MATHENMA=DS%(S,V)
4680 NEXT:NEXT:ZZ=MA-MI+1:REM HAVE GOT RANGE
4685 REM NOW PICK LEAST RISK
4690 VA=2:FORS=0TO3:FORV=0TO12
4695 IF(CA%(S,V)AND13)<>1THEN4710
4700 TV=11-CA%(4,V):GOSUB4720:XX=((DS%(S,V)-MI)/ZZ
+TV/100)*PR
4705 IFXX<VATHENVA=XX:NS=S:NV=V
4710 NEXT:NEXT:CD=13*NS+NV+1
4715 RETURN
4720 REM*CHECK ADJACENT DISCARDS*
4725 PR=1:REM SET PR TO MAX
4730 FORSL=0TO3:IF(CA%(SL,V)AND192)=64THENPR=PR-0.
2
4735 NEXT
4740 IFV=0THENPR=PR-0.2:GOTO4750
4745 IF(CA%(S,V-1)AND192)=64THENPR=PR-0.2
4750 IFV=12THENPR=PR-0.2:GOTO4760
4755 IF(CA%(S,V+1)AND192)=64THENPR=PR-0.2
4760 RETURN
4765 REM** SORT OUT HAND **
4770 POKE49160,120:POKE49161,0:REM TEMP
4775 POKE49164,229:POKE49165,0:REM J/S
4780 POKE49169,175:POKE49170,0:REM PTRS
4785 POKE49173,175:POKE49174,0
4790 POKE53248,175:POKE53264,0:POKE53249,175
4795 POKE49177,0:POKE49178,0
4800 SYS49183:REM WEDGE ON
4805 REM POSITION SPRITE
4810 POKE53269,1:CX=0
4815 POKE53248,PEEK(49169):POKE53264,PEEK(49170):P
OKE53249,PEEK(49173)
4820 IFPEEK(49177)=0THEN4815
4825 XC=PEEK(53248)+256*PEEK(53264):YC=PEEK(53249)
4830 IFCX=0THENX1=XC:Y1=YC:CX=1:FORI=1TO250:NEXT:P
OKE49177,0:GOTO4815
4835 CX=0:X2=XC:Y2=YC
4840 REM*WHICH CARDS?*
4845 X1=INT((X1-24)/49.3):Y1=INT((Y1-120)/65)
4850 X2=INT((X2-24)/49.3):Y2=INT((Y2-120)/65)
4855 X1=X1+1:X2=X2+1:W1=6*Y1+X1:W2=6*Y2+X2
4860 IFW1=W2THEN4895
```

Listing continued next page

```
4865  IFW1>12ORW2>12THENCX=0:GOTO4890
4870  P%(0)=P%(W1):P%(W1)=P%(W2):P%(W2)=P%(0)
4875  PI=W2:CD=255:CF=13:GOSUB2830:REM WIPE
4880  PI=W1:CD=P%(W1):CF=13:GOSUB2830:REM SWAP
4885  PI=W2:CD=P%(W2):CF=13:GOSUB2830:REM CRDS
4890  POKE49177,0:GOTO4815
4895  POKE53269,0:SYS49208:REM WEDGE OFF
4900  RETURN
4905  REM** PICK UP CARD **
4910  POKE49160,70:POKE49161,0
4915  POKE49164,100:POKE49165,0
4920  POKE49169,70:POKE49170,0
4925  POKE49173,100:POKE49174,0
4930  POKE53248,70:POKE53264,0:POKE53249,100
4935  POKE49177,0:POKE49178,0
4940  SYS49183:REM WEDGE ON
4945  POKE53269,1
4950  POKE53248,PEEK(49169):POKE53264,PEEK(49170):P
OKE53249,PEEK(49173)
4955  IFPEEK(49177)=0THEN4950
4960  XC=PEEK(53248)+256*PEEK(53264)
4965  X1=INT((XC-24)/49.3):X1=X1+1
4970  FORI=1TO12:IFP%(I)=255THENW1=I:I=12
4975  NEXT
4980  IFX1<>6THEN5005
4985  IFD1=255THENPOKE49177,0:GOTO4950
4990  CD=D2:OF=82:PI=6:CF=13:GOSUB2830:OF=442
4995  CD=D1:D1=D2:D2=255:PI=W1:CF=13:GOSUB2830
5000  P%(W1)=CD:GOTO5035
5005  IFDP<51THEN5020
5010  M$="END OF DECK... THIS HAND IS A DRAW":NN=11
:GOSUB3050:REM END OF DECK
5015  POKE53269,0:SYS49208:GOSUB6935:GOTO1435:REM C
LEAR ARRAYS BACK TO START
5020  DC=1:OF=82:PI=1:CF=13:GOSUB2830:OF=442:DC=0
5025  PI=W1:CD=D%(DP):CF=13:GOSUB2830
5030  P%(W1)=CD:DP=DP+1
5035  POKE49177,0
5040  POKE53269,0:SYS49208
5045  RETURN
5050  REM** DISCARD **
5055  POKE49160,120:POKE49161,0
5060  POKE49164,229:POKE49165,0
5065  POKE49169,175:POKE49170,0
```

```
5070 POKE49173,175:POKE49174,0
5075 POKE53248,175:POKE53264,0:POKE53249,175
5080 POKE49177,0:POKE49178,0
5085 SYS49183:REM WEDGE ON
5090 POKE53269,1
5095 POKE53248,PEEK(49169):POKE53264,PEEK(49170):P
OKE53249,PEEK(49173)
5100 IFPEEK(49177)<1THEN5095
5105 XC=PEEK(53248)+256*PEEK(53264):YC=PEEK(53249)
5110 X1=INT((XC-24)/49.3):Y1=INT((YC-120)/65)
5115 X1=X1+1:W1=6*Y1+X1:IFW1>12THENPOKE49177,0:GOT
O5095
5120 IFP%(W1)=255THENPOKE49177,0:GOTO5095
5125 PI=W1:CD=255:CF=13:GOSUB2830:OF=82:PI=6:CD=P%
(W1):IFA$="K"ORA$="C"THENDC=1
5130 GOSUB2830:OF=442
5135 P%(W1)=255:D2=D1:D1=CD
5140 POKE49177,0:POKE53269,0:SYS49208:REM WEDGE OF
F
5145 RETURN
5150 REM*KNOCK*
5155 CC=CC-CA%(4,NV):QK$=""
5160 IF(DP<26)OR(DP>47)THENGOSUB5200:GOTO5195
5165 IFCC<5ANDDP<30THENQK$="K"
5170 QM=0:QP=0:FORSK=0TO3:FORVK=0TO12
5175 TR=(CA%(SK,SK)AND12)=0
5180 QM=QM-TR:QP=QP-TRAND((CA%(SK,VK)AND16)=16):NE
XT:NEXT
5185 IFQM<3ANDQP>0THENQK$="":REM DON'T KNOCK
5190 IFQK$="K"THENGOSUB5200
5195 RETURN
5200 KF=1:DV=NV:DS=NS
5205 RETURN
5210 REM*ERASE CARD*
5215 FORI=0TO240STEP40:FORJ=0TO4:POKEB+I+J,32:NEXT
:NEXT
5220 RETURN
5225 REM *ERASE BOX*
5230 PRINTLEFT$(DD$,2);
5235 FORI=1TO7:PRINTLEFT$(R$,10)CC$:NEXT
5240 REM *CURSOR TO TOP LEFT OF BOX*
5245 DD=2:RR=10:GOSUB5250
5250 REM *ALL PURPOSE POSITION CURSOR**
5255 PRINTLEFT$(DD$,DD)LEFT$(R$,RR);
```

Listing continued next page.

```
5260 RETURN
5265 REM** DISPLAY MESSAGE **
5270 GOSUB5225:REM CLR/POSN
5275 IFA$="G"THENPRINT"     PLAYER GOING GIN    "
5280 IFA$="K"THENPRINT"     PLAYER KNOCKING    "
5285 RETURN
5290 REM**MARK PLAYERS MELDS**
5295 POKE49160,120:POKE49161,0:REM TEMP
5300 POKE49164,229:POKE49165,0:REM J/S
5305 POKE49169,175:POKE49170,0:REM PTRS
5310 POKE49173,175:POKE49174,0
5315 POKE53248,175:POKE53264,0:POKE53249,175
5320 POKE49177,0:POKE49178,0
5325 SYS49183:REM WEDGE ON
5330 REM POSITION SPRITE
5335 POKE53269,1:LC=0:CN=1:MT=0
5340 REM** LOOP TO INPUT CARD **
5345 M$="POINT TO CARDS-PRESS TWICE TO END ":GOSUB
3090
5350 POKE53248,PEEK(49169):POKE53264,PEEK(49170):P
OKE53249,PEEK(49173)
5355 IFPEEK(49177)=0THEN5350
5360 XC=PEEK(53248)+256*PEEK(53264):YC=PEEK(53249)
5365 REM*WHICH CARDS?*
5370 X1=INT((XC-24)/49.3):Y1=INT((YC-120)/65)
5375 X1=X1+1:W1=6*Y1+X1
5380 IFW1=LCTHEN5435:REM** MELD END - EXIT **
5385 IFW1>12THEN5425
5390 IF(P%(W1)AND128)=128THEN5425
5395 CB=CA:CA=P%(W1):IFCN=1THEN5415
5400 IFCN=2THENGOSUB5445:REM*SET MT*
5405 IF(CN=2)AND(MT=0)THEN5430:REM* ERROR*
5410 IFCN>2THENGOSUB5470:IFEE=1THEN5430:REM*ERROR*
5415 P%(W1)=P%(W1)OR128:LC=W1:MD(0,MP,CN)=P%(W1)AN
D127:CN=CN+1
5420 PI=W1:CD=P%(W1):DC=2:CF=CV%(MP):GOSUB2830:REM
 CHANGE FRAME COL
5425 POKE49177,0:GOTO5350:REM** NEXT CARD **
5430 CA=CB:GOTO5425:REM ** EXIT ERROR **
5435 POKE53269,0:SYS49208:REM WEDGE OFF
5440 RETURN
5445 REM* SET MT*
5450 IF(CA=CB+1)THENMT=1
5455 IF(CA=CB-1)THENMT=2
```

```
5460 IF(CA-13*INT(CA/13)=CB-13*INT(CB/13))THENMT=3
5465 RETURN
5470 EE=1:REM** CHECK TYPE**
5475 IFMT=1ANDCA=CB+1THENEE=0
5480 IFMT=2ANDCA=CB-1THENEE=0
5485 IFMT=3AND((CA-13*INT(CA/13)=CB-13*INT(CB/13))
)THENEE=0
5490 RETURN
5495 GETJU$:IFJU$<>""THEN5495
5500 M$="ANOTHER MELD (Y/N - S START AGAIN)? ":GOS
UB3090
5505 GETC$:IFC$<>"Y"ANDC$<>"N"ANDC$<>"S"THEN5505
5510 RETURN
5515 FOR HP=1TO12
5520 IF(P%(HP)AND128)=0THEN5540
5525 IFP%(HP)=255THEN5540
5530 PI=HP:CID=P%(HP):DC=2:CF=13:GOSUB2830:REM CHAN
GE FRAME COL
5535 P%(HP)=P%(HP)AND127
5540 NEXT
5545 RETURN
5550 REM** EXAMINE MELDS ***
5555 FO$="BAD":HT=0:REM NB OF CARDS
5560 FL$="GOOD":PT=0:REM POINTS TOTAL
5565 FORME=1TO3:REM CHECK MELD LENGTH
5570 IF(MD(LY,ME,0)<3)AND(MD(LY,ME,0)>0)THENFL$="B
AD"
5575 HT=HT+MD(LY,ME,0)
5580 NEXT
5585 HT=HT+MD(LY,4,0):REM ADD UNMELDED CDS
5590 IFHT=10THENFO$="GOOD"
5595 IF(FO$="BAD")OR(FL$="BAD")THEN5730:REM  EXIT
WHOLE ROUTINE
5600 REM*CALCULATE POINTS TOTAL*
5605 FORVV=1TOMD(LY,4,0)
5610 RE=MD(LY,4,VV)AND127:RE=(RE-1)-13*INT((RE-1)/
13):PT=PT+CA%(4,RE)
5615 NEXT
5620 REM*FIND POSSIBLE LAYOFFS FOR CBM*
5625 FORME=1TO3
5630 IFMD(LY,ME,0)=0THENME=3:GOTO5725:REM NO MELDS
 LEFT EXIT LOOP
5635 DI=MD(LY,ME,1)-MD(LY,ME,2):MO=DI-13*INT(DI/13
)
```

Listing continued next page

```
5640 IF(ABS(DI)>1)AND(MO<>0)THENPRINT"ERROR IN MD
ARRAY":STOP
5645 IFABS(DI)=1THEN5690:REM ROW MELD
5650 REM*COL MELD LAYOFF-IF ANY*
5655 Z2=0:TY=MD(LY,ME,1):TY=TY-13*INT(TY/13):IFTY=
0THENTY=13
5660 TY=4*TY+6*13
5665 FORVV=1TO4
5670 TY=TY-MD(LY,ME,VV)
5675 NEXT
5680 Z1=TY:LAY%(ME,0)=1:LAY%(ME,1)=Z1:LAY%(ME,2)=Z
2
5685 GOTO5725:REM NEXT MELD
5690 REM*ROW MELD LAYOFFS*
5695 IFDI<0THENZ1=MD(LY,ME,1)-1:Z2=MD(LY,ME,MD(LY,
ME,0))+1:REM ASCENDING MELD
5700 IFDI>0THENZ1=MD(LY,ME,1)+1:Z2=MD(LY,ME,MD(LY,
ME,0))-1:REM DESCENDING MELD
5705 TY=MD(LY,ME,1)-1
5710 IFINT((Z1-1)/13)<>INT(TY/13)THENZ1=0
5715 IFINT((Z2-1)/13)<>INT(TY/13)THENZ2=0
5720 LAY%(ME,1)=Z1:LAY%(ME,2)=Z2:LAY%(ME,0)=2:REM
ROW MELD
5725 NEXTME
5730 RETURN
5735 REM ARRAY LAY%() CONTAINS LAYOFFS
5740 REM PT IS TOTAL POINTS UNMELDED CARDS
5745 REM** DISPLAY PLAYERS MELDS **
5750 PRINTLEFT$(DD$,13)SPC(17)"?PLAYER?";
5755 DD=13:RR=1:FORMP=1TO3
5760 ML=MD(0,MP,0):IFML=0THENMP=3:GOTO5800
5765 DD=DD+2:GOSUB5250
5770 FORCN=1TOML
5775 CD=MD(0,MP,CN)AND127:S=INT((CD-1)/13):V=CD-13
*S
5780 OV$="  "+VV$(V)+SS$(S)
5785 PRINTRIGHT$(OV$,LEN(VV$(V))+3);
5790 IFCN=5THENDD=DD+1:GOSUB5250:DD=DD-1
5795 NEXT
5800 NEXT
5805 DD=15:RR=23:GOSUB5250
5810 ML=MD(0,4,0):IFML=0THEN5845
5815 FORCN=1TOML
5820 CD=MD(0,4,CN)AND127:S=INT((CD-1)/13):V=CD-13*
```

Listing continued next page

```
S
5825 OV$="   "+VV$(V)+SS$(S)
5830 PRINTRIGHT$(OV$,LEN(VV$(V))+3);
5835 IFCN=5THENDD=DD+1:GOSUB5250
5840 NEXT
5845 RETURN
5850 REM** MARK COMPUTERS MELDS **
5855 MP=0:FORS=0TO3:FORV=0TO12
5860  IF(CA%(S,V)AND1)=0THEN5885:REM NOT IN HAND
5865  IF(CA%(S,V)AND2)=2THEN5885:REM ALREADY DONE
5870  IF(CA%(S,V)AND4)=4THENGOSUB5900:GOTO5885:REM
DO ROW MELD
5875  IF(CA%(S,V)AND8)=8THENGOSUB5940:GOTO5885:REM
DO COL MELD
5880  GOSUB5975:REM NOT MELDED
5885 NEXT
5890 NEXT
5895 RETURN
5900 REM** DO ROW MELD **
5905 CN=0:MP=MP+1
5910 IFV+CN>12THEN5930
5915 IF(CA%(S,V+CN)AND4)=0THEN5930:REM END OF MELD
5920 CD=13*S+V+CN+1:MD(1,MP,CN+1)=CD:CA%(S,V+CN)=C
A%(S,V+CN)OR2
5925 CN=CN+1:GOTO5910:REM NEXT CARD
5930 MD(1,MP,0)=CN
5935 RETURN
5940 REM** DO COL MELD **
5945 ML=0:MP=MP+1:FORCN=0TO3
5950  IF(CA%(CN,V)AND8)=0THEN5960:REM NOT IN MELD
5955  CD=13*CN+V+1:MD(1,MP,ML+1)=CD:CA%(CN,V)=CA%(C
N,V)OR2:ML=ML+1
5960 NEXT
5965 MD(1,MP,0)=ML
5970 RETURN
5975 REM** DO UNMELDED CARD **
5980 CD=13*S+V+1:MD(1,4,MD(1,4,0)+1)=CD:MD(1,4,0)=
MD(1,4,0)+1
5985 RETURN
5990 REM** DISPLAY COMPUTERS MELDS **
5995 PRINT"▩▩"SPC(4)"MELDS"SPC(7)"▩COMPUTER▆"SPC(4
)"UNMELDED"
6000 DD=2:RR=1:FORMP=1TO3
6005 ML=MD(1,MP,0):IFML=0THENMP=3:GOTO6045
```

```
6010 DD=DD+2:GOSUB5250
6015 FORCN=1TOML
6020 CD=MD(1,MP,CN)AND127:S=INT((CD-1)/13):V=CD-13
*S
6025 OV$="   "+VV$(V)+SS$(S)
6030 PRINTRIGHT$(OV$,LEN(VV$(V))+3);
6035 IFCN=5THENDD=DD+1:GOSUB5250:DD=DD-1
6040 NEXT
6045 NEXT
6050 ML=MD(1,4,0):IFML=0THEN6090
6055 DD=4:RR=23:GOSUB5250
6060 FORCN=1TOML
6065 CD=MD(1,4,CN)AND127:S=INT((CD-1)/13):V=CD-13*
S
6070 OV$="   "+VV$(V)+SS$(S)
6075 PRINTRIGHT$(OV$,LEN(VV$(V))+3);
6080 IFCN=5THENDD=DD+1:GOSUB5250
6085 NEXT
6090 RETURN
6095 REM** BIG GREY BOX **
6100 PRINT""
6105 FORL=0TO39:POKESC+L,160:POKECO+L,15:NEXT
6110 FORM=1TO23
6115 L=0:POKESC+40*M+L,160:POKECO+40*M+L,15
6120 L=39:POKESC+40*M+L,160:POKECO+40*M+L,15
6125 NEXT
6130 FORL=0TO39:POKESC+24*40+L,160:POKECO+24*40+L,
15:NEXT
6135 FORL=0TO39:POKESC+11*40+L,160:POKECO+11*40+L,
15:NEXT
6140 RETURN
6145 REM** COMPUTER LAY OFF **
6150 MF=0
6155 LY=0:LX=1:AF$="N":ML=MD(1,4,0):IFML=0THEN6215
6160 FORCN=1TOML:CD=MD(1,4,CN):FD=0
6165 REM**IS CD IN LAY% ?**
6170 FORLP=1TO3
6175 IFLAY%(LP,0)=0THENLP=3:GOTO6200
6180 FORI=1TO2
6185 IF(CD=LAY%(LP,I))AND(FD<LAY%(LP,0))THENL1=LP:
I1=I:FD=LAY%(LP,0)
6190 IFFD<>0THENAF$="Y"
6195 NEXT
6200 NEXTLP
```

```
6205 IFFD<>0THENGOSUB6265:MF=1:REM MATCH FOUND
6210 NEXTCN
6215 IFAF$="N"ANDMF=1THENM$="COMPUTER LAYING OFF":
NN=11:GOSUB3050
6220 IFAF$="N"THENRETURN
6225 REM**LOOK FOR 0'S AND CLOSE UP**
6230 CN=1
6235 IF(MD(1,4,CN)=0)AND(CN<=ML)THENGOSUB6250:GOTO
6235
6240 CN=CN+1:IFCN<=MLTHEN6235
6245 MD(1,4,0)=ML:GOTO6155:REM NEXT PASS
6250 REM**CLOSE UP ARRAY**
6255 FORCX=CNTOML-1:MD(1,4,CX)=MD(1,4,CX+1):NEXT:M
L=ML-1
6260 RETURN
6265 REM**MATCH FOUND**
6270 IFFD=2THEN6290:REM ROW MELD
6275 REM ** COL MELD **
6280 MD(LY,L1,0)=MD(LY,L1,0)+1:MD(LY,L1,4)=CD
6285 GOTO6350:REM DONE
6290 REM** ROW MELD **
6295 I3=2*I1-3
6300 IFLAY%(L1,1)>LAY%(L1,2)THENI3=-I3:REM DESCEND
ING
6305 Z1=LAY%(L1,I1):Z2=Z1+I3
6310 LAY%(L1,I1)=Z1+(INT(Z1/13)=INT(Z2/13))*SGN(-I
3)
6315 MD(LY,L1,0)=MD(LY,L1,0)+1
6320 CV=MD(LY,L1,0)
6325 IFI1=2THENMD(LY,L1,CV)=CD:GOTO6350
6330 FORI2=CVTO1STEP-1
6335 MD(LY,L1,I2)=MD(LY,L1,I2-1)
6340 NEXT
6345 MD(LY,L1,1)=CD
6350 MD(LX,4,CN)=0
6355 RETURN
6360 REM **BLOCK - BN  COLOR -CC**
6365 DD=2+2*BN:RR=17:GOSUB5250
6370 PRINTCHR$(CC)TA$
6375 DD=3+2*BN:RR=17:GOSUB5250
6380 PRINTCHR$(CC)BA$CHR$(156)
6385 RETURN
6390 REM ** POINTER BLOCKS **
6395 J=9
```

Listing continued next page

```
6400 FORI=1TO3:IFMD(1,I,0)>0THENJ=J+1
6405 NEXT
6410 FORBN=1TOJ:CC=CC%(BN):GOSUB6360:NEXT
6415 RETURN
6420 REM**CLEAR TOP-HALF SCREEN**
6425 PRINTCHR$(19);:FORL=0TO8:PRINTW$;:NEXT
6430 RETURN
6435 REM** PLAYER LAY OFF **
6440 POKE49160,120:POKE49161,0:REM TEMP
6445 POKE49164,229:POKE49165,0:REM J/S
6450 POKE49169,175:POKE49170,0:REM PTRS
6455 POKE49173,175:POKE49174,0
6460 POKE53248,175:POKE53264,0:POKE53249,175
6465 POKE49177,0:POKE49178,0
6470 SYS49183:REM WEDGE ON
6475 M$="POINT TO CARD ":GOSUB3090
6480 POKE53269,1
6485 POKE53248,PEEK(49169):POKE53264,PEEK(49170):P
OKE53249,PEEK(49173)
6490 IFPEEK(49177)=0THEN6485
6495 XC=PEEK(53248)+256*PEEK(53264):YC=PEEK(53249)
6500 X1=XC:Y1=YC:FORI=1TO350:NEXT:POKE49177,0
6505 REM*WHICH CARDS?*
6510 X1=INT((X1-24)/49.3):Y1=INT((Y1-120)/65)
6515 X1=X1+1:W1=6*Y1+X1
6520 PI=W1:CD=P%(W1):DC=2:CF=0:GOSUB2830:REM CHANG
E FRAME COLOUR
6525 M$="POINT TO MELD ARROW BLOCK ":GOSUB3090
6530 POKE49160,50:REM UPPER HALF OF SCREEN
6535 POKE49177,0:REM CLEAR FIRE BUTTON
6540 POKE53248,PEEK(49169):POKE53264,PEEK(49170):P
OKE53249,PEEK(49173)
6545 IFPEEK(49177)=0THEN6540
6550 XC=PEEK(53248)+256*PEEK(53264):YC=PEEK(53249)
6555 IFYC<560RYC>104THENPOKE49177,0:GOTO6540
6560 IFXC<1580RXC>204THENPOKE49177,0:GOTO6540
6565 BN=INT((YC-56)/16)+1:IFBN>3THENBN=3
6570 POKE53269,0:SYS49208:REM WEDGE OFF
6575 CC=144:GOSUB6360:REM CHANGE BLOCK COLOR
6580 GETJU$:IFJU$<>""THEN6580
6585 M$="CORRECT (Y/N)?":GOSUB3090
6590 GETC$:IFC$<>"Y"ANDC$<>"N"THEN6590
6595 IFC$="Y"THEN6615
6600 PI=W1:CD=P%(W1):DC=2:CF=13:GOSUB2830:REM CHAN
```

```
6E FRAME COLOUR BACK
6605 CC=CC%(BN):GOSUB6360:REM RECOLOR BLOCK
6610 GOTO6435: REM START AGAIN
6615 REM ADD CARD TO MELD IF VALID
6620 I1=0
6625 FORLO=1TO2
6630 IFCD=LAY%(BN,LO)THENI1=LO
6635 NEXT
6640 IFI1=0THENCD=P%(W1):DC=2:CF=13:GOSUB2830:CC=C
CX(BN):GOSUB6360:GOTO6695
6645 ML=MD(0,4,0)
6650 FORLO=1TOML
6655 IFCD=MD(0,4,LO)THENCN=LO:LO=ML
6660 NEXT
6665 FD=LAY%(BN,0):L1=BN:LY=1:LX=9:GOSUB6265
6670 FORCX=CNTOML-1
6675 MD(0,4,CX)=MD(0,4,CX+1)
6680 NEXT
6685 MD(0,4,0)=ML-1
6690 PI=W1:P%(W1)=255:CD=255:DC=1:GOSUB2830:REM DE
LETE CARD
6695 RETURN
6700 REM**DISPLAY COUNTS**
6705 DD=5:RR=17:GOSUB5250:PRINTCHR$(18)"COUNT "CHR
$(146)
6710 DD=7:RR=18:GOSUB5250:PRINTPC
6715 DD=16:RR=17:GOSUB5250:PRINTCHR$(18)"COUNT "CH
R$(146)
6720 DD=19:RR=18:GOSUB5250:PRINTPP
6725 RETURN
6730 REM**DISPLAY END OF HAND***
6735 PRINTCHR$(147):POKE53281,6:REM SCR BCKGRD COL
6740 DD=1:RR=13:GOSUB5250:PRINTCHR$(158)"◤
    ◥"
6745 DD=2:RR=13:GOSUB5250:PRINT"◢ ▉GAME SO FAR◣ ▉"
6750 DD=3:RR=13:GOSUB5250:PRINT"◥◣         ▉"
6755 DD=5:RR=12:GOSUB5250:PRINT"HANDS PLAYED:";PG+
CG
6760 DD=7:RR=4:GOSUB5250:PRINTWIN$+" WON LAST HAND
:";PV;" POINTS"
6765 DD=9:RR=5:GOSUB5250:PRINT"◢PLAYER"
6770 DD=9:RR=25:GOSUB5250:PRINT" ◢COMPUTER"
6775 DD=11:RR=5:GOSUB5250:PRINT"HANDS WON"PG
6780 DD=11:RR=25:GOSUB5250:PRINT"HANDS WON"CG
```

Listing continued next page

```
6785 DD=12:RR=5:GOSUB5250:PRINT"POINTS"PS
6790 DD=12:RR=25:GOSUB5250:PRINT"POINTS"CS
6795 DD=15:RR=12:GOSUB5250:PRINTCHR$(158)"▧
     ▜"
6800 DD=16:RR=12:GOSUB5250:PRINT"▧ ▉PREVIOUS GAMES
▉"
6805 DD=17:RR=12:GOSUB5250:PRINT"▜▧                    ▉
▛"
6810 DD=19:RR=3:GOSUB5250:PRINT"POINTS TOTAL"AP
6815 DD=19:RR=23:GOSUB5250:PRINT"POINTS TOTAL"AC
6820 DD=22:RR=4:GOSUB5250:PRINT"▧GIN BONUS = 20
UNDERKNOCK = 10"
6825 DD=23:RR=4:GOSUB5250:PRINT"▧ GAME BONUS = 100
  POINTS AND    ";
6830 DD=24:RR=4:GOSUB5250:PRINT"▧  20 POINTS FOR E
ACH HAND WON    "
6835 DD=25:RR=14:GOSUB5250:PRINT"▧▉HIT ANY KEY";
6840 RETURN
6845 REM**END OF GAME DISPLAY**
6850 PRINTCHR$(147):POKE53281,7:PRINTCHR$(147):REM
  SCR BCKGRD COL
6855 DD=1:RR=14:GOSUB5250:PRINTCHR$(144)"▧
     ▜"
6860 DD=2:RR=14:GOSUB5250:PRINT"▧ ▉GIN RUMMY▧ ▉"
6865 DD=3:RR=14:GOSUB5250:PRINT"▜▧          ▛"
6870 DD=5:RR=13:GOSUB5250:PRINTCHR$(28)"▧
     ▜"
6875 DD=6:RR=13:GOSUB5250:PRINT"▧ ▉END OF GAME▧ ▉"
6880 DD=7:RR=13:GOSUB5250:PRINT"▜▧          ▛"
6885 DD=9:RR=12:GOSUB5250:PRINT"HANDS PLAYED:";HG
6890 DD=11:RR=17:GOSUB5250:PRINT"▧SCORES▉"
6895 DD=13:RR=5:GOSUB5250:PRINT"▧PLAYER"
6900 DD=13:RR=25:GOSUB5250:PRINT"▧COMPUTER"
6905 DD=15:RR=2:GOSUB5250:PRINT"THIS GAME"PS
6910 DD=15:RR=22:GOSUB5250:PRINT"THIS GAME"CS
6915 DD=16:RR=2:GOSUB5250:PRINT"RUNNING TOTAL"AP
6920 DD=16:RR=22:GOSUB5250:PRINT"RUNNING TOTAL"AC
6925 DD=22:RR=3:GOSUB5250:PRINT"WOULD YOU LIKE ANO
THER GAME? (Y/N)"
6930 RETURN
6935 REM** CLEAR ARRAYS FOR NEXT HAND**
6940 DD=25:RR=14:GOSUB5250:PRINT"▧▉PLEASE WAIT▉▉";
6945 FORI=0TO3:FORJ=0TO12:CA%(I,J)=0:DS%(I,J)=0:NE
XT:NEXT
```

Listing continued next page

```
6950 FORI=0TO1:FORJ=1TO4:FORK=0TO10:MD(I,J,K)=0:NE
XT:NEXT:NEXT
6955 FORI=1TO3:FORJ=0TO2:LAY%(I,J)=0:NEXT:NEXT
6960 D1=255:D2=255:KF=0
6965 RETURN
6970 REM*** SET UP TITLE PAGE ****
6975 PRINTCHR$(147)CHR$(142):POKE53281,1:POKE53280
,1
6980 PRINTSPC(5)"    "TAB(18)"  "TAB(25)"
6985 PRINTSPC(5)"    "TAB(18)"  "TAB(25)"
6990 PRINTSPC(5)"    "TAB(18)"  "TAB(25)"
6995 PRINTSPC(5)"    "TAB(18)"  "TAB(25)"
7000 PRINTSPC(5)"    "TAB(18)"  "TAB(25)"
7005 PRINTSPC(5)"    "TAB(18)"  "TAB(25)"
7010 PRINTSPC(5)"    "TAB(18)"  "TAB(25)"
7015 PRINTSPC(5)"    "TAB(18)"  "TAB(25)"
7020 PRINT
7025 PRINTSPC(1)"
7030 PRINTSPC(1)"
7035 PRINTSPC(1)"
7040 PRINTSPC(1)"
7045 PRINTSPC(1)"
7050 PRINTSPC(1)"    "CHR$(13)
7055 PRINTCHR$(13)SPC(19)"BY"CHR$(13)
7060 PRINTSPC(4)"MARY RADCLIFFE"CHR$(13)
7065 PRINTSPC(9)"GRAHAM CARPENTER"CHR$(13)
7070 PRINTSPC(18)"ANTONIA JONES";
7075 RETURN
7080 REM**COMMENTS PAGE**
7085 PRINTCHR$(147):POKE53281,6:PRINTCHR$(147)CHR$
```

```
(14):REM SCR BCKGRD COL/LCASE
7090 PRINTSPC(15)"⬛-⬛OMMENTS⬛-"
7095 PRINT:PRINT
7100 PRINT"   OE HAVE FOLLOWED THE RULES GIVEN IN"
CHR$(13)
7105 PRINTSPC(5)"⬛OAME ON ⬛ARDS⬛ (1965 ED)" CHR$
(13)
7110 PRINTSPC(9)"AS CLOSELY AS POSSIBLE":PRINT:PRI
NT:PRINT
7115 PRINTSPC(6)"!HE PROGRAM ⬛⬛⬛ /T! -!⬛!"
7120 DD=17:RR=4:GOSUB5250:PPINT"⬛!IN BONUS = 20 :
.NDERKNOCK = 10"
7125 DD=18:RR=4:GOSUB5250:PRINT"⬛ !AME BONUS = 10
0 POINTS AND    ";
7130 DD=19:RR=4:GOSUB5250:PPINT"⬛  20 POINTS FOR E
ACH HAND WON    "
7135 GETJU$:IFJU$<>""THEN7135
7140 DD=25:RR=14:GOSUB5250:PRINT"⬛!IT ANY KEY";
7145 GETC$:IFC$=""THEN7145
7150 RETURN
```

```
1000 REM ** LOAD BASIC LOADER **
1010 DATA160,2,177,71,141,65,195,200
1020 DATA177,71,141,66,195,200,177,71
1030 DATA141,67,195,169,1,174,64,195
1040 DATA160,1,32,186,255,173,65,195
1050 DATA174,66,195,172,67,195,32,189
1060 DATA255,169,0,162,255,160,255,32
1070 DATA213,255,96
1080 DATA7124:REM*CHECKSUM*
1090 CC=0
1100 FORI=49988TO50038
1110 READX:CC=CC+X:POKEI,X
1120 NEXT
1130 READX:IFCC<>XTHENPRINT"CHECKSUM ERROR"
```

```
1000 REM** TEST LOAD**
1010 DV=8:REM DISK
1020 POKE49984,DV
1030 INPUT"FILENAME";A$
1040 SYS49988:REM CALL ROUTINE
1050 END
```

```
1000 REM ** SAVE BASIC LOADER **
1010 DATA160,2,177,71,141,133,195,200
1020 DATA177,71,141,134,195,200,177,71
1030 DATA141,135,195,173,128,195,133
1040 DATA251,173,129,195,133,252,169,1
1050 DATA174,132,195,160,1,32,186,255
1060 DATA173,133,195,174,134,195,172
1070 DATA135,195,32,189,255,169,251,174
1080 DATA130,195,172,131,195,32,216,255
1090 DATA96
1100 DATA9781:REM*CHECKSUM*
1110 CC=0
1120 FOR I=50056TO50118
1130 READX:CC=CC+X:POKEI,X
1140 NEXT
1150 READX:IFCC<>XTHENPRINT"CHECKSUM ERROR"
```

```
1000 REM** TEST SAVE **
1010 DV=8:POKE50052,DV:REM DISK
1020 ST=50048:ED=50116
1030 SH=INT(SA/256):SL=SA-256*SH:REM START
1040 EH=INT(ED/256):EL=ED-256*EH:REM END
1050 POKE50048,SL:POKE50049,SH
1060 POKE50050,EL:POKE50051,EH
1070 INPUT"FILENAME";B$
1080 SYS50056
1090 END
```

```
1000 REM ** COPY BASIC LOADER **
1010 DATA173,210,194,205,208,194,173
1020 DATA211,194,237,209,194,144,78,173
1030 DATA208,194,133,251,173,209,194
1040 DATA133,252,173,212,194,133,253
1050 DATA173,213,194,133,254,173,210
1060 DATA194,133,247,173,211,194,133
1070 DATA248,173,214,194,133,249,160,0
1080 DATA165,247,197,251,165,248,229
1090 DATA252,144,31,177,251,166,249,240
1100 DATA8,133,250,177,253,145,251,165
1110 DATA250,145,253,230,251,208,2,230
1120 DATA252,230,253,208,2,230,254,76
1130 DATA10,195,96
1140 DATA17284:REM*CHECKSUM*
1150 CC=0
1160 FORI=49879TO49971
1170 READX:CC=CC+X:POKEI,X
1180 NEXT
1190 READX:IFCC<>XTHENPRINT"CHECKSUM ERROR"
```

```
1000 REM ** TEST COPY ROUTINE **
1010 FORI=7168TO7680
1020 POKEI,0:REM BLOCK OF 0S
1030 POKEI+1024,255:REM BLOCK OF 255S
1040 NEXT
1050 SH=INT(7168/256):SL=7168AND255:REM START ADDR
1060 EH=INT(7680/256):EL=7680AND255:REM END ADDR
1070 TH=INT(8192/256):TL=8192AND255:REM TO ADDR
1080 POKE49872,SL:POKE49873,SH
1090 POKE49874,EL:POKE49875,EH
1100 POKE49876,TL:POKE49877,TH
1110 POKE49878,0:REM COPY/SWAP
1120 SYS49879:CC=0:REM CALL ROUTINE
1130 FORI=7168TO7680
1140 CC=CC+PEEK(I+1024):REM CHECK DONE
1150 NEXT
1160 PRINTCC
```

```
1000 REM ** CLOCK BASIC LOADER **
1010 DATA173,166,2,240,10,169,128,13,14
1020 DATA221,141,14,221,48,8,169,127,45
1030 DATA14,221,141,14,221,169,127,45
1040 DATA15,221,141,15,221,173,208,195
1050 DATA41,128,141,208,195,173,209,195
1060 DATA32,28,197,13,208,195,141,11
1070 DATA221,173,210,195,32,28,197,141
1080 DATA10,221,173,211,195,32,28,197
1090 DATA141,9,221,169,0,141,8,221,120
1100 DATA173,20,3,141,214,195,173,21,3
1110 DATA141,215,195,169,76,141,20,3
1120 DATA169,196,141,21,3,88,96,120,173
1130 DATA214,195,141,20,3,173,215,195
1140 DATA141,21,3,88,96,173,216,195,201
1150 DATA6,240,3,76,8,197,169,255,141
1160 DATA216,195,173,213,195,240,243
1170 DATA173,11,221,170,41,128,208,5
1180 DATA169,1,76,111,196,169,16,141,38
1190 DATA4,173,212,195,141,38,216,169
1200 DATA13,141,39,4,173,212,195,141,39
1210 DATA216,138,41,16,32,14,197,141,28
1220 DATA4,173,212,195,141,28,216,138
1230 DATA32,22,197,141,29,4,173,212,195
1240 DATA141,29,216,169,58,141,30,4,173
1250 DATA212,195,141,30,216,173,10,221
1260 DATA170,32,14,197,141,31,4,173,212
1270 DATA195,141,31,216,138,32,22,197
1280 DATA141,32,4,173,212,195,141,32
1290 DATA216,169,47,141,33,4,173,212
1300 DATA195,141,33,216,173,9,221,170
1310 DATA32,14,197,141,34,4,173,212,195
1320 DATA141,34,216,138,32,22,197,141
1330 DATA35,4,173,212,195,141,35,216
1340 DATA169,46,141,36,4,173,212,195
1350 DATA141,36,216,173,8,221,105,48
1360 DATA141,37,4,173,212,195,141,37
1370 DATA216,238,216,195,103,214,195,74
1380 DATA74,74,74,24,105,48,96,41,15,24
1390 DATA105,48,96,160,255,56,200,233
1400 DATA10,176,251,105,10,141,217,195
1410 DATA152,10,10,10,10,13,217,195,96
1420 DATA42131 :REM*CHECKSUM*
1430 CC=0
```

```
1440 FORI=50138TO50481
1450 READX:CC=CC+X:POKEI,X
1460 NEXT
1470 READX:IFCC<>XTHENPRINT"CHECKSUM ERROR"
```

```
1000 REM** TEST CLOCK **
1010 POKE50128,128:REM AM/PM
1020 POKE50132,8:REM COLOUR
1030 POKE50133,1:REM DISPLAY
1040 POKE50129,4:REM HOURS
1050 POKE50130,30:REM MINUTES
1060 POKE50131,0:REM SECONDS
1070 SYS50138:REM CALL ROUTINE
```

```
1000 REM ** CHARGET BASIC LOADER **
1010 DATA76,70,197,76,92,197,162,2,189
1020 DATA67,197,149,124,202,16,248,96
1030 DATA162,2,189,171,227,149,124,202
1040 DATA16,248,96,133,251,134,252,186
1050 DATA189,1,1,201,140,208,13,189,2,1
1060 DATA201,164,208,6,165,251,201,95
1070 DATA240,14,165,251,166,252,201,58
1080 DATA176,3,76,128,0,76,138,0,165,45
1090 DATA166,46,56,229,43,176,1,202,133
1100 DATA251,138,56,229,44,166,251,32
1110 DATA205,189,169,167,160,197,32,30
1120 DATA171,32,115,0,208,251,76,121,0
1130 DATA32,66,89,84,69,83,13,13,82,69
1140 DATA65,68,89,46,13,0
1150 DATA14315:REM*CHECKSUM*
1160 CC=0
1170 FORI=50496TO50614
1180 READX:CC=CC+X:POKEI,X
1190 NEXT
1200 READX:IFCC<>XTHENPRINT"CHECKSUM ERROR"
```

```
1000 REM ** PARCOMS BASIC LOADER **
1010 DATA173,196,197,208,84,169,0,141,3
1020 DATA221,169,16,141,13,221,173,2
1030 DATA221,9,4,141,2,221,173,0,221,9
1040 DATA4,141,0,221,173,192,197,133
1050 DATA251,173,193,197,133,252,173
1060 DATA194,197,197,251,173,195,197
1070 DATA229,252,144,81,173,0,221,41
1080 DATA252,141,0,221,9,4,141,0,221
1090 DATA160,0,169,16,44,13,221,240,251
1100 DATA173,1,221,145,251,230,251,208
1110 DATA213,230,252,76,238,197,169,255
1120 DATA141,3,221,169,16,141,13,221
1130 DATA173,194,197,197,251,173,195
1140 DATA197,229,252,144,23,160,0,169
1150 DATA16,44,13,221,240,251,177,251
1160 DATA141,1,221,230,251,208,226,230
1170 DATA252,76,40,198,96
1180 DATA20181:REM*CHECKSUM*
1190 CC=0
1200 FORI=50629TO50763
1210 READX:CC=CC+X:POKEI,X
1220 NEXT
1230 READX:IFCC<>XTHENPRINT"CHECKSUM ERROR"
```

```
1000 REM ** PARAWEDGE BASIC LOADER **
1010 DATA173,84,198,208,61,169,0,141,3
1020 DATA221,169,144,141,13,221,173,2
1030 DATA221,9,4,141,2,221,173,0,221,9
1040 DATA4,141,0,221,173,80,198,133,251
1050 DATA173,81,198,133,252,173,24,3
1060 DATA141,85,198,173,25,3,141,86,198
1070 DATA120,169,188,141,24,3,169,198
1080 DATA141,25,3,88,96,169,255,141,3
1090 DATA221,169,144,141,13,221,173,24
1100 DATA3,141,85,198,173,25,3,141,86
1110 DATA198,120,169,234,141,24,3,169
1120 DATA198,141,25,3,88,96,169,144,44
1130 DATA13,221,240,36,173,1,221,145
1140 DATA251,230,251,208,2,230,252,173
1150 DATA82,198,197,251,173,83,198,229
1160 DATA252,144,49,173,0,221,41,252
1170 DATA141,0,221,9,4,141,0,221,108,85
1180 DATA198,169,144,44,13,221,240,246
1190 DATA177,251,141,1,221,230,251,208
1200 DATA2,230,252,173,82,198,197,251
1210 DATA173,83,198,229,252,144,3,108
1220 DATA85,198,120,173,85,198,141,24,3
1230 DATA173,86,198,141,25,3,88,108,24
1240 DATA3
1250 DATA25596:REM*CHECKSUM*
1260 CC=0
1270 FORI=50775TO50971
1280 READX:CC=CC+X:POKEI,X
1290 NEXT
1300 READX:IFCC<>XTHENPRINT"CHECKSUM ERROR"
```

```
1000 REM** 2BYTJOY BASIC LOADER **
1010 DATA120,173,20,3,141,29,192,173,21
1020 DATA3,141,30,192,169,71,141,20,3
1030 DATA169,192,141,21,3,88,96,120,173
1040 DATA29,192,141,20,3,173,30,192,141
1050 DATA21,3,88,96,173,27,192,205,16
1060 DATA192,240,3,76,65,193,169,255
1070 DATA141,27,192,162,0,160,0,185,2
1080 DATA220,141,28,192,169,224,153,2
1090 DATA220,185,0,220,72,173,28,192
1100 DATA153,2,220,189,8,192,221,21,192
1110 DATA189,9,192,253,22,192,144,18
1120 DATA189,8,192,157,21,192,189,9,192
1130 DATA157,22,192,104,74,72,76,162
1140 DATA192,104,74,72,176,13,222,21
1150 DATA192,189,21,192,201,255,208,3
1160 DATA222,22,192,189,21,192,221,12
1170 DATA192,189,22,192,253,13,192,144
1180 DATA18,189,12,192,157,21,192,189
1190 DATA13,192,157,22,192,104,74,72,76
1200 DATA207,192,104,74,72,176,8,254,21
1210 DATA192,208,3,254,22,192,189,0,192
1220 DATA221,17,192,189,1,192,253,18
1230 DATA192,144,18,189,0,192,157,17
1240 DATA192,189,1,192,157,18,192,104
1250 DATA74,72,76,1,193,104,74,72,176
1260 DATA13,222,17,192,189,17,192,201
1270 DATA255,208,3,222,18,192,189,17
1280 DATA192,221,4,192,189,18,192,253,5
1290 DATA192,144,18,189,4,192,157,17
1300 DATA192,189,5,192,157,18,192,104
1310 DATA74,72,76,46,193,104,74,72,176
1320 DATA8,254,17,192,208,3,254,18,192
1330 DATA104,74,176,5,169,1,153,25,192
1340 DATA200,232,232,224,4,240,3,76,91
1350 DATA192,238,27,192,108,29,192
1360 DATA35994:REM*CHECKSUM*
1370 CC=0
1380 FORI=49183 TO 49478
1390 READX:CC=CC+X:POKEI,X
1400 NEXT
1410 READX:IFCC<>XTHEN PRINT"CHECKSUM ERROR"
```

```
1000 REM***   TEST 2BYTJOY     ***
1010 REM**INITIALISE M/C ROUTINE**
1020 POKE49152,0:POKE49153,0:REM XMIN2
1030 POKE49154,0:POKE49155,0:REM XMIN1
1040 POKE49156,39:POKE49157,0:REM XMAX2
1050 POKE49158,39:POKE49159,0:REM XMAX1
1060 POKE49160,0:POKE49161,0:REM YMIN2
1070 POKE49162,0:POKE49163,0:REM YMIN1
1080 POKE49164,24:POKE49165,0:REM YMAX2
1090 POKE49166,24:POKE49167,0:REM YMAX1
1100 POKE49168,4:REM READ RATE
1110 POKE49177,0:POKE49178,0:REM CLEAR FIRE
1120 SC=1024:CO=55296:REM SRC/COL BASE
1130 POKE49169,0:POKE49170,0:REM DX2
1140 POKE49173,0:POKE49174,0:REM DY2
1150 POKE49171,39:POKE49172,0:REM DX1
1160 POKE49175,24:POKE49176,0:REM DY1
1170 SYS49183:REM INSERT WEDGE
1180 PRINTCHR$(147):REM CLEAR SCREEN
1190 REM***MAIN LOOP***
1200 X2=PEEK(49169)+256*PEEK(49170):REM X2 VAL
1210 Y2=PEEK(49173)+256*PEEK(49174):REM Y2 VAL
1220 S2=40*Y2+X2:REM SCREEN POSITION OF JOY2
1230 X1=PEEK(49171)+256*PEEK(49172):REM X1 VAL
1240 Y1=PEEK(49175)+256*PEEK(49176):REM Y1 VAL
1250 S1=40*Y1+X1:REM SCREEN POSITION OF JOY1
1260 F1=PEEK(49178):REM JOY1 FIREBUTTON
1270 F2=PEEK(49177):REM JOY2 FIREBUTTON
1280 POKE49177,0:REM CLEAR JOY2 FIREBUTTON
1290 POKE49178,0:REM CLEAR JOY1 FIREBUTTON
1300 REM***DISPLAY***
1310 POKESC+S1,42:POKECO+S1,1
1320 POKESC+S2,42:POKECO+S2,5
1330 IFF1=1THENPRINTCHR$(19)"F1":GOTO1360
1340 IFF2=1THENPRINTCHR$(19)"F2":GOTO1360
1350 GOTO1200
1360 SYS49208:REM REMOVE WEDGE
1370 END
```

```
1000 REM** PLOTSUB BASIC LOADER **
1010 DATA128,64,32,16,8,4,2,1,0,0,0,0,0
1020 DATA0,0,0,0,0,0,0,0,72,138,72,152
1030 DATA72,169,0,133,251,169,92,133
1040 DATA252,160,0,173,92,193,145,251
1050 DATA230,251,208,250,230,252,166
1060 DATA252,224,96,208,242,169,0,145
1070 DATA251,230,251,208,250,230,252
1080 DATA166,252,224,128,208,242,173,17
1090 DATA208,9,32,141,17,208,173,2,221
1100 DATA9,3,141,2,221,173,0,221,41,252
1110 DATA9,2,141,0,221,169,120,141,24
1120 DATA208,104,168,104,170,104,96,72
1130 DATA138,72,152,72,173,17,208,41
1140 DATA223,141,17,208,173,2,221,9,3
1150 DATA141,2,221,173,0,221,9,3,141,0
1160 DATA221,169,20,141,24,208,104,168
1170 DATA104,170,104,96,72,138,72,152
1180 DATA72,173,90,193,16,4,201,200,16
1190 DATA236,173,89,193,240,11,201,2,16
1200 DATA227,173,88,193,201,64,16,220
1210 DATA173,90,193,74,74,74,141,95,193
1220 DATA173,89,193,141,97,193,173,88
1230 DATA193,110,97,193,106,74,74,141
1240 DATA96,193,173,95,193,141,97,193
1250 DATA169,40,141,98,193,169,0,141,99
1260 DATA193,162,8,78,98,193,144,4,24
1270 DATA109,97,193,106,110,99,193,202
1280 DATA208,240,141,100,193,173,96,193
1290 DATA24,109,99,193,141,99,193,144,3
1300 DATA238,100,193,173,99,193,10,46
1310 DATA100,193,10,46,100,193,10,46
1320 DATA100,193,141,99,193,173,90,193
1330 DATA41,7,141,93,193,173,88,193,41
1340 DATA7,141,94,193,169,0,24,109,99
1350 DATA193,141,99,193,144,3,238,100
1360 DATA193,169,96,24,109,100,193,141
1370 DATA100,193,173,93,193,24,109,99
1380 DATA193,141,99,193,144,3,238,100
1390 DATA193,173,99,193,133,251,173,100
1400 DATA193,133,252,172,94,193,185,80
1410 DATA193,160,0,174,91,193,208,7,17
1420 DATA251,145,251,76,187,194,73,255
1430 DATA49,251,145,251,104,168,104,170
```

```
1440 DATA104,96
1450 DATA46296:REM*CHECKSUM*
1460 CC=0
1470 FORI=49488TO49856
1480 READX:CC=CC+X:POKEI,X
1490 NEXT
1500 READX:IFCC<>XTHENPRINT"CHECKSUM ERROR"




1000 REM** TEST PLOTSUB **
1010 REM CM BASE=96*256=24576
1020 POKE56,95:POKE55,255:CLR
1030 ER=0:COL=1:REM ER FLAG & COLOUR
1040 POKE49500,COL:POKE49499,ER
1050 PRINTCHR$(147)"PLEASE WAIT-COMPUTING CURVE"
1060 REM**COMPUTE DAMPED SINE CURVE**
1070 DIM Y(319)
1080 FORX=0TO319
1090 Y(X)=100-INT(99*EXP(-X/100)*SIN(10*X*π/180))
1100 NEXT
1101 SYS49509:REM INITITALISE PLOTSUB
1110 REM**PLOT AXIS**
1120 FORX=0TO319:Y=100:REM HORIZ LINE
1130 GOSUB1230:REM PLOTSUB
1140 NEXT
1150 FORX=0TO319
1160 Y=Y(X):GOSUB1230:REM PLOTSUB
1170 GETA$:IFA$<>""THENX=319:REM EXIT
1180 NEXT
1190 GETA$:IFA$<>CHR$(13)THEN1190
1200 SYS49594:REM END PLOTSUB
1210 PRINTCHR$(147):END
1220 REM***CALL M/C PLOTSUB***
1230 XH=INT(X/256):REM XHI
1240 XL=X-256*XH:REM XLO
1250 POKE49496,XL:POKE49497,XH:POKE49498,Y
1260 SYS49634:REM CALL PLOTSUB
1270 RETURN
```

Index